A Casebook of Cognitive
for Traumatic Stress Reac

Many people experience traumatic events and whilst some gradually recover from such experiences, others find it more difficult and may seek professional help for a range of problems. *A Casebook of Cognitive Therapy for Traumatic Stress Reactions* aims to help therapists who may not have an extensive range of clinical experience.

The book includes descriptions and case studies of clinical cases of cognitive behavioural treatments involving people who have experienced traumatic events, including:

- people with phobias, depression and paranoid delusions following traumatic experiences
- people with post-traumatic stress disorder (PTSD)
- people who have experienced multiple and prolonged traumatizations
- people who are refugees or asylum-seekers.

All chapters are written by experts in the field and consider what may be learned from such cases. How this learning can be applied more generally in cognitive behavioural treatments for traumatic stress reactions is also discussed.

This book will be invaluable to all mental health professionals and in particular to therapists wanting to treat people who have experienced traumatic events, allowing them to creatively apply their existing knowledge to new clinical cases.

Nick Grey is a Consultant Clinical Psychologist at the Centre for Anxiety Disorders and Trauma, South London & Maudsley NHS Foundation Trust, and the Institute of Psychiatry, King's College London. His clinical work is providing outpatient cognitive therapy to people with anxiety disorders.

'*A Casebook of Cognitive Therapy for Traumatic Stress Reactions* is the best book to date on this topic. This uniformly outstanding casebook thoughtfully illustrates creative and practical treatment guidelines derived from the latest trauma research. Therapist–client dialogues facilitate a three-dimensional appreciation of central therapy processes. Many topics glossed over in other PTSD manuals are afforded detailed discussion, such as how to manage suicidal ideation and how to choose treatment priorities when trauma reactions are co-morbid with other disorders. The chapter on the use of language interpreters in trauma therapy compassionately sets guidelines for assessing and addressing interpreters' emotional reactions so that these do not compromise client care or cause harm to the interpreter. I wholeheartedly recommend this book to every clinician, whether novice or expert, and predict it will quickly become one of the most dog-eared books on your desk from frequent and welcome use.'

Christine A. Padesky, PhD, Co-Founder, Center for Cognitive Therapy,
Huntington Beach, California, USA

A Casebook of Cognitive Therapy for Traumatic Stress Reactions

Edited by Nick Grey

Routledge
Taylor & Francis Group

LONDON AND NEW YORK

First published 2009
by Routledge
27 Church Road, Hove, East Sussex BN3 2FA

Simultaneously published in the USA and Canada
by Routledge
270 Madison Ave, New York, NY 10016

*Routledge is an imprint of the Taylor & Francis Group,
an Informa business*

Typeset in Times by
RefineCatch Limited, Bungay, Suffolk
Printed and bound in Great Britain by
TJ International Ltd, Padstow, Cornwall
Paperback cover design by Lisa Dynan

British Library Cataloguing in Publication Data
A catalogue record for this book is available from the British Library

Library of Congress Cataloging-in-Publication Data
A casebook of cognitive therapy for traumatic stress reactions /
edited by Nick Grey.
    p. cm.
  Includes bibliographical references.
1. Psychic trauma—Case studies.   2. Cognitive therapy—Case
studies.   I. Grey, Nick, 1970–   [DNLM: 1. Stress Disorders, Traumatic—
therapy.   2. Cognitive Therapy—methods. WM 172 C337 2009]
  RC552.T7C37 2009
  616.89'1425—dc22
                                                    2009001037

ISBN: 978-0-415-43802-5 (hbk)
ISBN: 978-0-415-43803-2 (pbk)

Contents

Tables

Figures

Contributors

Patricia d'Ardenne, Institute of Psychotrauma, East London NHS Foundation Trust, UK

Chris Brewin, Clinical, Educational & Health Psychology, University College London, UK

Richard A. Bryant, School of Psychology, The University of New South Wales, Sydney, Australia

Gillian Butler, Oxford Cognitive Therapy Centre, Oxford, UK

David M. Clark, Centre for Anxiety Disorders and Trauma, South London & Maudsley NHS Foundation Trust, and Institute of Psychiatry, King's College London, UK

Michael Duffy, Northern Ireland Centre for Trauma and Transformation, Omagh, UK

Anke Ehlers, Centre for Anxiety Disorders and Trauma, South London & Maudsley NHS Foundation Trust, and Institute of Psychiatry, King's College London, UK

Elly Farmer, National Clinical Assessment and Treatment Service, FreshStart, NSPCC, UK

Kate Gillespie, Northern Ireland Centre for Trauma and Transformation, Omagh, UK

Nick Grey, Centre for Anxiety Disorders and Trauma, South London & Maudsley NHS Foundation Trust, and Institute of Psychiatry, King's College London, UK

Ann Hackmann, Oxford Cognitive Therapy Centre, Oxford, UK

Rachel Handley, Centre for Anxiety Disorders and Trauma, South London & Maudsley NHS Foundation Trust, and Institute of Psychiatry, King's College London, UK

Emily A. Holmes, Royal Society Dorothy Hodgkin Fellow, Department of Psychiatry, University of Oxford, UK

Sally Hopwood, School of Psychology, The University of New South Wales, Sydney, Australia

Helen Kennerley, Oxford Cognitive Therapy Centre, Oxford, UK

Deborah A. Lee, Berkshire Traumatic Stress Service, Reading, UK

Sheena Liness, Centre for Anxiety Disorders and Trauma, South London & Maudsley NHS Foundation Trust, and Institute of Psychiatry, King's College London

Freda McManus, Oxford Cognitive Therapy Centre, Oxford, UK

Julie Mastrodomenico, School of Psychology, The University of New South Wales, Sydney, Australia

Michelle L. Moulds, School of Psychology, The University of New South Wales, Sydney, Australia

Martina Mueller, Oxford Cognitive Therapy Centre, Oxford, and Oxfordshire and Buckinghamshire Mental Health NHS Foundation Trust, UK

Paul Salkovskis, Centre for Anxiety Disorders and Trauma, South London & Maudsley NHS Foundation Trust, and Institute of Psychiatry, King's College London, UK

Ben Smith, Department of Mental Health Sciences, University College London and North East London Mental Health NHS Trust, UK

Pippa Stallworthy, formerly Traumatic Stress Clinic, Camden and Islington Mental Health and Social Care NHS Trust, and Royal Holloway, University of London. Now, Traumatic Stress Service, South West London and St Georges Mental Health NHS Trust.

Craig Steel, Department of Psychology, University of Reading, UK

Blake Stobie, Centre for Anxiety Disorders and Trauma, South London & Maudsley NHS Foundation Trust, and Institute of Psychiatry, King's College London, UK

Richard Stott, Centre for Anxiety Disorders and Trauma, South London & Maudsley NHS Foundation Trust, and Institute of Psychiatry, King's College London, UK

Jon Wheatley, Sub-department of Clinical Health Psychology, University College London, and Central & North West London NHS Foundation Trust, UK

Jennifer Wild, Centre for Anxiety Disorders and Trauma, South London

& Maudsley NHS Foundation Trust, and Institute of Psychiatry, King's College London, UK

Kerry Young, St Ann's Hospital, Haringey, and Sub-department of Clinical Health Psychology, University College London, UK

Foreword

Over the past three decades, significant progress has been made in the understanding and treatment of posttraumatic stress disorder (PTSD). A range of psychological treatments have been developed for this disabling condition. Research has identified factors involved in the development and maintenance of PTSD (for reviews see Brewin, Andrews & Valentine, 2000; Ozer, Best, Lipsey & Weiss, 2003). Among the most powerful predictors were cognitive factors such as negative idiosyncratic personal meanings (appraisals) of the trauma and its aftermath, characteristics of trauma memories and problematic coping responses (e.g., Kleim, Ehlers & Glucksman, 2008; Ehring, Ehlers & Glucksman, 2008).

Aided by the improved understanding of the development and maintenance of PTSD, clinicians and researchers have refined cognitive behavioural treatments (CBT) for this condition. These refinements have improved treatment efficacy (Öst, 2008). One development is that the importance of cognitive change during treatment has been increasingly emphasized and is now regarded by many theorists to be at the core of clinical change in this condition (e.g., Ehlers & Clark, 2000; Foa & Rothbaum, 1998; Resick & Schnicke, 1993). Another development is that the central role of the trauma in causing the patients' symptoms has been increasingly acknowledged, and leading CBT treatments for this condition now focus on the patients' memories of their traumatic events and the personal meanings of the trauma and its aftermath. Recent meta-analyses show that trauma-focused CBT programmes lead to large improvements in PTSD symptoms and other symptoms such as general anxiety and depression (Bisson, Ehlers, Matthews, Pilling, Richards, & Turner, 2007; Bradley, Greene, Russ, Dutra, & Westen, 2005; Cloitre, 2009). Treatment trials showed that, on average, 67% of patients who complete trauma-focused psychological treatments (and 56% of those who enter these treatments; intent-to-treat analysis) no longer meet diagnostic criteria for PTSD (Bradley et al., 2005). Thus, PTSD is a treatable condition.

Clinicians sometimes respond to the positive results of treatment research with scepticism. In clinical practice, clients do not neatly fall into diagnostic categories and they often have multiple problems. This raises the important questions of (1) whether the treatment methods studied in the research trials apply to clients seen in clinical practice and (2) how the methods need to be adapted to deal with a wide range of presentations and comorbidities. Encouragingly, there is now evidence addressing the first question. Trauma-focused CBT, delivered by trained therapists, has been shown to be very effective in unselected populations of PTSD patients (Brewin et al., 2008; Gillespie, Duffy, Hackmann & Clark, 2002; Duffy, Gillespie & Clark, 2007).

The current book addresses the second question. It brings together leading scientist-practitioners who illustrate how *Cognitive Therapy for PTSD* (Ehlers & Clark, 2000; Ehlers et al., 2003, 2005; Ehlers, Clark, Hackmann, McManus, Fennell & Grey, in press) and related trauma-focused CBT treatments can be adapted to treat a wide range of trauma reactions effectively. In particular, the chapters in this book address the following important clinical questions:

- *Trauma survivors may have a disorder other than PTSD (e.g., phobia or major depression) and may only have some, but not all of the symptoms of PTSD.* Should the intervention be trauma-focused in these cases? To what extent are techniques that target re-experiencing symptoms useful? (see Chapters 3 by Handley et al., and 6 by Wheatley et al.)
- *Trauma survivors often have comorbid disorders in addition to having PTSD.* How can the case formulation economically account for the different problems? To what extent are the comorbid disorders linked to personal meanings of the trauma? Are there common triggers for negative emotional responses? How can treatment best address PTSD and the comorbid conditions? (see Chapters 5 by Smith & Steel, 10 by Liness and 11 by Stobie)
- *Some patients develop symptoms that resemble those of PTSD after experiences that do not meet strict definitions for trauma.* How can the interventions be adapted to target these symptoms? (see Chapter 4 by Stott)
- *PTSD is usually only diagnosed after 1 month.* Can the treatment be successfully adapted as an early intervention? (see Chapter 2 by Moulds et al.)
- *Many patients with PTSD have been traumatised by more than one trauma.* How can these multiple experiences be addressed in treatment and where should treatment start? (see Chapters 13 by Stallworthy, 14 by Duffy & Gillespie, 16 by Young, and 17 by Mueller)
- *Patients with PTSD may be at significant risk, including suicidality, severe dissociation, or ongoing threat.* How can these be addressed in the context of cognitive interventions? (see Chapters 7 by Kennerley, 12 by Holmes & Butler, and 14 by Duffy & Gillespie)
- *Traumatized patients often have to live with long-lasting or permanent negative effects of the trauma such as physical disability or displacement.*

How can they be helped to live with these changes and rebuild their lives? (see Chapters 9 by Wild, 16 by Young and 17 by Mueller)

- *The mode of treatment delivery may need to be adapted to suit the needs of the trauma survivor.* Examples include working with interpreters, concentrating on the patient's shame or offering treatment as an intensive treatment rather than weekly sessions (see Chapters 8 by Grey, 15 by Lee and 18 by D'Ardenne & Farmer).

Each chapter includes detailed case descriptions. These illustrate how the individual case formulation that models the patient's particular constellation of problems guides therapy. They also illustrate that interventions that focus on changing problematic meanings of the trauma and on reducing re-experiencing symptoms are very helpful for a range of trauma-related problems. The book shows that *Cognitive Therapy for PTSD* and related treatment approaches are focused, but sufficiently flexible so that they can be adapted to the complexities of clinical practice.

Anke Ehlers

REFERENCES

Bisson, J., Ehlers, A., Matthews, R., Pilling, S., Richards, D., & Turner, S. (2007). Systematic review and metaanalysis of psychological treatments for posttraumatic stress disorder. *British Journal of Psychiatry, 190*, 97–104.

Bradley, R., Greene, J., Russ, E., Dutra, L., & Westen, D. (2005). A multidimensional meta-analysis of psychotherapy for PTSD. *American Journal of Psychiatry, 162*, 214–217.

Brewin, C.R., Andrews, B. & Valentine, J.D. (2000). Meta-analysis of risk factors for posttraumatic stress disorder in trauma-exposed adults. *Journal of Consulting and Clinical Psychology, 68*, 748–766.

Brewin, C.R., Scragg, P., Robertson, M., Thompson, M., D'Ardenne, P. & Ehlers, A. (2008). Promoting mental health following the London bombings: A screen and treat approach. *Journal of Traumatic Stress, 21*, 3–8.

Cloitre, M. (2009). Effective psychotherapies for posttraumatic stress disorder: a review and critique. *CNS Spectrums, 14 (Suppl 1)*, 32–43.

Duffy, M., Gillespie, K. & Clark, D. M. (2007). Post-traumatic stress disorder in the context of terrorism and other civil conflict in Northern Ireland: randomised controlled trial. *British Medical Journal, 334*, 1147–1150.

Ehlers, A. & Clark, D. M. (2000). A cognitive model of persistent posttraumatic stress disorder. *Behaviour Research and Therapy, 38,* 319–345.

Ehlers, A., Clark, D. M., Hackmann, A., McManus, F., & Fennell, M. (2005). Cognitive therapy for post-traumatic stress disorder: Development and evaluation. *Behaviour Research and Therapy, 43,* 413–431.

Ehlers, A., Clark, D. M., Hackmann, A., McManus, F., Fennell, M. & Grey, N. (in press). Cognitive Therapy for posttraumatic stress disorder: A therapist's guide. Oxford, UK: Oxford University Press.

Ehlers, A., Clark, D. M., Hackmann, A., McManus, F., Fennell, M., Herbert, C., & Mayou, R.A. (2003). A randomized controlled trial of cognitive therapy, a self-help booklet, and repeated assessments as early interventions for posttraumatic stress disorder. *Archives of General Psychiatry, 60,* 1024–1032.

Ehring, T., Ehlers, A., & Glucksman, E. (2008). Do cognitive models help in predicting the severity of posttraumatic stress disorder, phobia and depression after motor vehicle accidents? A prospective longitudinal study. *Journal of Consulting and Clinical Psychology, 76,* 219–230.

Foa, E.B. & Rothbaum, B.O. (1998). *Treating the trauma of rape: Cognitive-behavior therapy for PTSD.* New York: Guilford Press.

Gillespie, K., Duffy, M., Hackmann, A. & Clark, D. M. (2002). Community based cognitive therapy in the treatment of post-traumatic stress disorder following the Omagh bomb. *Behaviour Research and Therapy, 40,* 345–357.

Kleim, B., Ehlers, A. & Glucksman, E. (2007). Early predictors of posttraumatic stress disorder in assault survivors. *Psychological Medicine, 37,* 1457–1467.

Öst, L. G. (2008). Cognitive behaviour therapy for anxiety disorders: 40 years of progress. *Nordic Journal of Psychiatry, 62 (S47),* 5–10.

Ozer, E. J., Best, S. R., Lipsey, T. L., & Weiss, D. S. (2003). Predictors of posttraumatic stress disorder and symptoms in adults: A meta-analysis. *Psychological Bulletin, 129,* 52–73.

Resick, P.A. & Schnicke, M.K. (1993) *Cognitive processing therapy for rape victims.* Newbury Park, California: Sage.

Chapter 1

Cognitive therapy for traumatic stress reactions

An introduction

Nick Grey

Post-traumatic stress disorder (PTSD) is a common and disabling reaction to traumatic experiences. While clinical and research efforts have been focused on PTSD, other post-traumatic psychological difficulties include depression, panic disorder, and phobias. Cognitive therapy is a successful treatment for many disorders, including PTSD. Recent clinical guidelines have recommended the use of trauma-focused cognitive behaviour therapy for the treatment of PTSD (National Collaborating Centre for Mental Health (NCCMH), 2005). However, such guidelines, and the research trials on which their conclusions are based, do not cover all possible presentations of PTSD and traumatic stress reactions. Therefore clinicians are always working with some clients 'beyond the guidelines'. In such cases clinicians need to apply skills flexibly in empirically guided clinical interventions (Salkovskis, 2002). This involves careful assessment of phenomenology, individualized formulation, and the use and further development of strategies derived from efficacious and effective treatments. This casebook is intended as a resource for clinicians in devising such interventions.

This chapter introduces some basic information on PTSD, other psychological reactions to traumatic events, and associated comorbidity. It presents Ehlers and Clark's (2000) cognitive model of PTSD, the main treatment approaches that are derived from it, and reflections on how case and treatment descriptions can be used by clinicians to improve their practice.

TRAUMATIC STRESS REACTIONS

What is trauma?

The study of post-traumatic stress symptoms has often been a controversial area, subject to scientific, political, and legal influences (see Brewin, 2003), with some concern that the term 'trauma' is used too loosely, and colloquially even, and as such the term becomes meaningless. A formal diagnostic definition of a traumatic event requires that the individual 'experienced, witnessed, or was confronted with an event or events that involved actual or threatened death or serious injury, or a threat to the physical integrity of self or others' and that the person's 'response involved intense fear, helplessness, or horror' (American Psychiatric Association (APA), 1994).

Post-traumatic stress disorder

In order to meet formal DSM-IV diagnostic criteria (APA, 1994), following a traumatic event an individual needs to have one re-experiencing symptom, three avoidance or numbing symptoms, and at least two hyperarousal symptoms. However, factor analyses of traumatic stress symptoms have indicated that a four-factor structure (re-experiencing, avoidance, numbing, and hyperarousal) is a better fit to the available data than a three-factor structure (with avoidance and numbing combined together as in DSM-IV) (Foa, Riggs, & Gershuny, 1995).

A core feature of PTSD is the presence of intrusive memories of the event(s). Typically these intrusions are in the form of visual mental images but can also occur in other sensory modalities (Hackmann, Ehlers, Speckens, & Clark, 2004). One feature that distinguishes these traumatic memories from other autobiographical memories is that they are experienced as happening 'now' rather than as a memory of the past (Ehlers & Clark, 2000; Hackmann et al., 2004). Degree of 'nowness' of intrusive memories is a good predictor of chronic post-traumatic stress disorder after assault (Michael, Ehlers, Halligan, & Clark, 2005). Clinically there is a need to differentiate intrusions of (aspects) of the traumatic memory itself from rumination on the event(s) or sequelae of the event(s).

Epidemiology

The largest sample, from the US National Comorbidity Survey, found rates of exposure to traumatic events of 61% in men and 51% in women (Kessler, Sonnega, Bromet, Hughes, & Nelson, 1995). Rates of exposure in some non-western societies are higher due to greater exposure to natural disasters and warfare. In this sample the risk of developing PTSD in response to a traumatic event was 8% for men and 20% for women. Events such as rape and torture are associated with higher rates of PTSD than events such as accidents and natural disasters. Lifetime prevalence rates of PTSD in western community samples are usually around 5–10%. Kessler et al. (1995) found lifetime prevalence in women of 10.4% and in men of 5.0%. In a valuable epidemiological study in survivors of war or mass violence who were randomly selected from community populations, de Jong et al. (2001) found prevalence rates of PTSD of 37% in Algeria, 28% in Cambodia, 16% in Ethiopia, and 18% in Gaza. Higher rates of PTSD are found in refugees and asylum-seekers who have fled from their country of origin. Turner, Bowie, Dunn, Shapo, and

Yule (2003) examined a large group of Kosovan Albanian refugees in the UK and found 49% met criteria for PTSD.

Risk factors

While experiencing symptoms such as nightmares and flashbacks in the aftermath of traumatic events is common, most people recover from the early appearance of traumatic stress symptoms without any formal intervention and it is a subgroup that go on to develop chronic PTSD. Two thorough meta-analyses have provided strong evidence for particular risk factors for the development of PTSD such as post-trauma support and life stress, and peri-traumatic processes such as dissociation (Brewin, Andrews, & Valentine, 2000; Ozer, Best, Lipsey, & Weiss, 2003). Studies also indicate the role of post-traumatic cognitions as important predictors of the development of PTSD following road traffic accidents and assaults (e.g., Ehlers, Mayou, & Bryant, 1998). Recent longitudinal prospective studies have investigated the role of disorder-specific cognitive predictors derived from cognitive models of PTSD, depression and phobias in predicting the severity of symptoms of these three disorders following motor vehicle accidents (Ehring, Ehlers, & Glucksman, 2008) and assaults (Kleim, Ehlers, & Glucksman, 2008). These two studies showed that depression, phobia, and PTSD are correlated but distinct, and that symptoms are best predicted by the cognitive factors from the respective disorder-specific model, rather than other established predictors.

Other traumatic stress reactions

PTSD can only be formally diagnosed 1 month after the traumatic event. Within the first month individuals may meet diagnostic criteria for acute stress disorder (ASD) if they have the requisite number of symptoms, similar to those in PTSD, but also specifically requiring the presence of three dissociative symptoms.

If an individual has symptoms characteristic of PTSD without meeting the criterion A for the traumatic stressor, DSM would currently classify this as an adjustment disorder. A common example is the reaction to relationship break-ups or workplace bullying, in which no criterion A event has occurred but intrusive memories and nightmares relating to these events may occur.

In the PTSD literature a differentiation is often made between Type I trauma and Type II trauma. Type I trauma is essentially a one-off traumatic event such as a road traffic accident, assault, or natural disaster. Type II trauma refers to prolonged, repeated traumatic events such as repeated abuse or torture. Such circumstances may lead to more complicated traumatic stress presentations. Herman (1992) refers to this as 'complex trauma' character-ized by poor affect and impulse regulation, dissociation, somatization, and pathological patterns of relationships.

It has also been suggested that borderline personality disorder (BPD) is better conceptualized as a 'complex trauma' reaction. Certainly there are similarities in the criteria for BPD and 'complex trauma'. Furthermore, those people who could be diagnosed with BPD also often experience traumatic stress symptoms. However, epidemiological studies demonstrate that many individuals meet criteria for BPD without meeting criteria for PTSD, and that they are more likely to also meet criteria for a mood disorder, particularly depression, rather than PTSD (Zanarini et al., 1998).

The utility of the term 'complex trauma' is currently unclear. It is used in differing ways, all of which try to describe some sense of difficulty or profound impact on the client not fully captured by PTSD. It is preferable to describe the actual problems or symptoms an individual may have and to use an idiosyncratic psychological formulation. Models of depression, PTSD, and other anxiety disorders may be helpful in planning treatment approaches.

Epidemiology of other disorders following trauma

There is less research in this area as the focus has been on PTSD. In a very large sample of US veterans, PTSD was the most common disorder following trauma (13%), followed by any other anxiety disorder (6%), adjustment disorder (6%), and depression (5%) (Seal, Bertenthal, Miner, Sen, & Marmar, 2007). Twenty-five per cent of the sample had at least one diagnosis and of those 56% had more than one. In an Australian sample following physical injury and using conservative methodology, the most common disorders at 12 months post-injury were PTSD (10.4%), depression (10.1%), any substance use disorder (6.5%), phobia (3.6%), and panic disorder (2.3%) (O'Donnell, Creamer, Pattison, & Atkin, 2004). Half had comorbidity, most commonly depression and PTSD.

Comorbidity following traumatic experiences

The high levels of comorbidity in people with PTSD is acknowledged in DSM-IV (APA, 1994). The most common comorbid conditions are affective disorders (37–49%), substance-use disorders (27–45%), and other anxiety disorders (e.g. panic disorder, 13%) (Breslau, Davis, Andreski, & Peterson, 1991; Creamer, Burgess, & McFarlane, 2001; Kessler et al., 1995). It is unsurprising that there is high comorbidity because many symptoms overlap with other diagnoses. In most cases of comorbid depression or substance-use disorders, the PTSD was primary (Chilcoat & Breslau, 1998). In a large community sample in Chile, 71% of men and 90% of women who met criteria for PTSD also had another lifetime diagnosis (Zlotnick et al., 2006). In a review of comorbidity profiles, Deering, Glover, Ready, Eddleman, and Alarcon (1996) found that they differ according to the type of trauma experienced and the population studied. For example, the rates of substance-use disorders among combat veterans with PTSD is higher than those with PTSD from other traumatic events, and trauma involving physical suffering may be more likely to lead to somatization in PTSD.

ASSESSMENT

A comprehensive reference text addressing issues of assessment of traumatic stress reactions is Keane and Wilson (2004). Probably the 'gold standard' for assessing PTSD is the structured interview Clinician Administered PTSD Scale (CAPS; Blake et al., 1990), and for a range of diagnoses the Structured Clinical Interview for DSM-IV (First, Spitzer, Gibbon, & Williams, 1996). However, many people either do not meet specific diagnostic criteria, or meet criteria for many disorders. It is important to pay close attention to phenomenology and use an individualized formulation (e.g., Tarrier, 2006). Clinicians should not assume that intrusions indicate PTSD because intrusive memories occur in other disorders such as depression (Reynolds & Brewin, 1999) and, more broadly, intrusive images occur across many, if not all, disorders (see Holmes & Hackmann, 2004).

Self-report questionnaires also provide very helpful information and should be used to monitor progress session-by-session. Commonly used questionnaires for traumatic stress symptoms are the Revised Impact of Events Scale (IES-R; Weiss & Marmar, 1997) and the Posttraumatic Diagnostic Scale (PDS; Foa, Cashman, Jaycox, & Perry, 1997). Although beyond the scope of this chapter and book, there is particular interest in measures that may be used to screen large numbers of people, such as following disasters or terrorist attacks, in order to better direct available therapeutic resources. One such is the 10-item Trauma Screening Questionnaire (Brewin et al., 2002), which focuses on the re-experiencing and hyperarousal symptoms. Recent research suggests that other symptom combinations may work better and highlights the need for cross-validation research (Ehring, Kleim, Clark, Foa, & Ehlers, 2007). All self-report questionnaires need to be treated with caution, as when a person indicates that they have 'upsetting thoughts or images' coming into their head, this could mean vivid intrusions of aspects of the event itself, or could mean ruminations about the sequelae of the event. Further clarification in session is necessary.

In order to assess for particular cognitive themes, a commonly used questionnaire is the Posttraumatic Cognitions Inventory (PTCI; Foa, Ehlers, Clark, Tolin, & Orsillo, 1999). This has three factors: negative cognitions about the self, negative cognitions about the world, and self-blame. Used clinically, individual cognitions can be focused on in treatment and outcome tracked over time. Further open assessment of cognitive themes (e.g., 'have these events changed how you see yourself/others/the world? In what way?') and of potential maintaining factors such as avoidance, suppression, rumination, and taking precautions are more fully described in Ehlers et al. (2009) and briefly in a single chapter by Grey (2007a).

COGNITIVE MODEL OF PTSD

There are a number of broadly cognitive models of PTSD (Brewin & Holmes, 2003), including Emotional Processing Theory (Foa & Rothbaum, 1998), Dual Representation Theory (Brewin, Dalgleish, & Joseph, 1996) and Ehlers and Clark's (2000) cognitive model. Each of these models addresses key elements of PTSD, including alterations in memory functioning and specific appraisals during and following the traumatic events. The models are not mutually exclusive but have differing emphases.

Ehlers and Clark's (2000) model offers clear guidelines for therapy and has increasing empirical support in both efficacy and effectiveness studies with adults (Duffy, Gillespie, & Clark, 2007; Ehlers et al., 2003; Ehlers, Clark, Hackmann, McManus, & Fennell, 2005; Gillespie, Duffy, Hackman, & Clark, 2002) and a randomized controlled trial with children (Smith et al., 2007). Ehlers and Clark (2000) proposed that PTSD becomes persistent when traumatic information is processed in a way that leads to a sense of serious *current* threat. This can be a physical threat and/or a psychological threat to one's view of oneself. Due to high levels of arousal at the time of the trauma, the trauma memory is poorly elaborated, fragmented, and poorly integrated with other autobiographical memories, and can be unintentionally triggered by a wide range of low-level cues. In particular, there is no 'time-code' on the memory that tells the individual that the event occurred in the past. Thus, when the memory intrudes, it feels as if the event is actually happening again to some degree.

The persistence of the sense of current threat, and hence PTSD, arises from not only the nature of the trauma memory, but also the negative interpretations of the symptoms experienced (e.g. 'I'm going mad'), the event itself (e.g. 'It's my fault'), and sequelae (e.g. 'I should have got over it by now'; 'Others don't care about me'). Change in these appraisals and the nature of the trauma memory is prevented by a variety of cognitive and behavioural strategies, such as avoiding thoughts and feelings, places or other reminders of the event, suppression of intrusive memories, rumination about certain aspects of the event or sequelae, and other avoidant/numbing strategies such as alcohol and drug use (see Figure 1.1).

COGNITIVE THERAPY FOR PTSD

The aim of treatment derived from Ehlers and Clark (2000) is therefore threefold:

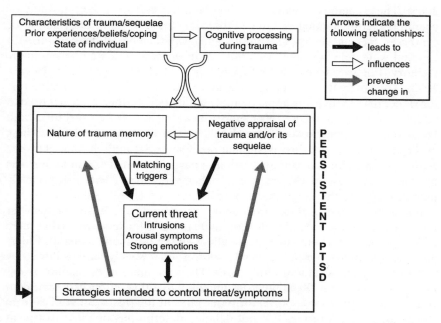

Figure 1.1 Cognitive model of PTSD. Reprinted from Ehlers and Clark (2000), with permission from Elsevier.

- To reduce re-experiencing by elaboration of the trauma memory and discrimination of triggers, and integration of the memory within existing autobiographical memory.
- To address the negative appraisals of the event and its sequelae.
- To change the avoidant/numbing strategies that prevent processing of the memory and reassessment of appraisals.

A wide range of both general and PTSD-specific cognitive-behavioural interventions can be used to achieve such changes (Ehlers & Clark, 2000; Ehlers et al., 2005, 2009; Mueller, Hackmann, & Croft, 2004).

There are multiple strategies used to help address the nature of the trauma memory. The most commonly used is that of 'reliving' the event; imaging and describing the event in the present tense in full detail with eyes closed. This is not used in order to allow habituation to any fear associated with the trauma memory, but in order to identify the main cognitive themes activated during, and after, the event(s). These are typically accessed at the most emotional, worst, moments of the traumatic experience ('hotspots'; Foa & Rothbaum, 1998). The cognitive themes in these hotspots are as likely to be related to psychological threat, e.g., 'I'm weak' or 'I'm to blame', as they are to physical threat, e.g., 'I'm going to die' (Grey & Holmes, 2008; Holmes, Grey, & Young,

2005). These cognitive themes can then be addressed with the full range of cognitive therapy strategies. Guided discovery leads to 'new' information or syntheses, such as 'it wasn't my fault', which can then be deliberately brought to mind while reliving again each hotspot in order to 'update' the traumatic memory (Ehlers & Clark, 2000; Ehlers et al., 2009; Grey, Young, & Holmes, 2002). Thus there is a direct interweaving of reliving and cognitive restructuring rather than them being applied purely sequentially. Other strategies used to address the nature of the trauma memory include using written narratives, and behavioural experiments with stimuli that trigger the trauma memory. These experiments allow stimulus discrimination of neutral stimuli that have become sensory triggers for the memory, such as a particular smell or sound that was present at the time of the trauma. Further experiments will also typically include revisiting the site of the trauma if it is possible and safe to do so.

For such changes to occur, treatment must provide a safe environment for the client. Therapists should allow up to 90 minutes for sessions so that there is enough time for clients to engage fully with the traumatic material. Ehlers and Clark's studies typically allow 12 sessions on a weekly basis, followed by 3 'booster' sessions on a monthly basis. The total amount of reliving across all sessions is about 90 minutes. Compared to other published treatment trials, there are very low (<5%) drop out rates in the treatment studies from Ehlers and Clark's group. For full detailed descriptions of these treatment strategies see Ehlers et al. (2009), and for a single chapter introduction see Grey (2007b).

Other cognitive behavioural treatments for PTSD have also been shown to be successful and the following texts may be helpful to clinicians: Foa, Hembree, and Rothbaum (2007), Folette, Ruzek, and Abueg (1998), Folette and Ruzek (2006), and Resick and Schnicke (1993).

'BEYOND THE GUIDELINES': EMPIRICALLY GROUNDED CLINICAL INTERVENTIONS

There are cognitive behavioural treatments of proven efficacy for PTSD (Foa, Keane, & Friedman, 2000; NCCMH, 2005). However, such clinical guidelines are based on those studies in which people formally meet diagnostic criteria for PTSD, rather than other presentations with similar symptoms. When a therapist is faced with a client for whom clear clinical guidelines have not been established, he or she must draw on a range of evidence and experience in order to provide treatment. This evidence will also include treatments of proven efficacy for other disorders, such as cognitive therapy for depression. Salkovskis (2002) described the interactions between theory, outcome research, experimental studies, and clinical practice and suggested that cognitive behaviour therapy (CBT) is best seen as a set of empirically grounded clinical interventions. Such interventions clearly draw on the therapist's existing skills, including careful assessment and formulation, and awareness of the role of the therapeutic relationship, and should be supported by ongoing supervision. Devising such interventions will inevitably draw on one's own clinical experience, but evidence can also be based on the cases of others (Edwards, Dattilio, & Bromley, 2004). Case-based reasoning (CBR) focuses on the use of analogy in the context of solving real-world problems, thus clearly having educational implications (Kolodner, 1997). CBR focuses on reasoning that is based on previous experience. One learns by 'acquiring' cases and 'indexing' them. Failure at applying an old case in a new situation triggers explanations that might result in reinterpreting old situations or discovering new kinds of interpretations, in the way one might consider why people do not improve with particular treatment approaches in order to better improve future treatment. Descriptions of relevant cases should be made available, highlighting issues to focus on, solutions to problems, and warning of potential pitfalls, allowing people then to try to tackle such cases themselves.

This book aims to provide descriptions of treatment of people with traumatic stress reactions in order for clinicians to use them as part of the material for their own empirically grounded clinical interventions. The subsequent chapters in this book describe adaptations of cognitive behaviour therapy for PTSD to presentations of broader traumatic stress reactions. Most of the chapters explicitly draw on the Ehlers and Clark (2000) cognitive model and the cognitive therapy for PTSD derived from it, either wholly or in part. The chapters include helping people who meet diagnostic criteria for acute stress disorder, travel phobia, depression, those who need help dealing with dissociative experiences, suicidal thoughts, and permanent disability, addressing PTSD from multiple traumatizations, such as from torture, in situations of civil conflict, and associated with shame, and adaptations of the manner of delivery, such as 'intensive' treatment and using interpreters. Inevitably, such a casebook cannot be entirely comprehensive. In some areas possible authors were not available and in other areas treatment interventions await further development. Such acknowledged gaps include post-traumatic substance use (see Najavits, 2002), and chronic pain, in which the role of mental defeat may be particularly important (Tang, Salkovskis, & Hanna, 2007). Drawing on theory, established efficacious treatments, and clinical experiences of oneself and others, treatment approaches for particular individuals can be developed. It is hoped that the treatment descriptions in this book can provide help with this.

RECOMMENDED READING

Ehlers, A., Clark, D.M., Hackmann, A., McManus, F., Fennell, M., & Grey, N. (2009). *Trauma-focused cognitive therapy for PTSD: A therapist's guide*. Oxford: Oxford University Press. In preparation.

INTERNET RESOURCES

Centre for Outcomes Research and Effectiveness: www.ucl.ac.uk/CORE
This site hosts very helpful 'competences maps' for provision of CBT and supervision. It also details specific competences needed to treat PTSD and other disorders.

International Society for Traumatic Stress Studies: www.istss.org
The largest professional organization focused on traumatic stress.

National Center for PTSD: www.ncptsd.org
This is a program of the US Department of Veteran Affairs, which maintains the free access Published International Literature on Traumatic Stress (PILOTS) database, which is the best place to start looking for trauma references.

National Institute for Health and Clinical Excellence: www.nice.org.uk
The NICE guidelines for PTSD provide a summary of PTSD assessment and treatment, and guide service provision within the UK National Health Service.

UK Trauma Group: www.uktrauma.org.uk
This includes listings of specialist UK trauma services.

REFERENCES

American Psychiatric Association. (1994). *Diagnostic and statistical manual of mental disorders* (4th ed.). Washington, DC: Author.

Blake, D., Weathers, F., Nagy, L., Kaloupek, D., Klauminzer, G., Charney, D., & Keane, T. (1990). *Clinician Administered PTSD Scale (CAPS)*. Boston: National Center for PTSD, Behavioural Sciences Division.

Breslau, N., Davis, G.C., Andreski, P., & Peterson, E.L. (1991). Traumatic events and posttraumatic stress disorder in an urban population of young adults. *Archives of General Psychiatry*, *48*, 216–222.

Brewin, C.R. (2003). *Posttraumatic stress disorder: Malady or myth?* New Haven: Yale University Press.

Brewin, C.R., & Holmes, E.A. (2003). Psychological theories of posttraumatic stress disorder. *Clinical Psychology Review*, *23*, 339–376.

Brewin, C.R., Andrews, B., & Valentine, J.D. (2000). Meta-analysis of risk factors for posttraumatic stress disorder in trauma-exposed adults. *Journal of Consulting and Clinical Psychology*, *68*, 748–766.

Brewin, C.R., Dalgleish, T., & Joseph, S. (1996). A dual representation theory of post-traumatic stress disorder. *Psychological Review*, *103*, 670–686.

Brewin, C.R., Rose, S., Andrews, B., Green, J., Tata, P., McEvedy, C., Turner, S., & Foa, E.B. (2002). A brief screening instrument for posttraumatic stress disorder. *British Journal of Psychiatry*, *181*, 158–162.

Chilcoat, H.D., & Breslau, N. (1998). Post-traumatic stress disorder and drug disorders. *Archives of General Psychiatry*, *55*, 913–917.

Creamer, M., Burgess, P., & McFarlane, A. (2001). Post-traumatic stress disorder:

Findings from the Australian National Survey of Mental Health and Well-being. *Psychological Medicine*, *31*, 1237–1247.

De Jong, J.T.V.M., Komproe, I.H., Van Ommeren, M., El Masri, M., Araya, M., Khaled, N., Van de Put, W.A.C.M., & Somasundaram, D.J. (2001). Lifetime events and posttraumatic stress disorder in 4 post conflict settings. *Journal of the American Medical Association*, *286*, 555–562.

Deering, C.G., Glover, S.G., Ready, D., Eddleman, H.C., & Alarcon, R.D. (1996). Unique patterns of comorbidity in posttraumatic stress disorder from different sources of trauma. *Comprehensive Psychiatry*, *37*, 336–346.

Duffy, M., Gillespie, K., & Clark, D.M. (2007). Posttraumatic stress disorder in the context of terrorism and other civil conflict in Northern Ireland: Randomised controlled trial. *British Medical Journal*, *334*(7604), 1147.

Edwards, D.J.A., Dattilio, F.M., & Bromley, D.B. (2004). Developing evidence-based practice: The role of case-based research. *Professional Psychology: Research and Practice*, *35*, 589–597.

Ehlers, A., & Clark, D.M. (2000). A cognitive model of posttraumatic stress disorder. *Behaviour Research & Therapy*, *38*, 319–345.

Ehlers, A., Clark, D.M., Hackmann, A., McManus, F., & Fennell, M. (2005). Cognitive therapy for posttraumatic stress disorder: Development and evaluation. *Behaviour Research and Therapy*, *43*, 413–431.

Ehlers, A., Clark, D.M., Hackmann, A., McManus, F., Fennell, M., & Grey, N. (2009). *Trauma-focused cognitive therapy for PTSD: A therapist's guide*. Oxford: Oxford University Press. In preparation.

Ehlers, A., Clark, D.M., Hackmann, A., McManus, F., Fennell, M., Herbert, C., & Mayou, R. (2003). A randomised controlled trial of cognitive therapy, self-help booklet, and repeated early assessment as early interventions for PTSD. *Archives of General Psychiatry*, *60*, 1024–1032.

Ehlers, A., Mayou, R.A., & Bryant, B. (1998). Psychological predictors of chronic posttraumatic stress disorder after motor vehicle accidents. *Journal of Abnormal Psychology*, *107*, 508–519.

Ehring, T., Ehlers, A., & Glucksman, E. (2008). Do cognitive models help in predicting the severity of posttraumatic stress disorder, phobia, and depression after motor vehicle accidents? A prospective longitudinal study. *Journal of Consulting and Clinical Psychology*, *76*, 219–230.

Ehring, T., Kleim, B., Clark, D.M., Foa, E.B., & Ehlers, A. (2007). Screening for posttraumatic stress disorder: What combination of symptoms predicts best? *Journal of Nervous and Mental Disease*, *195*, 1004–1012.

First, M.B., Spitzer, R.L., Gibbon, M., & Williams, J.B. (1996). *Structured clinical interview for DSM-IV axis I disorders, clinician version*. Washington, DC: American Psychiatric Press.

Foa, E.B., & Rothbaum, B.O. (1998). *Treating the trauma of rape: Cognitive behavioural therapy for PTSD*. New York: Guilford Press.

Foa, E.B., Cashman, L., Jaycox, L., & Perry, K. (1997). The validation of a self-report measure of posttraumatic stress disorder: the posttraumatic diagnostic scale. *Psychological Assessment*, *9*, 445–451.

Foa, E.B., Ehlers, A., Clark, D.M., Tolin, D.F., & Orsillo, S.M. (1999). The Post Traumatic Cognitions Inventory (PTCI): Development and validation. *Psychological Assessment*, *11*, 303–314.

Foa, E.B., Hembree, E.A., & Rothbaum, B.O. (2007). *Prolonged exposure therapy for PTSD: Emotional processing of traumatic experiences: therapist guide.* New York: Oxford University Press.

Foa, E.B., Keane, T.M., & Friedman, M.J. (Eds.) (2000). *Effective treatments for posttraumatic stress disorder: Practice guidelines from the International Society for Traumatic Stress Studies.* New York: Guilford.

Foa, E.B., Riggs, D.S., & Gershuny, B.S. (1995). Arousal, numbing, and intrusion: Symptom structure of PTSD following assault. *American Journal of Psychiatry, 152,* 116–120.

Folette, V., & Ruzek, J. (Eds.) (2006). *Cognitive behavioral therapies for trauma* (2nd ed.). London: Guilford Press.

Folette, V., Ruzek, J., & Abueg, F. (Eds.) (1998). *Cognitive behavioral therapies for trauma.* London: Guilford Press.

Gillespie, K., Duffy, M., Hackmann, A., & Clark, D.M. (2002). Community based cognitive therapy in the treatment of post-traumatic stress disorder following the Omagh bomb. *Behaviour Research & Therapy, 40,* 345–357.

Grey, N. (2007a). Posttraumatic stress disorder: Assessment. In S. Lindsay & G. Powell (Eds.), *The handbook of clinical adult psychology* (3rd ed.). London: Routledge.

Grey, N. (2007b). Posttraumatic stress disorder: Treatment. In S. Lindsay & G. Powell (Eds.), *The handbook of clinical adult psychology* (3rd ed.). London: Routledge.

Grey, N., & Holmes, E.A. (2008). 'Hotspots' in trauma memories in the treatment of posttraumatic stress disorder: A replication. *Memory, 16,* 788–796.

Grey, N., Young, K., & Holmes, E. (2002). Cognitive restructuring within reliving: A treatment for peritraumatic emotional 'hotspots' in post-traumatic stress disorder. *Behavioural and Cognitive Psychotherapy, 30,* 37–56.

Hackmann, A., Ehlers, A., Speckens, A., & Clark, D.M. (2004). Characteristics and content of intrusive memories in PTSD and their changes with treatment. *Journal of Traumatic Stress, 17,* 231–240.

Herman, J.L. (1992). *Trauma and recovery: from domestic abuse to political terror.* London: Pandora.

Holmes, E.A., & Hackmann, A. (2004). A healthy imagination? *Memory, 12,* 387–388.

Holmes, E., Grey, N., & Young, K.A.D. (2005). Intrusive images and 'hotspots' of trauma memories in posttraumatic stress disorder: An exploratory investigation of emotions and cognitive themes. *Journal of Behaviour Therapy and Experimental Psychiatry, 36,* 3–17.

Keane, T., & Wilson, J. (2004). *Assessing psychological trauma and PTSD* (2nd ed.). New York: Guilford Press.

Kessler, R.C., Sonnega, A., Bromet, E., Hughes, M., & Nelson, C.B. (1995). Post-traumatic stress disorder in the National Comorbidity Survey. *Archives of General Psychiatry, 52,* 1048–1060.

Kleim, B., Ehlers, A., & Glucksman, E. (2008). Predicting depression, phobia, and PTSD following assault with cognitive appraisal models: A structural equation modeling study. Submitted for publication.

Kolodner, J.L. (1997). Educational implications of analogy: A view from case-based reasoning. *American Psychologist, 52,* 57–66.

Michael, T., Ehlers, A., Halligan, S., & Clark, D.M. (2005). Unwanted memories of assault: What intrusion characteristics predict PTSD? *Behaviour Research and Therapy, 43,* 613–628.

Mueller, M., Hackmann, A., & Croft, A. (2004). Post-traumatic stress disorder. In J. Bennett-Levy, G. Butler, M. Fennell, A. Hackmann, M. Mueller, & D. Westbrook (Eds.), *Oxford guide to behavioural experiments in cognitive therapy*. Oxford: OUP.

Najavits, L. (2002). *Seeking safety: A treatment manual for PTSD and substance abuse*. New York: Guilford.

National Collaborating Centre for Mental Health. (2005). *Clinical guideline 26. Post-traumatic stress disorder (PTSD): The management of PTSD in adults and children in primary and secondary care*. London: National Institute for Clinical Excellence.

O'Donnell, M.L., Creamer, M., Pattison, P., & Atkin, C. (2004). Psychiatric morbidity following injury. *American Journal of Psychiatry, 161*, 507–514.

Ozer, E.J., Best, S.R., Lipsey, T.L., & Weiss, D.S. (2003). Predictors of posttraumatic stress disorder and symptoms in adults: A meta-analysis. *Psychological Bulletin, 129*, 52–73.

Resick, P., & Schnicke, M. (1993). *Cognitive processing therapy for rape victims: A treatment manual*. Newbury Park, CA: Sage.

Reynolds, M., & Brewin, C.R. (1999). Intrusive memories in depression and post-traumatic stress disorder. *Behaviour Research and Therapy, 37*, 201–215.

Salkovskis, P.M. (2002). Empirically grounded clinical interventions: Cognitive-behavioural therapy progresses through a multidimensional approach to clinical science. *Behavioural and Cognitive Psychotherapy, 30*, 1–10.

Seal, K.H., Bertenthal, D., Miner, C., Sen, S., & Marmar, C. (2007). Bringing the war back home: Mental health disorders among 103788 US veterans returning from Iraq and Afghanistan seen at Department of Veterans Affairs Facilities. *Archives of Internal Medicine, 167*, 476–482.

Smith, P., Yule, W., Perrin, S., Tranah, T., Dalgleish, T., & Clark, D.M. (2007). Cognitive-behavioural therapy for PTSD in children and adolescents: A preliminary randomized controlled trial. *Journal of American Academy of Child and Adolescent Psychiatry, 46*, 1051–1061.

Tang, N., Salkovskis, P, & Hanna, M. (2007). Mental defeat in chronic pain: Initial exploration of the concept. *Clinical Journal of Pain, 23*, 222–232.

Tarrier, N. (Ed.) (2006). *Case formulation in cognitive behaviour therapy: the treatment of challenging and complex cases*. Hove: Routledge.

Turner, S.W., Bowie, C., Dunn, G., Shapo, L., & Yule, W. (2003). Mental health of Kosovan Albanian refugees in the UK. *British Journal of Psychiatry, 182*, 444–448.

Weiss, D.S., & Marmar, C.R. (1997). The Impact of Event Scale – Revised. In J.P. Wilson, & T.M. Keane (Eds.), *Assessing psychological trauma and PTSD: A handbook for practitioners*. New York: Guilford Press.

Zanarini, M.C., Frankenburg, F.R., Dubo, E.D., Sickel, A.E., Trikha, A., Levin, A., & Reynolds, V. (1998). Axis I comorbidity of borderline personality disorder. *American Journal of Psychiatry, 155*, 1733–1739.

Zlotnick, C., Johnson, J., Kohn, R., Vicente, B., Rioseco, P., & Saldiva, S. (2006). Epidemiology of trauma, post-traumatic stress disorder and co-morbid disorders in Chile. *Psychological Medicine, 36*, 1523–1533.

Chapter 2

Cognitive therapy for acute stress disorder

Michelle L. Moulds, Sally Hopwood,
Julie Mastrodomenico, and Richard A. Bryant

The past decade has seen major advances in our understanding of the nature of acute trauma response, the optimal time post-trauma at which early intervention techniques should be implemented, and the utility of early intervention procedures in preventing chronic post-traumatic psychopathology. In this chapter we briefly overview the treatment outcome literature for acute stress disorder (ASD) and outline the cognitive treatment of a client who developed ASD subsequent to a motor vehicle accident (MVA). This case highlights the multifaceted needs of acutely traumatized clients, and the treatment outlined illustrates cognitive strategies for clinicians to apply.

ACUTE STRESS DISORDER (ASD)

Post-traumatic stress disorder (PTSD) is diagnosed if an individual reports clinically significant re-experiencing, avoidance, and arousal symptoms that are present for at least 1 month following a traumatic event. In DSM-IV (American Psychiatric Association, 1994), the diagnosis of ASD was introduced to describe stress reactions that occur in the *initial* month post-trauma. To satisfy criteria for ASD, an individual must: (a) be exposed to an objectively stressful event that involves actual or threatened death or serious injury, and report a subjective response to the stressor of helplessness and/or fear, and endorse: (b) three dissociative symptoms, (c) one re-experiencing symptom, (d) marked avoidance symptoms, and (e) marked arousal symptoms. In addition, symptoms must cause clinically significant distress or impairment, and occur between 2 days and 4 weeks post-trauma. The distinctive feature of the ASD diagnosis is the requirement that three of a possible five dissociative symptoms (including emotional numbing, decreased awareness of surroundings, derealization, depersonalization, and dissociative amnesia) be evident either at the time of the trauma or in the initial month after the trauma.

The rationale for the inclusion of ASD in DSM-IV (APA, 1994) was to facilitate the identification of individuals at risk of developing PTSD (Bryant & Harvey, 2000). Supporting this aim, prospective studies demonstrated the capacity of a diagnosis of ASD in the immediate weeks after trauma to predict later PTSD (e.g., Brewin, Andrews, Rose, & Kirk, 1999; Bryant & Harvey, 1998). Subsequently, a key goal for the trauma field was to investigate whether the provision of early intervention to individuals with ASD reduced the likelihood of chronic PTSD. A series of treatment outcome studies have provided a compelling evidence-base supporting the efficacy of cognitive behaviour therapy (CBT) for effectively treating ASD and therefore preventing PTSD (e.g., Bryant, Sackville, Dang, Moulds, & Guthrie, 1999; Bryant, Moulds, Guthrie, & Nixon, 2003; Bryant et al., 2008). The CBT protocol employed in these studies contained a combination of cognitive (e.g., cognitive restructuring) and behavioural (e.g., prolonged imaginal exposure, in vivo exposure) treatment strategies.

This chapter describes the treatment of a client (Mark) with ASD following a MVA. Mark was treated as part of a randomized controlled trial that compared the relative efficacy of cognitive restructuring and prolonged exposure (Bryant et al., 2008). Although in routine clinical practice cognitive restructuring would be delivered in combination with additional CBT techniques (e.g., reliving of the trauma memory, also referred to as prolonged exposure), in this chapter we focus solely on cognitive restructuring for ASD.

CASE EXAMPLE: MARK

Mark was a 41-year-old male who presented for psychological assessment following a MVA. He was employed as a truck driver and was married with two adult sons.

Mark was referred by his GP to the Centre for Traumatic Stress at Westmead Hospital, Sydney, 3 weeks after a MVA in which he collided with an oncoming vehicle. The young driver of the other vehicle died in the accident. Mark was taken by ambulance to accident and emergency at Westmead Hospital, and released later that evening. Physical injuries arising from the trauma were a mild closed head injury with brief loss of consciousness and bruising to his ribs. Mark reported ongoing neck pain and headaches at the time of assessment. Mark did not have any psychiatric history. On assessment, Mark presented as distressed, anxious, and tearful. He had blunted affect and limited spontaneous speech. He was hesitant in responding to questions, and provided only brief responses. He appeared reluctant to disclose some details; in particular, to elaborate on his emotional responses to the trauma and his post-trauma symptoms. His pre-treatment scores on assessment measures were CAPS-II, Frequency = 39, Intensity = 28, and BDI-II = 25.

Summary and case formulation

Mark reported symptoms consistent with a diagnosis of ASD (specifically: emotional numbing, derealization, depersonalization; nightmares, intrusive memories, distress on exposure to reminders of the MVA; avoidance of driving and of thinking about the accident; hypervigilance, insomnia, and irritability). He also reported uncued panic attacks, with onset following the trauma. He described low mood and a range of depressive symptoms consistent with a diagnosis of major depressive episode. His acute stress reactions appeared to be maintained by excessively negative appraisals of his symptoms (e.g., 'I'm going crazy') that exacerbated his anxiety and depression, and prompted extensive efforts to avoid the memory of the trauma, talking about the trauma, and returning to driving his truck. He experienced significant shame and frustration about his psychological symptoms (in particular, his angry outbursts and irritability with his family). Mark reported excessive guilt about the MVA, and frequently ruminated about how he could have avoided the accident and how he was solely responsible for the death of the other driver. Additional stressors secondary to the MVA (e.g., financial stress, employment uncertainty, compensation issues, physical injuries) were causing him further distress. Mark described a strong network of social support from family and friends; however, he reported feeling generally detached and withdrawn since the trauma. He had good insight into the extent of the impact of his symptoms on his functioning, and described being motivated to engage in therapy.

Cognitive treatment of ASD

As noted above, random allocation in a RCT for ASD being conducted at the time of Mark's referral resulted in him receiving treatment that exclusively contained cognitive restructuring. Treatment involved 5 × 90-minute therapy sessions. A summary of the treatment, and specific applications for Mark, is outlined below.

The focus of session 1 was on providing psychoeducation and introducing cognitive restructuring. Specific treatment components were as follows:

1   Feedback and normalization of ASD symptoms.
2   Presentation of treatment rationale and outline of treatment description.
3   Discussion of common trauma-related cognitive errors.
4   Introduction and demonstration of cognitive restructuring.

The primary goal of the first session was to normalize Mark's ASD symptoms. The need to normalize acute responses is underscored by evidence highlighting the importance of dysfunctional appraisals of symptoms (e.g., 'thinking about the accident over and over must mean that I am going crazy') in predicting chronic post-traumatic stress symptoms (e.g., Dunmore, Clark, & Ehlers, 2001; Ehlers, Mayou, & Bryant, 1998). Further, Mark voiced a number of cognitions in the assessment session that highlighted negative appraisals of his symptoms, including guilt about his irritability and detachment from his family ('I'm not a good father/husband'), anxiety about his intrusions ('They mean I'm losing control'), and his self-deprecating response following symptom exacerbation after attempting to return to work ('I shouldn't be affected by this event'). Accordingly, Mark received detailed feedback on his ASD reactions. Symptom clusters and examples of each were explained and normalized, as follows:

> Following a trauma, people often experience the sorts of problems you have told me about. We call this sort of problem post-traumatic stress. It means that after you have been through a traumatic experience, you tend to feel very scared, on edge and uncertain about things, and to think a lot about how dangerous the world is. This happens because when you go through a trauma, you learn that things around you can be harmful, and you tend to be on the lookout for other things that might hurt you again. People often think about their trauma a lot, dream about it, and feel uptight when reminded of it. People get very worked up after a trauma because they tend to be on the alert, waiting for the next bad thing to happen. These are all understandable responses to an event that has taught you to be wary of things around you. I want you to understand that all the sorts of problems that you are having are common considering what you've been through.

Let's talk about each of these reactions in more detail:

> *Intrusions* may be in the form of flashbacks or dreams, or memories popping into your mind when you don't want them. They serve the purpose of allowing the mind to process the trauma by playing it over repeatedly. The internal re-experiencing of the trauma also gives you plenty of occasions to learn what is dangerous and how to avoid it in future.
>
> *Emotional numbing* can occur at the time of the trauma or afterwards. It refers to feeling emotionally flat, feeling like you are in a daze, feeling the world is not quite real, or feeling like you are looking at yourself from the outside. These are signs that you are switched off inside, which is a way of trying to feel less distressed.
>
> *Avoidance* of thoughts, activities, places, and anything else that reminds you of the trauma is another common reaction. Avoidance is another attempt to minimize the hurtful memories of what happened and prevent it from happening again.
>
> *Physical arousal* refers to being hyperaware of your surroundings,

having trouble sleeping or concentrating, feeling restless and irritable, or having a sense of impending danger or doom. Physical arousal is a sign that even though the trauma is over, your body is still in alert mode and prepared for the worst, ready to fight or flee.

The second key goal of the initial treatment session was to present the rationale for cognitive restructuring, and to introduce the concepts of thinking errors and the process of cognitive restructuring. The establishment of a clear and coherent rationale for cognitive restructuring is essential. Many clients with ASD are extremely sensitive to the implication that their symptoms are 'all in their head'. Accordingly, it is essential that clinicians deliver a clearly explained, thorough rationale for any cognitive intervention, and that treatment does not proceed until the rationale is understood. To ensure comprehension, the clinician regularly checked Mark's understanding of the rationale for treatment, both during the first treatment session and throughout the course of therapy.

THERAPIST: In today's session we're going to focus on how having experienced a traumatic event may have changed the way you view yourself, other people, and the world in general. It is very common for people who have experienced trauma to perceive the world as dangerous, other people as unpredictable, and themselves as incapable of coping with their reactions and daily stressors. Have you noticed any changes in your thinking since the trauma?

MARK: Yeah, I keep thinking that it is not safe on the roads any more.

THERAPIST: So you see danger in a situation that you used to be comfortable in?

MARK: Yeah, well I used to love driving on roads.

THERAPIST: And have you noticed any changes in how you see yourself?

MARK: I don't trust myself any more. I don't understand how I can't cope with this . . . and I worry about how it is affecting my family.

THERAPIST: That's another good example of how our thoughts may change after a trauma. As well as seeing much more danger in the world, we often think differently about ourselves. And as our thoughts, feelings, and behaviours are all linked, the way you are thinking right now may be leading you to feel anxious, frightened, or down much of the time. So it is important for us look closely at these new thoughts and check out how accurate and how helpful they are. We will do this via a method called cognitive restructuring, or cognitive challenging. This type of therapy provides a way of identifying these new thoughts and beliefs, and evaluating how realistic and helpful they are. In this way we will discuss the meaning you attach to situations that cause you

	fear and anxiety. And this will help you to develop more realistic and helpful appraisals of the world and yourself, to assist you to cope better and recover.
MARK:	That would be good because I feel like I am not coping at the moment.
THERAPIST:	OK. Let me explain how our thinking affects how we are feeling. We constantly have thoughts come in to our minds, they tend to be automatic (that is we don't try to have them), and we are often not aware of them. However, how we *feel* in a situation depends on our *thoughts* in a situation. Let me give you an example . . . Imagine that you are walking down the road and you hear a sound in the bushes. You immediately think that there's a thug hiding in the bushes. What would you be feeling?
MARK:	Petrified.
THERAPIST:	That's how I would be feeling too. Most people would be very scared if they thought someone was in the bushes and may harm them. But what if you found out that it was only a cat in the bushes. What would you be feeling then?
MARK:	Oh that's no problem. I would just say to myself 'it's only a cat' and keep walking.
THERAPIST:	What different reactions did you notice within your self to these different perceptions?
MARK:	Well yeah, when I thought it was a thug I felt very scared, but there was no problem when I thought it was a cat.
THERAPIST:	OK, so it looks like it is what you *think* about an event that matters. It is not the noise that makes you scared but rather the thought that there is a thug in the bushes. Not only does this thought make you feel anxious, it influences your actions. For example, you might run away, call out for help, and avoid walking in that part of the neighbourhood in the future.
	Now as I explained earlier, our thinking tends to change after an accident. We tend to assume there is danger in a situation when there might not be. And as you can see, this leaves you feeling pretty anxious a lot of the time. And often we are not even aware of our thoughts, let alone how our thinking has changed. So what we need to do first is learn to identify the types of thoughts that you are having when you're in the car, and to start to notice the way that these thoughts make you feel more anxious and change your behaviour. Then we can spend some time together looking at how realistic and how helpful these thoughts are.

Once the client fully understands the rationale for targeting cognitions, the clinician should help them to identify examples of unhelpful cognitions that they have been experiencing since the trauma. Common examples include: 'It's only a matter of time before I have another accident', 'no one can be trusted', 'no place is safe', 'I have no control over what is going to happen to me', 'there is no point planning for the future'. As with cognitive therapy for any condition, the next important step is to explain the link between cognitions and emotions, as illustrated by the example above. The clinician should educate the client about unhelpful patterns of thinking (e.g., dichotomous thinking, overgeneralizing, emotional reasoning), and teach them to categorize their thoughts accordingly (a useful reference here is Resick & Schnicke, 1993). The final stage involves teaching clients to challenge their unhelpful trauma-related thoughts, and to consider more adaptive alternatives. Standard questions employed in cognitive challenging (e.g., 'what is the evidence for and against this thought?' 'is your thought based on feelings or facts?') can be employed (see Greenberger & Padesky, 1995; also Resick & Schnicke, 1993).

It is also important that clients monitor ratings of the *emotional impact* and *strength of belief* of both the initial thought and the new, alternative thought. Such careful monitoring allows both the clinician and the client to meaningfully compare the impact of both thoughts, and thus to gauge the effectiveness of cognitive challenging. Both the therapist and the client need to be realistic in their expectations about the process and speed of cognitive change. It is highly unlikely that a client like Mark will experience the thought 'I am responsible for the death of the other driver' with a belief rating of 100/100, and then reduce this rating to 0/100 after one session of cognitive challenging. Indeed, a thought such as this that is associated with extreme guilt may still be strongly believed (e.g., 85/100) following an entire therapy session devoted to challenging it. It is therefore essential that clinicians emphasize to clients that successful cognitive restructuring is dependent on continuing to collect evidence about the thought and repeatedly challenging unhelpful thoughts every time they arise. Further, clients should be encouraged to monitor the strength of their belief ratings and the degree of their emotional response to the thoughts whenever they occur. Thorough monitoring of these details between sessions provides valuable information about which cognitions have been successfully challenged, and which may be 'stuck points' that need to be addressed further in the session.

Finally, the clinician must also deliver a clear explanation for the need to complete cognitive monitoring. Some clients return for treatment sessions having not completed monitoring but saying that they did not need to, as they challenged their cognitions 'in their head'. For others, monitoring may represent having to complete yet another form; in the midst of paperwork about accident-related health/injuries, compensation claims, insurance, etc., clients with ASD may feel overwhelmed and therefore not comply with this important part of treatment. A clear rationale at the outset that highlights monitoring as central to successful treatment will maximize the likelihood of compliance.

Common trauma-related cognitions

Regardless of the type of trauma experienced, a number of cognitions are commonly reported by clients with ASD. We describe two examples from Mark's case.

(1) 'It's going to happen again'

Cognitions about experiencing another trauma play a significant role in the maintenance of ASD symptoms by promoting avoidance of trauma reminders and situations perceived to be dangerous (e.g., for Mark, resuming driving his truck), and by encouraging the use of safety behaviours in response to excessive hypervigilance to threat (e.g., repeatedly checking side mirrors to monitor other drivers). In such cases, cognitive restructuring should focus on attempts to reduce threat expectancy. At the beginning of treatment, Mark reported experiencing the thought 'It's going to happen again' every time he was travelling in the car as a passenger, and as treatment progressed, when he resumed driving. It had become clear from Mark's monitoring that this cognition was frequent and was causing him significant distress.

THERAPIST: Looking at your monitoring form from the past week, I can see that a very similar thought came up each time you had to ride in the car: 'I'm going to have another accident'. The fact that this thought arose repeatedly is a sign that it's one of the stuck points that we spoke about earlier. So let's start with this example today. Can you tell me what happened when you had this thought during the week?

MARK: OK. Well every time that I was about to get in the car I got really anxious. I felt for sure that I was going to have another accident. The thought that came into my mind was 'I'm going to have another accident – today could be the day'.

THERAPIST: I can see that this thought made you feel very anxious each time – either 90 or 100/100.

MARK: Yeah.

THERAPIST: And each time, how strongly did you believe that you were going to have another accident?

MARK: 100%, definitely sure.

THERAPIST: OK, it's understandable that this belief gets triggered so often after you've had such a nasty accident. But if it is causing you such high anxiety, it's worth having a look at how realistic it is. Let's weigh up the evidence.

MARK: OK, but I can tell you that the thought is completely realistic when I'm about to drive.

THERAPIST: Yes, I can see how much you believe the thought by taking a look at your monitoring – every time you had that thought in the past week, you wrote down that you believed it 100%. But let's explore it. OK, to begin with, how many trips have you taken in your car?

MARK: Do you mean ever? Well, I don't know, plenty I suppose. Hundreds? No, more likely thousands?

THERAPIST: Daily trips over the past 30 years?

MARK: Yeah, at least.

THERAPIST: That makes almost. . . . 11,000 trips, right?

MARK: Yeah, I suppose so.

THERAPIST: And how many accidents have you had?

MARK: Well, I've had the accident in the truck, and I've had about three dings in the car.

THERAPIST: So based on your past experiences, the chances of having another accident in the car are about 3 in 11,000, which is about 0.0003%. Does that surprise you?

MARK: I suppose so, when you look at it like that.

THERAPIST: So when you hop into a car you are judging that the risk of having another accident is 100%, which of course makes you feel very frightened, but when we look at the evidence we can make a guess that the risk is closer to 0.0003%. Let's go back to that original thought. Just by looking at the available evidence, how strongly do you now believe that you are going to have another accident?

MARK: Probably about 50%. It can't just go away. It's still strong and I can't help it. It's just how I feel.

THERAPIST: Sure. But just by looking at the evidence we've already shifted the degree that you believe that thought by 50%. It's a lot more realistic. And does that have any effect on your anxiety?

MARK: Well I don't know about being in a car. But I feel a bit relieved when I can see it like that.

THERAPIST: Terrific, that's the first step. Remember, you've been experiencing this thought since the accident happened, so it's not realistic to expect it to disappear. Also, it's easier to look at the evidence when we're sitting here together in the clinic – I'd predict that it would be much more difficult when you're actually in the car. But that's why it's important to persist and to challenge these difficult thoughts *every time* that they occur – especially when you're in the car. That's why it's also essential to keep a log of not only your thoughts, but also the belief and emotion ratings that go along with them. These details will allow us to reflect on the past week and to see when challenging your thoughts has been helpful, as well as which thoughts you're getting stuck on.

(2) 'If only I'd done things differently . . .'

Clients who have experienced a trauma commonly experience significant guilt about their actions and responses (or perceived lack thereof) during the traumatic event. A useful technique when challenging 'what if?' thoughts is to help the client to explore the effect and advantages/disadvantages of thinking in that way. Over time, the clinician's questioning can help the client to see that these types of ruminative thoughts only have a negative impact on their emotional state, and cannot change the fact that the trauma happened, nor alter its outcomes.

THERAPIST: I've noticed that there was another thought that you had many times this week: 'if I had done something differently the driver of the car would not have died'.

MARK: Yeah, that thought is often in my head.

THERAPIST: You have also written here that the thought makes you feel guilty and depressed.

MARK: Yeah (lowers head, teary).

THERAPIST: I can also see that every time the thought came into your head this week, your belief rating was 100/100.

MARK: Yes. Not surprising after what I did.

THERAPIST: I can see why that thought leads you to feel so awful. I think it would be useful for us to spend some time today evaluating it. Let's start by going back to what happened in the accident for a moment.

MARK: Well I was driving my truck, the highway was pretty busy and I saw this P-plater (provisional driver) pull out of his lane into mine.

THERAPIST: And what did you think at the time?

MARK: I thought it was a stupid move, but it seemed as if there was just enough room for him to overtake the car in front of him.

THERAPIST: I see . . .

MARK: Yeah, but for some reason he hesitated, tried to go back to where he was but couldn't (because there was another car behind him), so instead he froze and hit the brakes. Now I was doing 110 km and there was no way I could stop – not in a truck. He started to move into his lane but my truck hit directly into the driver's side of his car . . . and well . . . as you know, he died.

THERAPIST: OK, so since the accident you have been blaming yourself for the driver's death to some degree?

MARK: Not to some degree – completely. And all the time . . . I just keep trying to figure out why I didn't act differently so I could have avoided this horrible thing.

THERAPIST:	Do you think there were any other options available to you at the time?
MARK:	Yeah, I could have steered off the road to try and miss his car.
THERAPIST:	What would have happened if you chose to do that?
MARK:	The accident wouldn't have happened. Although, thinking about it, it probably wasn't really an option because my truck is so long that even if I had steered the front off the highway the car would have hit the side of the truck.
THERAPIST:	And what might have happened then?
MARK:	I guess maybe if I had gone off the highway quickly, the cars behind me might have hit the back of my truck and maybe even hit each other causing an even bigger accident.
THERAPIST:	Sounds like that wasn't really a good option.
MARK:	No, I suppose it wouldn't have been really.

The therapist then slowly helped Mark to realistically review all other options that he thought of during his periods of rumination. They also discussed how much time he had had to react and other factors that contributed to the death of the driver. Once they had looked at this evidence, the therapist helped Mark to consider the consequences of continuing to ruminate about his role in the accident.

THERAPIST:	It seems to me that it just wasn't possible for you to avert this accident.
MARK:	Yeah, but if I could have done something. . . .
THERAPIST:	OK, let's just slow it down for a moment and review what we have discussed. When you have the thought 'if I had of done something differently the driver of the car would not have died', it leaves you feeling guilty and depressed. However, when you think it through, it seems like the reality is that at the time there was no other feasible course of action that you realistically could have taken instead. Is that right?
MARK:	Yeah.
THERAPIST:	OK, it seems pretty clear that thinking this way is not helpful to you. Let's look at the advantages and disadvantages of thinking this way. What are some of the advantages?
MARK:	Maybe I could try to come up with something I could have done to avoid the accident. Not sure what else – that's probably it.
THERAPIST:	OK, now what are some disadvantages?
MARK:	Well, that it makes me feel depressed and guilty.
THERAPIST:	Yes, what else?
MARK:	Well it makes me feel like the accident was all my fault, and I suppose that maybe it wasn't completely my fault.
THERAPIST:	Good. Any other disadvantages?

MARK: It doesn't let me move on from the experience. And it makes me terrified about going back to driving the truck again, and I guess that stops me from getting back in to work again.

THERAPIST: OK, so it sounds like there are a few major disadvantages for you if you to continue to think this way. In fact, this is true of any thoughts that begin with 'what if . . .'. These types of thoughts are really just unanswerable questions. No matter how many times you ask them, they don't bring you closer to an answer. All that they do is have a negative effect on how you feel. Thinking this way can't change what happened in the past. What your thinking can change is how you will feel in the future.

MARK: I guess that's true.

Encouraging Mark to weigh up the advantages and disadvantages of his thinking was of course only the first stage of addressing this persistent thought. The clinician then proceeded to assist him to generate alternative, more adaptive thoughts to replace his unhelpful belief.

THERAPIST: So we've discovered that focusing on what you could have done to avoid the accident is unrealistic – any of your options probably would have caused a worse accident – and is unhelpful – it makes you feel depressed, guilty, and stops you from moving on. So what is a more helpful and realistic way of thinking about this?

MARK: What do you mean?

THERAPIST: When you notice that you start thinking this, what could you say back to yourself? I know that this is difficult for you to answer. Another way to think about it would be to consider what you might say to a friend who was in your position.

MARK: I could remind myself that realistically I couldn't have done anything that could have avoided an accident. It's probably more helpful to focus on getting better and getting back to driving.

THERAPIST: Exactly. And what would be the consequences of thinking in this way? Thinking about this alternative thought, how much do you now believe your initial thought that the accident was your fault?

MARK: Maybe 70%, no, more like 50%. It makes me feel a bit less guilty and more focused on the future right now. But tomorrow the guilt will still be there and I'll still believe the thought.

THERAPIST: I'm not surprised. Remember, this is a tough thought to tackle – it comes up over and over, and it makes you feel really guilty and depressed. So to expect that guilt to disappear right away really isn't very realistic. Instead, let's try out responding to the thought with the alternative that you just came up with. So every time you have the thought 'if I had done something differently the driver of the car would not have died', I'd like you to test out the alternative, and to note how much you believe the new thought each time.

MARK: I suppose I could give it a try. I'm not sure it will help with my guilt when I'm about to get in the car.

THERAPIST: I'm glad that you've agreed to give it a go. Suppose we treat it like an experiment. It sounds like your hunch is that replacing your thought with an alternative won't reduce your guilt, and that you're pretty convinced about that. The opposite prediction would be that responding to your thought with an alternative every time that it comes up would reduce your guilt ratings over time. So that we can test out these two options, I'd like you to be particularly careful to write on your monitoring form every time this thought occurs and you challenge it, and to note your emotion and belief ratings before and after. We can look at the outcome of the experiment next week.

MARK: OK.

Treatment outcome

Post-treatment, Mark reported improvements in terms of reductions in his post-traumatic stress symptoms, levels of depression and general anxiety. He had returned to driving, and although he reported still feeling anxious when behind the wheel, this anxiety was significantly less than pre-treatment, and was continuing to diminish. However, Mark's post-treatment responses on the assessment measures suggested only minimal treatment gains (CAPS-II: Frequency = 29, Intensity = 28, BDI-II = 38). A complicating factor that became apparent mid-treatment was Mark's disclosure that his feelings of shame about his symptoms had prompted him to underreport their severity pre-treatment. Thus, the minimal pre-/post-treatment differences indicated by his self-report measures could not be meaningfully interpreted. Nonetheless, it was encouraging that 6 months post-treatment, Mark's responses on the CAPS-II (i.e., Frequency = 15, Intensity = 13, BDI-II = 8) indicated sustained treatment benefits. This example highlights that one potentially critical impact of negative appraisals of ASD symptoms is underreporting in assessment, and stresses the need for clinicians to address these appraisals early in treatment to ensure accurate, meaningful assessment and engagement in treatment.

Discussion

There were obstacles encountered in the assessment and treatment of Mark that commonly arise in the management of acutely traumatized clients. First, on assessment, Mark was reluctant to disclose in detail the nature and extent of his cognitions and his ASD symptoms. He later reported that this was driven largely by his conviction that his symptoms indicated that he was indeed 'going crazy'. As rapport developed and therapy progressed, Mark responded to cognitive challenging of unhelpful metacognitive beliefs about his symptoms, and as a result became more open about his difficulties. A related challenge was Mark's self-imposed pressure to return to work quickly (i.e., in the week following the MVA). Unsurprisingly, the extent of his anxiety and avoidance prevented his return to work within this timeframe. This compounded his sense of shame about his symptoms ('*I shouldn't be so affected by this*') and served to exacerbate his guilt about not carrying out his role as the primary financial provider for his family ('*I have failed as a father and a husband*'). As treatment sessions progressed and these appraisals were challenged, it became apparent that such shame-related cognitions had further contributed to his reluctance to be completely open with the clinician about the extent of his distress and impairment. Thus, shifting key cognitions early in therapy had the important impact of increasing Mark's engagement in therapy, thereby maximizing potential treatment benefits.

A second challenge was dealing with multiple ongoing stressors at the time of treatment. Ongoing stressors are often deemed an obstacle to the application of acute intervention; in such cases the clinician should evaluate the client's resources before commencing with therapy in the acute period (see Bryant & Harvey, 2000). For Mark, such stressors included financial stress, uncertainty about his employment, unresolved legal issues following from the MVA and attending a range of follow-up appointments (e.g., with a physician regarding his head/neck injury, with a rehabilitation provider to address return to work issues). These additional stressors exacerbated Mark's anxiety and in turn maintained his ASD symptoms. The presence of ongoing stressors is common in ASD patients. Clinicians should be mindful of their potential impact, and be sure to address cognitions associated with them in the course of therapy, such as '*this is all too much, I can't handle all of these appointments*'.

As a result of random allocation in a treatment trial (Bryant et al., 2008), Mark's treatment was comprised of cognitive restructuring only. In routine clinical practice, however, cognitive restructuring would be delivered in combination with additional treatment components, most notably reliving of the trauma memory. It should be noted that early intervention for ASD will achieve optimal clinical gains when there is direct activation of the trauma memory. A recent ASD treatment study compared prolonged exposure versus cognitive restructuring found that patients who received prolonged exposure had greater symptom reduction post-treatment and at 6-month follow-up than patients who received cognitive restructuring (Bryant et al., 2008). Hence, reliving exercises should be integrated into therapy in order to maximize outcome. Reliving for patients with ASD should follow the same principles and procedures as reliving delivered to clients with PTSD. However, some clinical considerations are of increased relevance in the treatment of acute cases. For example, given that dissociative reactions are central to ASD, the clinician should be vigilant to any indicators that a client is not sufficiently engaged in the trauma memory (e.g., a lack of emotional activation evidenced by little or no shift in affect; for a detailed discussion, see Bryant & Harvey, 2000). Generally, however, reliving for patients with ASD should be implemented in the same way and with consideration of the same clinical issues that are relevant when treating PTSD. For example, decisions about the suitability of including reliving in treatment should be made with contraindications in mind (e.g., suicide risk, substance abuse) for both acute and chronic presentations.

CONCLUDING COMMENTS

Early intervention prevents individuals from unnecessarily suffering from distressing and disabling chronic PTSD. Intervening in the acute phase also has the significant advantage of preventing the establishment of entrenched avoidance responses and the development of secondary problems (e.g., use of drugs and alcohol to manage symptoms, depression, social withdrawal). Nonetheless, it is important to remain mindful of the fact that acute stress responses (e.g., hypervigilance, insomnia) are common in the immediate aftermath of trauma (in particular, the first 1–2 weeks following the event). For the majority, these reactions are transient, not sufficiently severe to satisfy criteria for ASD, and will naturally remit without intervention. In the initial weeks subsequent to a trauma, we recommend that clinicians adopt an approach of 'watchful waiting' (National Collaborating Centre for Mental Health, 2005). However, in cases in which symptoms persist and satisfy criteria approaching a month after the trauma, early intervention will very likely be indicated.

Ultimately, the decision to commence early intervention should be guided by each client's available resources. The presence of ongoing stressors (e.g., legal, physical, financial) that may compromise a client's capacity to manage the demands of therapy (in particular, the reliving component) may prompt a clinician to delay treatment. Similarly, if the trauma itself is unresolved (e.g., if there is an ongoing threat of domestic violence), pressing practical issues such as the client's safety and housing should of course take precedence. In the case of significant ongoing stressors, the most appropriate initial approach may be to apply problem-solving strategies that assist the client to manage their stressors and associated distress. In this sense, the best clinical decision may be to provide support and education about practical strategies that aim to promote coping with the immediate distress, and to defer the commencement of early intervention until these initial stressors have subsided.

Finally, it is important to make the distinction between CBT for ASD and critical incident stress debriefing (CISD; Mitchell, 1983). Debriefing is a form of early intervention that is most often administered in a single session to a group of individuals who have experienced a trauma. Evaluations of the efficacy of debriefing have yielded conflicting findings (Devilly, Gist, & Cotton, 2006; see also Rose, Bisson, & Wessely, 2003). An important distinction is that debriefing is typically offered to *all* individuals who are exposed to a trauma. The premise of debriefing is that all individuals who have been exposed to a trauma will benefit from discussing the event and their emotional responses to it. By comparison, early intervention in the form of CBT for ASD is offered to individuals who report clinically significant symptoms (i.e., that meet criteria for ASD) who, left untreated, would be at elevated risk of developing chronic PTSD.

This chapter has illustrated the application of cognitive therapy techniques for a patient with ASD. Cognitive strategies are a core ingredient of the CBT protocol for ASD that has received extensive empirical support from a host of treatment outcome trials conducted by Bryant and colleagues in Sydney. A challenge for the field is for independent clinical researchers in other trauma centres to replicate our finding that CBT delivered in the immediate weeks following trauma can prevent chronic PTSD.

REFERENCES

American Psychiatric Association. (1994). *Diagnostic and statistical manual of mental disorders* (4th ed.). Washington, DC: APA.

Brewin, C.R., Andrews, B., Rose, S., & Kirk, M. (1999). Acute stress disorder and posttraumatic stress disorder in victims of violent crime. *American Journal of Psychiatry*, *156*, 360–366.

Bryant, R.A., & Harvey, A.G. (1998). Relationship of acute stress disorder and posttraumatic stress disorder following mild traumatic brain injury. *American Journal of Psychiatry*, *155*, 625–629.

Bryant, R.A., & Harvey, A.G. (2000). *Acute stress disorder: A handbook of theory, assessment and treatment*. Washington, DC: American Psychological Association.

Bryant, R.A., Mastrodomenico, J., Felmingham, K., Hopwood, S., Kenny, L., Kandris, E., Cahill, C., & Creamer, M. (2008). Treating acute stress disorder: A randomized controlled trial. *Archives of General Psychiatry*, *65*, 659–667.

Bryant, R.A., Moulds, M.L., Guthrie, R.M., & Nixon, R.D.V. (2003). Treating acute stress disorder following mild traumatic brain injury. *American Journal of Psychiatry*, *160*, 585–587.

Bryant, R.A., Sackville, T., Dang, S.T., Moulds, M.L., & Guthrie, R.M. (1999). Treating acute stress disorder: An evaluation of cognitive behavior therapy and supportive counseling techniques. *American Journal of Psychiatry*, *156*, 1780–1786.

Devilly, G.J., Gist, R., & Cotton, P. (2006). Ready! Aim! Fire! The status of psychological debriefing and therapeutic interventions: In the work place and after disasters. *Review of General Psychology*, *10*, 318–345.

Dunmore, E., Clark, D.M., & Ehlers, A. (2001). A prospective study of the role of cognitive factors in persistent posttraumatic stress disorder after physical or sexual assault. *Behaviour Research and Therapy*, *39*, 1063–1084.

Ehlers, A., Mayou, R.A., & Bryant, B. (1998). Psychological predictors of chronic posttraumatic stress disorder after motor vehicle accidents. *Journal of Abnormal Psychology*, *107*, 508–519.

Greenberger, D., & Padesky, C.A. (1995). *Mind over mood: A cognitive therapy treatment manual for clients*. New York: Guilford Press.

Mitchell, J.T. (1983). When disaster strikes . . . The critical incident stress debriefing process. *Journal of Emergency Services*, *8*, 36–39.

National Collaborating Centre for Mental Health. (2005). *Clinical guideline 26. Posttraumatic stress disorder (PTSD): The management of PTSD in adults and children in primary and secondary care*. London: National Institute for Clinical Excellence.

Resick, P.A., & Schnicke, M.L. (1993). *Cognitive processing therapy for rape victims: A treatment manual*. Newbury Park, CA: Sage Publications.

Rose, S., Bisson, J., & Wessely, S. (2003). A systematic review of single psychological interventions ('debriefing') following trauma. Updating the Cochrane review and implications for good practice. In R. Orner, & U. Schnyder (Eds.), *Reconstructing early intervention after trauma: Innovations in the care of survivors* (pp. 24–39). Oxford: Oxford University Press.

Chapter 3

Travel, trauma, and phobia

Treating the survivors of transport-related trauma

Rachel Handley, Paul Salkovskis, Ann Hackmann, and Anke Ehlers

INTRODUCTION

Travelling by public and personal transport is an important part of modern life. Travel phobia is a common and disabling problem characterized by strong fear and avoidance of travel. It can interfere severely with the individual's occupational and social functioning. In clinical settings, fear of travel may present either as the main problem (i.e., as a specific phobia) or as part of another anxiety disorder (e.g., agoraphobia, claustrophobia). It may also develop as a response to experiencing a traumatic event when travelling (e.g., assault, terrorist attack, or severe accident). For example, it has been observed that driving phobias are common after road traffic accidents and can occur in the context of, or independently of, post-traumatic stress disorder (PTSD; Mayou, Bryant, & Ehlers, 2001).

Whereas the phenomenology of travel fears shares many features among these subgroups of patients (Blanchard & Hickling, 1997; Ehlers, Hofmann, Herda, & Roth, 1994), the concerns that lead people to be afraid of travel may be quite different. For example, whereas some people may be concerned mainly about the risk of being involved in an accident or attack on their lives while travelling, others may be concerned mainly about the risk of being suddenly incapacitated by anxiety, similar to the concerns of patients with panic disorder. Furthermore, travelling can activate social concerns, such as concerns about behaving in a way that would be embarrassing, thus overlapping in relevant concerns with social phobia. Cognitive behavioural therapy of travel phobia will thus need to be informed about the idiosyncratic cognitions that drive a patient's avoidance behaviour.

The treatment of two patients that fear the same travel situation, for example, fear of using underground trains, can therefore have a very different focus, depending on the content of the relevant concerns. Systematic exposure to feared situations is a core element of the treatment of situational phobias (Davey, 1997). However, the exposure exercises will need to be chosen carefully on the basis of the patient's concerns to maximize clinical benefit. Furthermore, as this chapter will show, treatment techniques that were developed for the treatment of panic disorder and post-traumatic stress disorder are often helpful in addressing the patient's relevant concerns. This is especially relevant for patients whose travel phobia was triggered by a traumatic event. The reason is that intrusive memories of the trauma are common among all trauma survivors, including those who do not meet diagnostic criteria for PTSD. Intrusive trauma memories have a 'here and now' quality that gives rise to a sense of current threat and predicts maintenance of symptoms (Michael et al., 2005). Furthermore, the interpretation of such memories as signs that one is going crazy or out of control (Ehlers & Clark, 2000; Ehlers & Steil, 1995) may lead to efforts to suppress these memories, which has the paradoxical effect of maintaining intrusive memories. Thus, in order to treat travel phobias after traumatic events, the therapist will need to map the patient's concerns in order to choose the appropriate methods of challenging them and may need to draw on recent advances in treating trauma memories.

We will illustrate how a cognitive formulation that takes into account cognitive elements of panic disorder and PTSD helps direct treatment of travel phobia after traumatic events, drawing on cases from the tragic events in London on 7 July 2005. On that day, four suicide bombers detonated explosive devices in London, killing 52 and injuring more than 770 passengers on three underground trains and a bus. Many commuters stayed away from the transport system in London in the following days, but most quickly returned to their old habits as time passed and fear gave way to necessity and convenience (Rubin et al., 2007). However, a substantial proportion of those who were directly involved in the events of that day developed PTSD, which usually included fearful avoidance of public transport (Brewin et al., 2008; Handley, Salkovskis, Scragg, & Ehlers, in press). Others developed travel phobia, which usually involved some symptoms of PTSD such as intrusive memories, but not the full syndrome (Handley et al., in press).

Mindful of the potential overlap in PTSD and specific phobia symptoms in the context of this large-scale trauma, the authors sought to develop a treatment protocol for individuals presenting with travel fear and avoidance based on existing specific phobia (Davey, 1997) and PTSD treatments. When the main problem more closely resembled travel phobia, patients were treated primarily using cognitive behavioural techniques for phobic avoidance, including:

- Formulation that the anxiety is due to patient's beliefs about negative events that may happen when travelling and that these beliefs are being maintained by safety behaviours.
- Challenging the beliefs by calculating the probabilities of the expected events.
- In vivo exposure with a cognitive rationale using behavioural experiments to test the predictions from the beliefs.

- Psychoeducation about the normal course of anxiety.
- Vicious circle model of panic attacks, identifying catastrophic mis-interpretations of bodily sensations at the core of panic attacks and behavioural experiments testing these interpretations.

When the main problem most closely resembled PTSD, the treatment incorporated further elements of cognitive therapy for PTSD (Ehlers & Clark, 2000; Ehlers, Clark, Hackmann, McManus, Fennell, & Grey, 2009), a model of treatment for PTSD which has a good evidence-base and has been successfully used for PTSD following terrorist events (Duffy, Gillespie, & Clark, 2007; Ehlers et al., 2003; Ehlers, Clark, Hackmann, McManus, & Fennell, 2005; Gillespie, Duffy, Hackmann, & Clark, 2002). The main add-itional interventions were those designed to reduce intrusive re-experiencing:

- Identifying threatening meanings of the trauma by imaginal reliving or narrative writing.
- Gaining a new perspective on these meanings by reconstructing what happened during the event and using cognitive restructuring to find alternative interpretations.
- Updating the moments in memory linked to the meanings by simul-taneously bringing into awareness the upsetting memory and the new meanings.
- Stimulus discrimination, i.e., identifying idiosyncratic low-level sensory cues that trigger memories of the bombings (such as loud bangs, smoky smells, darkness, the swaying, lurching, or halting of the vehicle and the sight of train tracks) and learning to discriminate the present triggers from those encountered during the trauma.
- Visit to the site of the trauma, taking in the difference between the 'then' (day of trauma) and 'now' (site as it appears today without the trauma).
- Imagery transformation of persisting intrusive memories.

The decision of when to include elements of PTSD treatment was based on presenting symptoms (i.e., whether the patient met diagnostic criteria for PTSD) and on theoretical considerations. Following the theoretical under-pinnings of the Ehlers and Clark (2000) model, it was expected that key indicators for the appropriateness of a PTSD treatment protocol would be:

'Nowness' of trauma memories and intensity of affect: High nowness and intense affect resembling that experienced during the bombing (e.g., freezing, fear, sadness, near fainting) in response to eliciting the memory of the bombing may indicate that the memory remained inadequately processed and is related to PTSD after trauma (Michael et al., 2005).

Poorly elaborated memory of the trauma: A particularly vague or disjointed account of the traumatic event, including memory gaps or uncertainty about the temporal course of the event, may indicate poor memory elaboration. There is no evidence of autobiographical memory problems in specific phobias.

Emotional numbing: This may also indicate strong avoidance or dissociation from the memories of the event and this seldom occurs in phobias.

Generalized negative meanings of the trauma: Negative cognitions in PTSD commonly extend to the self (e.g., a sense of permanent change or self-blame), the world (e.g., generalized expectations of being attacked), and the future (e.g., that one's life will be cut short). In contrast, negative cognitions in travel phobia might be expected to be confined to the dangers of public transport (Ehlers et al., 2007).

This chapter describes the treatment of two survivors of the London bombings from within a series of patients referred for treatment of fear and avoidance of transport situations; one with a primary diagnosis of travel phobia, the other with a primary diagnosis of PTSD. Both exhibited fear and avoidance of transport situations. Both exhibited some symptoms of re-experiencing and arousal. However, the differential diagnoses, formulations, and treatment protocols illustrate the importance of a range of interventions to treat both PTSD and phobias following trauma.

CASE OF SARAH: TRAVEL PHOBIA

Background

Sarah was travelling to work on the morning of 7 July 2005 when a bomb exploded in the adjacent carriage on her train. At the time, she thought that there was a fire on the train in which she would die and felt intensely fearful. During the trauma she felt that she could not breathe due to the soot-filled air and thought she was going to suffocate.

Assessment

Sarah's main diagnosis according to DSM-IV criteria was travel phobia. She reported excessive fear and avoidance of travelling on one particular tube line. As this was formerly part of her journey to work and the alternative route extended her journey, this caused significant interference in her day-to-day life.

Sarah also experienced repeated intrusive memories of being on the tube and of people screaming in the bombed carriage. She tried to avoid thinking about the trauma. She had some symptoms of heightened arousal, mainly comprising of hypervigilance for danger when travelling on the tube or in the car. However, these symptoms did not meet DSM-IV (American Psychiatric Association, 1994) or ICD-10 (World Health Organization, 1993) criteria for the disorder. She scored 14 on the Posttraumatic Diagnostic Scale (PDS; mild to moderate range for PTSD).

Sarah's initial account of 7 July 2005 was relatively detailed, with no apparent memory gaps. She did not become upset or avoid talking about her feelings on that day.

Treatment session one

Sarah's primary goals were to feel free from anxiety on the underground in general and in particular to be able to travel on the avoided tube line without feeling upset. She was also keen to be less upset by memories of the bombing. Sarah felt annoyed with herself for remaining upset and anxious a year after the bombings and some time was spent normalizing these reactions to a terribly traumatic event.

Cognitive formulation

The cognitive formulation was begun at assessment and developed further in session one and throughout treatment. Sarah recounted a recent episode of travel anxiety. She was walking through the bombing site underground station and saw a number of police officers. Their presence reminded her of 7 July and she began to feel anxious. As she descended into the tube she became more concerned that she would experience more detailed memories and mental images of that day and become upset. When travelling on the underground she tried to avoid thinking about the 7 July and planned to get off if she became upset. If she couldn't get off she thought that she might start crying, her heart would begin to beat faster, she would start sweating and feel trapped and self-conscious.

Thus, Sarah had three main cognitions about the dangers of using public transport. She believed that:

• Underground travel was dangerous due to possible future terrorist attacks.
• If she travelled on the underground, memories of the bombings would cause her to become overwhelmingly upset and anxious and other people would notice and think badly about her.
• If she travelled on crowded trains, she would find it difficult to breathe, not get enough air, and faint.

These beliefs were maintained by a range of avoidance and safety-seeking behaviours:

- Avoidance of the underground journey she had taken on 7/7.
- Sitting down and breathing deeply or getting out of the underground when memories of the bombings popped into her mind whilst travelling.
- Safety-seeking behaviours such as scanning tube carriages for potential bombers and packages, and getting off the tube if she felt she had identified such a risk. Their paradoxical role in maintaining her anxiety was discovered through Socratic questioning. Sarah's homework was to try to stop scanning tube carriages for 'suspicious' people and to try to allow any memories of 7 July to come and go.

Furthermore, the 'here and now' quality of her intrusive memories of being caught up in the bombings and finding it difficult to breathe (linked to the thought 'I'm going to run out of air, suffocate, and die') whilst waiting to be evacuated, and an image of herself covered in soot and crowded into an airless space, contributed to the belief that she would have trouble breathing and faint.

Interventions were designed to test out these negative predictions about the danger of transport, her memories, and her anxiety symptoms (see Table 3.1).

Table 3.1 Sarah: factors maintaining the travel phobia and interventions

Maintaining factors	Interventions
Belief 1: 'Travel is dangerous because there will be more terrorist attacks'	Calculating probabilities
Safety behaviour linked to belief 1: Check for potential bombers and suspicious packages	Drop checking
Belief 2: 'If I get memories of the bombings, I will become panicky and tearful (and other people will notice)'	Behavioural experiment: bring on memories with imaginal reliving
Safety behaviour linked to belief 2: avoid memories, leave tube if memories occur	Experiment with letting memories come and go
Belief 3: 'If I travel on a crowded train I will not be able to breathe and will faint'	Education about fainting and blood pressure
Safety behaviours linked to belief 3: sit down, breathe deeply or leave train	Drop behaviours
Maintaining image: intrusive image of herself on tube on the day of bombings, covered in soot, crowded in	Imagery transformation
Behaviour linked to beliefs 1 to 3: avoid underground travel on line used on the day of bombings	Travel on this line and let memories come

Session two

From her homework, Sarah learned that scanning underground carriages in fact increased her anxiety. However, she had found it difficult to allow the memories to come into her mind whilst on the tube without making an effort to push them away. Therefore, in order to further test the belief 'If I confront memories of 7 July I will become very upset, tearful, and panicky', a behavioural experiment was carried out. This involved intentionally bringing on vivid memories of the trauma through imaginal reliving (see Clark & Ehlers, 2004).

During the reliving Sarah felt upset and sad, but did not report feelings of fear. The memory felt only 20% as if it were happening now, rather than a memory from the past, but that she was also trying to push it away slightly. Therefore, a second reliving experiment was carried out in which she agreed to allow the memory to come 'close up'. During this second reliving the memory felt much more vivid and present (100% 'now'), but her main emotion was relief with very brief moments of fear at about 60%. She discovered that she did not feel as upset as she had expected or start crying if she allowed the memories 'close up'.

The therapist and Sarah then planned to travel together on the avoided underground line in the next session. She predicted that she would be reminded of 7/7, get upset or start crying, and that other people might see and think 'What's up with her?', and she would feel silly as a result. She also predicted that she would continue to think about 7/7 for the rest of the day and therefore feel anxious or tense.

To continue to process the memory of 7/7, and to test her belief that thinking about 7/7 would make her upset, anxious, and tense, Sarah was asked to listen to the reliving tape twice for homework.

Session three

The next session was conducted on the underground to test Sarah's prediction that if she travelled the same route as on 7 July, memories of the bombings would cause her to become overwhelmingly upset and anxious, and other people would notice and think badly about her. Several journeys were undertaken on the previously avoided line. Sarah and the therapist visited the station to which Sarah had been evacuated and she was encouraged to narrate the events of that day whilst noticing present differences. The next step was to travel together between this station and the next station (passing the site of the bombing). Finally, Sarah took this journey alone. Throughout these journeys, she allowed memories of 7/7 to come and go when they occurred spontaneously. In contrast to her expectations, she was not at all upset when travelling on this line. Normal anxiety responses were discussed, and Sarah was encouraged to report her anxiety levels at regular intervals.

Her peak anxiety (50%) throughout the session was experienced whilst on the platform anticipating the journey, and at the end of the in vivo session this was reduced to 15%.

Sarah learnt first, that her anxious anticipation of confronting the memories was worse than the reality, second, that her anxiety reduced when she remained on the underground and third, that she did not have an 'emotional' response to travelling on the previously avoided line.

For homework, Sarah agreed to travel home from work on the previously avoided line and then to try the journey to work which would involve retracing her steps of 7/7.

Session four

Following the in vivo session Sarah was able to travel to and from work via her old route with only mild anxiety between the stations closest to the bombing site. However, she was still avoiding this journey occasionally.

It became clear that Sarah was experiencing episodes of panic. Using a recent example of a time when she felt anxious on a crowded tube, her belief that she may be unable to breathe and faint, and corresponding safety-seeking behaviours were identified. The role of these behaviours in maintaining her fears was explored. Sarah also found it helpful to understand that fainting occurs when blood pressure drops, whereas anxiety actually causes blood pressure to rise. Sarah agreed to travel consistently on the previously avoided line for 2 weeks in order to target her remaining anxiety. She would review the panic cycle, including the evidence against the idea that anxiety could make her faint and, very importantly, drop the safety-seeking behaviours, which prevented the change in her beliefs.

Imagery work

Sarah's fear that she might not be able to breathe was sometimes accompanied by a mental image of herself in the tube on 7/7 when it had stopped, looking scared, covered in soot, and hemmed in by a crowd. This image created and reinforced the sense of being trapped. In order to alter the meaning of this image and the associated affect, Sarah recreated the image in her mind but transformed it so that train began moving again, the passengers looked clean and happy, and at the next stop she got out into a light tube station. She planned to practise the transformation of her image (and hence meaning) of being crowded in for homework.

Probabilities

Finally, to reinforce Sarah's resolve not to scan tube carriages for potential bombers, the probability of another bomb going off in a carriage as she travelled was calculated. She would then be able to remind herself of the tiny approximated risk of this feared event (which was less than 0.00000001%) when tempted to start scanning.

One-month follow-up session

Sarah's fear of fainting was now 0%. She had not even noticed when she had been on an underground train which stopped for a considerable amount of time in a tunnel. She still occasionally checked for suspicious packages, but she felt that this was no more than she, or other people, would have done before 7/7. She also felt OK talking about the events and did not worry that she would become upset.

A 'blueprint' or summary of what Sarah had learnt in treatment was completed. When asked what had been helpful in combating her fears she said that, 'in facing my fear now my fear has gone'.

Outcome

At the end of treatment, and at 1-year follow-up, Sarah was able to travel daily on the previously avoided line without anxiety and she did not avoid doing so. Her PDS score was 0.

CASE OF LISA: PTSD

Background

Lisa was travelling to work on the morning of 7/7 when a bomb exploded in her carriage. She found herself buried underneath other victims. She felt very fearful and helpless. She suffered injuries and subsequent scarring from embedded pieces of glass and shrapnel in her body, and tinnitus from the sound of the explosion.

Assessment

Lisa's symptoms met DSM-IV (American Psychiatric Association, 1994) criteria for PTSD. These included unwanted intrusive memories of the scenes she witnessed on the tube, often when she was trying to go to sleep. She sometimes experienced panic attacks and became very anxious and felt trapped in situations that reminded her of 7/7, such as travelling by public transport. She avoided thinking about where she was in the train and the feeling of being squashed by people. She could not recall some aspects of what she had seen on the train. Lisa was also having difficulty falling and staying asleep. She was more irritable, particularly with her partner's children, and hypervigilant for danger when on buses.

Lisa was fearful of and avoiding travelling on the underground and on crowded buses. However, these symptoms of travel phobia were clearly secondary to a diagnosis of PTSD. Her PDS score fell in the mild to moderate range for PTSD (18).

Treatment session one

Lisa's primary goal was to be able to go on the tube and feel completely OK. She was keen to think about 7/7 less, feel less distressed by the memories, and to feel less irritable and unhappy overall. Lisa was concerned by her reactions to the event and particularly annoyed at herself for being irritable with her loved ones. These responses were normalized in the context of the terribly traumatic event she had experienced, and she was given some written information on PTSD. An explanation for intrusive memories was shared with Lisa and she was encouraged to allow memories of 7/7 to come and go, rather than try to push them away.

Cognitive formulation

As before, the cognitive formulation was begun at assessment and developed throughout treatment. Lisa's intrusive memories and related sleep problems were seen as a sign that the trauma memory had not been fully elaborated and remained disjointed from knowledge about the final outcome of the situation. In particular, the intrusions were about moments when she believed she would have to see other people die and that she might suffocate and die herself, although neither of these things had happened. The poor memory elaboration was maintained by Lisa's avoidance of thinking about the trauma. It was clear from her account of her experience that the memory was disjointed. A range of situations that involved being squashed or crowded acted as triggers of intrusive memories.

Lisa reported two personal meanings of the trauma that created a general sense of current threat. First, she blamed herself for leaving the train after the bombing and not helping other trauma survivors who could not move. Second, she believed that the world had turned into a more dangerous place since the bombings. A range of behaviours, such as selective attention to bad news and unnecessary precautions, maintained this belief.

With respect to her fear of travelling, Lisa had two main cognitions about the dangers of using public transport. She believed that:

- Public transport was dangerous because another bomb was going to go off.
- Her reactions to memories of her traumatic experience, if triggered on public transport, would be dangerous as they would cause her to lose control of her emotions, get hysterical, and pass out.

These beliefs were maintained by the 'here and now' quality of her intrusive memories, by rumination, and her avoidance of public transport and crowded places.

Interventions were designed to elaborate and contextualize her trauma memories, challenge her excessively negative appraisals of the trauma and transport, and to help her change the strategies she was employing to try and reduce her sense of current threat that were in fact perpetuating it (see Table 3.2).

Table 3.2 Lisa: factors maintaining the PTSD and travel anxiety and interventions

Maintaining factors	Interventions
Intrusive memories of trauma lead to sense of threat in the 'here and now'	Elaborate memory by imaginal reliving and writing narrative Update trauma memory with what is known now Stimulus discrimination of triggers Site visit
Image of herself buried underground	Image transformation
Belief 1: 'I should have stayed with the people who could not move, feel guilty'	Cognitive restructuring (taking *own state at the time* into account) Imagery from other people's point of view
Belief 2: 'The world has generally become a more dangerous place since 7/7'	Distinguish between *feeling* more dangerous and *being* more dangerous
Maintaining behaviours linked to belief 2: selective attention to bad news and excessive precautions	Act as if things felt like before 7/7
Belief 3: 'Travel is dangerous because another bomb will go off when I am travelling on the tube'	Calculating probabilities and behavioural experiment (travelling)
Safety behaviour linked to belief 3: avoid travel, sit in particular place when travelling	Resume travelling, drop safety behaviours
Belief 4: 'If I have memories of the event I will lose control of my emotions, get hysterical and pass out or make a fool of myself'	Normalize memories Behavioural experiments: let memories come, let anxiety come, go to situations that bring on memories (crowded places)
Behaviours linked to belief 4: avoid memories, rumination, sitting down.	Let memories come and go, drop rumination, stand up

Sessions two to five

Memory work

Sessions two to five were mainly devoted to the reliving and updating of the trauma memory and beginning a narrative account of the trauma. Once the 'hotspots' in the memory were identified, the cognitions associated with these moments were explored and updated through verbal discussion of what Lisa knew now to be true that she did not know then. For example, Lisa believed at the time of the trauma that she would be stuck on the train and would lose control or become hysterical. However, with hindsight she knew that she did get off the train quickly and that far from losing control, she took control of her situation and freed herself from it. These new appraisals were then inserted into the memory in reliving. Imagery work was also used to correct and update excessively negative appraisals of what the people remaining in the carriage after she left would have experienced, reducing Lisa's sense of guilt for not staying to help or comfort them.

Sessions six to eleven

The next five sessions were mainly devoted to Lisa's travel anxieties and to further elaborating and contextualizing the trauma memory through in vivo work.

History of travel anxieties

Lisa had been on an underground train only once since 7/7, one week after the bombings. When the tube went into the tunnel she thought 'I can't get out of here, I'm committed to this' and got off the train at next stop. She feared that if she stayed on the underground, memories of 7/7 would come back and that she would get hysterical, start crying, pass out, get hot, and light-headed. After the failed bombing attempts two weeks later on 21/7, she felt there was more danger of it happening again.

Formulation of Lisa's travel anxiety

A recent occurrence of anxiety during a bus journey was explored in detail. Her anxiety had been triggered by her conviction that a man she saw had a bomb in his bag. Her anxiety on this journey was 85% and her belief that a bomb would explode was 75%. Safety-seeking behaviours and ruminative thoughts engaged in at other times were added to the formulation, and their role in maintaining the anxious cognitions was explored collaboratively through Socratic questioning (see Figure 3.1).

Lisa held two sets of fearful beliefs about going on buses and the tube:

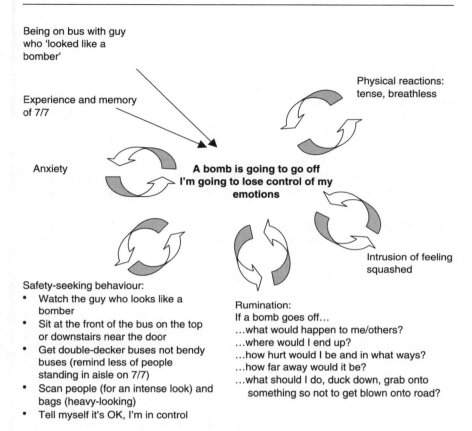

Being on bus with guy
who 'looked like a
bomber'

Experience and memory
of 7/7

Physical reactions:
tense, breathless

Anxiety

**A bomb is going to go off
I'm going to lose control of my
emotions**

Intrusion of feeling
squashed

Safety-seeking behaviour:
* Watch the guy who looks like a
  bomber
* Sit at the front of the bus on the top
  or downstairs near the door
* Get double-decker buses not bendy
  buses (remind less of people
  standing in aisle on 7/7)
* Scan people (for an intense look) and
  bags (heavy-looking)
* Tell myself it's OK, I'm in control

Rumination:
If a bomb goes off...
...what would happen to me/others?
...where would I end up?
...how hurt would I be and in what ways?
...how far away would it be?
...what should I do, duck down, grab onto
   something so not to get blown onto road?

Figure 3.1 Lisa's formulation of travel anxiety.

(i) that a bomb would go off or (ii) that she would get very anxious and that her symptoms of anxiety would be unpleasant and detrimental. Currently, the second set of fears was more troubling to Lisa. Her main fear was that a train she was travelling on would stop in a tunnel. She would feel 'tortured' not knowing when she would get off. She was concerned that this might undo the good that had happened already in treatment; she thought that 'stuff might go through my head [memories] and my body would feel horrible and tense'. She felt that this in turn would lead to her feeling more down, weaker, and less motivated.

Preparation for in vivo work

Although her belief in session that another bomb would explode on an underground train was low (her 'gut feeling' was that there was a 1/100 chance), it was helpful to calculate sequential probabilities and to compare her gut feeling to the calculated figure of 1/72,000,000.

Lisa was encouraged to drop her safety-seeking behaviours and look at people normally on buses. The end goal was to behave on transport as she had prior to 7/7, for example, sitting reading the paper on the underground. This was difficult at first and more behaviours were identified and targeted over the course of these sessions as she extended her travel from buses to tubes.

Through Socratic questioning Lisa discovered that the questions she ruminated on during travel in fact had no answers and tended to increase her belief that something bad was going to happen. Lisa was encouraged to notice when she was engaging in rumination, to assert that 'these questions have no answers', and then tell herself to 'stop'. Over time she found that an effective strategy to combat rumination, once she had noticed she was engaging in it, was to absorb herself in the here and now by looking out the bus window and turning her attention to the normal events and scenery outside.

In vivo work: behavioural experiments, stimulus discrimination, and journeys with the therapist

Lisa was encouraged to continue allowing memories of 7/7 to come and go even when she was anxious on transport in order to test out her belief that thinking about the trauma would cause her to get hysterical and that this would result in further catastrophe. Lisa gradually extended her travel for homework, taking bus and train journeys in rush hour, or when it was busy. Then she took an 'underground' journey on a section of the line that actually ran above ground level.

As she extended her travel, more triggers for the trauma memory were identified, such as crowded travel situations in which she would begin to feel trapped as she did on that day. Identifying the differences between these crowded situations and the extreme experience of being crushed on 7/7 was practised both in session and outside on transport for homework.

Similar memory triggers were identified in non-travel situations, such as when Lisa lay on the left side of her body. Stimulus discrimination exercises were extended to these situations and Lisa was creative in finding ways of recreating the sensation of being squashed (such as playing in the park with her children and having fun 'pile ons', in which they scrambled over her or placing books on her chest) and breaking the link to the memory of 7/7 through noticing the differences (such as 'I'm having fun with my kids', 'there is no danger here', 'I am not trapped' and 'no-one is hurt').

It was then planned that Lisa would go together with the therapist on the underground and return to the station to which she was evacuated on 7 July. Several journeys were made up and down the line on which the bomb had exploded, including the section between the stations closest to where the bomb exploded. Throughout these journeys safety-seeking behaviours were noticed and dropped. At the end of the session Lisa was able to complete her journey home on the same line on her own. Following this session, Lisa was encouraged to travel by tube daily and to continue noticing and dropping safety-seeking behaviours. She noticed, for example, that she had a tendency to sit in a particular place and to avoid the underground at rush hour.

Imagery work

As Lisa travelled more often on the underground, she noticed that she some-times had an intrusive memory of an image of the full underground train squashed and buried deep under rock with no way out, which had first occurred to her a split second after the bomb had exploded on 7/7. In order to alter the meaning of this image ('I'm trapped') and the fear that accompanied it, she transformed the image in session, 'zooming out' from the train in her mind's eye so that she could see all the underground stations and tunnels linking up everywhere. This new image was associated with the meaning that there were many ways out and therefore she was not trapped. She practised this new image for homework.

Session twelve

Anniversary planning and normalization

The final weekly session fell shortly before the first anniversary of 7/7, when there would be many more triggers for the trauma memory. Therefore, this session included planning for that day and preparing her for normal anniversary reactions.

Blueprint

A 'blueprint' or summary of what Lisa had learnt in treatment was com-pleted on which she noted that 'having problems doesn't mean I am weak', 'safety-seeking behaviours make me more anxious', and that in future she would build on treatment by trying not to fear anxiety itself.

Follow-up sessions

The follow-up sessions targeted remaining fears about becoming anxious, including her concern that she would pass out if she became anxious on the tube. Lisa tested out these beliefs by travelling on full trains at rush hour whilst dropping safety-seeking behaviours identified in session.

Finally, Lisa's more general cognition that 'the world is a dangerous place' was addressed. Lisa's attentional biases for 'bad news' were noted. Following previous work it was easy for Lisa to identify safety-seeking behaviours that were strengthening her sense of danger and vulnerability, such as taking excessive care crossing roads and going down escalators. She found it helpful to act 'as if' things felt as they did before 7/7.

Outcome

Lisa reported very few (and much less distressing) intrusive memories of 7/7. Additionally, she had returned to frequent tube travel. Her PDS score was 6 at the end of treatment and 3 at 1-year follow-up.

CONCLUSION

Following the London bombings many survivors reported fear and avoidance symptoms and met criteria for a range of disorders ranging from severe PTSD to specific phobia of transport situations. The cases described above illustrate the necessity of a careful cognitive formulation of the individuals' concerns underlying their travel fears in order to direct treatment choices. They also illustrate the clinical utility of indicators derived from the theoretical underpinnings of cognitive therapy for PTSD (Ehlers et al., 2005) to help direct treatment choices within these range of presentations.

When there is a phobic response after major trauma, cognitive behavioural techniques for reducing phobic avoidance are necessary and may be sufficient, as in the first case described. However, techniques from PTSD treatments, such as stimulus discrimination (Ehlers & Clark, 2000) may also be useful in these cases, as it may increase the chances that the confrontation with feared stimuli in vivo will be helpful. A further helpful technique derived from PTSD treatments was the use of imaginal reliving as a behavioural experiment to test the client's fears about what would happen if she allowed herself to think about the bombings (see Clark & Ehlers, 2004).

PTSD techniques designed to reduce intrusive re-experiencing, such as updating trauma memories and stimulus discrimination, may also be necessary when patients presenting with specific phobia after trauma find that exposure to the feared stimulus elicits an increase in intrusive and distressing memories of the trauma they experienced.

When PTSD is the main diagnosis after trauma, but fear and avoidance of trauma-related stimuli such as transport is prominent, treatment will need to aim at a reduction of phobic avoidance to enable patients to reclaim their lives. This may include dealing with beliefs about the physical effects of being anxious similar to those seen in patients with panic attacks. The second case described above illustrates the usefulness of a wide range of techniques for overcoming phobic avoidance.

Future directions

These patients formed part of a larger series of patients referred for treatment of fear and avoidance of transport situations following the London bombings. For the majority of patients, cognitive behavioural therapy for phobic avoidance was insufficient. Conversely, elements of cognitive therapy for PTSD were useful in the treatment of all patients. Imaginal reliving, updating trauma memory procedures, and imagery techniques sometimes used in PTSD treatment, such as updating fear cognitions during the trauma (e.g., 'I'm running out of air') by manipulating associated images (e.g., imagining a closed, dark, crowded underground tube with miles of rock overhead becoming light, bright and visibly connected to the outside world with air freely flowing through the tunnels), were powerful for identifying and updating current, specific fears on the underground such as suffocation. Stimulus discrimination techniques were a useful aid for in vivo work.

Recent research highlights the prevalence and importance of distressing memories and imagery in phobias (e.g., Hunt et al., 2004). It would be interesting to investigate the utility of using imaginal reliving and other imagery techniques commonly used in PTSD treatment in a series of patients with other specific phobias with an identifiable traumatic onset. There is perhaps a concern that using reliving techniques when there is not evidence of the full syndrome of PTSD may be unnecessarily traumatizing for patients. However, the clinical experience from this series of patients suggests that these techniques are not unduly distressing and in fact may be necessary when the patient begins to engage with the phobic stimuli again as trauma memories may become more apparent. Perhaps the diagnostic distinction between PTSD and specific phobia following trauma is not particularly valuable in trauma survivors, except to assist decisions about the main emphasis of treatment, which could, nevertheless, begin with an exploration of the trauma memory in both cases.

REFERENCES

American Psychiatric Association. (1994). *Diagnostic and statistical manual of mental disorders* (4th ed.). Washington, DC: APA.

Blanchard, E.B., & Hickling, E.J. (1997). *After the crash: Assessment and treatment of motor vehicle accident survivors*. Washington, DC: American Psychological Association.

Brewin, C.R., Scragg, P., Robertson, M., Thompson, M., d'Ardenne, P., & Ehlers, A. (2008). Promoting mental health following the London bombings: A screen and treat approach. *Journal of Traumatic Stress, 21*, 3–8.

Clark, D.M., & Ehlers, A. (2004). Posttraumatic stress disorder: From cognitive theory to therapy. In R.L. Leahy (Ed.), *Contemporary cognitive therapy* (pp. 141–160). New York: Guilford Press.

Davey, C.G.L. (1997). *Phobias: a handbook of theory, research and treatment.* Chichester: Wiley.

Duffy, M., Gillespie, K., & Clark, D.M. (2007). Posttraumatic stress disorder in the context of terrorism and other civil conflict in Northern Ireland: Randomised controlled trial. *British Medical Journal, 334,* 1147–1150.

Ehlers, A., & Clark, D.M. (2000). A cognitive model of posttraumatic stress disorder. *Behaviour Research and Therapy, 38,* 319–345.

Ehlers, A., & Steil, R. (1995). Maintenance of intrusive memories in posttraumatic stress disorder: A cognitive approach. *Behavioural and Cognitive Psychotherapy, 23,* 217–249.

Ehlers, A., Clark, D.M., Hackmann, A., McManus, F., & Fennell, M. (2005). Cognitive therapy for PTSD: Development and evaluation. *Behaviour Research and Therapy, 43,* 413–431.

Ehlers, A., Clark, D.M., Hackmann, A., McManus, F., Fennell, M., Herbert, C., & Mayou, R. (2003). A randomized controlled trial of cognitive therapy, self-help booklet, and repeated assessment as early interventions for PTSD. *Archives of General Psychiatry, 60,* 1024–1032.

Ehlers, A., Clark, D.M., Hackmann, A., McManus, F., Fennell, M., & Grey, N. (2009). *Cognitive therapy for PTSD: A therapist's guide.* Oxford: Oxford University Press. In preparation.

Ehlers, A., Hofmann, S.G., Herda, C.A., & Roth, W.T. (1994). Clinical characteristics of driving phobia. *Journal of Anxiety Disorders, 8,* 323–339.

Ehlers, A., Taylor, J.E., Ehring, T., Hofmann, S., Deane, F.P., Roth, W.T., & Podd, J. (2007). The Driving Cognitions Questionnaire: Development and preliminary psychometric properties. *Journal of Anxiety Disorders, 21,* 493–509.

Gillespie, K., Duffy, M., Hackmann, A., & Clark, D.M. (2002). Community based cognitive therapy in the treatment of post-traumatic stress disorder following the Omagh bomb. *Behaviour Research and Therapy, 40,* 345–357.

Handley, R.V., Salkovskis, P., Scragg, P., & Ehlers, A. (in press). Clinically significant avoidance of public transport following the London bombings: Travel phobia or subclinical posttraumatic stress disorder? *Journal of Anxiety Disorders.*

Hunt, M., Bylsma, L., Brock, J., Fenton, M., Goldberg, A., Miller, R., Tran, T., & Urgelles, J. (2006). The role of imagery in the maintenance and treatment of snake fear. *Journal of Behavior Therapy and Experimental Psychiatry, 37(4),* 283–298.

Mayou, R., Bryant, B., & Ehlers, A. (2001). Prediction of psychological outcomes one year after a motor vehicle accident. *American Journal of Psychiatry, 158,* 1231–1238.

Michael, T., Ehlers, A., Halligan, S., & Clark, D.M. (2005). Unwanted memories of assault: What intrusion characteristics predict PTSD? *Behaviour Research and Therapy, 43,* 613–628.

Rubin, G.J., Brewin, C.R., Greenberg, N., Hacker Hughes, J., Simpson, J., & Wessley, S. (2007). Enduring consequences of terrorism: 7-month follow-up survey of reactions to the bombings in London on 7 July 2005. *British Journal of Psychiatry, 190,* 350–356.

World Health Organization. (1993). *The ICD-10 classification of mental and behavioural disorders. Diagnostic criteria for research.* Geneva: World Health Organization.

Chapter 4

Tripping into trauma

Cognitive-behavioural treatment for a traumatic stress reaction following recreational drug use

Richard Stott

INTRODUCTION

Unwanted reactions stemming from recreational drug use may occur for a variety of reasons, including dose misjudgement, pharmaceutical impurity, drug intolerance, and idiosyncratic metabolism. Acute adverse reactions, lasting several hours or even days, are relatively common, and can include withdrawal syndromes, dehydration, and distressing emotional and perceptual disturbances.

Chronic adverse reactions to recreational drug ingestion, in the absence of ongoing usage, are less common, although these have been documented after use of hallucinogenic substances such as LSD (Abraham, 1983), psilocybin (mushrooms) (Espiard, Lecardeur, Abadie, Halbecq, & Dollfus, 2005), ecstasy (Van Kampen & Katz, 2001), and cannabis (Keeler, Reifler, & Liptzin, 1968). Of particular interest following hallucinogen use is the phenomenon of 'drug flashbacks' (Abraham, 1983), affecting a minority of individuals who have taken the substance, which can persist for months or even years after the ingestion. DSM-IV recognizes a syndrome called hallucinogen persisting perception disorder (HPPD; Flashbacks; American Psychiatric Association, 1994). The hallmark symptom here is re-experiencing of one or more perceptual symptoms of the original drug experience, such as geometric hallucinations, false perceptions of movement, or flashes of colour. The diagnosis is withheld if there is a failure in reality testing, as in a psychotic illness. Therefore, the person recognizes that the flashbacks are drug effects. The DSM-IV diagnostic criteria for HPPD are:

A   The re-experiencing, following cessation of use of a hallucinogen, of one or more of the perceptual symptoms that were experienced while intoxicated with the hallucinogen (e.g., geometric hallucinations, false perceptions of movement in the peripheral visual fields, flashes of colour, intensified colours, trails of images of moving objects, positive after-images, halos around objects, macropsia, and micropsia).

B   The symptoms in Criterion A cause clinically significant distress or impairment in social, occupational, or other important areas of functioning.

C   The symptoms are not due to a general medical condition (e.g., anatomical lesions and infections of the brain, visual epilepsies) and are not better accounted for by another mental disorder (e.g., delirium, dementia, schizophrenia) or hypnopompic hallucinations.

Interestingly, the HPPD criteria focus largely on visual phenomenology, following some of the major investigations in the area (Abraham, 1983). However, other authors have noted that intense emotions can accompany both the original drug experience and later drug flashbacks. Horovitz (1969) found that many people described the content of their drug flashbacks as derived from 'frightening imagery experiences during drug intoxication'. In a sample of college students, Matefy, Hayes, and Hirsch (1978) found that in addition to perceptual illusions there were substantial reports of flashbacks characterized by depersonalization, anxiety and panic, disorientation and confusion, auditory hallucinations, feelings of depression and paranoia. Abraham and Mamen (1996) found a correlated increase of visual disturbance and panic symptoms in a series of adults who were prescribed risperidone in an effort to treat HPPD. It is also noteworthy that not all re-experiencing of an initial drug experience is perceived as unpleasant (Matefy et al., 1978). Some enjoy the experience, or consider it emotionally neutral.

Conceptualizing the drug flashback phenomenon has been the subject of much theoretical speculation, including the possible role of neurological problems in the visual system (Abraham, 1983), attentional deficits (Keeler et al., 1968), learned role-enactment (Matefy, 1980), and breakthroughs of repressed ideas (Horovitz, 1969). Unfortunately, however, as Halpern and Pope (2003) comment, the data remain very unclear, due to a host of methodological problems and much of the research being conducted in the 1960s and 1970s prior to adequate definitions of the 'flashback', or to the introduction of DSM categorizations. McGee (1984) highlighted the similarities between drug flashbacks and a host of cued-retrieval memory phenomena, such as state-dependent retrieval, dream recall, and the re-experiencing in post-traumatic stress disorder (PTSD). Certainly, as in PTSD, drug flashbacks are often involuntary and triggered by certain stimuli, such as entering a darkened room (Abraham, 1983), becoming anxious, or simulating some of the original setting conditions of the drug experience, such as revisiting the site of the rock concert where the substance was taken. McGee concluded that flashbacks are best considered as memory phenomena and, as in other psychological traumatization, a number of investigators have concurred that the powerful emotions experienced during hallucinogen use may account for flashbacks (Wesson & Smith, 1976; Fischer, 1971).

The treatment of choice for such chronic drug flashbacks is still unresolved, with no large treatment trials and mostly anecdotal case series (Halpern &

Pope, 2003). Of these, most attention has been given to pharmacological treatment, including clonidine (Lerner, Finkel, Oyffe, Merenzon, & Sigal, 1998), benzodiazepines including clonazepam (Lerner et al., 2003) and a variety of other drugs. Matefy (1973) is one of the few authors to document a psychotherapeutic approach to treating such problems. He describes using a combination of relaxation and systematic desensitization strategies in treating a young man who had experienced recurrent LSD flashbacks five months after last ingestion. The symptoms were eliminated after 17 sessions, and recovery was maintained at 2-year follow-up. Interestingly, the patient's flashbacks had been accompanied by intense anxiety and were experienced as if being on a repeating unwanted 'high'. In addition, they could apparently be triggered by specific verbal cues emanating from the dialogue with his psychiatrist.

CASE OVERVIEW

Amelia, in her early 30s, presented for treatment at a specialist PTSD service having suffered from a longstanding traumatic reaction relating to the single ingestion of a drug named 'Bliss' at a night club 10 years previously. Bliss is a herbal preparation taken in tablet form, purportedly mimicking the effects of Ecstasy, its principal constituent extracted from the plant Common Sweet Flag (*Acorus calamus*), which is known to contain the active ingredient asarone. Asarone is understood to be a possible precursor to the hallucinogenic substance TMA-2. Sweet Flag itself has been used by many cultures over hundreds of years, for its stimulant, entheogenic (spiritual) and hallucinogenic properties. In Amelia's case, the precise purity and dose she ingested that evening remain unknown.

Amelia described the aftermath of taking the Bliss as follows. In the first hour of taking the pills, the air appeared to go solid, and she began to feel claustrophobic and terrified that she could not breathe. She left the nightclub and lay down on the grass outside. She saw a very bright white pinpoint of light, and felt as if she were looking at herself. Then she went and sat in the back of a car nearby, and remembers repeatedly opening and closing the door, believing that she must do so to have enough air to breathe. She started to feel that in fact she may be dead, and felt terror and despair that she had 'gone too far' and that 'a big part of me has been lost'. The following day she was disorientated, shocked, despairing, and again had a strong feeling that something about her was lost. In addition, she feared she had done herself physical brain damage. On day three, she felt a small degree of relief and comfort, but over the next 2 weeks she retained a persistent feeling that something may not be entirely right, and experienced some wariness about putting food in her mouth. However, life resumed to relative normality and she returned to college. Then, 3 weeks after the initial ingestion, Amelia had a terrifying day. In her college lecture room, the walls appeared to move. On her commute home, the train walls also seemed to move and she experienced dizziness and disorientation. That night, more visual hallucinations began. Amelia described these as 'layers of imagery, coming and going, intense, frightening, fast-moving, like computer graphics and brightly coloured'. These persisted night after night from that day onwards, typically when she shut her eyes to go to sleep. They were accompanied by a sense of horror, panic, and feeling out of control. She said they had a 'nightmarish quality'.

Ten years on, Amelia presented with a continuation of fast-moving, nightmarish, computer graphic-style imagery 4–5 nights per week when she shut her eyes. Once a week she would also have intrusive images with the same 'atmosphere' as her original experience (claustrophobia, despair, being dead). She ruminated constantly about what she had done to herself, and felt detached and alienated from others. She noticed that speaking about the events, or going back to the place where she took the drug, triggered anxiety, heart racing, despair, and shame. She showed major avoidance of socializing, and had not taken any further drugs since this time. She displayed elevated arousal by way of poor sleep, irritability, poor concentration, and jumpiness. An artist, Amelia had aimed to use her experiences to inspire her creative work. However, she felt her life was not progressing, her creative work was stalling and unfinished, others around were moving on with their careers, and she could not see her way forward. The primary focus of Amelia's own narrative centred upon the fact that the Bliss incident 10 years ago had altered her brain, and her life, irreparably. She scored 27 on the PTSD Diagnostic Scale (PDS: moderate/severe range), 22 on the Beck Depression Inventory (BDI; moderate range), and 38 on the Beck Anxiety Inventory (BAI; severe range).

FORMULATION AND TREATMENT

Formulating Amelia's history and current symptoms presented distinct challenges. Diagnostically, many features were suggestive of PTSD, including the repetitive intrusive phenomenology, avoidance and hyperarousal, and ruminative focus upon the devastating effect of the single episode of drug-taking on her life. However, her most florid, frequent, and upsetting images were the computer graphics, which had not been present, in Amelia's recollection, during the initial intoxication but only began 3 weeks later. Hence, the index traumatic event (or 'Criterion A' in the DSM-IV diagnosis) was in some question. Furthermore, the phenomenology of the computer-graphic imagery bore striking resemblance to the characteristics of hallucinogenic flashbacks in HPPD, with geometric hallucinations, fast-moving effects, bright colours and so on. Indeed, Amelia's imagery was triggered when she shut her eyes, and Abraham (1983) identified that a dark environment was the most common precipitant to hallucinogenic flashbacks. Nevertheless, one factor that weighed against diagnosing HPPD was, again, the fact that this visual experience was not recalled as being present during initial intoxication, a criterion of the diagnosis.

Cognitively, it seemed important to clarify the conceptualization by first charting the timeline of the core imagery and meaning elements in Amelia's account. Table 4.1 shows which elements were present at the time of intoxication, at the '3-week point', and causing ongoing distress. Using this as a template for discussion, a number of important observations emerged.

First, the '3-week point' saw the introduction of a new set of meanings about the *permanence* of damage caused by the drug. Although Amelia had, during intoxication, entertained thoughts about damage she was doing to her brain, she had assumed this would be a temporary effect. Only when the 3-week disturbance arose did this take on a more sinister meaning, i.e., that she had *irreparably* damaged her brain. This appeared also to coincide with the belief that she was inherently different and alien from others. A brief exploration of these beliefs revealed that Amelia considered her brain and/or her personality must be inherently flawed and weak to have been affected in this catastrophic way. She also suspected that others would not be able to comprehend this damage, and inevitably this would mean she was destined to a life of alienation.

This initial analysis demonstrated the rich web of cognitive material, much of it longstanding, which pertained to Amelia's difficulties. It also echoed the dominant narrative of her troubles that Amelia had brought to therapy. In essence, her story was that she had irreparably damaged her brain by taking the drug 10 years earlier, and this damaged brain caused her flashbacks, as well as her concentration lapses, being different, and social alienation. She had heard a certain amount of anecdotal information from friends and the internet about people going 'psychotic' after bad drug experiences. She dwelt

Table 4.1 Amelia: imagery and 'core meaning' elements timeline

	Emotion	Intoxication	Three weeks later	Now
Air solid	Terror	✓		
Piercing white light	Fear	✓		
Claustrophobia	Fear	✓	✓	✓
Not being able to breathe	Terror	✓	✓	✓
Computer-graphic imagery	Horror		✓	✓
Walls moving	Horror		✓	
Being dead	Sadness	✓	✓	✓
A part of me is lost	Despair	✓	✓	✓
Damaged brain	Despair	✓	✓	✓
Damaged brain irreparably	Despair		✓	✓
Am different/alienated	Sadness, shame		✓	✓
Life bleak, no way forward	Hopelessness			✓
Appear mad to others	Anxiety, shame			✓

extensively on these themes, and spoke as if everything in her life was hooked upon this one crucial moment.

It therefore seemed essential, early in therapy, to provide an alternative set of hypotheses that might help Amelia conceptualize her troubles. Following the Ehlers and Clark (2000) model of PTSD, we discussed the nature of traumatically encoded memories, and how unhelpful cognitions may get 'frozen in time'. Both reliving and a narrative account were then undertaken for the original memories, both of the original drug ingestion and the '3-week' disturbance. However, rather unusually for PTSD, this proved to have little impact on symptoms. Indeed, when voluntarily brought to mind, the events carried relatively little emotion, but rather triggered a ruminative train of thought involving, once again, sadness, shame, and the feeling of difference.

Therapy therefore moved to an exploration of appraisals, and in particular Amelia's beliefs about brain damage. For example, did she know others with brain damage, what were its typical origins, what symptom profiles might be seen, what did it mean for the future, and, crucially, what evidence was she using to nurture her own belief that she had brain damage? It transpired that Amelia had muddled the concept of brain damage with 'psychosis', and some basic education clarified these issues. However, the exploration revealed an underlying fear of complete madness, and Amelia believed her mind was constantly in danger of letting her down, especially in social situations.

Discussion of a number of recent social encounters revealed an informative pattern of social processing, for example when going out for drinks or for dinner with friends. A typical sequence would involve Amelia feeling self-conscious that, as she assumed it to be, everyone else could see her 'damaged' self. She would find it hard to concentrate and focus properly on conversations, lose track of what was being said, fear she would not be coherent, become rather quiet and withdrawn as a result, and spend much time feeling exposed and like a failure. From time to time, her friends would ask her if she was feeling OK. Amelia interpreted her inability to focus, quietness, and her friends' enquiries as evidence she was indeed brain damaged or going mad. Drawing upon elements of Clark and Wells's (1995) model of social anxiety, it was thus hypothesized that undue attentional focus upon herself, together with misattribution of others' comments (which referred to her mood rather than any brain damage), conspired to lead her erroneously to conclude that brain damage was not only present but visible and obvious to others.

By session five, a new formulation was made; a modified version of the 'vicious flower' model, as used in the formulation of health anxiety (e.g. Salkovskis, Warwick, & Deale, 2003). In the centre were the key cognitions ('My brain is permanently damaged', 'I am different and alien'). Four petals, the hypothesized maintaining processes, were drawn. These were:

1   The intrusion of graphic imagery and pushing away of these images.
2   Mood changes associated with the cognitions.

3   Idiosyncratic processing of social interactions, including a heightened self-focus.

4   Rumination on the cognitive themes of damage, hopelessness, as well as dwelling on the subjects in her creative work (see Figure 4.1).

An analogy was offered of the flower unable to survive without its petals. We agreed that we would work to analyse whether the evidence better fitted this formulation of destructive *ideas* maintained by a set of cognitive and behavioural processes (Theory B), or better fitted her original formulation of an irreparably damaged brain (Theory A).

This reformulation was undoubtedly the turning point in therapy. Whereas the previous discussions had, individually, shifted things little, the vicious flower represented the first genuinely plausible alternative account, centred upon longstanding destructive *ideas*, rather than longstanding destruction. Clinically, it appeared that this moment in therapy was also the first to truly motivate Amelia's curiosity, and for her to contemplate a radical shift in perspective. She offered the observation that often it is said that if a person is repeatedly told something about themselves, they begin to believe it – it 'sticks'. 'And that is exactly what I have done to myself for 10 years – but it doesn't make it true!' Whilst initially she held only partial conviction in this idea, Amelia resolved that, if this new perspective was valid, she owed it to herself to prove properly that her brain was fit and healthy, and she could do anything she wanted to with her life.

From this point, Amelia became noticeably more active, both within and

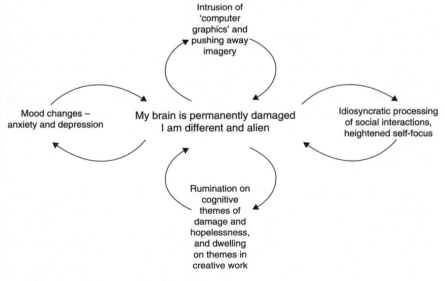

Figure 4.1 Amelia's 'vicious flower' formulation.

outside the sessions. She engaged willingly in homework assignments to initi-
ate social interactions as behavioural experiments, looking for robust evidence
whether others thought she was brain damaged, keeping her attention external
to herself whilst she did so. She also resolved to make a plan to complete her
artistic work and to consider how her future art might be inspired by experiences other than her trauma. She also agreed, as an experiment, not to push
away any unwanted imagery but to disattend, and note any change in the
frequency and intrusiveness of the graphics.

A rapid drop in Amelia's intrusive symptoms followed, and this appeared
to be further self-reinforcing, as it was obvious to her that a symptomatic
drop coinciding with a change of mental perspective was sure-fire evidence
to fit her new 'Theory B' rather than 'Theory A'. Between sessions five and
seven, her disturbing graphic imagery abated completely, and her levels of
anxiety and mood improved dramatically, together with an increase in her
perceived levels of having 'come to terms' with the trauma from 20% to 65%.
Importantly also, her belief that she had irreparably damaged her brain
dropped to 15% from a previous rating of 100%.

The remainder of therapy was devoted to seeking further evidence to consolidate the new perspective Amelia had engaged with. A more in-depth
exploration of her social-evaluative concerns was also undertaken, as Amelia
felt that her social withdrawal since the trauma had left her with a habitual
lack of confidence in social situations. Her sense of 'lost years' was also
discussed in light of her many years of struggling with this issue, and the
understandable sense of sadness and 'difference' that ensued as a result. As
therapy drew to a close, Amelia felt there was still some 'work in progress' in
respect of rebuilding of her confidence socially, and consolidating her direction in her working life after some significant stagnation. However, she felt
'unhooked' from the trauma, free from the intrusive graphic images, free to
turn her attention to future plans, and without the belief that her brain was
damaged or that she was inherently and problematically different from
others. At the end of 12 sessions of treatment and at 3-month follow-up, she
scored 8 on the PDS (mild range), 10 on the BDI (mild range), and 8 on the
BAI (none/minimal range).

DISCUSSION

This case involved the successful psychological treatment of a woman with a
chronic adverse reaction following the traumatic ingestion of a recreational
drug. Whilst undoubtedly a terrifying episode in her memory, her symptom
profile was not classic of PTSD, and a competing diagnosis was hallucinogen
persisting perception disorder (HPPD). Nevertheless, sufficient features were
present to warrant an attempt at using a trauma-focused and anxiety-based
cognitive approach.

The cognitive examination undertaken early in therapy showed that the bizarre experiences at the '3-week point' changed the meaning of her drug experience from a time-limited unpleasant experience into a truly traumatic moment that changed her brain forever. It was never entirely clear exactly what occurred in her college classroom when the walls seemed to move. One possibility, given the associated dizziness, is that she experienced symptoms of panic. However, Amelia's attribution was catastrophic and the seeds of her uncertainty were sown. The visual hallucination that evening was also something of a mystery. Possibly it was a delayed hallucinogenic after-effect, as has been documented previously (Abraham, 1983), or possibly her heightened anxiety had already sensitized her to attending closely to otherwise innocuous visual stimuli. Cognitively, however, this represented the final straw for Amelia, cementing her beliefs of brain damage and difference that were to dominate the next 10 years.

This 'change of meaning' process has been documented in other cases of PTSD, and constitutes one explanation for the delayed onset of symptoms sometimes observed after trauma (Ehlers & Clark, 2000). For example, a victim of a near-miss assault might become chronically traumatized only months later when they discover the perpetrator was a serial rapist. However, it is the *appraisal* of new information or experience that is crucial in such rescripting of traumatic meaning. In Amelia's case, the new information was unsettling but ambiguous; it was Amelia's catastrophic interpretation that led to the chronic traumatization.

Another interesting feature of this case is that the reliving, attempted in the early stages of treatment, did not result in intrusive symptom reduction. In more classic cases of PTSD, reliving typically offers a powerful therapeutic strategy to reduce the frequency and distress of intrusive re-experiencing symptoms. One crucial difference in Amelia's case was the fact that the repetitive intrusive imagery did not obviously represent re-experiencing of a traumatic memory element. Another possibility follows from the notion that intrusive PTSD imagery usually carries traumatic content from on or just before the worst moments of the trauma. However, in Amelia's case it may have been less the *content* of the intrusive imagery than the *occurrence* of this bizarre imagery that carried the destructive meanings. This hypothesis is supported by the observation that it is common for patients with PTSD to experience high levels of arousal when voluntarily bringing to mind intrusive imagery in treatment. However, notably, Amelia did not show very significant levels of arousal when describing the content of her 'computer graphic' image voluntarily. It seemed therefore that it was possibly the repetitive involuntary occurrence of such imagery that gave rise to the problematic appraisals and to her distress. In support of this idea, Ehlers and Steil (1995) found that idiosyncratic meanings surrounding the occurrence, as well as the content, of intrusive material contribute to the maintenance of PTSD.

Given these observations, other treatment strategies might profitably have been attempted in this case. In particular, there was relatively little direct work done on the bizarre imagery itself. It might have been fruitful to simulate this imagery, and perhaps simulate the random occurrence of such imagery, to purposefully activate her emotional system with the aim of contextualization, or perhaps conducting an imagery transformation to link with more benign meaning. Instead, however, it was felt important to 'follow the cognitions' and discover what was informing and maintaining them. However, there does remain something of a puzzle, perhaps, in understanding the mechanism by which the intrusive imagery, or 'drug flashbacks' actually abated. Certainly the cessation of visual disturbances correlated with a number of other changes, notably the drop in belief of brain damage. It may therefore be that this drop in belief simply motivated a reduction in the counterproductive behavioural response to push imagery out of the mind. However, it is also likely that the belief drop represented a further 'change in meaning' process for the trauma. The original memory therefore once again assumed relatively benign, and time-limited characteristics – a direct reversal therefore of the cognitive process that occurred at the delayed-onset '3-week point'. Theoretical insight into how such cognitive material can later affect the status of a traumatic memory without specifically working upon the memory itself may be offered by the UCS revaluation phenomenon (Davey, 1989). Research in this area has demonstrated that the strength of conditioned response to a given stimulus in humans can be moderated by information relating to an unconditioned stimulus which is acquired in the *absence* of direct contact with the conditioned stimulus.

Another tactic that might have been employed in this case would have been to conduct a functional analysis to examine more closely the setting conditions in which the intrusive imagery was triggered. A clear trigger offered by Amelia was that of the dark, and specifically when she closed her eyes at night. However, imagery was not triggered every time she shut her eyes and therefore a more fine-grained analysis and monitoring might have pointed to more specific cues. It then might have been possible to offer some stimulus discrimination training, as is suggested in the Ehlers and Clark (2000) approach. This process helps facilitate an appropriate reattribution of benign triggers (e.g., darkness) with such themes as safety (not threat), nowness (not a past incident), normality (not horror), and so forth. It is believed this process can inhibit the involuntary triggering of unwanted stimuli when such cues are encountered.

It is unclear whether such alternative approaches would have reached the same endpoint. However, it does seem likely that a necessary component of treatment would have been to facilitate a shift in Amelia's beliefs about having permanent brain damage. Indeed, possibly the most fundamental transformation made by Amelia in treatment involved entertaining a new meta-perspective on her troubles – i.e., a maintenance conceptualization centring upon problematic beliefs rather than a damaged brain. In this respect, the model followed some of the ideas from a health anxiety approach (e.g., Salkovskis & Bass, 1997). A vicious flower formulation was shared and allowed Amelia to contemplate the cluster of counterproductive cognitive and behavioural processes that kept the beliefs alive. The approach also borrowed from the social phobia model of Clark and Wells (1995) in identifying that Amelia was making erroneous judgements in respect of others' views of her, owing to a self-focused attentional bias and selective processing of social feedback.

A final question is the extent to which the successful cognitive-behavioural approach adopted in this case might generalize to the treatment of drug flashbacks more generally. Only one previous case in the literature describes a psychological approach to such problems (Matefy, 1973), and this used a behavioural rather than a cognitive approach. Whilst the principal thrust of substance misuse policy will understandably be to tackle drug *dependence*, and its associated social problems, it would be valuable to be able to assist the significant minority of individuals who experience chronic perceptual and emotional disturbances, and appear to be traumatized by an episode of substance use. This case demonstrates some of the similarities to and differences from classic PTSD treatment that might be encountered when adopting a trauma framework to conceptualize the problems. Most importantly, perhaps, it demonstrates the usefulness of adopting a cognitive approach, i.e., centring the formulation around an analysis of the key cognitions responsible for maintaining the disorder.

REFERENCES

Abraham, H.D. (1983). Visual phenomenology of the LSD flashback. *Archives of General Psychiatry, 40*, 884–889.

Abraham, H.D., & Mamen, A. (1996). LSD-like panic from risperidone in post-LSD visual disorder. *Journal of Clinical Psychopharmacology, 16*, 238–241.

American Psychiatric Association. (1994). *Diagnostic and statistical manual of mental disorders* (4th ed.). Washington, DC: APA.

Clark, D.M., & Wells, A. (1995). A cognitive model of social phobia. In: R. Heimberg, M. Liebowitz, D.A. Hope, & F.R. Schneier (Eds.), *Social phobia: Diagnosis, assessment and treatment*. New York: Guilford.

Davey, G.C.L. (1989). UCS revaluation and conditioning models of acquired fears. *Behaviour Research and Therapy, 27*, 521–528.

Ehlers, A., & Clark, D.M. (2000). A cognitive model of posttraumatic stress disorder. *Behaviour Research and Therapy, 38*, 319–345.

Ehlers, A., & Steil, R. (1995). Maintenance of intrusive memories in posttraumatic stress disorder: A cognitive approach. *Behavioural and Cognitive Psychotherapy, 23*, 217–249.

Espiard, M., Lecardeur, L., Abadie, P., Halbecq, I., & Dollfus, S. (2005). Hallucinogen persisting perception disorder after psilocybin consumption: A case study. *European Psychiatry, 20,* 458–460.

Fischer, R. (1971). The flashback: arousal-statebound recall of experience. *Journal of Psychedelic Drugs, 3,* 31–39.

Halpern, J.H., & Pope, H.G. (2003). Hallucinogen persisting perception disorder: What do we know after 50 years? *Drug and Alcohol Dependence, 69,* 109–119.

Horovitz, M.J. (1969). Flashbacks: Recurrent intrusive images after the use of LSD. *American Journal of Psychiatry, 126,* 565–569.

Keeler, M.J., Reifler, C.B., & Liptzin, M.B. (1968). Spontaneous recurrence of marijuana effect. *American Journal of Psychiatry, 125,* 384–386.

Lerner, A.G., Finkel, B., Oyffe, I., Merenzon, I., & Sigal, M. (1998). Clonidine treatment of hallucinogen persisting perception disorder. *American Journal of Psychiatry, 155,* 1460.

Lerner, A.G., Gelkopf, M., Skladman, I., Rudinski, D., Nachshon, H., & Bleich, A. (2003). Clonazepam treatment of lysergic acid diethylamide-induced hallucinogen persisting perception disorder with anxiety features. *International Clinical Psychopharmacology, 18,* 101–105.

Matefy, R.E. (1973). Behavior therapy to extinguish spontaneous recurrences of LSD effects: A case study. *The Journal of Nervous and Mental Disease, 156,* 226–231.

Matefy, R.E. (1980). Role-play theory of psychedelic drug flashbacks. *Journal of Consulting and Clinical Psychology, 48,* 551–553.

Matefy, R.E., Hayes, C., & Hirsch, J. (1978). Psychedelic drug flashbacks: Subjective reports and biographical data. *Addictive Behaviours, 3,* 165–178.

McGee, R. (1984). Flashbacks and memory phenomena: a comment on 'Flashback phenomena – clinical and diagnostic dilemmas'. *Journal of Nervous and Mental Disease, 172,* 273–278.

Salkovksis, P.M., & Bass, C. (1997). Hypochondriasis. In D.M. Clark, & C.G. Fairburn (Eds.), *Science and practice of cognitive behaviour therapy.* New York: Oxford University Press.

Salkovskis, P., Warwick, H.M.C., & Deale, A. (2003). Cognitive-behavioral treatment for severe and persistent health anxiety (hypochondriasis). *Brief Treatment and Crisis Intervention, 2003,* 353–367.

Van Kampen, J., & Katz, M. (2001). Persistent psychosis after a single ingestion of 'Ecstasy'. *Psychosomatics, 42,* 525–527.

Wesson, D.R., & Smith, S. (1976). An analysis of psychedelic drug flashbacks. *American Journal of Drug and Alcohol Abuse, 3,* 425–438.

Chapter 5

'Suspicion is my friend'

Cognitive behavioural therapy for post-traumatic persecutory delusions

Ben Smith and Craig Steel

INTRODUCTION

Within this chapter we will consider the potential for certain complex post-traumatic reactions to be categorized as symptoms consistent with a diagnosis of schizophrenia. Schizophrenia is the most commonly diagnosed form of psychotic disorder. Symptoms include hallucinatory experiences, which are commonly auditory, but may also be visual, olfactory or tactile, and delusions, which often occur in the form of paranoid beliefs. Fenigstein (1996) described paranoia as a disordered mode of thought dominated by an intense, irrational, but persistent mistrust or suspicion of people and a corresponding tendency to interpret the actions of others as deliberately threatening or demeaning. Before an individual is diagnosed with schizophrenia, they have often suffered a long period of distress within which they feel confused and threatened. Upon diagnosis the standard treatment is administration of anti-psychotic medication.

In recent years, a number of predominantly UK-based clinical researchers have publicized the potential for an individualized formulation-based cognitive behavioural approach to schizophrenia (e.g., Morrison, 2002; Kingdon & Turkington, 2005). Such an approach, as for other disorders, is based on the integration of developmental experiences and current beliefs and behaviours. The aim is to develop a personal account of the development and maintenance of currently distressing experiences that is less threatening than the beliefs that are currently held. This aim is particularly relevant for people diagnosed with schizophrenia, as their current explanations are usually limited to, for example in persecutory delusions, either (a) 'It is all true, people are out to get me' or (b) 'I am insane, I cannot trust my thoughts, I must take medication for ever'. Although current UK guidelines suggest cognitive behavioural therapy should be available to everyone suffering from schizophrenia (National Collaborating Centre for Mental Health, 2002), current resources fail to meet this demand.

Associations between trauma and psychosis

A number of studies report high levels of traumatic events to have occurred within individuals with psychosis (e.g., Shevlin, Houston, Dorahy, & Adamson, 2008), and others report comorbid post-traumatic stress disorder (PTSD) rates of between 15 and 40% (McFarlane, Bookless, & Air, 2001; Mueser et al., 2004). Large epidemiological studies report that varied forms of disadvantage, or having been bullied or severely abused, are associated with a significantly increased likelihood of developing a psychotic disorder (e.g., Bebbington et al., 2004). The most striking finding was that those who had been sexually abused were over 15 times more likely to develop psychosis than those who had not.

Understanding the associations between traumatic events and psychotic symptoms

It is argued that an individual who develops a psychotic disorder is likely to have had the type of adverse and traumatic life events that would predispose an individual to the development of anxiety or depression. The critical distinction is often that the individual has some unusual perceptual experiences that are confusing, and are appraised in a manner that is distressing. Garety, Kuipers, Fowler, Freeman, & Bebbington (2001) propose a cognitive model of the positive symptoms of psychosis that highlights the role of appraising unusual perceptual experiences. In this model it is proposed that in a negative social-cognitive context often characterized by negative schematic beliefs and trauma history, emotional changes occur in response to intrusive anomalous experiences. This emotional state then influences the content of these phenomena. Biased conscious appraisal processes (e.g., externalization and jumping to conclusions biases) contribute to the individual's appraisal of experiences being external in origin. Social isolation contributes to the acceptance of the psychotic appraisal by reducing access to alternative, more normalizing explanations. Symptoms are then maintained by negative schematic beliefs and normal belief confirmation processes.

Evidence for associations between trauma and psychosis

Despite the developments in cognitive theory, the role of the content of traumatic life events within currently distressing psychotic symptoms remains poorly understood. Hardy et al. (2005) found that in their sample of 75 people with psychosis, 53% reported a traumatic event that still impacted upon them negatively. Of that group, almost half (45%) exhibited an emotional theme (e.g., threat, guilt) within the content of the auditory hallucinations that corresponded to the emotional theme of the traumatic event; 12.5% experienced hallucinations in which the content was specifically linked to the content of the traumatic event. There are other reports also linking traumatic events to a wider variety of psychotic symptoms (e.g., Read, Agar, Argyle, & Aderhold, 2003).

For some people diagnosed with a psychotic disorder, it may be that traumatic events induce strong emotion and that this emotional disturbance subsequently triggers information-processing abnormalities and psychosis. However, others may be more vulnerable to the development of post-traumatic intrusions, and these intrusions may form the onset and maintenance of their symptoms. In line with this possibility, Steel, Fowler and Holmes (2005) propose that individuals with high levels of schizotypal personality traits exhibit an information-processing style that makes them particularly vulnerable to re-experiencing a past event as an intrusive memory. More specifically, they exhibit a weakened ability to integrate information into a spatial and temporal context. Within cognitive models of PTSD, such weakened contextual integration is thought to occur temporarily during a traumatic event (Brewin et al., 1996; Ehlers & Clark, 2000). Thus, when such individuals experience a trauma, they are particularly likely to engage in a form of information processing that results in trauma-related intrusions. Frequent trauma-related intrusions may result in a confused state of consciousness, in which the individual may be unsure of the link between the intrusions and past events, and fail to identify the intrusion as a memory. In such circumstances, they may appraise the intrusive phenomena within the context of their prior schizotypal beliefs (e.g., clairvoyance and telepathy) and conclude that someone, or something, is actively interfering with their mind. Whilst this account may contribute to the understanding of how trauma-related intrusions may develop within vulnerable individuals, it is again the appraisals of such experiences that are critical within the occurrence of a psychotic presentation.

This research suggests that in clinical settings a thorough assessment of an individual's trauma history and the impact of this on their beliefs, assumptions, and thoughts will be important when conceptualizing their psychotic symptoms. Despite this, there are only a few existing accounts of how to conduct such a clinical intervention (e.g., Callcott, Standart, & Turkington, 2004; Kevan, Gumley, & Coletta, 2007). On that basis the case example presented here aims to describe the process of cognitive behavioural therapy (CBT) within a case of psychosis in which trauma is a key part of the formulation. We illustrate how understanding and validating experiences of trauma, and incorporating them into an individualized formulation of psychosis, can shape the CBT intervention. The case shows how CBT techniques developed for post-traumatic stress disorder (PTSD) can be adapted for work in psychosis.

CASE EXAMPLE

Presentation

Tim was 23 years old and had been resident in the UK for 2 years when we started CBT sessions. He had migrated from a central African country and was living in the UK with his cousin, with whom he had a difficult relationship. Until recently Tim had been studying towards a professional qualification at a local college and had also been working full time on a cash-in-hand basis. Tim was seeking asylum. He was not receiving benefits or housing and was very dependent on his cousin.

Tim had a diagnosis of paranoid schizophrenia, had recently been admitted to hospital, and was taking anti-psychotic medication. His primary symptoms were described as persecutory beliefs that people he knew either personally (his cousin and his friends) or through work were out to sabotage his success. He believed that these people spoke about him behind his back and were conspiring to ruin his life. He was also hypervigilant of others' actions and words. He believed that others tried to slander him and put him down. Tim spent long periods of time ruminating about his persecution and getting depressed. He would often use alcohol to cope.

At assessment Tim endorsed his persecutory beliefs with 70% belief conviction and a subjective distress rating of 5/10. He was also, however, willing to entertain the idea that he had had a 'nervous breakdown'. Tim explained that this could have been the result of recently losing his job and the stress that he had experienced. This belief was rated at 50% belief conviction, but was far more distressing (9/10) than the persecutory belief.

Tim also reported having heard auditory hallucinations. These included the voices of his cousin and his friends. The voices made negative comments about him (to one another) and particularly referred to his inactivity and lack of employment. The voices repetitively said 'He is lazy, look at him, he is a failure'. At initial assessment he reported that although the voices had been present just before his admission, he was no longer hearing them. Tim believed that his cousin had been using some mechanism (which Tim did not properly understand) to transmit these voices. He reported no previous voice-hearing experiences.

Assessment measures

Two established psychometric measures of the positive symptoms of psychosis were used to formally assess Tim's symptoms and are reported here. First, the Scale for the Assessment of Positive Symptoms (SAPS: Andreasen, 1984) is a 35-item, 6-point (0–5) rating instrument for the assessment of the positive symptoms of psychosis. Symptoms are rated over the last month. Second, the Psychotic Symptom Rating Scales (PSYRATS: Haddock,

McCarron, Tarrier, & Faragher, 1999) is a 17-item, 5-point scale (0–4) multi-dimensional measure of delusions and auditory hallucinations. The dimensions of symptoms (e.g., distress, pre-occupation, conviction) over the last week are rated. Tim's post-traumatic stress symptoms were not formally measured at baseline as he had not received a diagnosis of PTSD and had not disclosed his trauma history at this stage.

Before CBT sessions began, Tim scored as follows on the SAPS: Auditory Hallucinations 0 (None); Persecutory Delusions 3 (Moderate); Delusions of Reference 3 (Moderate); Mind Reading 2 (Mild); Global Rating of Delusions 3 (Moderate). On the PSYRATS he scored as follows: Hallucinations Sub-Scale 0 (Maximum 24, Minimum 0); Delusions Sub-Scale 14 (Maximum 24, Minimum 0).

Background information

Tim reported his upbringing as harsh. He was an only child and he and his parents moved from the city to a rural village when he was 5 years old. He was taught that to be productive and provide for your family was essential and 'The mark of a man'. He was bullied and struggled at school due to poor behaviour and started drinking at an early age. In his late teens he was violently attacked by a vigilante group and nearly died. He later learnt from a friend that this attack was planned from within his village in an attempt to rid the village of 'People like you, your sort, a social nuisance'. He became suspicious at this point in his life and stated that 'From that point onwards suspicion was my only friend'.

Transcript from session two

TIM: Growing up the other kids did not want to associate with me. I was always the outsider and I knew they didn't think much of me. The big thing that happened was that when I was 17 I was attacked by a mob returning home from college late one evening. I was walking home in the pitch dark and then suddenly a huge mob came out of nowhere and flew at me. I remember thinking 'Why, why, why?' during the attack and just lying there taking the hits. I was so scared, I thought 'They are going to get the knives out, I will be killed' – but they didn't. It was a warning. No one spoke at all during or after it. It was like a wall of silence. They beat me so badly I was in hospital for over a week. They were trying to kill me, or trying to make me leave – to show me that they hated me and that they would ruin me – could ruin me – at any time. The mob involved people I called my friends. They never warned me that the attack was being planned, that I had been singled out for this punishment beating. Afterwards, I kept asking myself 'How did it get to this?' and 'Why did no one warn me?' Most of my friends were native to that village – my family were immigrants. It just shows you that your so-called friends will sell you down the river and that you can't trust anyone.

THERAPIST: It sounds terrifying. What sense did you make of the attack?

TIM: They sold me out. It was after that that I got so suspicious. Suspicion to me became like a protection. You keep an eye out. To counter the conspiracies out there to get you, to ruin you. You have to stay one step ahead you see. Suspicion protects me. I do it consciously. The incident with the mob changed me. I realized that I needed to be strong and to analyse even the smallest thing. If I noticed anything abnormal, then I needed to keep an eye on it.

Tim reported experiencing intrusive involuntary recollections of the mob attack approximately two to three times a week. Intense fear accompanied the memories and triggered ruminative thinking about why the attack had occurred in the first place.

Recent hospital admission

This transcript illustrates how Tim was conceptualizing this recent period of his life.

Transcript from session three

TIM: It was just before Christmas and I had been working so hard, 14 to 16 hours a day. I was also living with my boss who was originally a friend of my cousin's. Then suddenly there was no work after Christmas and I had money worries and I had rent arrears. One day my cousin and boss and another guy came to my room and told me to move out – now. Also, that I owed money. I felt like they were ganging up on me, my independence was challenged, they were accusing me of misusing money and of drinking.

THERAPIST: What did you make of that?

TIM: I couldn't believe it, it was a shock, I felt like my trust had been shattered, I felt betrayed. My cousin showed no understanding, no sympathy, no remorse – I felt they were laughing at me.

THERAPIST: So, how did you respond?

TIM: I slept rough for weeks to show them that I could handle it – the test they were running on me. That I was not so stupid as not to

	see what they were doing. It was freezing cold. I felt in a daze like I was losing my mind, shattered, deserted and lost.
THERAPIST:	That sounds awful. You must have had a lot of time to think.
TIM:	I kept asking myself 'Why?' I dwelt on this a lot. I was thinking 'Maybe this is just the beginning of more humiliations and tests to come', and 'What does he have planned for me next?' I was feeling humiliated. People were trying to make me look as if I knew nothing, they were pushing me. These people who should be closest to you, should love you. They are the worst.
THERAPIST:	What you are describing sounds extremely traumatic and stressful. How did you cope with it all at the time?
TIM:	I didn't cope really. I started to think that maybe I am crazy. I was starting not to be able to concentrate, I got lost in my mind, and in the end my cousin got me admitted to hospital. In hospital I thought that maybe I have lost my mind but that does not explain his actions. My nervous breakdown was due to him conspiring against me. I thought I could trust my own cousin – you cannot trust anyone. Once I was out of hospital in order to defend myself I drank, hid away, didn't sleep and thought about it all. Then I started to get very vigilant for any signs. It was like another chapter for me. First the mob and my friends and now my cousin. Suspicion is my friend even if no one else is. You have to trust your instincts to keep safe.

Initial formulation

It was helpful to draw both on cognitive models of PTSD (e.g., Ehlers & Clark, 2000) and psychosis (e.g., Garety et al., 2001). First, the mob attack seemed a very important and traumatic event that had (by Tim's own account) led to significant changes in the way Tim processed information (i.e., filtered through suspicion). Second, there was evidence of links between Tim's attempt to understand this event peri-traumatically ('Why, why, why?'), post-traumatically ('They were showing me they could ruin me'), and his appraisals following his job loss in the UK ('Why?' and 'This is just the beginning of more humiliations and tests to come'). Third, the strategies adopted by Tim of suspicion, hypervigilance, and avoidance were functioning to prevent change both in Tim's appraisals and memories of the mob attack. It seemed that Tim's hypervigilance for threat meant that very subtle and small indications, filtered through his suspicious mind set, very rapidly became hard evidence of an ongoing conspiracy (e.g., words people used, looks they gave him) and therefore of current threat. This reasoning style was hypothesized to be maintaining Tim's persecutory beliefs.

Tim's emotional state was one of depressed and anxious exhaustion and was hypothesized to prime him for negative interpretations of day-to-day events. His social isolation was providing him with few opportunities to disconfirm his persecutory beliefs. Tim's auditory hallucinations were also thought to have contributed to his low mood, and indeed led to an understandable search for meaning (i.e., 'What are these voices?') and hence to the conclusion that this was yet another mechanism through which his downfall was being operationalized. Finally, memories and thoughts of Tim's attack regularly intruded into his consciousness, with the associated peri-traumatic emotions (fear) and cognitions ('Why, why, why?') indicating that this memory remained poorly integrated with his other autobiographical memories, and maintaining a sense of current threat.

Initial treatment strategies

In response to Tim's low mood, isolation, and inactivity we made a plan to gradually increase his pleasurable and valued activities, allowing him to 'reclaim his life' (Ehlers & Clark, 2000). He re-commenced his studies towards his professional qualification (mornings) and joined an established gardening programme with a local Mind organization (afternoons). He also resolved to reduce his alcohol intake. Tim responded well. He quickly reported that his mood had improved and that he was busier. Importantly, Tim had met new people at Mind, something he was ordinarily very anxious about. He reported that 'Meeting friendly people helps. I felt like I belonged. I didn't feel judged. I was thinking positively. My mood was better.' Tim stated that 'The foundations of my recovery will be activity and trusting people.' This paved the way for Tim to engage in further behavioural experiments as he tested out his predictions that others could not be trusted.

Formulation development

As Tim's mood improved, he began to reflect on his experiences the previous Christmas. He noted that 'My cousin has always been a bit of a bully – maybe he took advantage of my situation and crushed me. The intensity of it triggered me off into paranoia and I got confused.' The therapist reinforced this idea that Tim may have understandably run away with these initial paranoid ideas beyond the facts. Also, that the confusion and emotion at the time may have led to him thinking in this way. Tim and the therapist began to ask themselves 'Are we sure you were accurate in your perceptions when you were in that state?'

Tim also noted that since the mob incident aged 17 he had noticed that it mattered to him greatly what people thought of him and noted that 'The mob knocked my trust in people completely. I now assume that people will take advantage and are not to be trusted.' The therapist encouraged Tim to reflect on whether this was a fair assumption. An idiosyncratic model (see Figure 5.1) was developed collaboratively.

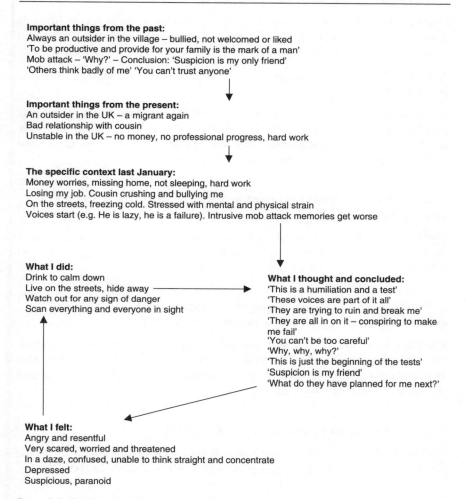

Important things from the past:
Always an outsider in the village – bullied, not welcomed or liked
'To be productive and provide for your family is the mark of a man'
Mob attack – 'Why?' – Conclusion: 'Suspicion is my only friend'
'Others think badly of me' 'You can't trust anyone'

Important things from the present:
An outsider in the UK – a migrant again
Bad relationship with cousin
Unstable in the UK – no money, no professional progress, hard work

The specific context last January:
Money worries, missing home, not sleeping, hard work
Losing my job. Cousin crushing and bullying me
On the streets, freezing cold. Stressed with mental and physical strain
Voices start (e.g. He is lazy, he is a failure). Intrusive mob attack memories get worse

What I did:
Drink to calm down
Live on the streets, hide away
Watch out for any sign of danger
Scan everything and everyone in sight

What I thought and concluded:
'This is a humiliation and a test'
'These voices are part of it all'
'They are trying to ruin and break me'
'They are all in on it – conspiring to make me fail'
'You can't be too careful'
'Why, why, why?'
'This is just the beginning of the tests'
'Suspicion is my friend'
'What do they have planned for me next?'

What I felt:
Angry and resentful
Very scared, worried and threatened
In a daze, confused, unable to think straight and concentrate
Depressed
Suspicious, paranoid

Figure 5.1 Collaborative formulation for Tim.

Treatment

The formulation highlighted important areas for intervention, influenced both by cognitive models of psychosis and PTSD. The tasks overlapped across sessions.

1 To talk through the mob attack in detail so that it stops intruding into my mind

The cognitive model of PTSD (Ehlers & Clark, 2000) was shared with Tim, including a rationale to update and elaborate his trauma memories. Tim gradually talked through the mob attack in detail in the first person, present tense. He then repeatedly listened to an audiotape of his account.

2 To check that the conclusions I drew following the attack still hold true today

It was clear that the mob attack had changed Tim's view of other people and had led to suspicion. Each of his conclusions from the mob attack were gently scrutinized to ensure that they were a fair reflection of events and to consider whether they applied in the present day.

3 To continue to meet new people and remain active with an open mind

Tim's attendance at the Mind centre provided many opportunities for him to test out whether or not his beliefs and conclusions about other people held true.

4 To check that the way I think these days is fair, even-handed, and reasonable and isn't outdated

The thinking style that Tim had adopted following his recent hospital admission was scrutinized. The conclusions that he drew at that time were approached in the same way as his post-mob attack conclusions, including the influence of Tim's longstanding beliefs.

Tim's developing psychological insight

This transcript illustrates how the shared formulation and cognitive behavioural interventions were beginning to influence Tim's thinking style.

Transcript from session ten

TIM: I have spent a lot of time at the Mind centre this week. Talking to people there helps, it reduces the mental strain.
THERAPIST: Why do you think that is?
TIM: I think you have to limit the isolation. Your mind is like a train on a track and unless someone talks to you, knocks you off course, then you can't get off that track, you can't get things right in your mind, the track will determine where you end up without other people's input.
THERAPIST: So once you are on that track it is very hard to go in any other direction unless you get another perspective?
TIM: Yes. In that state you can begin to count everything in life as a

problem. I have done that for years since the attack really. But if you discuss this with someone you realize that you think of these things in one way only, that you never diversify from that view.

THERAPIST: That makes a lot of sense. It sounds like you got into that state partly by being so isolated. Do you think your emotions also play a part?

TIM: Yes I do. Speaking to others allows you to revise your suspicions but isolating yourself gives you no hope of that. Also, feeling so scared just makes it impossible to think straight.

THERAPIST: That sounds very important indeed. What is the lesson to be learnt for the future do you think?

TIM: I have to slow down my thinking. Also, in the past I would go it alone. I would go at things fast and aggressively and I would think 'Don't trust others – trust yourself only'. Life had taught me that.

THERAPIST: And has that changed a little recently, the trust in others?

TIM: Yes, I have met some good people recently, who can clearly be trusted.

THERAPIST: So, are we saying that the attack was skewing your view of other people more than was deserved. Is that right Tim or am I mis-understanding?

TIM: That is right. When you are vulnerable you get suspicious and shut down. The bad things in my life like the attack make me very sensitive and vulnerable. I need to watch this. Instead of being suspicious and trying to analyse things yourself you need to open up. With suspicion there is no communication, which makes it even worse. You can lose perspective as it escalates in your mind. It is tempting when you notice something to think immediately 'What is that?' 'Watch out for that!'

THERAPIST: So your trust has come back because you are now watching out for the suspicion rather than seeing it as your only friend?

TIM: Yes.

THERAPIST: Thinking back, where do you think that extra suspicion came from in the first place?

TIM: From the way in which I lost everything in one go. First my pride and self-respect after the humiliating attack, then last Christmas when I was on the streets. In both cases no one was explaining to me why this was all happening. I had to work it out myself.

THERAPIST: And why do you think that you ended up feeling so suspicious rather than, say, angry?

TIM: I was so upset I couldn't understand it all, I went into hyper-drive thinking, thinking, thinking. I was hearing the voices too, which kept calling me a failure and lazy. It just felt so personal and like an attack. I did feel angry but more I felt that maybe this was just the beginning, the threat was still there, so suspicion helps then – it keeps you safe.

THERAPIST: When you look back now at the period after Christmas last year, and the incidents with your cousin, does it still feel suspicious?

TIM: I know that him treating me so badly made me suspicious.

THERAPIST: Rather than that he set out to ruin you in collaboration with others?

TIM: Yes. He did behave very badly to me though. What I was forgetting is that he is very harsh. I mistook that for some kind of nasty plan – it is just his way. But at the time you start to get suspicious.

THERAPIST: We were also speaking about the mob attack last week in quite some detail. It sounded as if the discussions we have had about it had changed your view a little . . .

TIM: For years I was convinced they were all in on it, but I realize now that the leaders were to blame. I was just a good target. I fitted the bill. The others followed them because they were scared, they had to. Those who organized the mob were bad – not all of those who took part – it was a mob mentality – you can't say no. When I got in touch with that guy from the village recently he confessed that they had been misled by the village elders and forced to take part. He said sorry and you could see he felt awful about it.

THERAPIST: Is that important information both in terms of what you said about your cousin and the mob?

TIM: Yes. Not *everyone* is a threat.

Ending therapy and outcomes

At session 10 of CBT, Tim again completed the psychosis outcome measures. He now scored zero on all the measures taken at the initial assessment. In addition, a summary table of his changes in thinking was drawn up (see Table 5.1).

After 12 CBT sessions, Tim was informed that he was to be deported from the UK. His relationship with his cousin had deteriorated and he was no longer willing to support him. He decided to voluntarily return home rather than wait in stressful circumstances contesting his immigration status. Despite this, in the 2 months prior to him leaving he was housed in four separate towns in the UK and interviewed by officials on six occasions. We put together a 'blueprint' for the future. This was a summary of what he had learnt in the CBT sessions and was accompanied by the formulation diagram and the original thinking/revised thinking table.

Table 5.1 Tim's summary of his 'revised thinking'

Original thinking:	Revised thinking:
You can't trust anyone.	You can trust some people, just not everyone.
You have to analyse even the smallest thing to be strong.	No. That way you lose perspective and strength and it escalates in your mind. You need others' perspectives too.
Suspicion is my only friend.	I have other friends. Relegate the suspicion.
Why was I attacked without warning?	Many of those who took part in the mob were forced to and were misled.
They were all showing me they could ruin me.	A small number of powerful people who hated outsiders organized the mob. It wasn't everyone.
These voices are part of the plan to ruin me (e.g. He is lazy, he is a failure).	The voices were part of the mental strain, the nervous breakdown. I just felt such a failure.
They are all in on it, running tests on me, conspiring to make me fail.	My cousin is just cold and harsh. I mistook that for some kind of nasty plan.
You can't be too careful.	You can be too careful. Don't avoid people as it just makes it worse.

In the 16th and final session of CBT, just prior to Tim being deported, his scores on all sub-scales of the SAPS and on the hallucinations sub-scale of the PSYRATS remained at zero. He now scored 6 (Maximum 24, Minimum 0) on the PSYRATS delusions sub-scale. In the context of his imminent deportation, Tim was experiencing a slight return of his pre-occupation with persecutory ideas. Despite this, he endorsed these beliefs with only a 5–10% belief conviction and a subjective distress rating of 2/10. His belief that he had experienced a stress-induced nervous breakdown was now endorsed at 90% belief conviction with a subjective distress rating of 2/10.

Tim now only reported experiencing intrusive involuntary recollections of the mob attack less than once a week and these were no longer accompanied by intense fear. Interestingly, Tim's imminent deportation had not given rise to an increase in his PTSD symptoms. The memory of the mob attack had been placed properly in the past as an adverse event of late adolescence rather than as a real, current, and imminent threat.

Tim emailed the therapist once he had returned home. 'I am struggling to adapt to the new environment but I still try to use CBT to take care of myself. I am working again in order to regain my mental strength and earn some money.'

DISCUSSION

Tim's case shows clear and meaningful links between traumatic events and the content of psychosis, such as Tim's post-traumatic shift to a suspicious thinking style. Morrison et al. (2005) have proposed that for some individuals paranoia is a useful survival strategy following repeated interpersonal trauma. Beliefs such as 'If I were not paranoid others would take advantage of me' and 'It is safer to be paranoid' and 'My paranoia protects me' may be employed as a deliberate strategy for managing interpersonal threat. Tim's beliefs that 'Suspicion is my only friend' and 'You can't be too careful' acted as a survival strategy and it was important to reappraise these as 'I have other friends. Relegate the suspicion' and 'You can be too careful' respectively. A crucial factor in Tim's ability to reappraise these powerful cognitions were the behavioural experiments he undertook at the Mind centre. His contact with trustworthy people allowed for Socratic questioning in-session to fully maximize the learning points he gained from his contact with these new people.

Negative post-traumatic cognitions are a central feature of cognitive models of PTSD (e.g., Ehlers & Clark, 2000) and of Tim's presentation. Campbell and Morrison (2007b) specifically found that negative post-traumatic cognitions were associated with psychotic experiences. Individuals who have more adverse psychological adjustments to trauma (rather than trauma exposure per se) may be more vulnerable to psychosis. Cognitions such as 'This is just the beginning of the tests' and 'They were all showing me they could ruin me' illustrate how Tim was processing the trauma of the mob attack in a manner that maintained current threat. These cognitions along with Tim's beliefs that paranoia would keep him safe (e.g., 'You have to analyse even the smallest thing to be strong') help us understand the content of his psychosis.

Reappraising the meaning of the traumatic event and enhancing self-esteem may be important. Interpersonal trauma such as bullying may add to the propensity to experience psychosis or, alternatively, psychotic-like experiences in adolescence may lead to an interpersonal context of peer hostility and rejection (Campbell and Morrison, 2007a). Tim was perceived by the villagers as an outsider and a social nuisance, and this seems to have led to the original attack.

Tim's status as an asylum seeker in the UK is another important factor to consider in understanding the triggers for his psychosis. Fazel, Wheeler, and Danesh (2005) suggest that refugees settled in western countries could be about 10 times more likely to have PTSD than the general population in those countries, with much psychiatric morbidity. It is plausible to hypothesize that the relative insecurity of seeking asylum over having refugee status may further increase this risk.

In clinical settings in the UK there are also anecdotally observed high levels of 'traumatic-psychosis' in migrant populations. The reasons why are unclear. Hypotheses include greater trauma exposure in this group, greater levels of social stress and isolation, or culturally unacceptable appraisals of psychotic experiences that lead to a diagnosis of schizophrenia. It is important to stress that in Tim's case a careful, sensitive, and appropriately timed CBT intervention for trauma-psychosis achieved success despite these apparent hurdles.

Garety et al. (2001) emphasize the role of emotion in the development, and importantly the maintenance, of psychotic symptoms and empirical evidence supports this assertion (e.g., Smith et al., 2006). Tim's case formulation clearly illustrates how he was experiencing strong emotions peri-traumatically, post-traumatically, and in the build up to his hospital admission. Reducing the intensity of his emotional response and the frequency of his intrusive trauma memories was achieved by talking through the mob attack in detail. Clinicians often fear overloading clients with too much emotion by discussing trauma in detail, meaning that an important and useful therapeutic strategy goes unused. A very slow and gentle approach to the account of the mob attack was taken with Tim. We discussed the fact that a written narrative account was an alternative to the imaginal reliving and Tim knew at all stages that he could adopt this approach at any time. With care and attention to the emotional wellbeing of clients, reliving techniques can be adapted and used in trauma-psychosis. It would not be used if the person was acutely psychotic, and a shared rationale for such memory work is imperative.

Tim developed a less threatening explanation of his distressing experiences. He is now able to find the internal explanation of a 'nervous breakdown' far less distressing. CBT for psychosis should therefore be inherently non-judgemental and validating of experiences. A key part of such formulation-driven CBT is the integration of the experience of psychotic disorder into an acceptable explanation that promotes understanding and self-worth. This will sometimes include the integration of traumatic events as well as prior beliefs, appraisals, and subsequent maintenance factors. This case illustrates how trauma work can feature in CBT for psychosis. This is different from promoting 'insight' which, on its own, may be associated with depression (Watson et al., 2006). With the growing evidence of an association between trauma and psychosis, clinicians need to ask people with psychotic symptoms about past exposure to traumatic events, and be willing to help with post-traumatic symptomatology if it presents.

The evidence base for such work with people with psychotic symptoms is just developing, but such approaches should not be dismissed simply due to formal diagnostic status.

ACKNOWLEDGEMENTS

Many thanks to Tim. This work was supported by a programme grant from the Wellcome Trust (No. 062452).

REFERENCES

Andreasen, N.C. (1984). *The Scale for the Assessment of Positive Symptoms (SAPS)*. Iowa City, IA: University of Iowa.

Bebbington, P.E., Bhugra, D., Brugha, T., Farrell, M., Lewis, G., Meltzer, H., Jenkins, R., Lewis, G., & Meltzer, H. (2004). Psychosis, victimisation and childhood disadvantage: Evidence from the Second British National Survey of Psychiatric Epidemiology. *British Journal of Psychiatry*, *185*, 220–226.

Brewin, C.R., Dalgleish, T., & Joseph, S. (1996). A dual representation theory of PTSD. *Psychological Review*, *103*, 670–686.

Callcott, P., Standart, S., & Turkington, D. (2004). Trauma within psychosis: Using a CBT model for PTSD in psychosis. *Behavioural and Cognitive Psychotherapy*, *32*, 239–244.

Campbell, M., & Morrison, A.P. (2007a). The relationship between bullying, psychotic-like experiences and appraisals in 14–16-year-olds. *Behaviour Research and Therapy*, *45*, 1579–1591.

Campbell, M., & Morrison, A.P. (2007b). The psychological consequences of combat exposure: The importance of appraisals and post-traumatic stress disorder symptomatology in the occurrence of delusional-like ideas. *British Journal of Clinical Psychology*, *46*, 187–201.

Ehlers, A., & Clark, D.M. (2000). A cognitive model of posttraumatic stress disorder. *Behaviour Research and Therapy*, *38*, 319–345.

Fazel, M., Wheeler, J., & Danesh, J. (2005). Prevalence of serious mental disorder in 7000 refugees resettled in western countries: A systematic review. *Lancet*, *365*, 1309–1314.

Fenigstein, A. (1996). Paranoia. In: C.G. Costello (Ed.), *Personality characteristics of the personality disordered*. New York: John Wiley and Sons.

Garety, P.A., Kuipers, E.K., Fowler, D., Freeman, D., & Bebbington, P.E. (2001). A cognitive model of the positive symptoms of psychosis. *Psychological Medicine*, *31*, 189–195.

Haddock, G., McCarron, J., Tarrier, N., & Faragher, E. (1999). Scales to measure dimensions of hallucinations and delusions: The psychotic symptom rating scales (PSYRATS). *Psychological Medicine*, *29*, 879–889.

Hardy, A., Fowler, D., Freeman, D., Smith, B., Steel, C., Evans, J., Garety, P.A., Kuipers, E., Bebbington, P., & Dunn, G. (2005). Trauma and hallucinatory experience in psychosis. *Journal of Nervous and Mental Disease*, *193*, 501–507.

Kevan, I., Gumley, A., & Coletta, V. (2007). Post-traumatic stress disorder in a person with a diagnosis of schizophrenia: Examining the efficacy of psychological intervention using single N methodology. *Clinical Psychology & Psychotherapy*, *14*, 229–243.

Kingdon, D., & Turkington, D. (2005). *Cognitive therapy of schizophrenia*. New York: Guilford Press.

McFarlane, A.C., Bookless, C., & Air, T. (2001). Posttraumatic stress disorder in a general psychiatric inpatient population. *Journal of Traumatic Stress, 14*, 633–645.

Morrison, Anthony P. (2002). *A casebook of cognitive therapy for psychosis.* New York: Brunner-Routledge.

Morrison, A.P., Gumley, A.I., Schwannauer, M., Campbell, M., Gleeson, A., Griffin, E., & Gillan, K. (2005). The Beliefs about Paranoia Scale: Preliminary validation of a metacognitive approach to conceptualizing paranoia. *Behavioural and Cognitive Psychotherapy, 33*, 153–164.

Mueser, K., Salyers, M., Rosenberg, S., Goodman, L.A., Essock, S., Osher, F.C. et al. (2004). Interpersonal trauma and posttraumatic stress disorder in patients with severe mental illness: Demographic, clinical, and health correlates. *Schizophrenia Bulletin, 30*, 45–57.

National Collaborating Centre for Mental Health. (2002). *Clinical guideline 1. Schizophrenia: Full national clinical guidelines on core interventions in primary and secondary care.* London: National Institute of Clinical Excellence.

Read, J., Agar, K., Argyle, N., & Aderhold, V. (2003). Sexual and physical abuse during childhood and adulthood as predictors of hallucinations, delusions and thought disorder. *Psychology and Psychotherapy: Theory, Research and Practice, 76*, 1–22.

Shevlin, M., Houston, J., Dorahy, M., & Adamson, G. (2008). Cumulative traumas and psychosis: An analysis of the National Comorbidity Survey and the British Psychiatric Morbidity Survey. *Schizophrenia Bulletin, 34*, 193–199.

Smith, B., Fowler, D., Freeman, D., Bebbington, P.E., Bashforth, H., Garety, P.A., Kuipers, E., & Dunn, G. (2006). Emotion and psychosis: Links between depression, self-esteem, negative schematic beliefs and delusions and hallucinations. *Schizophrenia Research, 86*, 181–188.

Steel, C., Fowler, D., & Holmes, E.A. (2005). Trauma related intrusions and psychosis: An information processing account. *Behavioural and Cognitive Psychotherapy, 33*, 1–14.

Watson, P.W.B., Garety, P.A., Weinman, J., Dunn, G., Bebbington, P.E., Fowler, D., Freeman, D., & Kuipers, E. (2006). Emotional dysfunction in schizophrenia spectrum psychosis: The role of illness perceptions. *Psychological Medicine, 36*, 761–770.

Chapter 6

Imagery rescripting for intrusive sensory memories in major depression following traumatic experiences

Jon Wheatley, Ann Hackmann, and Chris Brewin

INTRODUCTION

The cognitive behavioural treatment of depression has changed little since the cognitive model was originally developed (Beck, Rush, Shaw, & Emery, 1979). Cognitive behavioural therapy (CBT) has been shown to be as effective as antidepressants in the short term, but has the advantage of helping to prevent relapse. However, only around 25% of patients treated with CBT recover and remain well for 1 year, leaving many patients at risk of further relapse (Roth & Fonagy, 2005). There is often a chronic relapsing course, with a 50% probability of relapse after just one depressive episode (Paykel et al., 1995), rising to 70–80% after two episodes (Judd, 1997).

The mixed outcomes for CBT might be due to the fact that depression is often treated in a standardized way, even though individuals may present very differently. It may be that there are specific cognitive and behavioural processes maintaining symptoms of depression in individual cases. A more precise understanding of these processes might help us to design more effective treatments to target them. Perhaps rather than standard treatment packages for depression, specific strategies could be aimed at the symptoms shown by an individual patient.

Brewin and colleagues have conducted a number of studies investigating the role of memories of distressing life events in depression. In the first study (Kuyken & Brewin, 1994), 86% of a sample of women with major depressive disorder and a history of childhood sexual abuse reported having had intrusive memories of the abuse in the past week. In the second study, Brewin, Hunter, Carroll, and Tata (1996) found that intrusive memories were characteristic of depressed men and women, and could involve many different events, including loss of loved ones and interpersonal crises. A third, longitudinal study (Brewin, Reynolds, & Tata, 1999) revealed that the presence of high levels of intrusive memories predicted whether or not patients remained depressed at follow-up. The implication is that frequent intrusive memories may maintain depression and could therefore be a potential target for therapy.

Both depression and post-traumatic stress disorder (PTSD) may involve the repeated involuntary experience of intrusive memories about distressing past events. PTSD is classified as an anxiety disorder characterized by feelings of fear and a strong sense of current threat, leading to symptoms such as an exaggerated startle response (Ehlers & Clark, 2000). In a recent study of depressed patients (Patel et al., 2007), intrusive memories were associated with high levels of distress and interference with daily life. Depressed patients reported that although the memories were distressing and had implications for current appraisals and actions, there was little sense of current threat. This study also found lower levels of dissociation than is typical of patients presenting with PTSD. We suggest that idiosyncratic appraisals of traumatic events may give rise to different presentations, with fear-related appraisals more likely to lead to anxiety and appraisals of loss more likely to lead to depression.

Two studies have directly compared the experience of intrusive memories in PTSD and depression (Birrer, Michael, & Munsch, 2007; Reynolds & Brewin, 1999). In these studies both groups of patients described their memories as having similar frequency, duration, vividness, and associated distress and reported experiencing similarly intense emotions and sensations to those that they had felt at the time of the original events. Relative to intrusions in depression, the intrusions of PTSD patients are more likely to be visual, to have a sense of 'nowness', and to be accompanied by an out-of-body experience. This suggests that the phenomenology of the two disorders, although similar, differs because of the greater likelihood of dissociation in PTSD, possibly resulting in distortions in time or space when the event is re-experienced.

This chapter describes two cases in which a presentation of clinical depression appeared to be maintained by frequent intrusive memories of past distressing events. In the first case we outline a brief intervention targeting a single intrusive memory of loss from the patient's recent past. In the second case we describe a longer intervention for a patient troubled by memories of many distressing events from her childhood. Both cases were treated using imagery rescripting as the sole intervention, rather than the verbal discussion, cognitive challenge, and behavioural activation change methods that are more traditionally used in CBT for depression.

Imagery rescripting

Imagery rescripting of distressing early memories has been used to treat patients with personality disorders and survivors of childhood abuse (Edwards, 1990; Smucker, Dancu, Foa, & Niederee, 1995; Smucker & Dancu, 1999/2005; Arntz & Weertman, 1999; Young, Klosko, & Weishaar, 2003; Weertman & Arntz, 2007) but not routinely for Axis I disorders such as depression. Under the description of 'imagery rescripting' a variety of procedures have been used. Most studies present an experiential approach, in which the memory is relived and then pictured again from different perspectives. Careful questioning from the therapist prompts for changes of perspective (similar to guided discovery in cognitive therapy) by asking questions such as 'How does that look through the eyes of your adult self?'; 'If you were there now what would you like to do?'; and 'What needs to happen in the image for you to feel better about this?' Therapists vary in the nature of the rationale given to patients.

Our own rationale and procedure

Our own approach is based closely on the work of Arnzt & Weertman (1999), Hackmann (1998) and Smucker (1999, 2005). It is primarily an experiential technique with a cognitive rationale. The rationale we give to patients is that intrusive memories can be thought of as 'ghosts from the past'. In this we also draw on the theoretical models of PTSD provided by Ehlers and Clark (2000) and Brewin (Brewin, Dalgleish, & Joseph, 1996; Brewin, 2001). Prior to treatment we explain the procedure roughly as follows: 'Traumatic events may leave us with distressing images and memories that haunt us and colour our experience of the present. Sometimes these distressing memories are stored with the meaning they had at the time of the event and we may believe that these distressing memories say a lot about the kind of person we are. Some of our beliefs about these events may be unhelpful, distorted, or out-of-date. These memories need to be updated so that they find their proper place amongst your other memories. The best way to do this is for us to access the memories by re-experiencing them in your imagination. We can then try to transform them by reflecting on their meanings and using creative imagery so that they become less distressing.'

We assume that memories do not always accurately reflect events and can be thought of as constructed rather than completely veridical. We have therefore found it useful to ask questions such as 'Is the image you experience based on an actual event?' or 'How closely does the image in your mind's eye correspond to what actually happened?' Having identified the intrusive memory or image, the basic procedure is as follows.

1   The patient is helped to bring the memory image fully into awareness. The patient is encouraged to close their eyes during the imagery exercise and to use the first person, present tense, e.g., 'I am at home, sitting in the garden . . .'. The patient needs to visualize *and* verbalize the distressing memory. The therapist's role is to help the patient activate the entire memory network: visual, verbal, emotional, kinaesthetic, and olfactory, asking for details of any sensory experience, emotions, and meanings given to events. The therapist intervenes to help the patient stay with the image, ask for more detail, and elaborate on thoughts and feelings about what is happening in the imagery.

2 The therapist helps to elicit and clarify any meanings given to the events held in memory.

3 Once the memory has been brought 'online', the therapist then asks the patient what needs to happen (in the image) in order to reduce the toxic affect associated with the memory. The aim is to help the patient construct a competing image that has strong associative links to the distressing image, but will effectively compete with it. In order for the rescripted image to win the retrieval competition over the distressing memory, it must be easy to remember and to retrieve, and involve positive affect. This may require several attempts until a successful rescript can be imagined.

4 Once an alternative imaginary scenario has been created, this rescripted scene is then practised in the patient's imagination until affect lowers and any toxic beliefs based on the original event begin to change. It is important to take belief and affect ratings before and after rescripting as this is the therapist's manipulation check and sometimes powerful shifts in degree of belief can take place in a single session. These ratings are also useful because different memories may be associated with similar emotions and beliefs, which can also be tracked.

5 The therapist checks whether any new memories emerge and repeats the procedure if necessary.

The length of sessions should be 60–90 minutes, depending on how much prompting is needed for the patient to access the memory network and bring it 'online'. We suggest leaving enough time to debrief and for the patient's mood to return to baseline before the session ends. It is important not to rush imagery work, and therefore it should be started early in the session to allow sufficient time to rescript and then debrief. Several sessions may be needed to complete the process of rescripting a single memory.

Our clinical experience is that patients' distress levels and the frequency of intrusive memories may show an initial increase after the first or second treatment session as they are allowing more emotional material that may previously have been avoided into their awareness. Imagery has been shown to be more powerfully linked to emotion than verbal thoughts (Holmes & Mathews, 2005). We would therefore advise some caution in using imagery techniques when there are concerns about high suicide risk. However, we would not suggest that suicidal patients be automatically excluded from imagery rescripting (see Holmes & Butler, chapter 12 this volume). Following the initial increase in distress, we have found that patients usually begin to show improvement as they gain a sense of mastery and control over their intrusive memories and as the meaning of the memories is transformed.

Images are often frozen at the worst point, and it can be clinically useful to encourage the patient to run the memory on past this point (Hackmann, 1998) by asking questions such as 'What would happen next if you allowed the image to continue?' We suggest that the idea of rescripting alternative outcomes should be introduced as early as possible, ideally towards the close of the first session so that the patient is at least considering the possibility of change. We find it useful to ask the patient to think about what their distressed self may have needed. Some helpful questions to ask the patient when planning a rescript are: 'How did you need to feel at the time? More in control? Protected?', 'What do you need to happen in the image in order to feel that way?', 'What would you like to happen next?', 'What should have happened?', or 'What would have helped if you had known it at the time?'

It is sometimes helpful to ask the patient to try to imagine their present-day self going back in time to assist the past self in their distress. Depending on the nature of the intrusive memory, the self that intervenes may be a 'survivor self' or a 'compassionate self'. The therapist may then facilitate a dialogue between the patient's distressed self and their 'survivor' self. If the memory is from childhood, the adult self might intervene to protect or nurture the distressed child. If the memory is more recent, the present-day self can perhaps enter the image to reassure the distressed self that they will pull through. Some useful questions are: 'Can you visualize yourself, the survivor today, entering into the scene? Where are you, and what do you see? Is there anything that you, the adult would like to do or say to the distressed you? Can you see yourself doing/saying that? How does the distressed you respond? How are others around you responding? What else would you like to do or say? Is there anything that you want to tell your distressed self? How does the distressed you feel about you the survivor you of today being there? What's happening now in the imagery between the distressed you and the survivor you?'

Patients may also imagine intervention from other people, such as people whom the patient trusts, or that have shown them compassion in their past or present (perhaps friends, relatives, or teachers). Alternatively, the rescript could incorporate the patient's spiritual viewpoint. In order to win the retrieval competition, the patient simply has to be able to vividly imagine an alternative outcome. We are asking patients to imagine what should have happened, even if this did not and perhaps could never have happened in real life.

If the patient finds it hard to generate alternative outcomes, then it may be a good idea to start with more 'basic' transformations, such as changing the perspective from which a scene is viewed or its physical dimensions, and then build up to more creative transformations. Some questions to help with this might be: 'What would the scene look like projected onto a cinema screen or seen from a moving train?', 'Imagine yourself looking at the image as though it is on a television, then switching it off, making it smaller or dimmer.' 'Freeze the image, and make it black and white.' Another option is to start with transforming non-emotional material, such as imagining a kettle starting to boil; the gradual build up of sound, steam, heat, etc. The patient could then perhaps try to imagine something impossible happening, like the steam heading back into the kettle.

If during rescripting the patient becomes very distressed, then they can be asked to practise neutral or grounding imagery such as describing what they had for breakfast that day or imagining themselves in a favourite place. If the patient is emotionally avoidant, it might be useful to construct a hierarchy of avoided material, ranked from most to least threatening. Then the patient can be encouraged to experiment with allowing the least threatening material into their awareness for short periods.

The new image that is created in therapy often has emergent properties and it may take the patient by surprise. It is important that the therapist does not guide too much and gives the patient time to allow new ideas to emerge. Sometimes just holding the distressing image in awareness may lead to change as images rarely remain static. There may also be spontaneous shifts in perspective, such as 'That was wrong – that shouldn't have happened'. For example, asking the patient to imagine themselves as a small child may help them to feel compassion towards themselves.

CASE EXAMPLE 1: WORKING WITH A SINGLE DISTRESSING MEMORY FROM ADULT LIFE IN A BRIEF INTERVENTION

'Mary', a woman in her early 40s, was haunted by persistent distressing images of her father who had died from cancer 5 years ago. She met DSM-IV (American Psychiatric Association, 1994) criteria for major depressive disorder. Her depression was so severe that she had given up work several months prior to treatment. She had no previous history of depression or other psychological problems.

Mary described two recurrent related distressing images. The first was based on a memory of finding her father fallen to the floor in the hospice where he was being treated, unable to get back up. The second image was of her father's face when he was most unwell. Both images were associated with a sensation Mary described as 'feeling' his bony body as she reached for him and a smell she described as a 'hospital smell'. The key cognitions associated with these memories were: 'I'm alone, I've lost my ally' and 'I must be mad to have these pictures in my mind'. She also reported 'depression about depression', believing that her illness meant that she was a failure because she had been forced to give up work and felt unable to cope with life.

Mary was first encouraged to relive the memory as if it was happening again right now. During this procedure, Mary realized that the worst thing about the image was that her father had been helpless and a shadow of his former self towards the end of his life. As his illness had progressed, his face had become shrunken and drawn, and he had lost his curly hair.

Mary was asked to 'run the image on' past the moment at which it had become 'stuck' and imagine where she thought her father was now. She felt immediate relief as she formed a picture of him in the afterlife looking healthy. In her mind's eye she saw what she described as his 'proper fat' face before his illness, with a full head of hair. In the next session she incorporated this mental picture with other positive memories of her father, finally arriving at an elaborated image. She pictured him at his workbench, wearing a green T-shirt with a pencil behind his ear and a flat cap on. He was listening to her, smiling and advising her on her problems. As she imagined this scene, Mary described a spontaneous sensation of feeling her father's 'normal' fleshy hand on hers. When she pictured this she spontaneously reported smelling the saw-dust of her father's workspace. Following the session she put some sawdust in a small bowl next to a photograph of her father. This illustrates how the sense of smell can be used clinically to anchor a rescripted image. At the next session Mary reported having had a dream in which she had 'heard' her father telling her what a good job she'd done bringing up her children, and how much they valued her. She reported that the illness memories of her father now seemed to be static, whereas the memory of her father in his workshop seemed vibrant, colourful, and dynamic. As she put it, 'the illness images are still and grey, but the healthy image is full of action, colour, and life'.

One meaning of the distressing memory had been that Mary had lost her strongest ally. Her father had been the only member of her family who had shared her values of compassion. She had felt understood by her father, who had in the past helped her stand up to her critical mother and siblings, with whom she was often in conflict. After working on the memories of her father, Mary was able to recognize that she did have several close friends who also valued her warmth and generosity. She was able to imagine her father, her children, and her friends standing alongside her whilst her mother and her siblings stood on the other side of the room. 'Looking' between the two sides, Mary decided that she was much better off where she was. This challenged the meaning of the original intrusive memory that she was alone. She reported no further distressing intrusive memories.

Result and outcome

Mary responded very quickly to imagery rescripting. Her score on the Beck Depression Inventory (BDI) dropped from the severe range (34) to just 9 (below the clinical cut-off) after just three treatment sessions, and she no longer met criteria for major depression. These gains were maintained and even improved at follow-up, with her BDI score dropping to 3 after 3 months, 2 after 6 months and 0 a year after treatment. We believe that Mary responded so well to this treatment for the following reasons. First, her intru-sive memories were from a single event and she had many other positive memories of her father available. Second, she had held strong meta-cognitive appraisals of the intrusions ('I must be mad to have these pictures in my mind') and therefore had been relieved to discover that they were only images and that she could alter them. Following treatment Mary no longer believed she was alone or mad, and she began to make significant behavioural changes. She took on voluntary work and began studying for a degree.

CASE EXAMPLE 2: WORKING WITH MULTIPLE MEMORIES FROM EARLY LIFE

Imagery rescripting may be a more complex task when there are several intrusive memories. We have found that multiple memories are often linked in terms of their meaning and sensory components, even when related to events from different stages of a patient's life.

'Jen', a woman in her mid 30s, had a history of depression including many previous hospital admissions and significant suicide attempts, the most recent of which she had barely survived. At initial assessment she expressed high suicidal ideation and her score on the BDI was 44 (severe range). She met DSM-IV criteria for major depressive disorder as well as post-traumatic stress disorder, with depression being the most prominent feature of her presentation. She showed rumination interspersed with intrusive memories from childhood. These intrusions were of episodic memories with associated affect of sadness and helplessness. Although she met criteria for PTSD, she did not experience any of the fear-related symptoms such as flashbacks, nightmares, hypervigilance, or startle response. However she did have intrusive memories from age 6–11 of witnessing her parents being violent towards each other. Examples were images of her father holding an electric drill against her mother's head, or her mother smashing a bottle over her father's head. Jen recalled how during such incidents one parent would typically have been screaming at her to call an ambulance or the police, whilst the other would have been shouting at her to stay away from the telephone. These memories were associated with feelings of being frozen and unable to decide how to act. Key cognitions associated with the memories were: 'I'm helpless and incapable', 'I can't make a decision how to act because whatever I choose to do will be wrong', and appraisal of the experience of having intrusive memories: 'I will never be happy because I have these scenes in my mind'. Her appraisals of these memories were associated with strong suicidal ideation. Jen also attempted to block out the memories with frequent binges of drug and alcohol use. As a small child she had sometimes avoided witnessing her parents' arguments by hiding in a cupboard, and as an adult she would often stay in bed for days at a time when feeling most depressed.

To help her imagine herself as a child, Jen chose to bring old photographs of herself and her parents along to the therapy sessions. In treatment, Jen was first asked to imagine herself entering the house where her parents had fought, viewing the scenes depicted in her intrusive memories from an adult perspective. She imagined looking into the eyes of herself as a little girl and this allowed her to 'see' how scared and helpless her child self had been. She then chose to bring a compassionate figure (her aunt) into the image to tell her parents that they were putting their little girl in an impossible situation. She imagined the aunt telling her parents that the child looked scared and that they had to stop fighting. The aunt then reassured the little girl that her parents would survive (as a child Jen had feared that they might kill each other). Jen decided that what she needed next (as a child) was for her aunt to take her away from her parents' home. However, she was worried that if she left the house then her parents would kill each other. Jen then remembered how she had used to halve her pocket money each week and put it into her parents' jacket pockets in the hope that this might stop them fighting. This allowed her to feel some compassion for her 'child' self, and she now felt inclined to intervene herself. She imagined herself from the present day entering the image to give her child self the message that 'your parents are strong enough to look after themselves, they are very angry but they are not going to kill each other'. Jen was also asked to imagine someone whom she felt genuine compassion for. She chose a cousin who had Down's syndrome, and imagined hugging him. Following this she was able to imagine her adult self hugging herself as little girl. At this point in treatment Jen started to grieve that she had not got the help that she had needed as child. She felt great sadness that her parents had been so preoccupied with their marital problems that they had not been able to notice or soothe her distress.

Jen also reported another specific memory. Whilst on holiday in Greece at the age of 10, she had witnessed her parents have a blazing row as a crowd gathered to watch. Her parents had stormed off in opposite directions and Jen had been left alone in the crowd, unable to decide which parent to follow. The affect associated with this memory was of feeling terribly alone and helpless. During the rescript, Jen imagined her adult self first covering up the little girl's ears so that she could not hear the horrible things that her parents were shouting at each other. She then decided that she wanted to take herself off for an ice-cream as a little girl. In her imagination, she 'discovered' that the child had been worried that each parent would assume that she was with the other one and be cross with her for taking sides. She therefore imagined her adult self telling each parent that the little girl was with her before sitting the parents down together with a cup of tea to talk it over. Jen's parents separated when she was 11, and she reported a further intrusive memory of saying goodbye to her father as he left the family home. At the time she had felt abandoned and during the rescript she imagined her adult self comforting herself as a child, explaining that her parents needed to separate and that this was for the best.

In a subsequent session Jen reported an intrusive memory from her adolescence. This was a new intrusion that had not been reported at assessment. The memory was of a time that her mother had found laxatives that the young Jen had been using to control her weight. The intrusive image was of her mother's face looking angry and screaming at her for being so stupid. The meaning of the memory was that she had let her mother down and that she had gotten things wrong once again. She imagined her adult self comforting her adolescent self, while her therapist entered the image to tell her mother that her child had good reasons for dealing with her emotions this way. Jen then recalled how she had been fond of a school headmaster at that time in her life and she was able to imagine him giving her parents a bad report on their parenting skills.

Result and outcome

After 19 sessions Jen no longer met criteria for major depressive disorder or post-traumatic stress disorder. Her score on the Beck Depression Inventory had halved from an average of 33 over baseline to 16.5 over her final two sessions. All gains were fully maintained and even improved at follow-up, with her BDI score dropping to well below the clinical range: 9 at 3 months, 2 at 6 months, and 0 at 1 year.

Jen began to make many behavioural changes and started doing voluntary work that eventually led to a career change. These activity changes were not planned or discussed in the treatment sessions, but were spontaneously generated by the patient. At 1-year follow-up Jen showed a slight increase in her anxiety levels because she was doing more things that she had previously avoided.

Following treatment, Jen continued to report intrusive memories of child-hood events, but these were infrequent and did not cause distress or interfere with her functioning. She was able to reappraise the memories of her parents fighting and now believed that there was nothing she could have done at the time to help them. She no longer believed that she had been abandoned by her father and acknowledged that her parents had been unable to live together and needed to separate. She reflected that her parents had both been able to move on with their lives and that now she could do so too. The distressing events of her past no longer seemed to hold such relevance for her personal actions and happiness. Prior to treatment, Jen had reported believing that she had been so damaged by childhood events that she couldn't ever be normal, and that this frequently made her feel hopeless and suicidal. Towards the end of treatment, she reflected that although she knew the inter-ventions of the imagery rescripting had only taken place in her imagination, it felt as if they actually had happened. At follow-up she reported 'I feel as if a weight has been lifted from my mind. I feel more grown-up. I don't feel dependent or unable to make decisions any more. It's like I've salvaged my self, my soul.'

REVISITING MEMORIES: SUMMARY, CONCLUSIONS, AND FURTHER QUESTIONS

Imagery rescripting allows patients to revisit specific scenes from memory which carry general meanings about themselves and others. A successful rescript works on several different levels. It challenges the idea that the distressing past event is the basis of a rule for life, rather than being seen as an exception. It challenges the meaning of key self-defining memories, including meta-cognitive appraisals of the experience of the intrusions themselves. It also provides an emotional experience of what should have happened at the time (but did not). Bringing these scenes 'on-line' and imagining alternative outcomes enables the patient to experience being in control or being worthy of love and compassion (Hackmann, 2005; Lee, 2005). As Jen reported following treatment, she knew that the rescript only happened in her imagination, but her appraisals of past events and of herself had changed because of them.

Events are interpreted in the light of experience and traumatic memories may be stored with their original meanings (Ehlers & Clark, 2000). These memories and their meanings may be best accessed through imagery. This might result in some spontaneous restructuring, such as 'it's only a memory' or 'it wasn't my fault'. Rescripting of these highly emotional past events may reduce the ease with which negative representations of self are accessed. The two cases described here show that imagery rescripting can be an effective and sometimes rapid treatment for depressed individuals with high-frequency intrusive memories relating to stressful events that are now in the past.

It seems that both cognitive and behavioural change are possible through using imagery techniques. Belief change and symptom reduction were achieved here using an experiential technique in which beliefs were not directly challenged, and it may be that evidence supporting depressive beliefs may not need to be rationally disputed. In these two examples patients were guided to use their imagination to help them see beyond the depressive beliefs encapsulated in their intrusive memories. Imagery rescripting helped them to attend to information that might challenge negative beliefs, such as positive memories of experiences that contradict the toxic meanings of their intrusions, and to incorporate this information into the memory network. In the first case, Mary was helped to attend to positive memories of her father and this allowed her access to evidence that her children and friends valued the same qualities that her father had once valued. In the second case, Jen was able to feel empathy for the distressing position that her parents had placed her in and to update her appraisals of the traumatic events. Strikingly, both patients showed significant behavioural changes without any traditional behavioural experiments or activity scheduling being part of the treatment. Cognitive change was achieved by altering the meaning of the memory by working within the sensory memory system, using questions to prompt for change.

Working with imagery may not be suitable for every patient. It is likely that only very frequent intrusions might maintain the disorder. Patients who report intrusive memories may have encoded information in a sensory way and may retrieve it in a similar way. Creating competing sensory representations may therefore be more effective than verbally challenging the meanings of the memories. Such patients might respond better to imagery work than to written thought diaries and verbal challenging. Successful imagery treatment seems to depend on the extent to which the emotional memory system can be brought 'online' in the therapy session and this might be more difficult with some depressive presentations, particularly if there is strong emotional avoidance.

A theoretical framework that can help us understand how and why imagery rescripting might work is the retrieval competition hypothesis. In a recent reformulation of CBT, Brewin (2006) has suggested that emotions and behaviour are under the control of alternative memory representations that compete for retrieval. They may take the form of general semantic knowledge (e.g., 'I am a bad person') or images and memories related to specific auto-biographical incidents. Rather than memories being directly modified by therapy, alternative positive semantic and episodic memories are created to compete with any dominant negative memories. The retrieval competition hypothesis views imagery rescripting as constructing or strengthening competitor memories that are similar enough to be retrieved by reminders but different enough to evoke positive feelings. The two cases reported here seem to fit with this hypothesis, as therapy helped them to create an alternative sensory representation to challenge the meanings of their most toxic memories.

One important empirical question is whether it is necessary in treatment for the patient to relive the whole memory in detail or whether simply accessing key fragments of the memory might be enough. This is currently unanswered, so we will need to be guided by idiosyncratic formulations and clinical intuition. It may be useful for the patient to access the entire memory at least once in order to identify the most toxic aspects of the memory and the key meanings that might be attached. However, in some cases, when a distressing event such as childhood abuse was very prolonged and/or repeated over time, it may not be necessary or desirable to run through the entire memory. We suggest that the patient only needs to relive enough of the memory to activate any affect and associated beliefs that need to be targeted in treatment. It may be enough simply to allow the beginning point of the memory into awareness, for example for the patient to 'hear' the sound of an abuser's footsteps as they approach. The patient will know what this signals and what would have happened next, and we can then spare them the distress of reliving the whole trauma (Arnzt & Weertman, 1999; Arnzt & van Genderem, 2009). Remember that rescripting is not the same as exposure treatment and patients only need to allow enough of the toxic material into awareness for any transformation to be meaningful. Judgements about how much 'toxic' material it is necessary to relive before rescripting will vary on a case by case basis.

The aim of rescripting is to help the patient construct a competing image that has strong associative links to the distressing memory but will effectively compete with it and will be easy to remember and retrieve. The competing image must also involve positive affect and challenge any toxic meanings of the memory for the patient. Suggesting possible transformations to the patient or directing them too much may be less powerful than a transformation that the patient generates for themselves. We propose that if patients are helped to develop their own alternative image, this promotes a greater sense of mastery than if the alternative image is suggested by the therapist. The aim of questioning by the therapist is to help patients find a transformation that works for them, and it may take many trials before a satisfactory rescript is reached. Sometimes distressing images fail to shift until a particular transformation is hit upon, which may be nothing to do with the prompts of the therapist. In this way the process is similar to Socratic questioning of verbal thoughts, in which many questions might fail to lead to a change in perspective before a new possibility opens up to the patient. Patients often report that a transformation just 'comes to them' all of a sudden. The aim is to arrive at a rescripted image that is meaningful and emotionally salient to the patient, and that is at least as powerful as the original image.

Imagery rescripting may be used as part of a broader CBT treatment package for depression. For example, if a patient is severely depressed and unmotivated, then it might make clinical sense to begin treatment with activity scheduling before moving on to imagery rescripting once there has been some improvement in symptoms. Another idea might be to follow up any successful rescripts of distressing memories with behavioural experiments designed to extend any belief change into the 'real world'. However, the two cases reported here show that imagery rescripting can work as a stand-alone treatment, and that both behavioural and cognitive change can occur as a result of working with imagery. The fact that treatment gains were well maintained at a year's follow-up suggests that using imagery rescripting to target frequent intrusive memories could help reduce the risk of relapse in those cases in which distressing memories may be maintaining depression.

ACKNOWLEDGEMENTS

This study was undertaken with the support of a Medical Research Council strategic grant to Chris Brewin and Adrian Wells. It was also supported by the Camden and Islington Mental Health and Social Care Trust, who seconded Dr Wheatley and received a proportion of funding from the NHS Executive.

REFERENCES

American Psychiatric Association. (1994). *Diagnostic and statistical manual for mental disorders* (4th ed.). Washington, DC: APA.

Arntz, A., & Weertman, A. (1999). Treatment of childhood memories: Theory and practice. *Behaviour Research and Therapy, 37*, 715–740.

Arnzt, A., & van Genderem, H. (2009). *Schema therapy for Borderline Personality Disorder*. Chichester: Wiley.

Beck, A.T., Rush, A.J., Shaw, B.F., & Emery, G. (1979). *Cognitive therapy of depression*. New York: Wiley.

Birrer, E., Michael, T., & Munsch, S. (2007). Intrusive images in PTSD and in traumatised and non-traumatised depressed patients: A cross-sectional clinical study. *Behaviour Research and Therapy, 45*, 2053–2065.

Brewin, C.R. (2001). A cognitive neuroscience account of posttraumatic stress disorder and its treatment. *Behaviour Research and Therapy, 39*, 373–393.

Brewin, C.R. (2006). Understanding cognitive behaviour therapy: A retrieval competition account. *Behaviour Research and Therapy, 44*, 765–784.

Brewin, C.R., Dalgleish, T., & Joseph, S. (1996). A dual representation theory of posttraumatic stress disorder. *Psychological Review, 103*, 670–686.

Brewin, C.R., Hunter, E., Carroll, F., & Tata, P. (1996). Intrusive memories in depression. *Psychological Medicine, 26*, 1271–1276.

Brewin, C.R., Reynolds, M., & Tata, P. (1999). Autobiographical memory processes and the course of depression. *Journal of Abnormal Psychology, 108*, 511–517.

Edwards, D.J.A. (1990). Cognitive therapy and the restructuring of early memories through guided imagery. *Journal of Cognitive Psychotherapy, 4*, 33–51.

Ehlers, A., & Clark, D.M. (2000). A cognitive model of posttraumatic stress disorder. *Behaviour Research and Therapy, 38*, 319–345.

Hackmann, A. (1998). Working with images in clinical psychology. In A.S. Bellack, & M. Hersen (Eds.), *Comprehensive clinical psychology* (Vol. 6, pp. 301–318). New York: Elsevier.

Hackmann, A. (2005). Compassionate imagery in the treatment of early memories in Axis 1 anxiety disorders. In P. Gilbert (Ed.) *Compassion: Conceptualisations, Research and Use in Psychotherapy*. London: Brunner-Routledge.

Holmes, E.A., & Mathews, A. (2005). Mental imagery and emotion: A special relationship? *Emotion, 5*(4), 489–497.

Judd, L.L. (1997). The clinical course of unipolar major depressive disorders. *Archives of General Psychiatry, 54*, 989–991.

Kuyken, W., & Brewin, C.R. (1994). Intrusive memories of childhood abuse during depressive episodes. *Behaviour Research and Therapy, 32*, 525–528.

Lee, D. (2005). The perfect nurturer: using imagery to develop compassion within the context of cognitive therapy. In P. Gilbert (Ed.) *Compassion: Conceptualisations, Research and Use in Psychotherapy*. London: Brunner-Routledge.

Patel, T., Brewin, C., Wheatley, J., Wells, B., Fisher, F., & Myers, S. (2007). Intrusive images and memories in major depression. *Behaviour Research and Therapy, 45*, 2573–2580.

Paykel, E.S., Ramana, R., Cooper, Z., Hayhurst, H., Kerr, J., & Barocka, A. (1995). Residual symptoms after partial remission: An important outcome in depression. *Psychological Medicine, 25*, 1171–1180.

Reynolds, M., & Brewin, C.R. (1999). Intrusive memories in depression and post-traumatic stress disorder. *Behaviour Research and Therapy, 37*, 201–215.

Roth, A., & Fonagy, P. (2005). *What works for whom? A critical review of psychotherapy research* (2nd ed.). New York: Guilford.

Smucker, M.R., & Dancu, C. (1999/2005). *Cognitive-behavioural treatment for adult survivors of childhood trauma: Imagery rescripting and reprocessing*. Lanham, MD: Rowman & Littlefield (Original work published 1999).

Smucker, M.R., Dancu, C., Foa, E.B., & Niederee, J.L. (1995). Imagery rescripting: A new treatment for survivors of childhood sexual abuse suffering from post-traumatic stress. *Journal of Cognitive Psychotherapy, 9*, 3–17.

Weertman, A., & Arntz, A. (2007). Effectiveness of treatment of childhood memories in cognitive therapy for personality disorders: A controlled study contrasting methods focusing on the present and methods of focusing on childhood memories. *Behaviour Research and Therapy, 45*, 2133–2143.

Young, J.E., Klosko, J.S., & Weishaar, M.E. (2003). *Schema therapy: A practitioner's guide*. New York: Guilford.

Chapter 7

Cognitive therapy for post-traumatic dissociation

Helen Kennerley

INTRODUCTION

Dissociative reactions are not uncommon following trauma for both 'type I trauma' (single or few events) and 'type II trauma' (chronic, multiple events) (Terr, 1991; Rothschild, 2000). Clinical work is confounded by there being no agreed cognitive-behavioural model of dissociation to guide us, and by the wide and sometimes confusing range of clinical presentation. Clinicians must rely heavily on using a general understanding of the processes of dissociation, from psychological and neuropsychological literature, combined with a good functional analysis of a client's presenting problems, to guide them in their interventions.

What is dissociation?

At first his thoughts were of the huge administrative stress of moving home, but then they wandered to his plans for the flat. In his mind's eye, he saw himself in the sunny living room with his Sunday papers and fresh coffee. Snug in his dressing gown, feet up, listening to jazz. Relaxed, pleased with what he had created, enjoying where he was . . .

Fran heard what the doctor said and, strangely, felt nothing. She realized the implications of the diagnosis, but felt detached and a little unreal. She drifted through the rest of the day feeling calm – and yet emotional in an intellectual way.

The deadline was approaching. Phil recalled sitting at his desk, focused on the project, but he had no idea that it was now two in the morning or that his favourite piece of music had finished playing some time ago.

These examples support the notion that dissociation should not be considered inherently pathological and often does not lead to significant distress, impairment, or help-seeking. The *Diagnostic and Statistical Manual of*

Mental Disorders (DSM-IV; American Psychiatric Association (APA), 1994) describes dissociation as a disruption in the usually integrated functions of consciousness, memory, identity, or perception of the environment, which might be sudden or gradual, chronic or transient. It defines the following presentations:

- Dissociative amnesia: loss of memory for a discrete period of time that is too extensive to be 'forgetting'.
- Dissociative fugue: confusion of identity with an associated amnesia.
- Depersonalization disorder: persistent sense of strange unreality concerning the self.
- Dissociative identity disorder (DID): experience of two or more distinct 'personae' with degrees of amnesia associated with each.
- Dissociative disorder not otherwise specified (DDNOS) that includes, for example, trance states, derealization, psychogenic stupor.

DSM-IV-TR (APA, 2000) also recognizes that dissociation is often an aspect of acute stress disorder (ASD), post-traumatic stress disorder (PTSD), somatization disorder, panic disorder, schizophrenia, depression, and borderline personality disorder (BPD). Other states that are considered to be dissociative include: age regression, identity alteration, pseudo hallucination, emotional numbing, and post-traumatic flashback (Steinberg, 1995).

However, pathological amnesic states should not be confused with normal forgetting or incomplete encoding of information, psychogenic amnesia, organic amnesia, or straightforward reluctance to disclose information (McNally, 2005). Hence the need for thorough assessment, flexible formulation, recognition of the importance of the therapeutic relationship as a vehicle for encouraging openness, and seeking supervision when we are uncertain of the clinical picture.

In summary, dissociation is currently an 'umbrella' term describing various altered states of consciousness, some of which are not obviously similar. For example, some states involve a 'tuning out', or distancing or suppressing an experience (e.g., functional amnesias, lack of affect, depersonalization, or derealization), while some states appear to reflect the opposite, an intense state of being highly 'tuned in' to an experience (e.g., flashbacks, daydreaming, hypnotic states). This chapter concerns itself with forms of dissociation that are associated with trauma and that can lead to significant distress, impairment, or help-seeking.

Post-traumatic dissociation

An association between dissociative symptoms and traumatic events has been widely documented (e.g., Cardena & Spiegel, 1993; Freinkel, Kooperman, & Spiegel, 1994). Dissociative presentations are more likely to occur following the more 'severe' traumatic experiences (Zatzick, Marmar, Weiss, & Metzler, 1994), particularly if the experience involves personal threat (Chu, 1998).

Dissociation is a key aspect of ASD, in which the sufferer can experience: emotional numbing, being in a daze, derealization, depersonalization, and inability to remember aspects of what happened during or immediately after the trauma. ASD has been identified as a risk factor or precursor for PTSD, and, specifically, peri-traumatic dissociation as a risk factor for PTSD (e.g., Birmes et al., 2001). However, Murray, Ehlers, and Mayou (2002) suggest that persistent dissociation rather than peri-traumatic dissociation best predicts PTSD.

Childhood trauma is also linked with a tendency towards a dissociative style of information processing in adulthood (e.g., van der Kolk & van der Hart, 1989; Waller et al., 2000). It is suggested that a traumatized child might develop this style of information processing in order to minimize the emotional impact of the experience and that it can become habitual.

Flashbacks

The post-traumatic flashback is the dissociative phenomenon for which we have the best cognitive-behavioural (Ehlers & Clark, 2000; Brewin et al., 1996) and neurobiological (for an overview, see McNally, 2003) understanding. This intense memory (or parts of memory) is intrusive and so vivid as to feel as if the event were actually happening again to some degree. Such memories can comprise various sensory experiences, such as visual images, bodily sensations, smells, and sounds, which recreate recollections with *apparent* verisimilitude, i.e., the intensity of the experience conveys a *sense* of the memory reflecting an accurate account of an experience. There has been little comparison of type-I trauma and type-II trauma flashbacks, but in my own experience, the latter often meld into a 'generic' recollection, particularly if the trauma suffered was during childhood. Recollections from childhood may not be as predominantly visual as type-I trauma memories, and also seem more prone to distortion, sometimes even becoming a metaphor for actual events (see below). Flashbacks may not reflect an event accurately. They are memories, and as such are *reconstructive*, thus can change with each recollection (McNally, 2003). However, they can capture relevant personal meaning as is apparent in the following:

'I am in a bubble filled with the sounds and smells and tastes and fear and revulsion. In the bubble it's childhood and I experience it all over again. Something in my mind knows that the real world is outside of the bubble but I can't focus on that, only on what's happening to me again. It is awful.'

'All at once I see just their faces: his looking at me in that steely way and hers laughing. She wasn't there with him then but I can see her now. Right there. I can smell his breath and feel him on me. It's disgusting. I feel dirty . . .'

A characteristic of flashbacks is that they are dissociated for time, but they can be dissociated in other ways too. For example, a client had a powerful flashback of receiving painful medical treatment in childhood that was without auditory or visual recollection. She described a feeling of: '. . . burning orange all through my body with the hottest red in my heart. It takes over and it is a horrible, garish bright colour. I can't say it's pain – it's colour and shape and sensation and it's worse than any pain that I've known as an adult.'

Models, categories, and mechanisms of dissociation

Outside flashbacks, clinicians face greater challenges in understanding the processes underpinning dissociative symptoms. Proposed models and mechanisms are not necessarily mutually exclusive or conflicting: they often reflect attempts to understand a complex phenomenon from different angles.

Models

A spectrum of dissociation. This simple notion proposes that each type of dissociative experience can be expressed at a non-pathological level through to highly dysfunctional states (e.g., Kennerley, 1996). For example: mild derealization during the excitement of one's wedding through to extreme and disorientating derealization that promotes concerns about sanity or sense of self; temporary emotional numbing on hearing bad news through to a chronic lack of affect; a pleasant but intense recollection of an exciting event the night before through to uncontrollable and unwanted flashbacks of a traumatic scene. This view offers an often useful and reassuring simplification for clients, that the sufferer is experiencing a normal but exaggerated experience that can be 'harnessed' and brought back within non-pathological boundaries.

Dissociation as an interruption of information processing. The common elements of information processing models are:

1   A point of 'data collection' when sensory stimulus impinges on the organism.
2   A means of deriving meaning of the stimulus. This is generally taken to be a multi-modal network of sensory, cognitive, and emotional brain processes interlinking to inform each other. For example, if I see and hear that I am walking past a snarling dog ('data collection'), I am able to cross-check generic information that I have about dogs, specific memories that I have about dogs, and my own feelings about them with projections

of what might happen if I was bitten etc. I have a rich inner experience that conveys a subjective meaning about the situation: 'I am in danger'.

3   An emotional response appropriate to the derived meaning. In response to the above, I would feel fear and act accordingly, giving the dog wide berth.

Dissociation occurring at different points in this process may result in different types of dissociative phenomena (Kennedy et al., 2004; Kennerley, 2004).

1   Dissociation at the point of 'data collection' might well result in apparent amnesias as a full sensory experience would not be laid down – this is a 'genuine' amnesia rather than a functional or true traumatic amnesia. The information will not have been stored and therefore cannot be retrieved. For example, attention can be impaired during trauma, and a victim might only encode details of an assailant's weapon and not the face or peripheral details.

2   Dissociation at the point of deriving meaning – when the full multi-modal network failed to communicate – might result in flashbacks or in lack of affect linked with recollections, for example, because all relevant aspects of the experience are not 'communicating'.

3   Disruption at the point of retrieval could underpin functional amnesias or depersonalization, whereby the multi-modal processes have been effective but the derived meaning is so personally distressing as to trigger some form of detachment. Waller, Quinton, and Watson (1995) observed that women with anorexia nervosa tend to achieve emotional numbing before experiencing a full emotional response (peri-retrieval), while women with bulimia nervosa achieve (via binge-eating) emotional numbing after experiencing unwanted emotion (post-retrieval).

Categories

Allen (2001) distinguished dissociative responses representing 'detachment' and 'compartmentalization'. Detachment is an altered state of consciousness characterized by a sense of separation, such as is seen in out-of-body experiences (OBE), depersonalization, and derealization. Compartmentalization is described as a deficit in ability to control psychological or physiological processes, as is evident in dissociative amnesias, DID, or conversion disorders.

Factor analysis studies of the Dissociative Experiences Scale (DES, Berstein & Putnam, 1986; for a review, see Holmes et al., 2005) have revealed other possible categorizations for dissociative phenomena, namely: (i) depersonalization/derealization; (ii) amnesia; and (iii) absorption. The latter refers to a state of fully engaged attention that is limited in scope. An everyday example of this would be concentrating on a piece of music and not realizing that a friend had entered the room.

A further clinically relevant distinction is between 'psychological' and 'somatoform' dissociation (Waller et al., 2000). 'Psychological' dissociation is characterized by a failure to integrate psychological aspects of an experience (e.g., not linking relevant emotions with recollection; being unable to recall certain events or aspects of events), while 'somatoform' dissociation describes a set of adaptive psychophysiologic responses to physical trauma that can, for example, be manifest as absence of pain despite injury. Somatoform dissociation is associated with childhood trauma involving physical contact and/or trauma, and psychological dissociation associated with a wider range of non-contact forms of trauma.

Mechanisms

The *defensive mechanism* (van der Kolk & van der Hart, 1989) proposes that dissociation decreases the awareness of the impact of trauma so that the victim can better function in the short term. For example, emotional numbing allowing the road traffic victim to get his family to safety away from a burning car (dissociation at the point of deriving meaning), lack of pain from an injured limb permitting a soldier to move away from a source of threat (dissociation at the point of data collection). It is argued that continued decreased awareness can impede adequate processing of trauma memories and result in pathological post-traumatic dissociation (Spiegel, Kooperman, Cardena, & Classen, 1996).

A different suggestion is that peri-traumatic dissociation is a *compensatory mechanism to marked physiological arousal* (Freidman, 2000; Marmar, Weiss, & Metzler, 1998). The evidence for this comes from indirect sources, such as the finding that yohimbine, which increases arousal, can precipitate flashbacks in trauma survivors (Southwick et al., 1993), that hyperventilation can induce dissociative responses in recent trauma victims (Nixon & Bryant, 2006) and that peri-traumatic panic symptoms account for most of the variance of peri-traumatic dissociation (Bryant & Panasetis, 2005).

These two views are not incompatible: there may be a functional basis to peri-traumatic dissociation that can become dysfunctional if it becomes habitual *and* this phenomenon could be heightened by arousal.

Some conclusions

Dissociation remains ill-defined. The term embraces a collection of differing presentations, which are related by the fact that they illustrate a *dis*-association of information processing. It seems likely that there is a distinction to be made between the presentations that indicate Detachment and those that indicate Compartmentalization. Within Compartmentalization we see Absorption (which is a form of 'tuning in' to a limited aspect of our experience) and we see a 'tuning out' phenomenon that is quite specific and that would include post-traumatic amnesias, and traumatic memories that lack emotion. The experience of Compartmentalization can incorporate the two – for example, in DID a person 'tunes in' to one aspect of self, whilst detaching from other aspects of self (perhaps to differing degrees), and in flashbacks we often see acute 'tuning in' to one aspect of an experience whilst being temporally detached (see Figure 7.1)

From theory to practice

A richer understanding of the different types of presentation of dissociative phenomena and the processes that underlie them is pertinent to clinical work, from engagement through to relapse management. Clinicians first have to create the right environment to engage the client, usually by showing an empathic understanding of the problem and presenting a compelling rationale for treatment. The theory can enhance our understanding of the client's experience and offer possibilities for change. During assessment and conceptualization, the theory can help us appreciate dissociative *processes* and this can fuel hypotheses for testing and also guide us in teasing out crucial maintaining cycles.

Providing information on the non-pathological basis of dissociation helps clients who cannot otherwise understand their experiences. The models also indicate necessary changes: put simply, if the client is detaching too much, we need to help her/him 'tune in'; if they are 'tuning in' excessively, then they need to learn to decentre, re-focus, or review. The latter is crucial to flashback management.

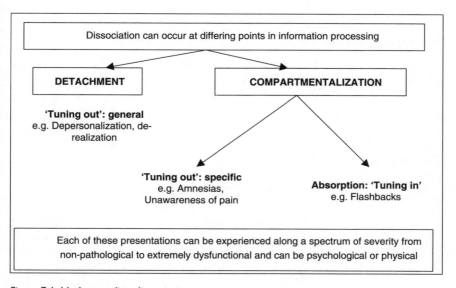

Figure 7.1 Understanding dissociation.

CASE EXAMPLES

Moira: childhood type-II trauma

At the age of 57, Moira began to have traumatic flashbacks from childhood. For 40 years she had regarded herself as stable and content, but 3 months earlier she had been contacted by Tamsin, a daughter whom she had given up for adoption weeks after birth. Moira had been excited about meeting her, but extremely shocked to recognize features of her father in Tamsin's face. For Moira this was undeniable confirmation that Tamsin was her father's child, something that she 'had refused to think about for over 40 years'. She began to have flashbacks of her childhood and teenage experiences of abuse and her mood deteriorated rapidly. At assessment, she was very depressed and suicidal. She described two types of post-traumatic dissociation: chronic emotional numbing, which had begun in childhood and continued until she met Tamsin, and delayed post-traumatic flashbacks of her childhood trauma. She described these as 'vivid and immediate'. They evoked a level of affect that she was not used to managing; she felt overwhelmed, helpless, and afraid.

Moira's physical abuse began as far back as she could remember and continued until she left home; her sexual trauma probably began when she was 4 or 5 years old. At 15 she fell pregnant and gave birth to Tamsin. Her parents forced her give the child up for adoption. She left home soon after, and met and married Roger, who is devoted to Moira and their children. She was aware that she was not an 'emotional' person and Roger would comment on her lack of anger and joy. Nonetheless, she was not unhappy and she said that she had been 'entirely satisfied' with her adult life.

Brief formulation

During the period of her abuse, Moira had been able to detach emotionally and this helped her (apparently) cope with her traumatic experiences. Emotional numbing continued into her adult life and had possibly kept the intense memories of assault at bay. She had severed contact with her parents and, again, this might have enabled her to avoid provoking traumatic memories. Once these memories had been awakened, by the meaning of Tamsin's appearance, the recollections themselves seemed to prompt further remembering.

She had two or three 'composite' flashbacks, representative memories of several incidents. The fundamental meaning of each was similar: 'I am disgusting and dirty and have done something to deserve this – therefore I am bad' and 'You cannot trust anyone. If your vulnerability is apparent, you will be hurt.' The content of the flashbacks promoted high levels of fear, which in turn exacerbated the flashbacks. The personal meaning of these memories fuelled depression, which was also exacerbated by increased fear.

Moira had a dichotomous experience of emotions, in which she was either emotionally numb or felt overwhelmed. Until recently this had suited her, as she was able to remain emotionally numb, guided by an intellectual appreciation of how she should feel and behave. Recently she had been decreasingly able to attain numbness – which terrified her, as she believed that her emotions were escalating out of control. Thus, she strived to regain emotional detachment and remained unconfident that she could tolerate and moderate affect.

Management

Initially we agreed to target the depression due to her strong suicidal impulses. However, following the assessment and formulation, the impulses diminished as she felt more hopeful, so we focused on her flashbacks. We began with a simple explanation of the neurobiology of flashbacks, using a very minimal diagram of the brain to illustrate the interruption of communication between the amygdala and sensory cortices. This helped Moira appreciate that her brain was 'doing what it was programmed to do' in its initial processing of an emotionally laden event, that the process had become arrested, and that treatment would aim to contextualize the flashback memories. As talking about the content of her flashbacks precipitated dissociation, we engaged in a graded exposure to these through use of a written narrative (Resick & Schnicke, 1993). Moira began by writing a very detached and dispassionate account of her childhood experiences in the past tense, third person, and devoid of emotional content. Once she achieved this without slipping into a flashback, she added a little more emotional content. Thus a phrase such as: 'he told her that she must not tell anyone or he would kill her' became 'he told her that she must not tell anyone or he would kill her and she believed him and was frightened'. Our intention was to systematically increase the vividness of the recollection until Moira was able to describe her flashbacks in first person, present tense with full exploration of the emotional content and meaning. Interestingly, this was unnecessary because by session six the flashbacks had disappeared. After writing a detached account Moira found herself feeling angry with the father who had so abused his child. She said: 'a penny dropped: I wasn't bad, it wasn't my fault. He abused me and he had no right to'. In doing so she changed the meaning of the flashbacks. They then became less disturbing and less frequent, her feelings of self-loathing diminished, and her mood improved. We hypothesized that as the affective impact of the flashback reduced, her brain was able to more efficiently process and contextualize her recollections, and they were held, not as flashbacks, but as 'regular' memories.

Moira's striving to stay in an emotionally 'flat' state was driven by a fear that if she began to allow herself to feel emotions she would find them uncontrollable and overwhelming and 'have a nervous breakdown'. We devised a behavioural/emotional experiment to test her prediction. First, she learnt grounding skills (Kennerley, 1996) to give her confidence that she could restore her mind and physiology to a calm state. Then she systematically worked up a hierarchy of increasingly emotionally evocative images. For example, her hierarchy for 'sadness' began with hearing that a neighbour's cat had been killed, and moved on to learning that a neighbour's elderly spouse had died, and so on, up to an image of herself giving up Tamsin for adoption. She spent time dwelling on the least evocative image and when she grew confident that she could tolerate this, she moved on to the next set in the hierarchy. She began this in sessions and continued the task as homework. Within two weeks she was able to allow herself to feel sad, angry, and happy, and was convinced that it was safe to do so.

Comment

Moira's therapy lasted only eight sessions. It is of note that she had had 40 years of being in a safe, supportive, and loving environment, and was within this environment during her therapy. This had helped her develop a positive belief set – which we built on – and probably gave her confidence in engaging in difficult tasks. Her recovery highlights that contextualization of flashbacks can be achieved in several ways. It is important to evolve the best approach for your client, drawing on knowledge of the psychology and neurobiology of memory. Moira's story also reminds us of the utility of the basic 'tool kit' of the cognitive therapist and that a relatively simple behavioural experiment using a graded approach was sufficient for her to modify her emotional numbing.

Laura: type-I and type-II trauma

Laura was an in-patient in her early 20s, admitted because of her suicidal depression. She had also been given a diagnosis of Borderline Personality Disorder (BPD). She reported having experienced sexual, emotional, and physical abuse in childhood at the hands of her father and his uncle, while her mother had 'turned a blind eye'. She had also been raped by a virtual stranger six months earlier, and it was during this experience that flashbacks of child-hood abuse surfaced. She was experiencing flashbacks from the distant and recent past, self-loathing, and high anxiety in response to a range of triggers. As a child she recalled dissociating to cope with her trauma: having pleasant out-of-body experiences (OBEs), 'floating up and away from my body and circling the room – feeling light and ethereal and calm'. Now she tried to manage the painful memories, self-loathing, and anxieties by inducing a similar dissociated state through direct self-injury (cutting and burning), indirect self-injury (exercising to the point of injury, provoking physical assault by her father), binge-eating, and self-starvation. She had also dealt with her traumatic home life by adopting a different persona when she left the house for school, and later for work. This persona was 'confident and competent', and Laura felt that she owed her academic and work successes to this 'other self'. She was clear that this 'other Laura' was not the 'real' her, and she said that she had no sense of being a person in her own right. In fact, she wondered what it would be like to feel that one existed. She was now distraught that she could not access the 'other Laura', and felt hopeless to deal with her problems 'alone'.

Laura's dissociative presentations were: flashbacks of repeated child-hood trauma (type-II trauma); flashbacks of adult rape (type-I trauma); out-of-body experiences; lack of a sense of identity; emotional numbing.

Brief formulation

As a child, Laura used dissociative strategies to cope with trauma: she achieved OBE during molestation, was able to 'detach' from negative emotions, and developed a fragmented sense of self in order to repress the reality of her life. This served her well in that she achieved at school and at work, she had a (superficial) social network, and suffered no flashbacks. However, during her adult rape, the memories returned, and persisted. She was not able to detach from them and the affect that the memories triggered became intense and she grew depressed and suicidal. She attempted to manage the flashbacks, fear, and self-disgust by inducing different forms of dissociation through self-harm. Cutting gave her rapid stress relief combined with an exhilarating OBE, reinforcing the behaviour. Starvation promoted a reliable state of emotional detachment, while binge-eating was initially exhilarating and then promoted 'mental and emotional oblivion'. These dissociation-triggering strategies had evolved as stress management techniques, but they had the longer term consequences of undermining her positive sense of self and prevented her from learning more adaptive ways of dealing with stress, and prevented the memories from being processed. Also, these behaviours increased her self-loathing, which fuelled depression and precipitated further attempts to dissociate (see Figure 7.2).

Laura also had a fragmented sense of self. She did not meet criteria for DID, but she was aware of different aspects of herself. She had no amnesias and had been able to exert control over this. We conceptualized her frag-mentation as her having a core sense of 'Bad Laura' that felt quite robust and that she avoided experiencing by accessing aspects of 'Competent Laura' that felt fragile. The main aspects of 'Competent Laura' were 'the efficient worker' (which she felt was no longer available to her) and 'the pleasant person' (friend, patient, customer etc.) which she could still access at times. She saw the 'competent' self as a device for concealing the 'bad' self, and she tried very hard to remain in 'competent' mode. However, the onset of the flash-backs had undermined her ability to do so and her self-loathing, self-harm, and depression worsened.

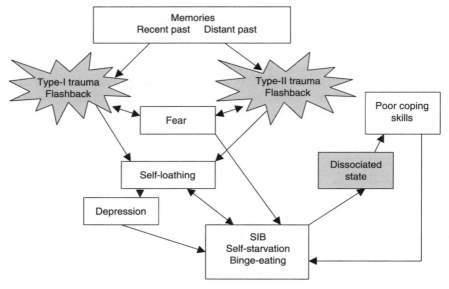

Figure 7.2 Formulation for Laura.

Management

Our priority was safety, and Laura agreed a contract to refrain from self-harm between sessions. The driving force behind her impulses to kill or injure herself was her strong conviction of badness, which, because of her fragmented sense of self, was not modified by a sense of positive personal qualities.

Laura found discussing the content of the flashbacks overwhelming. Hence some preparatory work was necessary. First, Laura learnt grounding skills: an image of a safe, soothing place that she could think of in order to resume a sense of calm and safeness, and a grounding object (a small humorous gift given to her by work mates), which conveyed to her the message that she was adult with adult friends who liked her. In addition, the object made her smile and this was incompatible with feeling sad or fearful. By learning to tap into feelings of calm, safeness, adulthood, and humour, she developed the ability to offset the negative feelings triggered by the flashbacks and by her sense of 'badness'. Next, we began to challenge her profound sense of 'badness' by encouraging the integration of her experiences of personal and professional competence using schema-change strategies (for a review, see Beck, Freeman, Davis, & Associates, 2004). Over several months, she was able to modify her sense of 'badness', and as she did so, she reported feeling less 'fragmented', more aware of having a sense of who she was, and she became less depressed. She was then able to talk about her traumatic memories in detail, as her fear of flashbacks had decreased. We successfully used re-living to manage the vivid recollection of her recent rape, and imagery restructuring to moderate the more generic recollections of childhood abuse (Layden, Newman, Freeman, & Byers-Morse, 1993). This further improved her mood.

Despite the improvement in her mood and the diminished intensity and frequency of her flashbacks, she retained the urge to self-injure, and to starve and binge when stressed. We reviewed her formulation and she agreed that it would be helpful to develop a wider repertoire of coping strategies. We first built on her grounding skills as alternative ways to achieve a sense of calm and soothing, and particularly focused on developing a positive somatic image that conveyed the sense of Laura being: 'in charge, okay, cool'. In this image, she imagined herself in the position of the sitting Buddha and she felt a cool, soft, silvery breeze drifting from the top of her head, through her torso and limbs, bringing with it a pleasant heaviness, calm, and strength. She began to access this visceral image rather than cutting in order to achieve an OBE. Next we further developed her skills in cognitive challenging so that she used constructive self-talk to acknowledge and address her negative cognitions. Finally, she learnt to become more mindful and tolerant of her negative emotions (Linehan, 1993). The more dramatic ways of dealing with stress continued to remain compelling, but Laura now had a wider coping repertoire and could draw on strategies that were, ultimately, more helpful. As her use of self-harming behaviours diminished, so her mood improved and her sense of identity strengthened.

Comment

Laura was in therapy for over a year, as her presentation was complex (she had a diagnosis of personality disorder and multiple presenting problems) and she lived in a dysfunctional environment (close to her family, who promoted the belief that she was 'bad', and who put her at risk of physical harm). Therapy for her post-traumatic dissociative problems could only occur in parallel to working systemically, with attention given to interpersonal processes, and helping her manage a generally negative view of herself, the world, and the future.

While Laura agreed to holding a therapy contract, which gave her extra motivation to resist urges to harm herself, some clients cannot resist the urge and will break contracts. This can promote a sense of failure and risk undermining the working alliance. In such cases other means of increasing motivation and engaging ambivalent clients need to be explored (e.g., Miller & Rollnick, 1991).

It is common for clients to find that the substitute behaviours for self-injury are not nearly as rapid and dramatic in effect as the problem behaviours themselves, and this should be normalized for the client. The aim is to find safe responses that will be sufficiently similar to render the urge resistible.

Finally, we used many grounding and benign imagery techniques in our work, and it is important that the therapist monitors their use to ensure that they are not developing into unhelpful safety-seeking behaviours. For example, using a grounding object as a 'lucky charm', or a grounding image such as a 'neutralizing' image for a disturbing visual intrusion.

Kelly: Type-1 trauma in childhood

At the age of 10, Kelly witnessed her mother's murder. Kelly hid in a cupboard and endured the terror of hearing the murderer prowl around the house. During the murder and when she hid, her eyes were tightly shut to try to block out the horror of her experiences.

It was not until adulthood that she began to have panic attacks and the 'strange episodes' that brought her to therapy. Her partner complained that she was frequently 'not with it: spaced out', when she was not able to communicate with him. She had little or no recollection of these brief periods. She also described times when she was overwhelmed by a 'black memory' of being in the cupboard and periods of profound detachment. At assessment, Kelly was in an almost chronic state of emotional dissociation rather like the shock experience following an accident or after hearing very bad news. She now hardly ate and had lost a great deal of weight.

Her dissociative experiences comprised derealization, some episodes of which were linked with panic attacks, occasional 'trance states', and flashbacks with a physiological 'hot spot'. Her flashback experience was predominantly visceral: 'black in the pit of my stomach: sick overpowering black that oozes through my body. I can't put a word to it but I know that it is what I felt then and it is as if I am back there. I cannot bear it.'

Brief formulation

Kelly had apparently coped with childhood trauma through emotional dissociation and cognitive avoidance. Now, traumatic memories re-emerged, possibly triggered by her son's 10th birthday, which marked the onset of her panic attacks and periods of derealization – the latter possibly being an exaggeration of her childhood coping strategies as well as being part of the panic symptoms. Fear, promoted by the flashbacks, contributed to their maintenance, because heightened arousal would impede memory processing. Panic attacks triggered about half the flashbacks. She also had a 'constant fear' of having a flashback – fuelling more panic attacks and chronic detachment. Monitoring by her partner revealed that derealization could escalate into a 'trance state' and, again, we hypothesized that high anxiety, associated with detachment, could both maintain it and impair memory processing – explaining her lack of awareness when 'spaced out'. Her panic-related cognitions were typically catastrophic: 'What's that sensation? Oh God, I am going to have another flashback!' Escalating anxiety provoked physiological sensations and detachment, which exacerbated her extreme thinking. The derealization and trance states enhanced her fear, as she concluded: 'I am going mad, my life is falling apart and my husband will leave me and take the children . . .' (see Figure 7.3).

Management

Sharing the formulation and explaining the phenomena of flashbacks, derealization, and trance states reduced Kelly's fears and panic episodes. Her detachment diminished following psycho-education, but Kelly felt that she was still in a detached state half the time. Despite monitoring by both Kelly and her partner, it was difficult to find a pattern, outside the panic attacks, and it seemed most likely that random anxious thoughts were the trigger for 'spacing out' and relatively simple cognitive techniques for re-evaluating or distracting from the thoughts helped. She also began feeling more 'with it' when she was encouraged to eat more. Learning to control hyperventilation, including using controlled breathing, helped her further manage derealization and reduce panic episodes. As hyperventilation can provoke flashbacks, the use of illustrative over-breathing should be avoided or used with caution, and the therapist needs to ensure that controlled breathing does not become an unhelpful safety behaviour.

Although controlling hyperventilation reduced Kelly's flashbacks, they remained a problem. In order to contextualize the flashbacks, she felt she needed to assure herself that the feeling would pass and she would be okay. However, she had no conviction in this and so we embarked on a 'visceral' restructuring exercise (see Kennerley, 1996), whereby she learnt to transform the 'black feelings'. Prompted by Socratic questions such as: 'What is happening in your body right now?', 'How do you want to feel in your body?', 'How

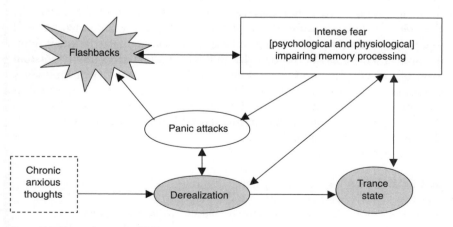

Figure 7.3 Formulation for Kelly.

could you make that happen?', she described the 'blackness' gathering into a hard ball that collected in the pit of her stomach. When asked: 'What do you want to do with this feeling?', she described it floating from her body leaving behind a sensation of golden warmth. She was encouraged to stay with this positive sensation in the session. Her subsequent assignment was to rehearse it several times a day, so that she became able readily access it. In this way she developed confidence in the belief that the 'black' sensations would pass. Once she achieved this, she fully engaged in re-living and soon completely overcame her flashbacks.

Comment

Kelly had eight sessions of treatment. Like Moira, she had both intra- and inter-personal resources, an actively supportive partner, and many of the dissociative problems were managed by basic psycho-education and anxiety management. This reminds us of the necessity of the therapist understanding the psychological and neuro-psychological processes of dissociation. Again, 'basic' CBT strategies were invaluable, but the therapist needs to tailor them to the client, as in the case of the visceral imagery work here.

CONCLUSIONS

As there is no well-established model of dissociation and few management guidelines for CBT practitioners (other than for flashbacks), we have to fall back on generic skills in assessment and conceptualizations in order to guide our practice. This must be informed by a good understanding of information processing, memory, and the organization of dissociative processes. We can then use our wide repertoire of cognitive and behavioural skills and tailor them according to the maintaining cycles of our conceptualizations. For example, if avoidance (behavioural or emotional) plays a part, then we need to devise achievable forms of exposure; if anxiety contributes to a maintaining cycle, then we use our knowledge of the best CBT interventions for that form of anxiety. The work clearly needs to be in the context of a sensitive empathic therapeutic relationship. This is particularly pertinent when working with clients who have been the victims of inter-personal trauma for whom the therapeutic relationship may be an especially important aspect of therapy (Middle & Kennerley, 2001).

REFERENCES

Allen, J.G. (2001). *Traumatic relationships and serious mental disorders*. New York: John Wiley and Sons.

American Psychiatric Association. (1994). *Diagnostic and statistical manual of mental disorders* (4th ed. DSM-IV). Washington, DC: American Psychiatric Association.

American Psychiatric Association. (2000). *Diagnostic and statistical manual of mental disorders* (4th ed. DSM-IV-TR). Washington, DC: American Psychiatric Association.

Beck, A.T., Freeman, A., Davis, D.D., & Associates. (2004). *Cognitive therapy of personality disorder*. New York: Guilford Press.

Berstein, F.M., & Putnam, F.W. (1986). Development, reliability and validity of a dissociation scale. *Journal of Nervous and Mental Disease, 174*, 727–735.

Birmes, P., Carreras, D., Charlet, J.P., Warner, B.A., Lauque, D., & Schmitt, L. (2001). Peritraumatic dissociation and posttraumatic stress disorder in victims of violent assault. *Journal of Nervous and Mental Disease, 189*, 796–798.

Brewin, C.R., Dalgleish, T., & Joseph, S. (1996). A dual representation theory of post traumatic stress disorder. *Psychological Review, 103*, 670–686.

Bryant, R.A., & Panasetis, P. (2005). Panic symptoms during trauma and acute stress disorder. *Behaviour Research and Therapy, 39*, 961–966.

Cardena, E., & Spiegel, D. (1993). Dissociative reactions to the San Francisco Bay Area earthquake of 1989. *American Journal of Psychiatry, 150*, 474–478.

Chu, J.A. (1998). Dissociative symptomatology in adult patients with histories of childhood physical and sexual abuse. In J.D. Bremner, & C.R. Marmar (Eds.), *Trauma, memory and dissociation* (pp. 179–203). Washington, DC: American Psychiatric Press.

Ehlers, A., & Clark, D.M. (2000). A cognitive model of posttraumatic stress disorder. *Behaviour Research and Therapy, 38*, 319–345.

Freidman, M. (2000). What might the psychobiology of PTSD teach us about future approaches to pharmacotherapy? *Journal of Clinical Psychiatry, 61*(suppl. 7), 44–51.

Freinkel, A., Kooperman, C., & Spiegel, D. (1994). Dissociative symptoms in media eyewitnesses of an execution. *American Journal of Psychiatry, 157*, 1335–1339.

Holmes, E.A., Brown, R.J., Mansell, W., Fearon, R.P., Hunter, E.C.M., Frasquilho, F., & Oakley, D.A. (2005). Are there two qualitatively distinct forms of dissociation? A review and some clinical implications. *Clinical Psychology Review, 25*, 1–23.

Kennedy, F., Clarke, S., Stopa, L., Bell, L., Rouse, H., Ainsworth, C., Fearon, P., & Waller, G. (2004). Towards a cognitive model and measure of dissociation. *Journal of Behaviour Therapy and Experimental Psychiatry, 35*(1), 25–48.

Kennerley, H. (1996). Cognitive therapy of dissociative symptoms. *British Journal of Clinical Psychology, 35*, 325–340.

Kennerley, H. (2004). Lies, damn lies and information processing. Workshop given at the BABCP annual conference, Warwick.

Layden, M.A., Newman, C.F., Freeman, A., & Byers-Morse, S. (1993). *Cognitive therapy of borderline personality disorder*. Boston: Allyn and Bacon.

Linehan, M.M. (1993). *Cognitive behavioural treatment of borderline personality disorder*. New York: Guilford Press.

McNally, R.J. (2003). *Remembering trauma*. Cambridge, MA: Belknap Press, Harvard University Press.

McNally, R.J. (2005). Debunking myths about trauma and memory. *Canadian Journal of Psychiatry, 50*, 817–822.

Marmar, C.R., Weiss, D.S., & Metzler, T.J. (1998). Peritraumatic dissociation and posttraumatic stress disorder. In J.D. Bremner, & C.R. Marmar (Eds.), *Trauma, memory and dissociation* (pp. 229–247). Washington, DC: American Psychiatric Press.

Middle, C., & Kennerley, H. (2001). A grounded theory analysis of the therapeutic relationship with clients sexually abused as children and non-abused clients. *Clinical Psychology and Psychotherapy, 8*, 198–205.

Miller, W., & Rollnick, S. (1991). *Motivational interviewing: Preparing people to change addictive behaviour*. New York: Guilford Press.

Murray, J., Ehlers, A., & Mayou, R. (2002). Dissociation and post-traumatic stress disorder: Two prospective studies of road traffic accident survivors. *British Journal of Psychiatry, 180*, 363–368.

Nixon, R.D.V., & Bryant, R.A. (2006). Dissociation in acute stress disorder after a hyperventilation provocation test. *Behavioural and Cognitive Psychotherapy, 34*, 343–349.

Resick, P.A., & Schnicke, M.K. (1993). *Cognitive processing therapy for rape victims: A treatment manual*. Newbury Park, CA: Sage.

Rothschild, B. (2000). *The body remembers: The psychophysiology of trauma and trauma treatment*. New York: Norton.

Southwick, S.M., Krystal, J.H., Morgan, C.A., Johnson, D.R., Nagy, L.M., Nicolaou, A.L., Heninger, G.R., & Charney, D.S. (1993). Abnormal noradrenergic function in posttraumatic stress disorder. *Archives of General Psychiatry, 50*, 266–274.

Spiegel, D., Kooperman, C., Cardena, E., & Classen, C. (1996). Dissociative symptoms in the diagnosis of acute stress disorder. In L.K. Michelson, & W.J. Ray (Eds.), *Handbook of dissociation: Theoretical, empirical and clinical perspectives* (pp. 367–380). New York: Plenum Press.

Steinberg, M. (1995). *Handbook for the assessment of dissociation: a clinical guide*. Washington, DC: American Psychiatric Press.

Terr, L.C. (1991). Childhood traumas: an outline and overview. *American Journal of Psychiatry, 148*, 10–20.

van der Kolk, B.A., & van der Hart, O. (1989). Pierre Janet and the breakdown of adaptation in psychological data. *American Journal of Psychiatry, 146*, 1530–1540.

Waller, G., Hamilton, K., Elliott, P., Lewendon, J., Stopa, L., Waters, A., Kennedy, F., Lee, G., Pearson, D., Kennerley, H., Hargreaves, I., Bashford, V., & Chalkley, J. (2000). Somatoform dissociation, psychological dissociation and specific forms of trauma. *Journal of Trauma and Dissociation, 1*, 81–98.

Waller, G., Quinton, S., & Watson, D. (1995). Dissociation and the processing of threat-related information. *Dissociation, 8*, 84–90.

Zatzick, D.F., Marmar, C.R., Weiss, D.S., & Metzler, T.J. (1994). Does trauma-linked dissociation vary across ethnic groups? *Journal of Nervous and Mental Disease, 182*, 576–582.

Chapter 8

Intensive cognitive therapy for post-traumatic stress disorder

Case studies

Nick Grey, Freda McManus, Ann Hackmann, David M. Clark, and Anke Ehlers

INTRODUCTION

There is good evidence from randomized controlled trials that cognitive therapy (CT) for post-traumatic stress disorder (PTSD) (Ehlers et al., 2009) is an effective treatment (Duffy, Gillespie, & Clark, 2007; Ehlers, Clark, Hackmann, McManus, & Fennell, 2005; Ehlers et al., 2003). Furthermore, CT has been successfully disseminated to routine clinical settings in which, in contrast to randomized trials, no exclusion criteria are applied (Duffy et al., 2007; Gillespie, Duffy, Hackmann, & Clark, 2002). Finally, CT has been shown to work for acute and chronic PTSD following from one or two events (Ehlers et al., 2003, 2005), and for very chronic PTSD following multiple traumas (Duffy et al., 2007). The efficacy and effectiveness of CT for PTSD is in line with the finding from recent meta-analyses that trauma-focused cognitive behaviour therapy (CBT) is effective in the treatment of PTSD (e.g., Bisson et al., 2007). Other effective forms of trauma-focused CBT are Foa's Prolonged Exposure (Foa & Rothbaum, 1998; Foa et al., 2005) and Resick's Cognitive Processing Therapy (Resick & Schnicke, 1993).

CT for PTSD has typically been provided in up to 12 weekly sessions (mean 10 sessions) of up to 90 minutes each, followed by up to three follow-up sessions on a monthly basis. Some patients find it difficult to engage in lengthy psychological treatment because it requires a significant commitment of time and emotion (Bisson et al., 2007) and others may not be able to attend weekly appointments due to work/family commitments or distance from the treatment centre. A second concern with sessions being spaced out is that in the early stages of CBT for PTSD some patients may initially experience an increase in symptoms, especially re-experiencing, following exposure sessions. Delivering treatment in a more intensive format may minimize any negative effects and lead to greater acceptability of the treatment.

Ehlers and Clark's clinical research group has developed a form of CT for PTSD in which the majority of the treatment is completed within 1 week. This is described in detail in Ehlers et al. (2009) and has been shown to be as acceptable and effective as weekly CT in a pilot series of 14 cases (Ehlers et al., in preparation a) and in a randomized controlled trial (Ehlers et al., in preparation b). Intensive treatment approaches have also shown promise in other disorders, including specific phobias (Öst, 1989), panic disorder (Clark, 1996; Deacon & Abramowitz, 2006), agoraphobia (Hahlweg, Fiegenbaum, Frank, Schröder, & Witzleben, 2001), and OCD (Abramowitz, Foa, & Franklin, 2003; Oldfield & Salkovskis, 2008; Storch et al., 2007), indicating that intensive versions of CBT may be as effective as more traditional service delivery models.

This chapter describes the assessment, formulation, and treatment of two patients who received CT for PTSD in an intensive format. Typically CT for PTSD covers the following: the first session or two cover normalization of symptoms, starting 'reclaiming your life' (assignments designed to re-engage the patient with meaningful activities that were important to them before the trauma, such as meeting friends or exercise), and the formulation and rationale for working on the trauma memory. The next session will include imaginal reliving of the trauma (Foa & Rothbaum, 1998) (or narrative writing in some cases) to access the problematic moments in the trauma memory, identification of hotspots, and peri-traumatic cognitive themes. Following sessions interweave working on the trauma memory directly (e.g., using reliving, narrative writing, stimulus discrimination of sensory triggers of intrusions, site visit, and behavioural experiments) with work on changing excessively negative post- and peri-traumatic appraisals using a mixture of verbal and imaginal cognitive therapy techniques. The same therapeutic procedures are used in intensive CT for PTSD, but they are carried out within a week, followed by a session 1 week later and up to three follow-ups at monthly intervals.

CASE 1: MARK

Background

Mark was a 31-year-old professional who had had a motorcycle accident 9 months prior to being referred. During the accident Mark had been knocked off his bike when a car pulled out from a side road. He slid down the road into the path of an oncoming bus, which he feared would run him over. In fact he stopped just before the bus. Mark made a good physical recovery, but he had not been back to the site of the accident and rarely rode his motorbike.

At the time of referral Mark was having nightmares, in which the accident was replayed, three times a week and he experienced daily intrusive memories. He tried to push these intrusions out of his mind. Mark reported being very irritable and having weekly angry outbursts, which worried him as he feared he may become like his volatile father. His mood was very low and he had daily suicidal ideation, but no specific suicidal plans. At assessment Mark scored 44 on the PTSD Diagnostic Scale (PDS; severe range), 40 on the Beck Depression Inventory (BDI; severe range), and 35 on the Beck Anxiety Inventory (BAI; severe range).

Outline of sessions

Day 1: morning 2.5 hours

Treatment began by identifying Mark's goals, which were to reduce the frequency of his nightmares, to improve his mood, and to ride his motorbike again. In order to develop a formulation of Mark's PTSD based on the cognitive themes in his presentation, he was asked to describe his intrusions, their meaning, and his appraisals of the trauma and its sequelae in detail.

Mark's intrusions tended to be replays of some aspect of the accident, typically the physical sensation of 'sliding down' and lying on the road waiting for the ambulance. Intrusions appeared both spontaneous and triggered by reminders of the accident. Mark responded to the intrusions by trying to suppress them and ruminating about why the accident had happened, and what it meant that he still was not over it, e.g., 'Why me? Life is crap. I should be over it by now.' The rumination further decreased Mark's mood, which led to further rumination, and was interpreted as 'proof' that life was indeed 'crap'. Furthermore, Mark's avoidance of cycling and of his thoughts and feelings about the accident may have prevented change in the relatively unprocessed nature of his traumatic memories and negative appraisals.

From the therapist's perspective, the discussion indicated the following treatment goals according to the Ehlers and Clark (2000) model:

1   To access the moments in memory that gave Mark an ongoing sense of threat in traffic situations and the ongoing sense that 'life is crap', and update these moments with information that contradicts these meanings.
2   To change the problematic meanings of the accident (cycling is [too] dangerous, life is crap) and of Mark's reactions since the accident ('I should be over it by now').
3   To reverse thought suppression, rumination, and avoidance of the accident site and cycling. To re-engage in activities that were an important part of Mark's life before the event.

The discussion of the maintaining factors led to a rationale for discussing the trauma memory in order to help it become 'properly archived'. The therapist also normalized Mark's reaction since the trauma. Mark noted that his self-criticism and negative appraisals of his reactions to the trauma prompted further avoidance and lowered mood.

Day 1: afternoon 2 hours

Mark 'relived' the accident in imagination – describing it in detail, with eyes closed, in the present tense, including not just what happened but his thoughts and feelings at the time. He did this twice, taking about 10 minutes each time. He began just before the accident and continued the reliving until the point at which he felt safe again (when the ambulance arrived). He reported afterwards that it had felt 90% vivid and 90% as though it was happening again right now ('nowness'). He identified four worst moments (hotspots) (see Table 8.1).

Mark made some connections between the feelings he had during the accident and earlier childhood experiences. The loneliness and sadness he experienced while on the ground at the end of the accident was the same as he felt at the end of the contact visits that he had had with his father when he was a young child. He also realized that the worst thing about his being angry now was that his father had had a volatile temper, and Mark feared he was becoming like him. This sense of 'becoming his father' also reinforced his belief that 'life is crap'. The therapist suggested an alternative interpretation of Mark's anger: that irritability is a common symptom of PTSD and would be likely to reduce when memory was better processed.

Homework was to begin 'reclaiming his life' by going swimming, an activity Mark had previously enjoyed but had stopped since the accident.

Day 2: morning 2 hours

Mark described again the whole event in imaginal reliving. His rated it as 100% vivid and 90% 'nowness'. The hotspots remained those described above. He reported that he believed that life was full of crap 100% during the

Table 8.1 Mark's hotspots

Hotspot	Appraisal	Feeling	'New' updating information
Sliding down the road	'This is it. I'm going to die.'	Empty	'I don't die'
Wing mirror breaking off	'I'm losing everything'	Sad	'My life gets back on track and I don't lose everything.'
Bus looming	'I'll be run over'	Scared	'I'm not run over.'
Lying on ground at end	'I'm all alone'	Scared, lonely and sad	'I'm not alone. People help me and my girlfriend comes to see me at hospital very quickly. This isn't the same as when was I a child.'
	'Life is crap'	Sad	'There's lots of evidence that life is good and not full of crap.'

trauma itself, and still believed it 80% when reflecting on it during the session. Mark's evidence for the belief that 'life is crap' was reviewed, as this was the most upsetting appraisal. He recalled feeling this way during his childhood, particularly because his parents separated and his father was very critical and physically abusive. Life had felt hard and unfair to Mark. Mark felt very alone, both as a child and also when he himself divorced two years prior to the accident. These feelings were re-activated while lying on the ground awaiting the ambulance.

Day 2: afternoon 2.5 hours

Evidence for and against Mark's belief that 'life is full of crap' was systematically elicited and discussed. This reduced his belief to 40%. The belief change was further reinforced with a reverse role play, the therapist being Mark, and Mark defending the idea that life had some positives. Mark agreed to collect evidence on an ongoing basis that perhaps life wasn't simply full of crap. Next, the evidence regarding Mark being alone at the end of the trauma was reviewed. During the discussion, Mark realized that people did help him, an ambulance was called, and his girlfriend arrived very quickly at the hospital. Mark concluded that whilst he may have been alone physically at that moment, he was not alone emotionally, and certainly not in the way he had experienced as a child.

This discussion provided information that could be used to update the hotspot when Mark was lying on the ground. Some further brief discussion also provided information to update his other hotspots, such as that he was not run over and that he did not die. He completed a further reliving of the accident, and at the hotspots he vividly brought to mind this 'new' information. For example, when visualizing the moment when he was lying on the ground feeling alone and that life was 'full of crap', he 'updated' this memory with the information that life is not solely full of crap, and that he was not alone. He did this verbally and also by bringing into the reliving imagery an image of his girlfriend rushing to meet him at hospital, which encapsulated these new meanings. He rated that the belief 'I'm alone' changed from 90% (original reliving) to 20% (during the updating procedure), and the belief that 'life is full of crap' reduced 100% (original reliving) to 20% (during updating). This session was crucial to Mark's progress and he reported feeling exhausted but also 'lighter' as a result.

As his appraisal that 'life is full of crap' had prevented him from planning for his future since the accident, homework aimed at strengthening the belief change in the session further by reintroducing plans for the future. Mark was to plan both short-term enjoyable activities but also to discuss longer-term plans with his girlfriend.

Day 3: morning 2 hours

We discussed again the change in meanings of the last hotspot and did a further reliving, with the new updated information brought to mind while focusing on the image of lying on the road. He now rated 'I'm alone' at 10% and 'life is full of crap' at 15%.

Day 3: afternoon 2.5 hours

Since the accident Mark had avoided the site of the accident for fear of having another accident – he knew that logically it wasn't very likely but it *felt* about 70–80% likely. The main therapy task for this session was for the therapist to accompany Mark to the site in order to help Mark further process the memory by deliberately reconstructing what happened on the day while looking at the site, by focusing on similarities and differences between the day of the accident and the way the site looked today, to test his belief that another accident would occur, and overcome his avoidance. As he approached the site, Mark became increasingly anxious. At the site itself, Mark was gently guided to describe the accident and to 'walk' the therapist through what had occurred. Mark recalled previously forgotten details, including the level of help given by passers-by and that in fact he had been lying alone in the road for a shorter time than he had previously remembered. No further accident occurred at the site and Mark's belief that another accident would happen reduced to 5%.

For homework Mark was encouraged to get his motorbike in working order and use it.

Day 4: 2 hours

Although Mark reported feeling much brighter and more easily able to reflect on the accident without intense distress, he continued to be distressed by irritability and anger. He was still angry with the other driver, and tended to 'blow up' at any perceived signs of thoughtlessness from others, including his girlfriend. The therapist initially merely empathized and normalized Mark's reactions, but then raised the question of whether there was any malicious intent on the part of the other driver. Initially Mark believed the driver must have deliberately pulled out in front of him, but in reviewing the evidence, he moved towards the conclusion that he may have been simply a poor driver rather than actively seeking to injure Mark. In addition, reviewing the consequences of his anger helped Mark see that staying angry was hurting himself and his partner rather than the other driver.

For homework Mark was to reverse his avoidance of talking about the accident, starting by discussing it with his girlfriend. It was hoped that this would also help her to better understand what he had been experiencing, and thus be better able to avoid acting in ways that Mark perceived as thoughtless but which were more likely born out of ignorance of his difficulties.

Day 5: 2 hours

Mark described the accident in reliving, and said it felt 'less heavy'. He began constructing a 'final' written account of the event, which included the updates of the hotspots. We also started his 'blueprint', summarizing what he had learned in treatment and how he could continue his progress in the future.

One-week session: 1 hour

This session occurred 2 weeks after the intensive week due to difficulties in scheduling. Mark had passed the site of the accident daily on public transport and felt indifferent to it. He had completed the narrative and communication with his partner had improved considerably. Mark rated his belief that 'life's full of crap' at 5% and 'I'm alone' at 0%. He scored 1 on the PDS, 0 on the BDI, and 1 on the BAI.

One-month follow-up: 30 minutes

Mark had returned to riding his motorbike and was very busy at work. He had had no nightmares since the end of the intensive week.

Three- month follow-up: 1 hour

Mark had ridden past the site of the accident without incident. We completed the blueprint in session.

Six- month follow-up: 45 minutes

Mark reported that he was now engaged to his girlfriend. He had also been subjected to verbal abuse in a 'road rage' incident while on his motorbike. A bystander came to his support. This reinforced the fact that he was not alone. He described that he had not got angry himself and had not experienced any intrusive memories of his accident.

Long-term outcome

At an 18-month follow-up point Mark scored 2 on the PDS, 2 on the BDI, and 0 on the BAI, and had no nightmares. He reported that life was going well for him.

CASE 2: HANNAH

Background

Hannah was a 30-year-old nurse who had been badly injured on a holiday abroad, 10 years previously. She had experienced a cannabis-induced psychosis, which caused her to believe that 'people were out to kill her', and that in order to 'maintain her dignity and sense of control' she must kill herself. She jumped off a road bridge into the path of oncoming traffic. Hannah suffered extensive injuries, including multiple fractures and internal damage. In the hospital emergency room, a hospital porter sexually abused her as she was taken to and from X-rays and other investigations. Hannah made a reasonable physical recovery and had no previous or further history of psychotic episodes.

Hannah met criteria for PTSD, which had had immediate onset with vivid distressing intrusive memories while in hospital. She had weekly nightmares of falling, felt emotionally numb, and detached from others. Following the trauma she also met criteria for panic disorder with agoraphobia. She avoided underground trains, aeroplanes, and long car journeys for fear of a crash or 'losing control'. She had had no previous treatment and reported 'this event made me who I am' and 'I can't remember the old me'.

At assessment Hannah scored 28 on the PDS (moderate range), 22 on the BDI (moderate/severe range), and 33 on the BAI (severe range).

Outline of sessions

Day 1: 2.5 hours

Hannah's main goals were to no longer have intrusions of her experience, to be able to 'feel emotions', and to engage and feel attached to people.

Several maintenance cycles were identified. Hannah suppressed strong emotions, especially those related to the accident, and suppressed the intrusions when they occurred. In addition, Hannah concealed her negative feelings from family and friends, which had the effect that they did not know when she needed support. This left Hannah feeling misunderstood and lonely. Hannah said that if she did allow her feelings 'out', she would 'feel like a bad person'. In addition, she said that if she feels happy, she thinks something bad will happen ('don't get smug; pride before a fall') and therefore tries to 'keep a lid on emotions'. The cognitive theme of being a bad person was also reflected in the intrusive images that Hannah experienced. Together with the associated meanings, these were: standing at the top of the bridge – 'I'm going to be killed, I must be bad if they want me dead'; lying on the road and being put on stretcher – 'it's my fault, I'm a bad person'; and sexual abuse at hospital – 'my body responded, which is disgusting and makes me a bad person'. In addition, she had post-traumatic appraisals of a similar theme 'it's my fault, I'm a bad person, I shouldn't have been taking drugs'. She rated her belief that she was bad at 80% and level of shame at 90%.

From the therapist's perspective, the initial assessment indicated the following treatment goals according to the Ehlers and Clark (2000) model:

1   To access the moments in memory that gave Hannah the sense that she was to blame for what had happened to her and that she was a bad person and to update these moments with information that contradicts these meanings.
2   To change the problematic meanings of the trauma ('I am bad, I am to blame') and of having and showing emotions ('bad things are going to happen').
3   To reverse suppression of emotions and memories. To disclose feelings to others.

Furthermore, beliefs ('I am losing control, there is going to be a crash') and safety-behaviours (mainly avoidance of public transport) linked to Hannah's panic disorder needed to be taken into consideration.

In this session, the fact that over-control of emotions had not allowed the normal processing of the trauma memory was discussed and a rationale for imaginal reliving was derived (the metaphor of a conveyor belt). Hannah agreed to start 'processing' the memory by writing a narrative of the trauma for homework, as there was not sufficient time remaining in the session to begin imaginal reliving.

Day 2: 2.5 hours

Hannah had begun writing a narrative but had focused on the days before the event. She reported that she had felt numb writing it. In the session Hannah described the traumatic events in imaginal reliving from shortly before arriving at the bridge to when she left the first hospital she was in. This took 30 minutes. She reported that the images were 70% vivid, but that she was still detached from the emotion. The most vivid moments of the experiences were those moments that matched her intrusions. In order to attempt to 'get in touch' with the feelings, Hannah agreed to write about these worst moments in detail for homework.

Day 3: 2.5 hours

Hannah had not written anything further for homework. She brought in a sketchbook of pictures that she had drawn very soon after the event in order cope with the intense feelings she was experiencing at that time. These drawings illustrated her feelings of shame and guilt. They meant to her that she was a bad person and that she was to blame for what had happened. She said that looking at the pictures again led her to experience the same feelings that she had had both during and soon after the event. She had not drawn anything related to the sexual abuse, as she felt it was simply too disgusting and shameful.

The most disgusting aspect of the abuse for Hannah was that her body had had a sexual response. She interpreted this to mean that she is a bad person (rated at 80%) and also that this sort of thing would only happen to a bad person. She became distressed when discussing this. She also reported that she dissociated at the time of the abuse, having an out-of-body experience, watching herself from above. We discussed that such a sexual response and/or dissociation are both typical responses to traumatic, sexually abusive situations, and that perhaps her feelings of detachment now were partly a continued use of (broadly speaking) a 'dissociative' coping style when experiencing strong emotion.

Hannah also reported that her sex life was still affected by the abuse, as when she was touched in particular ways it triggered the memory of the abuse and also a dissociative response. We discussed how Hannah could attempt to break the link between being touched in certain ways and the abusive experience by deliberately triggering the memory with this touch and discriminating the differences between the abuse and the touch of her partner, both in terms of sensations and context. Stimulus discrimination of sensory triggers of intrusive memories, discriminating between 'then' and 'now', is a particularly helpful way of reducing re-experiencing (Ehlers et al., 2005, 2009). For Hannah, the differences that she decided to focus on are shown in Table 8.2.

Hannah's homework was to discuss this with her partner and for her to focus on these differences when the memory was activated when with her partner.

Day 4: 3.5 hours

We tried again to access the Hannah's emotions during the trauma through reliving and to update the moment when she experienced arousal with the

Table 8.2 Hannah's stimulus discrimination of a sensory trigger

Then	Now
Touched in particular way	
Couldn't move	Can move
Didn't want it to happen	I've chosen to be with partner
No choice what he did	I have control over what happens
Couldn't speak	Can speak
Very very ill	Healthy
He's sick, not normal	{Partner} is normal
Just 20 then	30 now

information that this is a normal human response. Hannah said that she was still emotionally numb, but that the memory was now even more detailed.

It was not possible to visit the site of the traumatic events as they happened abroad. However, in order to try to access more of the memory and the associated emotions and meanings, we went to a bridge over a busy road near the treatment clinic. Hannah reported that the memory was very vivid. She described the traumatic event while we were there. We stayed for 30 minutes. Initially, feelings were present, but after describing the event she reported that she again felt emotionally numb.

Back at the clinic we tried reliving the part of the trauma by the bridge and in the road again, together with the update that she didn't in fact die in the road. It was more detailed, but she reported that the emotions were somewhat distant still. In order to better access Hannah's feelings and the associated meanings, for homework she agreed to draw pictures representing the hotspots of her experience, and also to draw a current overall representation of being a bad person.

Day 5: after weekend – 2 hours

Hannah brought these pictures to the session and reported that while drawing she had experienced the emotions more strongly than in imaginal reliving. This included a representation of the abuse she had experienced. She also said that she had felt a little better about the moments of sexual abuse, as it became clearer to her while actually drawing it that it was not her fault, that she was incapacitated on a hospital bed, and that even though her body had responded physically, this did not make her a bad person. She represented this changed meaning in her picture by making her abuser reptilian in character, which indicated that it was in fact his fault. She rated her overall shame now at 70% and 'I'm bad' at 60%.

However, the drawings and the associated emotional experience also increased the shame that Hannah felt between sessions. She thought she was 'a failure for being so stupid' and that it was shameful and disgusting that she let herself 'get to that state'. The context of Hannah's drug use was discussed. Hannah reported that she had felt inferior to others at her fee-paying school as she was singled out by other pupils for being on a scholarship and teased about various things, including her accent. In addition, she had had no contact with her father throughout her childhood as her parents were estranged. She reported feeling his loss keenly. As a teenager she had really enjoyed dance music and clubbing, and during this time she had fallen in love with a man who started using recreational drugs himself and supplied them to Hannah. She greatly enjoyed recreational drug use. The drugs also made her physically thinner, for which she received compliments, which was the first time she could remember being praised. Some time later, a close friend was killed in a road traffic accident. She used drugs to cope with her grief at that time. Two months later she went on an enjoyable holiday, including using recreational drugs. Soon after the holiday her personal relationship broke up and she was feeling low in mood. In order to try to feel better again, she went on holiday with a friend, during which she had the psychotic experience. This discussion helped to place the traumatic experiences in context, rather than it being an isolated event, as it had seemed when purely experiencing the intrusive images and trying to avoid thinking about the circumstances of the trauma. She rated her level of shame and belief 'I'm bad' at 50% after this discussion. We discussed the need to be kinder and more compassionate to herself in general.

Day 6: 2.5 hours

We discussed Hannah's panic attacks in which the strong physical sensations of anxiety she felt made her believe that she was going to 'lose control' or that other bad things might happen (70%). In addition to establishing a panic vicious circle and discussing safety behaviours, we went to an underground station. Hannah 'felt' with 70% conviction that something would happen, like a bomb exploding. We discussed the realistic likelihood and she realized that the chances were much less than 0.01%. Following this discussion she did not 'hold back' or suppress the panicky feelings in any way, and she discovered that in fact she neither lost control nor did any other catastrophes occur. Her belief that something bad would happen reduced to 1%. The high levels of emotions experienced by Hannah on days 5 and 6 acted as behavioural experiments to test her belief that if she did not suppress her emotions generally, then she would 'lose control'.

For homework over the week to the next session, Hannah decided to do more drawings that encapsulated her new outlook on the trauma, and also incorporated being compassionate to her self. She also decided to talk to a close friend about how she was really feeling and the events she had experienced (including the sexual abuse). This expressing and experiencing of emotions was also set up as a behavioural experiment to test her beliefs about losing control.

One week later: 2 hours

Hannah scored 8 on the PDS (none/minimal range), 10 on the BDI (none/minimal range), and 7 on the BAI (none/minimal range). Hannah reported that she had not yet done the drawings as it 'didn't feel right yet'. She still blamed herself fully for the traumatic event and also felt ashamed. We discussed again the context of both her drug use and the traumatic event. On a responsibility pie chart, her perceived degree of responsibility changed from 70% to 25%, once she had taken other factors into account, including her early experiences at school and with her father, her old boyfriend, and the grief of losing a friend. She rated her shame at 25% and 'I'm bad' at 20%.

One-month follow-up: 75 minutes

Hannah reported that she was no longer fully blaming herself or feeling ashamed. She said she felt she could view the trauma in a broader context. In order to better emotionally experience the changed meanings, Hannah did further drawings that reflected compassion for herself. She reported that she no longer regarded herself as disgusting and shameful, but as being unwell at the time. She rated her shame at 10%. She also reported that she had been on the London Eye for the first time, and had enjoyed it rather than feeling panicky.

Two- and three-month follow-ups: 90 and 45 minutes

These sessions focused on identifying Hannah's qualities and strengths, and incorporating these in a blueprint. Hannah had told friends about her experiences and she had received a supportive response. She reported feeling warmth towards others and had even made some new friends via her child's nursery. She drew further pictures to encapsulate her new sense of no longer feeling alone and detached, but feeling connected to others and able to experience emotions more fully. She reported that her sex life had improved and that she did not feel ashamed about the abuse or her physiological response to it. At the end of treatment she rated 'I'm bad' at <5% and her shame at 0% and no longer had intrusive images of the experience. She scored 3 on the PDS, 0 on the BDI, and 1 on the BAI.

Long-term outcome

At 1-year follow-up, Hannah reported that life was going well. She scored 9 on the PDS (none/minimal range), 2 on the BDI (none/minimal range), and 3 on the BAI (none/minimal range).

DISCUSSION

These two cases show how an intensive form of CT for PTSD can produce rapid and enduring clinical benefits. In both cases the traumatic event activated and confirmed beliefs that had been established in childhood ('I'm alone' and 'life is crap' for Mark, and 'I'm bad' for Hannah), but the intensive treatment focusing on the recent trauma was successful nevertheless. Although the individualized treatment protocol meant that different interventions were used for Mark and Hannah, there are common principles

Table 8.3 Summary of intensive treatments

	Mark	Hannah
Traumatic event	Motorcycle accident	Attempted suicide while in delusional state
Main symptoms	Nightmares, flashbacks, irritability/anger, avoid site	Detached/numb, overgeneralized threat 'fear of death'
Duration since trauma	9 months	10 years
Main intrusions	'Sliding down onto the road'	Nightmares of falling and hospital 'experience'
Key cognitions	Life is crap I'm all alone	I'm to blame I'm a bad person Bad things are likely to happen to me
Comorbidity	Major depression	Panic disorder with agoraphobia
Day 1	*Monday a.m.: 2.5 hours* Initial interventions, formulation and rationale *Monday p.m.: 2 hours* Standard reliving – 2×10 min	*Tuesday a.m.: 1.5 hours* Initial interventions, formulation and rationale *Tuesday p.m.: 1 hour* Initial interventions, formulation and rationale
Day 2	*Tuesday a.m.: 2 hours* Standard reliving 13 min; initial exploration of 'crap' and 'alone' *Tuesday p.m.: 2.5 hours* Formal CT on 'life is crap' and 'I'm all alone'; reliving with updates 13 min	*Wednesday a.m.: 2.5 hours* Reliving 30 min and discussion of hotspots
Day 3	*Wednesday a.m.: 2 hours* Reliving with updates 10 min *Wednesday p.m.: 2.5 hours* Site visit	*Thursday a.m.: 2.5 hours* Discussion of hospital abuse, discrimination of triggers for current relationship
Day 4	*Thursday p.m.: 2 hours* Anger and relationship	*Friday a.m.: 3.5 hours* Reliving 20 min; 'site visit' to a bridge; reliving with updates 15 min
Day 5	*Friday p.m.: 2 hours* Reliving 10 min, narrative, start blueprint	*Monday a.m.: 2 hours* Longitudinal formulation to help put drug use and trauma in context
Day 6	–	*Tuesday a.m.: 2.5 hours* Panic work, sequential probabilities and going on underground.
1 week	*1 hour* General review and blueprint	*2 hours* Responsibility pie chart

Follow-ups (3)	30+60+45 minutes General review and blueprint	75+90+45 minutes Compassionate imagery and drawings; blueprint. Reliving with updates 10 min
Total treatment time	Week: 18.5 hours Follow-ups: 2.25 hours	Week: 17.5 hours Follow-ups: 3.5 hours
Amount of imaginal reliving	Standard: 4 times, total 43 min With updates: 2 times, total 23 min	Standard: 2 times, total 50 min With updates: 2 times, total 25 min
PDS scores:		
Assessment	44	28
I week after treatment	I	8
Long-term follow-up	2	9
BDI scores:		
Assessment	40	22
I week after treatment	0	10
Long-term follow-up	2	2

guided by the treatment model. Treatment focused on maintenance cycles that prevented a change in these appraisals (rumination for Mark, suppressing and concealing emotions for Hannah) and on widening the client's perspective by taking other evidence into account (indicators that life is not all bad for Mark; factors that contributed to her own behaviour before and during the trauma and increasing awareness of the wrong-doing of others for Hannah). New insights from the discussion were linked in memory to the worst moments of the trauma through verbal reminders, imagery, or drawings ('updating trauma memories'). For Hannah, who tended to dissociate when reminded of the trauma, special efforts had to be made to access the relevant moments in memory, including a visit to a similar site and drawings of the experience. Visits to the site of the trauma or similar situations and stimulus discrimination assignments were used to help Mark and Hannah 'take in' that the trauma was over and that triggers of re-experiencing and a sense of current threat were different to those encountered during the trauma, and occurred in a different, safe context. Both Mark and Hannah had comorbid disorders (depression, panic disorder with agoraphobia) that had a link in meaning with those involved in the PTSD (life is crap for Mark, bad things are going to happen to me for Hannah) and were addressed within the PTSD treatment by targeting the relevant beliefs and behaviours (reclaiming your life for Mark, behavioural experiments reversing safety behaviours for Hannah). For both Mark and Hannah, social factors helped them take advantage of this form of treatment, including supportive partners and stable jobs and housing.

Treatment and practical considerations of intensive CT for PTSD

Therapy relationship

The therapeutic relationship is inevitably affected by the intensive nature of the sessions. For some people issues regarding trusting the therapist and being emotionally avoidant make it harder for them to engage in memory work at such an early stage. The message is given that the week can help set things up, but that the hard work for the patient is likely to continue in the weeks and months ahead.

Taping of sessions

In CT for PTSD, all sessions are recorded for the client to listen to between the sessions. Clearly it would not be possible to listen to such lengthy recordings each night with intensive CT. Typically we ask clients to listen to one or two segments of tape after the week in order to consolidate parts. However, we still recommend recording all the sessions so that access to this material is available and the client can keep copies for future reference.

Homework

After several hours of therapy each day, expecting patients to do emotionally demanding homework is usually unrealistic, and possibly unhelpful. In the first few days of treatment the homework is usually based around the patient simply looking after themselves well, and trying to reclaim their life by re-engaging in one or two enjoyable activities, such as playing with their children more, doing exercise, or watching a favourite film or TV programme. It is possible to schedule in homework time during the week, such as allowing a morning for the patient to complete a written narrative and meeting in the afternoon. We have observed that the first month after the end of the intensive week is an important time for the patient to consolidate gains and put new approaches to the test. For this reason we try to ensure that a fairly full and comprehensive list of homework tasks is agreed with the patient at the end of the week, with timescales identified.

Scheduling

Initially when providing these treatments, they were offered Monday to Friday. We now prefer to schedule them starting on the Tuesday (or even Wednesday), to have a weekend within the week, and ending on the following Monday or Tuesday. This allows the patient the opportunity to do suitable homework on the weekend and/or have a break. However, some patients may only be able to attend Monday to Friday. When possible, we have tried to ensure that the therapist also organizes his or her week such that there is flexibility in the use of the days, and that one is not rushing to meetings or seeing other patients immediately afterwards.

On the days of intensive treatment, breaks are taken as necessary. Typically, this may mean having a short tea break in the morning and then longer for lunch. This can be negotiated together with the patient, and to fit in with the demands of the session that day. The therapist takes lunch separately from the patient. We very rarely meet for longer than 5 hours in a single day, with 3–4 hours being more typical.

We have found that we have had a better reaction from patients at assessment when introducing this treatment as a 'daily' treatment option rather than an 'intensive' treatment, which may have pejorative connotations. Patients are advised to organize in advance their lives during the treatment week so that they can fully focus on the treatment for that week. This may involve taking the week off work, arranging childcare, and telling family and friends so that they can provide support.

When Ehlers and Clark's clinical research group piloted the treatment, they used two therapists throughout the sessions in order to both provide support and supervision, and provide a learning experience to more therapists. In the randomized controlled trial only one therapist was used. Therapists wishing to trial this form of CT for PTSD may find it best to try it at first with two therapists. One option would be to use a more experienced therapist together with a less experienced therapist or trainee. This could provide a time-efficient learning experience for trainees to observe the variety of techniques used to address PTSD.

Supervision

A crucial element of CT for PTSD is weekly supervision for therapists. For the intensive treatment, supervision is arranged for the end of each day, for up to 30 minutes. This is an additional factor to consider when scheduling such treatments.

'Intensive' daily treatment and weekly treatment compared

There are a number of possible advantages to intensive treatment over standard CT for PTSD. For people who find it difficult to attend therapy sessions on a weekly basis, for reasons including remote location, and demands of work and/or family life, taking 1 week to do most of the therapist-assisted work may be attractive. There are also therapeutic reasons that may favour an intensive form of treatment. There are likely to be fewer intervening life events, which in some instances can take up much therapy time. There is likely to be less forgetting of material, and the need to 'catch up' each week. Meeting each day can help overcome avoidance by building therapeutic momentum. If there are increased intrusions in response to starting treatment, this distress may be minimized by meeting regularly. Finally, the intensive treatment can help people get better quicker. Aside from the reduced overall disability and loss of amenity, this may be important if negative consequences are being exacerbated by the PTSD, such as being unable to work or the avoidance of important situations such as receiving medical treatment.

Weekly sessions may have advantages for patients who have no elements of their previous life in place, such as a relationship or job, as weekly treatment allows the patient more opportunity to reclaim their lives while working with the therapist. If the patient has severe agoraphobia it may be easier to overcome with weekly sessions. Weekly sessions may also allow more opportunity for working on avoidance. The longer-term follow-up results of the recently completed trial will be important in determining whether weekly treatment does work better for some individuals with particular circumstances.

Intensive treatment can also have greater emotional impact on the therapist, both positively and negatively. Seeing a person overcome a severe problem in a short space of time is a remarkable therapy experience. On the other hand providing intensive CT for PTSD is emotionally demanding, particularly if rapport is not easily established and the therapeutic relationship is problematic in some way. A further difficulty of the intensive treatment is scheduling one's other clients around it, ensuring access to daily supervision, and dealing with cancellations.

Future developments

Gillespie and Duffy have recently started testing the utility of an intensive treatment with people who have experienced many traumatic events. Intensive CT for PTSD related to childhood events remains to be investigated.

In some settings there may be questions as to how such a treatment may be funded. As the therapy hours are the same, the overall costs are the same as for weekly treatment. Within our own UK NHS setting, we were able to establish a new care option to provide intensive treatment without great problem. Simply 'adding up' the total of the sessions the person could have, but providing them in quick succession, may be acceptable to people or organizations funding treatment.

A possible development from this treatment is the option of 'semi-intensive' treatment, in which there is a flexible combination of perhaps two or three intensive days to focus on memory work nearer the beginning, followed by more weekly sessions than the full intensive treatment, but fewer than the full standard treatment.

Overall, the experiences with the intensive treatment have been positive.

At the very least, the cases here suggest that having to stick to weekly sessions of the same duration may not always be the only way to help people.

ACKNOWLEDGEMENTS

The development of weekly and intensive CT for PTSD was funded by the Wellcome Trust (grant 069777, Ehlers & Clark).

REFERENCES

Abramowitz, J.S., Foa, E.B., & Franklin, M.E. (2003). Exposure and ritual prevention for obsessive-compulsive disorder: Effectiveness of intensive versus twice-weekly treatment sessions. *Journal of Consulting and Clinical Psychology*, *71*, 394–398.

Bisson, J.I., Ehlers, A., Matthews, R., Pilling, S., Richards, D., & Turner, S. (2007). Psychological treatments for chronic post-traumatic stress disorder. *British Journal of Psychiatry*, *190*, 97–104.

Clark, D.M. (1996). Panic disorder: From theory to therapy. In P.M. Salkovskis (Ed.), *Frontiers of cognitive therapy* (pp. 318–344). New York: Guilford Press.

Deacon, B., & Abramowitz, J. (2006). A pilot study of two-day cognitive behaviour therapy for panic disorder. *Behaviour Research and Therapy*, *44*, 807–817.

Duffy, M, Gillespie, K., & Clark, D.M. (2007). Post-traumatic stress disorder in the context of terrorism and other civil conflict in Northern Ireland: Randomised controlled trial. *British Medical Journal*, doi:10.1136/bmj.39021.846852.BE (published 11 May 2007).

Ehlers, A., & Clark, D.M. (2000). A cognitive model of posttraumatic stress disorder. *Behaviour Research and Therapy*, *38*, 319–345.

Ehlers, A., Clark, D.M., Hackmann, A., Grey, N., Wild, J., & McManus, F. (in preparation a). Intensive cognitive therapy for PTSD: A feasibility study.

Ehlers, A., Clark, D.M., Hackmann, A., McManus, F., & Fennell, M. (2005). Cognitive therapy for PTSD: Development and evaluation. *Behaviour Research and Therapy*, *43*, 413–431.

Ehlers, A., Clark, D.M., Hackmann, A., McManus, F., Fennell, M., & Grey, N. (2009). *Cognitive therapy for PTSD: A therapist's guide*. Oxford: Oxford University Press. In preparation.

Ehlers, A., Clark, D.M., Hackmann, A., McManus, F., Fennell, M., Herbert, C., & Mayou, R. (2003). A randomised controlled trial of cognitive therapy, self-help booklet, and repeated early assessment as early interventions for PTSD. *Archives of General Psychiatry*, *60*, 1024–1032.

Ehlers, A., Hackmann, A., Grey, N., Wild, J., Deale, A., Liness, S., Albert, I., Stott, R., & Clark, D.M. (in preparation b). A randomized controlled trial of intensive and weekly cognitive therapy and emotion-focused supportive therapy in the treatment of chronic posttraumatic stress disorder.

Foa, E.B., & Rothbaum, B.O. (1998). *Treating the trauma of rape: Cognitive behavioural therapy for PTSD*. New York: Guilford Press.

Foa, E.B., Hembree, E.A., Cahill, S.P., Raunch, S.A.M., Riggs, D.S., Feeny, N.C., &

Yadin, E. (2005). Randomized trial of prolonged exposure for post-traumatic stress disorder with and without cognitive restructuring: Outcome at academic and community clinics. *Journal of Consulting and Clinical Psychology, 73*, 953–964.

Gillespie, K., Duffy, M., Hackmann, A., & Clark, D.M. (2002). Community based cognitive therapy in the treatment of post-traumatic stress disorder following the Omagh bomb. *Behaviour Research and Therapy, 40*, 345–357.

Hahlweg, K., Fiegenbaum, W., Frank, M., Schröder, B., & Witzleben, I. (2001). Short- and long-term effectiveness of an empirically supported treatment for agoraphobia. *Journal of Consulting and Clinical Psychology, 69*, 375–382.

Oldfield, V., & Salkovskis, P. (2008). Time-intensive cognitive-behaviour therapy for obsessive-compulsive disorder: a case series and matched comparison group. Submitted for publication.

Öst, L.G. (1989). One-session treatment for specific phobias. *Behaviour Research and Therapy, 27*, 1–7.

Resick, P., & Schnicke, M. (1993). *Cognitive processing therapy for rape victims: A treatment manual.* Newbury Park, CA: Sage.

Storch, E.A., Geffken, G.R., Merlo, L.J., Mann, G., Duke, D., Munson, M., Adkins, J., Grabill, K.M., Murphy, T.K., & Gooman, W.K. (2007). Family-based cognitive-behavioural therapy for pediatric obsessive compulsive disorder: Comparison of intensive and weekly approaches. *Journal of American Academy of Child and Adolescent Psychiatry, 46*, 469–478.

Chapter 9

Cognitive therapy for post-traumatic stress disorder and permanent physical injury

Jennifer Wild

INTRODUCTION

A high percentage of people who suffer trauma survive with permanent physical injury. Fifteen per cent of motor vehicle accidents in the UK result in permanent serious injury (Department for Transport, 2008) and 53% of physical assaults involving knife crime result in permanent injury (Davenport & Davis, 2008). Examples of injury include severe scarring, loss of limbs, paralysis, loss of sight, nerve damage, and chronic pain. Physical injury is a robust risk factor for post-traumatic stress disorder (PTSD) (e.g., Blanchard et al., 1995; Koren, Norman, Cohen, Berman, & Ehud, 2005) and appears to result in more severe PTSD than when there is no injury following trauma (e.g., Mayou, Tyndel, & Bryant, 1997). The injury is a constant reminder of what happened, inducing flashbacks, intrusive memories and ongoing upset more frequently than when reminders are external to one's body and less frequently encountered. Whereas patients with PTSD without injury are more likely to discover that the trauma is an event in the past without enduring implications, this is not the case for those with physical injury. For these patients, the physical injury often means that the trauma has had and continues to have lasting implications. Further, individuals with permanent injury have the additional challenge of adjusting to their disability and the associated problems this may incur, such as depression, job loss, and reduced quality of life.

Cognitive therapy (CT) for PTSD has three main goals: to reduce re-experiencing symptoms, modify negative appraisals, and to change strategies that maintain the patient's sense of threat (Ehlers & Clark, 2000; Ehlers, Clark, Hackmann, McManus, & Fennell, 2005). The treatment is adapted in those cases in which physical injury has occurred so that it may focus on helping clients to establish and claim their current lives, rather than 're-claim' all aspects of their previous lives. Early in treatment, the cognitive therapist will help sufferers to re-think their life's goals to fit with their change in abilities. The cognitive therapist will likely address negative appraisals of how the patient views their appearance and their life, with extensive focus on discovering what has and what has not changed. In so doing, the therapist may draw on CT for depression to address negative appraisals about how one perceives their life, grief work to address loss of functioning, and CT for social phobia to help the sufferer to see themselves in a realistic fashion as opposed to in a distorted way.

This chapter presents the cognitive therapy of Maryanne, a young woman who suffered septic shock that resulted in the loss of her legs. Unlike many patients who suffer PTSD and physical injury, Maryanne's treatment drew on all, rather than some, of the suggested components above for PTSD and physical injury. There were many elements that made Maryanne's case complex, factors thought to predict chronic PTSD: the duration of her trauma was lengthy (6 months), her trauma memory was disorganized due to loss of consciousness and pain medication at the time of the trauma, she was involved in ongoing litigation, and she also suffered comorbid agoraphobia.

CASE EXAMPLE: MARYANNE

Maryanne was a 27-year-old woman who suffered a medical misdiagnosis that resulted in septic shock, loss of hearing, and the amputation of her legs below the knee when she was 24 years old. At the time of assessment, she had been married for three years and was living with her husband. She had met her husband just before her trauma and they were married when she had physically recovered. Prior to her trauma, she had been working as a legal assistant. She had not worked since the trauma. She had a close relationship with her mother, whom she saw most days and who would accompany her when she went out. Maryanne was born with a congenital heart problem that necessitated antibiotic treatment when she had any dental treatment. Maryanne had seen the same dentist since she was a child and had always been given antibiotics.

Trauma

When Maryanne was 24 years old, she contacted her dentist for a routine check-up. The dentist cleaned her teeth. Maryanne enquired about antibiotics and was told it was unnecessary to administer them. The next day, Maryanne collapsed. She was taken to the hospital, where it was queried she may be suffering endocarditis, an infection of the heart, which was never further investigated. She was given standard headache medication and sent home. She collapsed again the following day, and was rushed to hospital. When she awoke, she was in a hospital bed with nursing staff busy around her. A tracheotomy had been performed to help her breathe and she was on intravenous antibiotics. She was suffering pain in her lower legs where she had lost circulation to her lower limbs. Despite the administration of antibiotics, she was told they would have to be amputated. She also suffered a reaction to the high dose of antibiotics and lost her hearing. Maryanne was in hospital for six months and was in and out of consciousness whilst the doctors treated her endocarditis and leg infection. Much of this time, she was unable to hear the nursing staff and believed as a result of the pain she experienced that they were intentionally trying to torture her. One year after she was discharged from hospital, she received cochlear implant surgery, which restored 60 per cent of her hearing. She also had prosthetic limbs that enabled her to walk with a stick.

Diagnostic assessment

Maryanne described intrusive memories of her stay in hospital about twice per week. She recurrently experienced images of nurses looking at her in a cruel and cold manner. These were triggered by talking or thinking about the trauma, reading about similar events on the internet, or seeing hospital programmes on television. She also described flashbacks to being in hospital when she was reminded of it. She was tearful throughout the assessment and, in particular, in response to thinking about and talking about her trauma. As a result, she avoided thinking about the trauma and her symptoms as much as possible. She also avoided going out to socialize with friends. This was in part due to her 40 per cent loss of hearing, feeling more vulnerable as a result of her reduced mobility, and the sense of threat she experienced as a result of her trauma. Maryanne no longer engaged in exercise. This was due to her perception that people would stare at her and think badly of her body. She described feeling more irritable now than before the trauma, and being hypervigilant when she went out. She also described strong startle responses, in part due to her reduced hearing and being unclear as to which noises represented danger and which were innocuous, and also due to heightened physiological responding as a result of the trauma.

Maryanne also suffered agoraphobia symptoms, rooted in socially anxious beliefs that people would stare at her if she was on her own, and also in trauma beliefs about being in more danger now than before the trauma. She therefore avoided leaving her house, unless accompanied by her mother. Maryanne said that she felt down and sad, although she did not meet formal criteria for depression.

Maryanne scored 30 on the Posttraumatic Diagnostic Scale (PDS; Foa, Cashman, Jaycox, & Perry, 1997), which is in the moderate to severe range. She scored 23 on the Beck Depression Inventory (BDI; Beck, Rush, Shaw, & Emery, 1979), which falls in the moderately depressed range.

Sessions one and two: Cognitive assessment and formulation

In these sessions, the therapist's main focus was to identify Maryanne's primary symptoms and the factors maintaining them, the worst moments of the trauma and the linked appraisals, and how different areas of her life had been affected by the trauma. The therapist had an additional three goals. The first was to instil a sense of optimism about what treatment could offer and to actively engage Maryanne in treatment. The second was to identify Maryanne's short- and long-term goals, and the third was to identify trauma themes that may have relevance to how future experiments were planned.

Maryanne's primary symptoms were recurrent, upsetting memories of nurses with cold, uncaring faces. She also had intrusive images of seeing her blackened legs for several months before they were amputated. When the images popped up, Maryanne thought she was going crazy. She tried hard to avoid them or she dwelt on why her trauma happened. Avoidance made her images pop up more frequently and dwelling caused her to fail to run the trauma on past its worst point, as well as making her feel down. Maryanne identified five worst moments during her traumatic experiences. Three were concerned with how nurses interacted with her and her belief that she was being tortured. One concerned a misunderstanding over a hospital procedure and her appraisal that she was dying. The fifth concerned the consultant who told her that she needed to have her legs amputated. She concluded that her life was over.

Almost all areas of Maryanne's life had changed since the trauma. She described a rocky relationship with her husband. She was no longer working, exercising, or socializing.

Specific appraisals that Maryanne made at the time of the trauma and continued to make afterwards influenced her feelings and her behaviour, and maintained her distress. Through much of Maryanne's trauma, she had no ability to hear and this coupled with physical pain caused her to believe that the nursing staff were torturing her. Consequently she believed she could not trust nursing staff and that people in general could not be trusted. These appraisals made her feel unsafe and she concluded that the world is dangerous and it is safer to stay at home than to go out. She therefore avoided going out as much as possible. At home, she avoided hospital programmes on television because they brought back intrusive memories of her worst moments of the trauma, which included images of 'being tortured' by her nurses. When these memories popped to mind, Maryanne thought she was going crazy. She also felt helpless like she did in hospital and to feel safe she would push them out of her mind. She would avoid leaving the house to avoid danger and to avoid the possibility that people would stare at her prosthetic legs and think badly of her. Sometimes when the memories popped up she would spend some time questioning why she went to the dentist and why the dentist failed to give her antibiotics. She would picture different endings to her trauma, compare them with what happened, and conclude that she could not accept the way her body had changed. This caused her to feel low. As Maryanne had been in and out of consciousness during her hospital stay, her memory was disorganized. That is, she was unable to easily remember the sequence of events in hospital and many details. She could not easily remember information that did not fit her fears of being tortured in hospital. Consequently, she felt distressed when memories of nurses came to mind. Further, they likely came to mind frequently because her memory was poorly organized.

To normalize what Maryanne was suffering and to address her belief that her reactions meant that she was going crazy, she was told that what she was experiencing was entirely normal given the ordeal she had suffered, that post-traumatic stress symptoms are a normal reaction to an abnormal event. She was also given written information about PTSD.

Maryanne's goals were to 'move on' from the trauma and to be 'carefree' again. 'Moving on' would mean she would feel less irritable, find herself work, have a more peaceful relationship with her husband, be able to talk about the trauma without crying, and to be able to exercise again. To be 'carefree' again would mean having more spontaneity in her life and not always going out with her mother. The therapist was able to help her to conclude that addressing her trauma symptoms would help her to reach her goals.

Maryanne had themes of helplessness and loss of personal power linked to her trauma because, whilst unconscious, significant medical decisions were made without her consent. Thus, in addition to addressing her PTSD symptoms, the therapist aimed to give Maryanne the opportunity to make choices in session and enough information to feel informed in making them. This involved frequent checking with her that she understood the therapist's suggestions, and frequent seeking of her opinion as to what she thought would be a good way to test a particular problematic belief, or a good way to move forward.

Maryanne was given a rationale (e.g., Ehlers & Clark, 2000) for focusing on her trauma memory in future sessions and then suggestions for homework activities. As Maryanne's hearing was impaired, she was not given audio tapes of the sessions to listen to. Maryanne identified going to the gym for 15 minutes to walk on the treadmill as a manageable and nurturing activity.

Sessions three to twelve: Maintaining factors

The treatment targeted the factors maintaining Maryanne's sense of threat and distress: a disorganized trauma memory, hotspot appraisals, rumination, socially anxious beliefs about her appearance and how people would respond if she went out, and her loss.

Disorganized trauma memory

Maryanne had endured a lengthy trauma, during which she was in and out of consciousness for six months. As such, her trauma memory was disorganized. That is, she remembered events in hospital out of sequence. Further, she failed to easily remember details of interactions with nurses who were helpful. In sessions three to four, therefore, the therapist had Maryanne slowly take her through the trauma, while she wrote out the narrative. They had time to discuss what happened when and to focus on the order in which events happened. The complete narrative was typed out for Maryanne with space for her to make changes. Her homework from session four, in addition to going to the gym, was to read the narrative and to fill in any gaps.

Hotspot appraisals

The therapist addressed hotspots clearly linked to distorted beliefs before addressing those concerned with loss and fear of dying. Thus, Maryanne's worst moments involving interactions with nurses were addressed first.

'*I am being tortured' and calling on experts*: A nurse attended session five to give information to correct Maryanne's appraisals about being tortured. Maryanne had believed that when the nurses washed her legs, they were intentionally trying to torture her. She believed this with 100% conviction throughout the trauma and when recalling it in session. The therapist had contacted a colleague who had been a former nurse in Accident and Emergency and asked if she would meet with Maryanne to answer any questions she may have about hospital procedures and nurses. The therapist briefly told the nurse about Maryanne and what she had endured. She asked her to answer Maryanne's questions honestly.

The nurse explained that nurses have standard procedures that they must perform several times a day. They do them so often that sometimes they forget to explain them to patients. This does not necessarily mean that they do not care about the patient. They do it unknowingly because they forget it is a frightening and new experience for the patient. The nurse also explained that washing Maryanne's legs, which was an excruciating procedure, would have been necessary, and many of the nurses would have been vigilant about keeping her legs clean because of the small possibility that doing so would heal her leg infection and avoid amputation. Thus, the nurses were not trying to torture her with their rigid cleaning regime. Rather they were trying to help her. With this new information, Maryanne believed her original thought that they did not care about her and were trying to torture her with 0% strength. The conversation with the nurse was video-recorded and the recording was given to Maryanne to view again at home.

'*I did not die*': Maryanne had one hotspot about a fear of dying. The therapist considered this a straightforward hotspot as Maryanne had not died. She addressed it in session seven after they had successfully updated appraisals concerned with torture.

'My life is over': Maryanne believed that her life was over when the consultant told her that she needed to have her legs amputated. She believed that she would be bed-bound for the rest of her life or in a wheelchair forever. The therapist approached this hotspot in session nine after Maryanne's PTSD had improved somewhat, leading her to feel less depressed and more positive about her life. Having already addressed many hotspots, Maryanne was able to generate new information to update this one with minimal prompting from the therapist.

Table 9.1 shows Maryanne's five hotspots, her original appraisals at the time of the trauma, and her new information generated in therapy.

Rumination

Maryanne estimated that she spent about two hours a day dwelling on why she had gone to the dentist and why the dentist had forgotten to give her antibiotics. The therapist guided Maryanne to discover that when she dwelled on these questions, she felt worse, and it stopped her from focusing on how she could move forward in her progress, as well as stopping her from running the trauma on past its worst point. Maryanne's triggers included delays in getting dressed in the morning due to reduced mobility, intrusive memories of

Table 9.1 Maryanne's hotspots with appraisals and new information

	Situation	Appraisals	New information
#1	Two nurses washing me	'I am being tortured. It doesn't make any sense. They're doing it purposely to cause pain. They're not listening to my screams and cries. They must want to hurt me.'	The nurses were washing my legs regularly because there was a possibility that it would help to clear up the infection and save my legs from being amputated. They couldn't actually hear my screams and cries because I had had a tracheotomy. No sound was coming out of my mouth when I screamed. I didn't know this and they didn't know that they were hurting me. They were trying to be helpful. It just happened to cause a lot of pain.
#2	Nurses wheel me out of my room and put a needle in my arm	'I am going to have an operation and die. They haven't given me any anaesthetic. I will feel huge amounts of pain. I'll die.'	It was not an operation. The nurses were doing something minor like taking blood. It was a misunderstanding on my part because I couldn't hear. The nurses didn't know what I was thinking so had no idea that I needed reassurance and that I had grossly misunderstood the situation. I didn't feel any pain and I didn't have an operation at that time.

(Continued overleaf)

Table 9.1 Continued

	Situation	Appraisals	New information
#3	Nurse insists on washing me before rolling me	'He doesn't care about me. He's making me do something against my wishes. Why? I am powerless. No one's fighting for me. Something painful, bad, and uncomfortable is going to happen and no one's going to stop him. I am all alone.'	The nurse had a procedure to follow, which had nothing to do with whether or not he cared about me. He wasn't trying to cause me pain. He had been told to wash my feet and then roll me. My parents were there and they were not reacting when he washed me because it wasn't a dangerous procedure. It was a painful and uncomfortable one. There was a possibility that cleaning my feet could save my legs so it had to be done.
#4	A nurse puts an intraven- ous solution in my hand	'She's poisoning me. I'm going to die.'	I was on morphine for the pain in my legs. On one occasion when I woke up at night, I noticed a nurse in my room, changing my intravenous solution. They did this most nights but most nights I was sleeping and didn't notice them doing this. Because I was on morphine, I thought she was changing the solution with a poisoned one. I now know she simply changed the solution. She wasn't poisoning me and I didn't die.
#5	The consultant tells me I need an operation to amputate my legs	'My life is over. I'll be bed-bound for the rest of my life, or in a wheelchair forever.'	At the time, I thought that my life was over and that I'd need a wheelchair for the rest of my days. Walking again seemed like an impossibility. I thought my life was over. The reality, however, was that whilst my life HAD changed, it was far from over. It just meant that I would need to learn new skills (like walking, sitting down, etc.). My life wasn't over, it had simply changed. I was not bed-bound and I do use a wheelchair now, but only as a computer chair! I did manage to walk again, so it wasn't an impossibility. I am proud of how far I've come. Whilst life will never be the same again, I have achieved a lot and I am walking proof that there is indeed life after amputation.

being in hospital, feeling suddenly wobbly on her prosthetic legs, and seeing a pair of high-heeled shoes. She would then think of her abilities before the trauma and begin to question, 'Why did I go to the dentist? Why didn't I push to have antibiotics more forcefully when I went? Why did the dentist forget to give me antibiotics?' Then she would imagine different endings to the trauma, compare them with what actually happened, and start to feel quite down.

Below is an example of an answer to one of Maryanne's 'why' questions that she and the therapist worked on together.

'Why did I go to the dentist?'

'I went to the dentist because it had been two years since I had had a check-up and I wanted to get my teeth cleaned. At the time, I had no idea that my dentist would make a huge error in judgement. I had seen her for 21 years and I had always trusted and relied on her opinion. There was no reason not to on this occasion. If I had known that she would make a mistake that would put me in hospital, I would not have gone. But it was impossible for me to know that in advance and giving myself a hard time about it now is assuming I had information that I simply did not have. That is hindsight bias. I didn't have the information before I went. It is important to have good oral hygiene and it made sense to see my dentist after a gap of two years. I have learned that when I ask 'why' questions like this, I start to feel down and what is more helpful is thinking about 'how'. 'How can I feel better right now, what will help?' Looking at my list of activities to do when I spot dwelling will help. This list suggests telephoning my mother or my niece, catching up on my e-mails, or logging onto the amputee forum.'

Socially anxious concerns

To address Maryanne's fears of how people would respond to her when she went swimming, the therapist constructed a survey for others to complete. Maryanne believed that people would stare at her for several minutes, think that she had a contagious disease, and would then immediately leave the swimming pool. The survey questions are reproduced below.

Please take a few moments to answer the following questions. Thank you.

1   If you went to your local gym for a swim and saw a young woman who had no legs below her knees get into the pool and swim some laps, what would you think?
2   How much out of 100% would you believe 'It's a shameful thing. She must have a disease and I could catch it.'?
3   Would you feel uncomfortable being in the same pool? If so, how much? (out of 100%) And why?

4   Would you leave?
5   Would you stare at her? If so, for how long?
6   What, if any, judgements would you make?
7   What do you think generally of people who have lost their limbs below the knees?

All respondents indicated that they would feel impressed by someone who was swimming with no legs. Two out of seven respondents indicated that they would look and that they would look because they were not used to seeing someone without legs, but that they would not stare and after a few seconds would return to their own exercise programme. The survey results indicated that how others would respond was much different to how Maryanne felt they would respond. It was the final push for her to start swimming. The swimming exercise was set up as a behavioural experiment, described below.

Behavioural experiments

Maryanne thought that if she went swimming, people would stop and stare and then leave the pool. She had an image of how others would respond: shocked faces, disbelief, frowns, and looks of disgust. The behavioural experiment asked her to predict the likelihood that other people would stare and to specify for how long. She was asked to predict the likelihood that others would leave the pool. She was then encouraged to swim and to look up and around when getting into the pool to gain accurate information about how many people were leaving and how many people looked disgusted. She went swimming three days later. Her swimming session went well and she concluded that what she imagined had no relation to what actually happened, that perhaps her fearful feelings were unrelated to how she actually appeared. She arranged to make swimming a regular part of her fitness routine. Experiments like this helped to update her distorted image of how others would respond when they saw her without legs.

Reliving with imagery updating

Maryanne had a negative image of having black and rotten legs when she lay in bed. The trigger was lying down (as she had been in hospital). When the image recurred, she opened her eyes and focused on what is different now in her surroundings. She was also encouraged to look at a photo of herself at this time. She had one in which she was standing smiling with her husband. Looking at the photo helped to discriminate between the past image and the present reality. In reliving, when Maryanne got to the point of the trauma where the nurses were roughly washing her blackened legs, she was encouraged to bring in the new information that she knew now about why nurses are sometimes rough, and then to imagine how she looks now, able to stand free of pain. The aim was to run the image on past its worst point to what is real and current, widening the gap between the past memory and the present day.

Loss

Maryanne felt loss about not being able to feel sand beneath her toes and not being able to wear high-heeled shoes. She was also on ongoing medication to keep her blood from clotting too much, which meant she could no longer have biological children.

To help Maryanne come to terms with these losses required focusing her on what she had lost and empathizing with her to encourage her to grieve in therapy. Maryanne's therapist acknowledged the intense sadness that she no longer would feel sand on her toes or wear high heels, or have biological children.

When Maryanne had expressed some sadness over these losses and had also experienced some successes in therapy, such as feeling less distressed by hotspots, and gaining pleasure from going to the gym regularly, the therapist then explored which of her appraisals linked to loss were in fact accurate, which needed updating, and what she had lost that could be replaced. This meant looking at the meaning of what she perceived she had lost. This came late in therapy in session ten.

While Maryanne could not now experience sand on her toes, she identified that she could still go to a beach, go swimming, and feel sun on her face. In terms of motherhood, the therapist encouraged her to think about what it means to be a mother, and in particular what she had been looking forward to in having biological children. Maryanne said that she had really wanted to have a baby to nurture and love. She was less attached to the idea of a toddler and a teenager. Motherhood was much more about loving and nurturing a small being. Maryanne was asked if there was a way she could introduce this into her life now. For example, could she love and nurture one of the many babies already in the world who needs a loving and caring parent? Could she love and nurture a project that is important to her? She was encouraged to think about the ways in which she could create love and nurturance in her life now.

In relation to high-heeled shoes, Maryanne had thought 'I can't wear high heels' and had felt sad. She discovered in the course of therapy that she could wear high heels of two inches. Although she could not wear stiletto heels, she was pleased that she could wear some heels and this new information modified her appraisal to 'I can't wear stiletto heels, but I can wear heels and I have some very funky shoes, some are high heeled and about two inches high.' The updated appraisal reduced her feelings of loss about womanhood.

Outcome

In Maryanne's twelfth and final session, her score on the PDS was 1, in the mild PTSD range, and her score on the BDI was 3, in the minimally depressed range. She no longer met criteria for PTSD or agoraphobia.

DISCUSSION

Cognitive therapy for PTSD is adapted in those cases in which physical change and injury has occurred. There is more emphasis on helping patients to claim a new life rather than simply reclaim their old life. Further, as these clients have experienced loss, many sessions may focus on this, and the order in which hotspots are addressed may differ from patients without injury.

Such complexity may lead to the cognitive assessment and formulation requiring more sessions than usual to complete. In addition to identifying the thoughts and behaviours that maintain the patient's anxiety and distress, the key goals of this are to instil optimism, plan goals, and to consider themes from the trauma that may influence how experiments are set up later in therapy. Homework following this is more likely to include nurturing activities and exercise to address low mood rather than listening to the audio recording of the session.

Much of cognitive therapy is about addressing maintaining factors. Key ones for those with PTSD and permanent change are the nature of the trauma memory, rumination, and appraisals linked to loss and social anxiety. If there has been loss of consciousness and extensive hospital stays, then the therapist will likely need to call on medical experts, such as nurses or doctors, to provide information that can update distorted appraisals linked to pain or treatment in hospital.

Often patients with permanent physical injury have experienced a loss of consciousness at the time of their injury. As such, there may be gaps in their memory of the trauma, which may be more disorganized than clients with PTSD without injury. Constructing a written narrative helps the client and therapist to work together to organize the events in memory in sequence, to identify gaps in the memory, and when possible, to decide on the likely course of events and plausible information that could fill gaps in memory.

Hotspots

One of the most important decisions the cognitive therapist can make in treating clients with PTSD and physical injury is deciding in which order to address hotspots. Patients with physical injury will have hotspots about loss, such as loss of functioning, loss of limbs, or loss of a pain-free life. As loss is difficult to address, clinicians are encouraged to modify clearly distorted appraisals, which tend to be easier to update, before addressing those to do with loss. This will help to update some hotspots early on in treatment, reduce intrusive memories associated with those hotspots, and simultaneously give clients a sense of achievement and relief before approaching issues of loss. Addressing appraisals linked to loss requires considering all that has and has not changed and positive possibilities that are currently occurring, such as new courses, relationships, and career ideas, and even the positive experience of therapy. It makes most sense to address these once the client has positive experiences to draw on and these may occur during the course of therapy in conjunction with homework exercises.

Body image

Socially anxious and body dysmorphic-type fears are common among patients with PTSD and physical change. They often have distorted images of how they think they look, often believing that physically they appear as they did at the time of the trauma. It is as if their image of themselves today is a frozen fragment of their worst-looking moment during their trauma. They also typically believe other people will respond to them in a negative, rejecting way because they feel different. It is necessary to update their distorted image of how they think they look with a current and realistic one. It is also necessary to address their fears of how they think other people will respond to them. Doing so requires drawing on techniques from cognitive therapy for social phobia, notably: video feedback in which the therapist elicits patients' predictions of what they think they will see when they look at a video of themselves and compares it with what they actually see after watching the video following cognitive preparation (e.g., Harvey, Clark, Ehlers, & Rapee, 2000). Other CT for social phobia techniques include behavioural experiments and surveys. Behavioural experiments will help to disconfirm patients' distorted beliefs about how others will respond to them. Surveys will do the same and are intended to gain objective information about how others would respond to the patient in a hypothetical scenario or how others actually perceive the patient. Photo surveys, for example, will generate information about how others view the patient's physical appearance, which can be compared with their own perception. Reliving with imagery updating may also be used to discriminate between how the patient thought they looked during the trauma and how they look now.

Loss

Cognitive therapy for PTSD and physical change will require addressing loss. Patients may have lost some functioning, their former dreams, and a way of life they enjoyed. With loss comes grief and addressing loss requires allowing the patient to grieve. Empathy is obviously crucial as is the need to courageously confront the loss, to identify what patients feel they have lost, what it means to them, and to consider alternatives, when appropriate. It is important to consider what is really lost, what is not, and what can be replaced over time.

Anger

One area that has not been addressed in this chapter and that does feature in those with permanent change is anger and beliefs to do with the world being unfair. These beliefs did not feature in Maryanne's presentation, although they could have given that the injury she suffered was preventable. These appraisals will likely feature in other patients with physical change and it will be necessary to address them in the way that cognitive therapists address anger generally: to identify exactly who the client is angry at and what they are angry about. It will be necessary to modify any distortions in their appraisals of other people's behaviour to make them less personal, if appropriate. For example, Maryanne thought that the nurses were intentionally trying to torture her, which made her feel scared, although equally she could have felt angry. It was necessary to update this appraisal to make it less personal. This reduced her fear and would have reduced her anger had the original appraisal resulted in anger. In addressing anger it is important to empathize with the patient and gently introduce the idea that everyone makes mistakes and that bad things can happen to good people. Some clients will feel less angry having thought about the trauma and others' behaviour in new ways. Some will continue to feel angry and it may be necessary to look at the advantages and disadvantages of staying angry and what it would mean to let go of their anger. If there are any distorted appraisals about letting go of anger, such as 'If I am no longer angry, the trauma will be forgotten', then the therapist will need to address these and modify accordingly.

Pain

Maryanne did not experience chronic pain, which may be a feature of those with PTSD and permanent injury. Chronic pain in the context of PTSD is a difficult clinical problem. Certainly some patients may benefit from specific treatment focused on their pain and responses to it. Such treatment may be provided in specialist pain clinics. Currently it is unclear whether such treatment is best delivered before, after or integrated with treatment for PTSD. There are further specific links between PTSD and pain, such as the role of mental defeat (Tang, Salkovskis, & Hanna, 2007), which also require further investigation.

Litigation

Maryanne was involved in litigation, and this can be a complicating factor in treating patients with PTSD. It was unnecessary to address this with Maryanne because her primary goal was to be free of symptoms and her recovery from PTSD had no bearing on the outcome of her court case. Some patients may believe that should they recover, then their compensation will be reduced. This may be true and the therapist must help the client to look at the pros and cons of prolonging their suffering by delaying their treatment.

Effects on the therapist

Loss is painful to confront for both client and therapist. The therapist needs to focus the patient at times on painful memories and feelings. This can be difficult when the reality of what they have lost is sad. It is crucial to have supportive supervision where the therapist can express their own feelings about the patient's loss so they may return to sessions with renewed capacity to approach painful thoughts and feelings. It may be helpful for the therapist's caseload to be varied. It is also important that the therapist nurtures themself outside of work, so they have a balance in their own life and have the emotional capacity to offer support to others. Feelings of burn-out are high in the helping profession and the therapist should know the early signs, such as beginning to feel uncaring towards clients, unvalued in their role, and extremely fatigued, so they know when to take a break themselves.

CONCLUSION

This chapter conceptualized PTSD and permanent injury in terms of factors that cause and maintain trauma-related distress and anxiety. These included appraisals linked to hotspots and loss, rumination, socially anxious beliefs, and a disorganized trauma memory. A complex case was presented, which illustrated cognitive therapy of a young woman with PTSD and permanent physical injury. Successful treatment involved addressing the maintaining factors, some of which are different to those that maintain PTSD in patients without injury, such as appraisals and avoidance linked to socially anxious concerns. Other important considerations were presented, such as an emphasis on structuring goals, identifying what has and what has not changed, the order in which to address hotspots and when to modify appraisals linked to loss. The chapter also briefly considered the emotional impact on the therapist of treating individuals with permanent injury who have clearly experienced loss. The ultimate goal in cognitive therapy for PTSD and permanent injury is creating a new direction in patients' lives, one which includes an understanding that whilst life may have changed, it is far from over. Much of this understanding may come late in therapy when many of the PTSD symptoms have been addressed and patients are no longer avoiding the possibility of a new future. They are creating it.

ACKNOWLEDGEMENTS

This therapy was funded by the Wellcome Trust. I would like to thank Professor Anke Ehlers for her continuous support. I would also like to express my gratitude to Maryanne and the other patients I have treated who have suffered permanent physical injury. They have encouraged thinking about best ways to facilitate recovery in those with injury, which has been a rewarding experience.

REFERENCES

Beck, A.T., Rush, A.J., Shaw, B.F., & Emery, G. (1979). *Cognitive therapy of depression*. New York: Guilford Press.

Blanchard, E.B., Hickling, E.J., Mitnick, N., Taylor, A.E., Loos, W.R., & Buckley, T.C. (1995). The impact of severity of physical injury and perception of life threat in the development of post-traumatic stress disorder in motor vehicle accident victims. *Behaviour Research and Therapy*, *33*, 529–534.

Davenport, J., & Davis, J. (2008). Surgeon: One in three of trauma patients has been knifed. *Evening Standard*, 2 June.

Department for Transport. (2008). Road casualties in Great Britain: Quarterly provisional estimates Q3 2007. Department for Transport, London, 7 February.

Ehlers, A., & Clark, D.M. (2000). A cognitive model of posttraumatic stress disorder. *Behaviour Research and Therapy*, *38*, 319–345.

Ehlers, A., Clark, D.M., Hackmann, A., McManus, F., & Fennell, M. (2005). Cognitive therapy for PTSD: Development and evaluation. *Behaviour Research and Therapy*, *43*, 413–431.

Foa, E.B., Cashman, L., Jaycox, L., & Perry, K. (1997). The validation of a self-report measure of posttraumatic stress disorder: The Posttraumatic Diagnostic Scale. *Psychological Assessment*, *9*, 445–451.

Harvey, A.G., Clark, D.M., Ehlers, A., & Rapee, R.M. (2000). Social anxiety and self-impression: Cognitive preparation enhances the beneficial effects of video feedback following a stressful social task. *Behaviour Research and Therapy*, *38*, 1183–1192.

Koren, D., Norman, D., Cohen, A., Berman, J., & Ehud, E.M. (2005). Increased PTSD risk with combat-related injury: A matched comparison study of injured and non-injured soldiers experiencing the same combat events. *American Journal of Psychiatry*, *162*, 276–282.

Mayou, R., Tyndel, S., & Bryant, B. (1997). Long-term outcome of motor vehicle accident injury. *Psychosomatic Medicine*, *59*, 578–584.

Tang, N., Salkovskis, P., & Hanna, M. (2007). Mental defeat in chronic pain: Initial exploration of the concept. *Clinical Journal of Pain*, *23*, 222–232.

Chapter 10

Cognitive therapy for post-traumatic stress disorder and panic attacks

Sheena Liness

INTRODUCTION

Despite evidence that panic attacks are prevalent in people with post-traumatic stress disorder (PTSD; Falsetti & Resnick, 1997, 2000; Bryant & Panasetis, 2001), and national comorbidity studies demonstrating elevated rates of comorbid panic disorder among men and women with PTSD in the US (Kessler, Sonnega, Bromet, Hughes, & Nelson 1995), studies addressing the interrelationship of these two disorders are limited. However, a number of recent studies have investigated comorbid PTSD and panic attacks. Vujanovic, Zvolensky, and Bernstein (2008) found a differential significance of anxiety sensitivity (AS) physical concerns predicting panic symptoms and AS psychological concerns predicting PTSD. Treatment studies have reported successful CBT for comorbid PTSD and panic attacks in women compared to a control condition (Falsetti, Resnick, & Davis, 2008), in Cambodian refugees (Hinton, Hoffmann, Pitman, Pollack, & Barlow, 2008), and using predominantly interoceptive exposure (Wald & Taylor, 2008).

This chapter describes the treatment of someone with both PTSD and panic attacks. Treatment combined cognitive therapy (CT) for PTSD (Ehlers & Clark, 2000; Ehlers, Clark, Hackmann, McManus, & Fennell, 2005) and cognitive therapy for panic disorder (Clark, 1986, 1996). CT for PTSD focuses on reducing the sense of current threat that is maintained by the unelaborated nature of the trauma memory, the (negative) appraisals of the trauma and its sequelae, and the (usually avoidant) strategies used to cope that prevent change in the appraisals or nature of the trauma memory. CT for panic disorder focuses on the key cognitive theme of the catastrophic misinterpretation of bodily sensations. Such interpretations can also lead to an increase in the sense of current threat experienced as part of PTSD, and hence help to maintain PTSD. The case focuses on key clinical issues on commencing treatment with two equally disabling problems, and outlines the assessment, formulation, and interventions used.

CASE EXAMPLE – SUSAN

Susan was a 30-year-old journalist who had extensive experience of working in war-torn and politically difficult areas. Throughout her journalist career she had dealt with tense and difficult situations, and had felt in danger for her life previously. She believed she always had the ability to talk her way out of danger. She also believed her work to be worthwhile in alerting people to the horrors and crimes in the world and so enable aid and international interventions. Since her traumatic experience she continued to work as a journalist but on home affairs only and often turned down assignments she perceived to hold an element of danger. Her company was supportive, she also had a close circle of friends, and had no prior psychiatric history.

Trauma

Five years previously, Susan was part of a group of journalists that flew into an African country. On arrival, they realised that they were in a politically tense and extremely dangerous situation. The next day, they were taken, by locals, to view the aftermath of a massacre. They witnessed gruesome and horrific scenes, including mutilated bodies in an open grave. On returning to the main town that evening, they pitched their tents in a seemingly safe area. As night progressed, they were surrounded by the sound of gunfire and explosions, which came nearer and nearer. Susan felt terrified. Her heart was racing and she felt nauseous. She feared that they were surrounded by the same tribe that had carried out the massacre, and experienced images from the massacre scene. She felt unable to move or lift her arms and lay as flat as she could on the floor to avoid being hit by any stray bullets.

Assessment: PTSD and panic disorder

Susan described feeling relieved initially on leaving that country, but that she soon began to experience frequent nightmares, flashbacks, and intrusions. At assessment she met diagnostic criteria for PTSD. She had intrusive images of bodies from the massacre on a daily basis and frequent nightmares. Flashbacks were triggered by reminders such as passing butchers' shop windows, and attending barbeques. Her heart pounded and she felt sick. She avoided watching television news reports and violence on TV. She was highly anxious when out, hypervigilant for danger, and thought something bad was about to happen. She also avoided colleagues associated with her time in that country. She was socially withdrawn, emotionally numb, and had difficulty sleeping and concentrating. She compared herself negatively to her work colleagues who seemed unaffected, believing this meant she was weak.

Susan also met diagnostic criteria for panic disorder with mild agoraphobia. In order to gain a detailed chronology of her difficulties a timeline was reviewed with Susan. She had experienced her first panic attack 1 year prior to first seeking referral, which was 3 years since the traumatic experiences. Onset for her panic attacks was at a music festival when sleeping in a tent in a crowded field. She suddenly felt trapped, that she couldn't breathe and feared she was going to suffocate and collapse. Later that week she experienced a panic attack on an underground train and she then began to avoid enclosed spaces for fear of further attacks. Soon after, on a flight for work, she experienced an unexpected panic attack and she thought she was about to die. She had a period of severe agoraphobia, having difficulty leaving the house, and experiencing regular panic attacks, some triggered by reminders of her traumatic experiences, but also some out of the blue. She also started to wake in the night panicking following trauma-related nightmares, which would be accompanied by a feeling of utter terror. Similarly, enclosed spaces, such as public transport, lifts, and driving in tunnels, led to feeling trapped and would trigger a panic attack. Panics seemingly unrelated to the trauma would start with noticing a change in bodily sensations, such as her heart racing and a change in her breathing. These panic attacks were not accompanied by the same feeling of terror.

At assessment Susan scored 38 on the PTSD Diagnostic Scale (PDS; severe range), 22 on the Beck Depression Inventory (BDI; moderate range). Key panic-related beliefs were: I am going to suffocate (90%), I am going to faint (90%), and I will lose control/go crazy (80%). She was experiencing three or four panic attacks each week.

Susan's goals were to not have intrusive images, memories, and nightmares, and to be able to walk past butchers' shops and go to street markets without feeling sick. She also wanted to stop having panic attacks and to be able to travel on public transport. A long-term goal was to be able to resume her journalist work abroad. An overall goal was also to get back to 'the person she had been' prior to this experience.

Treatment session one

The first treatment session focused on education and normalising of PTSD symptoms, starting 'reclaiming her life', and working collaboratively towards a cognitive formulation.

Normalising

Susan believed that her frequent intrusions and flashbacks to the trauma were a sign that she was going crazy. She also believed that the flashbacks, intrusions, and her panic attacks meant that she was a weak person. Time was spent in the session explaining common reactions to traumatic events and the nature of PTSD symptoms. This included an explanation of the nature of the trauma memory that causes re-experiencing. She was also given an information leaflet at the end of the session, outlining common symptoms and difficulties related to PTSD, to further reinforce what had been covered in the session.

Reclaiming her life

In the first, and each subsequent, session there was some discussion of how best to reclaim/rebuild her life, including homework plans. The aim was to keep a focus on the overall goals of therapy, by reconnecting with the person she was before the trauma. This would increase her activity levels, hopefully improving mood, but also help to put the traumatic event in context and more clearly in the past, rather than feeling it was ever-present.

Cognitive formulation

As the initial trauma was the onset of Susan's difficulties and trauma-related triggers caused panic attacks, we began with conceptualising the PTSD symptoms. Susan described events in detail and chronologically, and problematic appraisals were elicited.

When Susan first came across the mass grave, she experienced a sense of derealization; the surroundings seemed silent with very clear pictures but no sound. Her main emotions were of horror and disbelief. She also felt sick and detached. There was a dreadful smell in the air, putrid and sweet, with flies everywhere. Many bodies had been burned and limbs and body parts were scattered on the ground. In addition to the disbelief, Susan thought about her role and responsibilities as a journalist, and that she needed to take pictures and gather information. While local people were crying and being sick, she felt numb, derealized, and detached. She worried she was losing touch with reality and going mad. This was also the main feeling in her current intrusions. She thought 'what kind of person have I become to have lost touch with humanity'. She described the horror destroying her faith in people. She had been to many war-torn countries, but this was beyond the 'conventions of war'.

A different set of problematic beliefs were elicited from the traumatic night spent in the tent. As night descended, Susan had become aware of the sheer number of rats everywhere. She could hear them scurrying around the tent, sounding like hundreds of them. She worried they would bite through the tent, bite her, and she would contract cholera. She also feared running out of water and that they would die of dehydration. As night continued, gunfire started that seemed to get nearer and nearer to where they were camping. She could hear gunmen in the compound and the sound of twigs cracking nearby. Gunfire was spraying intermittently and randomly around them. She now felt extremely vulnerable, terrified, and her heart was racing. She felt paralysed with fear and unable to call out to her colleagues, so was unaware of their circumstances. She decided to lie as flat as possible so stray bullets would not hit her, fearing that they were all going to die. She also thought the gunfire was coming from the same group that had carried out the massacre and had images from the massacre, including the putrid smell, making her feel sick.

She also described feeling guilty. She said she had persuaded her colleagues to go to the site of the massacre on a tip-off. She now thought 'I'm naive, I'm irresponsible. We're all going to die and it will be my fault.' She had also held the belief that she could always talk herself out of a tricky situation, but here she felt out of control, out of her depth, small, defenceless, and 'surrounded by hell'.

Problematic appraisals

From this initial exploration of the trauma, the following worst moments and related appraisals were identified. While witnessing the scene of the massacre, she thought that terrible things had happened there and that she had 'lost touch with humanity'. This was associated with a feeling of disbelief, that she was 'going crazy', feelings of horror and detachment, that she was 'out of control', and associated feelings of fear and nausea. While in the tent, she thought that she was 'going to be bitten by rats and contract cholera' and felt vulnerable and terrified, and that she would be 'shot with a stray bullet and would die'. She felt afraid, that it was all her fault, and felt guilty.

Disorganized trauma memory

The relatively unprocessed nature of her traumatic memories served to maintain her current sense of threat and hence PTSD symptoms (Ehlers & Clark, 2000). Susan's trauma was long in duration. She had never spoken about it in detail to anyone or gone through the sequence of events in her own mind. Whenever parts of the memory popped into her mind, her key strategy had been to push them away, partly driven by her belief that she was going crazy. As such, there were gaps in her memory and fragments that did not 'tie together'.

Maintaining strategies

A key strategy employed by Susan was one of avoidance. She avoided talking about the traumatic event, had been unable to read the article she wrote at the time, and avoided thinking about it. If thoughts or memories popped into her mind, she would push them away. She avoided butchers' shops, watching or reading the news, and walking through street markets. She also avoided her colleagues who had also experienced this event. When out, she was hyper-vigilant, always sat near exits for an easy escape, and at night she kept her bedroom door open. She also always kept her trainers on at home so that she was ready to run at the first sign of danger. A pictorial representation of the formulation is shown in Figure 10.1.

Addressing images of the massacre

As the traumatic event was lengthy, attempting to 'relive' the entire account in one session would have been problematic. We divided the trauma into two sections, 'the massacre' and 'the tent', as there were different themes in each part, and addressed each in turn. Work on the trauma memory was closely interwoven with work on the problematic appraisals and meanings (e.g., eliciting meaning of worst moments, exploring images, sensations, and corresponding emotions, and bodily reactions linked to the worst moments; Ehlers et al., 2005).

As Susan's most frequent and distressing intrusive image was a scene from the massacre, we explored this image first. This image also triggered panic attacks, and encapsulated key meanings for her. The image was of a pit filled with bodies, limbs, charred and disembodied. Susan was worried that if she focused on the image and described it, she would have a panic attack and lose control. Losing control for her meant at worst she would completely lose touch with reality, go mad, and end up in hospital. She believed this 90%. She also believed that she might 'fall into' the image and get trapped in it, and then it would never end. She believed this 80%.

Describing the image was set up as a behavioural experiment to test out these specific predictions. Susan started by describing the image like a painting, with very bright colours, but out of focus. She was gradually able to notice new details, such as a child's shoe. She then agreed to draw the image

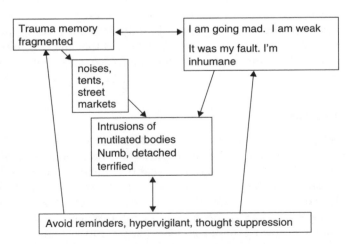

Figure 10.1 Susan's PTSD conceptualization (Ehlers & Clark, 2000).

on a whiteboard in the therapy room. During this she reported feeling distressed, numb, disoriented, and that she could smell the putrid sweet smell, and hear the buzzing of flies. However, eventually she was able to piece the scene together as a whole.

She learnt that even when bringing the image consciously into her mind, she did not lose control, go mad, run out of the room, 'fall into the image' and get trapped in it, or end up in hospital. She now rated these beliefs at 30%. She had still experienced some sense of losing control and rated this now as 30%. At the end of the session, she said 'I have spent too much time pushing it away, if I stay with it, it doesn't get worse and out of control and it is easier to face it'. For homework she agreed to listen to the tape of the session and also to practise bringing the image into focus at home. She also volunteered to start reading newspapers again.

Discriminating stimuli that triggered memories of the massacre

She returned the following week reporting that overall the image had been less distressing, less vivid, less threatening, and that she felt less afraid of it. She agreed to work further on the image in the session, and once again brought it to mind, described it in detail, and drew it on the whiteboard. She had similar beliefs that she might lose control and go mad (30%). When describing the image she still experienced a sense of disorientation and numbness, and could smell the putrid smell and hear the flies. At this point we introduced the technique of *stimulus discrimination of sensory triggers* (Ehlers et al., 2005). The numbness, disorientation, and smell made her feel that the events were happening again right now and that she was 'back in the trauma memory', and she needed to discriminate that it was in fact a memory and not the present moment. While keeping the image in mind, she brought into her attention stimuli in the therapy room, the noise of the room and traffic outside, and reminded herself that this was simply an image of a traumatic memory and not actually happening now. We also sprayed her favourite perfume in the session to show that the putrid smell is 'in the memory' and not really present now. Once again she did not lose control, go mad, or run out of the room, and these beliefs now reduced to 10%.

'I'm inhumane'

While she reported finding such discrimination helpful, she became distressed and said 'I was inhumane, I felt nothing, I was removed and detached whilst others were crying and sick'. She believed that at the time there was something wrong with her reaction and therefore something inherently wrong with her as a person. She believed this 75%. The rest of the session was spent discussing this belief and finding alternative evidence.

Evidence for:

- I felt nothing. I was numb, detached, disorientated.
- I was inhumane.
- Others were crying, others were sick, and I felt nothing.

Evidence against:

- No one knows how anyone might react in the face of such a horrific scene, it was my way of coping.
- Although a lot of people were crying and sick, not everyone was.
- The local people were crying for friends and family.
- I am a journalist and have seen similar scenes before and have been trained to be professional in these situations. I needed to maintain some sense of detachment to log information to write the article.
- My father shouted at us a lot as children and I tend to detach and disengage in difficult situations.
- Although I felt nothing at the time, I have suffered since then and felt sick and upset regularly.
- The fact I chose these places to work in the first place shows my humanity, and I want to go back to see what good work has been done to help recovery.

At the end of this discussion she rated 'I am inhumane and there is something inherently wrong with me as a person' at 20%.

Behavioural experiments

Subsequent sessions involved allocating some time to addressing the massacre to monitor frequency of intrusions and degree of conviction in associated beliefs. Susan also undertook behavioural experiments, practising stimulus discrimination if the memories came to mind, such as walking past butchers' shops and walking through street markets. She also read a charity brochure at home with pictures from the country in which the trauma occurred. We also went together in session to an anatomical museum exhibition in which some body parts triggered intrusions and Susan further used stimulus discrimination strategies. During the course of therapy she had to write an article on atrocities in another country, which she managed without difficulty. She also went on holiday with a friend to another part of Africa, where she reported seeing a different side to Africa from previous assignments she had had there.

Addressing the tent experience

Susan described ('relived') her experience in detail with eyes closed in the first person present tense. Susan rated her anxiety at 80%, the memory at 90%

vivid, and that it was as if it was happening again right now 80% ('nowness'). She had a number of 'hotspots' during the course of the night (see Table 10.1). She agreed to listen to the tape as homework, record her distress, vividness, and nowness, and write down any new information that came to light. Susan found listening to the tape distressing, although slightly less so than in session. It had felt less 'now' and more 'like a memory'. Susan also remembered further details. At the end, UN soldiers had intervened, the militia had withdrawn, and the next day the UN enabled them to leave. This 'completed the scene' for her. In her memory she was stuck in the tent, surrounded by gunfire, about to die, whereas now she had not died, the UN had intervened, and she and the others had flown to safety.

Through discussion, we collaboratively identified important information that she knew now but that she was not aware of at the time, nor when re-experiencing the trauma memory (see Table 10.1).

Susan agreed to listen to the tape of the session again, and also to write a narrative including this new information within the account. At the next session we reviewed her narrative and she reported seeing the experience in a different context now. Susan described the events in a further reliving, also incorporating the new and updated information within the reliving, by bringing it to mind at the worst moments (Ehlers et al., 2005). The distress, vividness, and nowness were much reduced (30%) and she continued to bring the updating information to mind when she experienced intrusive memories.

Addressing panic attacks

At session nine, we focused specifically on treatment of Susan's panic attacks. From the work so far, she reported a reduction in the frequency and intensity of her unexpected panic attacks in the day, but she continued to experience them at night, and also in specific situations, such as on public transport. As Susan had clearly experienced her first panic in a tent at a music festival, with similar feelings and sensations as to the tent in the trauma, it was possible that by processing this traumatic memory it reduced the number of possible trauma-related triggers for her panic attacks.

We derived collaborative panic conceptualizations for a number of specific panic attacks, eliciting key misinterpretations of bodily sensations and maintaining strategies (Clark, 1986, 1996). An example is shown in Figure 10.2.

During a panic attack, Susan felt dizzy and had difficulty breathing and interpreted these sensations as signs that she was going to faint/collapse and suffocate. These two beliefs also fed into an overall belief that she would lose control. Work on her panic involved exploring these beliefs in detail, generating alternative, non-catastrophic interpretations by discussion and carrying out behavioural experiments to test out some of her anxious predictions (Clark, 1996).

Table 10.1 Susan's hotspots and 'updating information'

Situation	Thought/meaning	Emotions	Updating information: 'what I know now in reality'
As nightfall descends, rats scurrying around the tent	I am going to be bitten by rats and contract cholera.	Anxious	The rats didn't bite through the tent, they didn't bite me and I didn't contract cholera.
Intermittent gunshots	The shooting is near – I can't move – I can't move my arms there are gunmen in the grounds spraying bullets – I am a walking target. He could hit me – I will be shot with a stray bullet. We are all about to die. I'm not ready to die.	Terrified, helpless	There was nothing else I could do – If I had got up and moved around I could have been shot – I did the best thing. The bullets didn't hit me, I didn't die. My colleagues didn't die. The gunmen were chased off by the UN and we all escaped safely. We are all alive.
	It is my fault. I will be responsible for my colleagues' deaths – are they ok?	Nauseous/sick, out of control	This was no different from any other assignment – they didn't have to come. None of my colleagues died. They all left safely.
	We are running out of water. We'll die from dehydration.		We did get dehydrated but got supplies from the UN – we didn't die.
Images of massacre	We are going to end up the same.		They didn't attack us or hurt us, we are all alive and safe.

I'll suffocate (90%)

In a panic attack, Susan believed that her perceived breathing difficulties were a sign that she was running out of air (such as on the underground or in a tunnel) and that her throat was constricting. She believed that there was only so much air available in spaces such as lifts and tunnels, and that this could run out. She was also worried that her lungs could just shut down at night. The main evidence for these beliefs was her strong feelings at the time. We discussed the actual mechanism of the lungs and breathing, including what

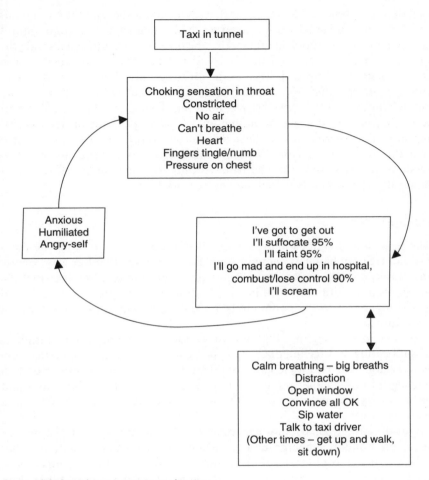

Figure 10.2 Susan's panic conceptualization.

happens when we are sleeping. We also discussed that airtight enclosed spaces actually are with gaps and cracks in walls and windows.

In-session behavioural experiments – I'll suffocate: First, Susan demonstrated how she breathed during a panic attack to prevent herself from suffocating. She focused on her breathing and also worked hard to take in more air, which then resulted in over-breathing. We both started to deliberately breathe in this way and both started to get sensations of finding it difficult to breathe. We then tried to hold our breath for as long as we could to see if we could deliberately run out of breath. Susan learned that the automatic reflex to breathe 'kicked in'.

Out-of-session behavioural experiments – I'll suffocate: We then went to the lift in the clinic and Susan rated that she believed she could run out of air in it and suffocate at 95%. First she went in alone and when the doors shut, I sprayed air freshener outside the door, which she was able to smell inside the lift in seconds. She realised that it could not be airtight. We then experimented with going up and down in the lift to test how long it would take to run out of air. After 20 minutes, Susan agreed that there was more than enough air in the lift for two people; however, she expressed doubts if the lift was full. She agreed to me 'rounding up' people to pack the lift to capacity, repeating the experiment to test whether she would run out of air. She learned that this was not the case. Work on this belief was carried out over two sessions. At the end of this she believed only 30% she could suffocate in a panic attack, but clearly we still had more work to do.

I'll faint (90%)

The sensation of suffocating often spiralled into a sensation of feeling dizzy and faint. Susan had never actually fainted but believed that this was because she always escaped or sat down at just the right moment. We discussed the mechanism of fainting, which involves a drop in blood pressure to the head and compared it to the pounding heart and raised blood pressure during a panic attack.

In-session experiment – I'll faint: In session we brought on the sensations of suffocating and feeling dizzy by hyperventilating and later spinning on a swivel chair. When Susan felt she would faint we stood up, and even stood on one leg, to test whether she would in fact faint. After these discussions and in-session experiments, her belief that she would faint in a panic attack had reduced to 40%.

Out-of-session behavioural experiments – I'll faint: Our next session was spent on London Underground travelling on busy trains and testing her beliefs that she would run out of air, suffocate, faint, and lose control. New safety-seeking behaviours were noticed when out, such as on the tube Susan kept her hands in her pockets, which she believed helped her stay in control; she also had a bottle of water that she frequently sipped from believing it helped her breathe. She agreed to get rid of her water and take her hands out of her pockets to more fully test whether she would in fact suffocate or lose control.

I'll lose control, go crazy (80%)

Susan worried that in a panic attack she would 'freak out', start shouting, run around madly, and at its worst go insane. We explored what this would consist of, what it would look like, how it would happen, and what kind of things do cause people to lose control in public and the differences between them and her.

In-session experiment – I'll lose control, go crazy: In session Susan tried to 'lose control/go crazy' and found that she could not make it happen. As this belief was also triggered by her main intrusive trauma image, the earlier work in therapy helped provide evidence against this belief. Susan did try to again induce feelings of unreality by deliberately bringing the image to mind and found that she still did not go crazy.

After the panic work, Susan came to the following conclusions.

- It is difficult to faint or pass out during a panic attack as my heart is pounding and the blood pressure rising.
- There is no need to focus on my breathing or try to regulate it – I know my lungs breathe on their own quite capably when I am asleep, and if I try to deliberately suffocate, I can't.
- I know I am not going crazy or mad. Even at its worst, I did not lose control and no one noticed.
- She also had a flight booked and had some anxious thoughts about being trapped on the plane but said – It doesn't matter that I can't get off. I have been trapped in a small room, trapped in my office at work, on the tube, and in my car in a tunnel and I did not lose control, suffocate, or go crazy.
- If I get the intrusive memory, I know I won't get trapped in it – it is just my memory.

Overarching beliefs

Susan had developed further problematic beliefs since the traumatic event. They occurred consistently in both the trauma and panic-focused work. Susan reported at various points in therapy that she felt weak and useless (initial belief rating 80%). This belief was identified when exploring the massacre, the tent overnight, and also in relation to her panic attacks. We discussed the evidence regarding this belief using a thought record.

Evidence for I'm weak and useless:

- I haven't got over it.
- I'm not tough enough – I'm too sensitive.
- My colleagues just carried on and were fine.
- I can't use the tubes, I don't like loud noises.
- I can't do the work I want to do, and often say no to offered assignments.
- I no longer see my friends or have hobbies or interests.

Evidence against the belief:

- I am getting over it.
- I now have fewer intrusions and panic attacks.

- I am not going crazy, but I was suffering from PTSD.
- My colleagues did not actually just carry on and be fine – thinking about it, the photographer said he had had enough and left – he had worked as a news photographer for 20 years, one of the aid workers turned to alcohol, another colleague's behaviour became erratic and he was sacked.
- Others were clearly as affected as I was.
- I am starting to use the tubes again.
- I am also starting to take on new assignments at work and can see the possibility in going back to some of the war-torn countries to report on the rehabilitation taking place.
- Not liking loud noises is understandable and related to my PTSD.

Following this Susan re-rated her belief that she was weak and useless at 20%. She continued to collect evidence against it during follow-up sessions.

A further belief discussed was that 'people are basically bad and happy to carry out evil tasks' (85% belief). We used a continuum to work on this idea with 'really good people' at one end and 'really bad/evil people' at the other end, and explored who would be categorised where along the continuum. The outcome of this discussion resulted in Susan deciding that actually the majority of people were in the centre of the continuum, with different hypotheses of what might make someone good or bad, or do good or bad deeds. She also came to the realization that those who had carried out the massacre were not necessarily in themselves evil. They would have been poor people, recruited as mercenaries, possibly enforced to enlist, and paid to fight and kill, probably based on propaganda and brain washing. She now believed 'people are basically bad and happy to carry out evil tasks' at 10%. She also reported that 'people have not changed – it is just that I am more aware of such events'.

Outcome

Treatment lasted 18 sessions with three monthly follow-up sessions. Sessions were an average of 90 minutes in duration. At the end of treatment, Susan reported much improvement and that she felt she was returning to the person she used to be. She had been able to watch and read news coverage of terrorist bombings. She was using underground trains and driving through tunnels daily. She had taken flights. She remained uncertain about resuming duties as a foreign correspondent but had taken on work abroad in areas where rehabilitation work was taking place.

At the end of treatment, Susan scored 6 on the PDS (minimal range), and 2 on the BDI (minimal range). Her belief ratings were 'I am going to suffocate' 10%, 'I am going to faint' 0%, and 'I will lose control/go crazy' 0%. These scores were all maintained at 3-month follow-up. Her panic attacks had reduced to a single limited symptom attack each month.

DISCUSSION

The case example demonstrated the effective treatment of someone experiencing trauma and panic symptoms. When presented with two equally troublesome problems, key questions are where to begin, how to formulate, where do the symptoms overlap/differ, and in particular where to start in treatment? We started with the trauma because Susan's intrusions were so distressing and also among the triggers for panic attacks. However, there is no doubt that her panic attacks were of equal severity and caused equal distress, and that it was the panic attacks that had led her to seek treatment. We do not know what might have happened had we started therapy focusing on panic first, but this is a key point for future research. There are occasions when clients are unwilling to engage in any work on their trauma memory because of panic fears, such as they might faint or have a heart attack while describing events. Had this been more strongly the case for Susan, we would have started treatment with a specific focus on these beliefs and her panic attacks. That said, although the strategies are described sequentially, clearly the PTSD and panic symptoms were interconnected and themes addressed will affect both sets of problems. In any treatment this can be guided by the individual formulation and through discussion with the client.

Wald and Taylor (2008) demonstrated people with PTSD experienced marked anxiety symptoms and trauma memories during interoceptive exposure (IE) exercises, and that IE reduces PTSD symptoms. The type of IE exercises used in this study were those used in treating panic disorder, such as jogging on the spot, spinning, and hyperventilation. This study indicates the interrelationship between the processes, symptoms, and effective treatment of these two disorders. It is possible that IE targets panic misinterpretation of symptoms and memory processing/stimulus discrimination in PTSD concurrently. Susan's case incorporated some separate treatment strategies for PTSD and panic, and some, like IE, that targeted both at the same time. Future research could focus on refining and improving this.

The onset of Susan's panic attacks is of interest. Staying in a tent at a crowded music festival where there were a lot of people and noise was clearly enough of a matching cue to trigger similar feelings from her experience when trapped in the tent during the trauma. Although this was a one-off incident, it was from here that she went on to develop panic attacks, both in relation to trauma stimuli and also out of the blue. This reinforces the importance of exploring the onset of panic and the first panic attack in particular.

Diagnosis is a further point of discussion. Susan did report experiencing panic attacks out of the blue. She also had related avoidance and fear of future panic attacks, hence meeting diagnostic criteria for panic disorder with mild agoraphobia. However, it could be that her panics were not in fact out of the blue but triggered by covert trauma stimuli, in line with the theory of perceptual priming (Ehlers & Clark, 2000) in which even low-level stimuli that are associated with the traumatic event can trigger trauma memories. So, whilst Susan experienced panic attacks travelling on tubes, in tunnels, and in her sleep as out of the blue because of the different context, it could be low-level trauma stimuli such as the sensation of breathlessness or memories she was not aware of from the tent were in fact triggering the attacks. However, whilst work on trauma memories alone did reduce the frequency and intensity of her panic attacks to a degree, these still required further panic-focused interventions.

ACKNOWLEDGEMENT

I would like to thank Susan for giving her consent for this chapter and acknowledge the work of Anke Ehlers and David Clark.

REFERENCES

Bryant, R.A., & Panasetis, P. (2001). Panic symptoms during trauma and acute stress disorder. *Behaviour Research and Therapy*, *39*, 961–969.

Clark, D.M. (1986). A cognitive approach to panic. *Behaviour Research and Therapy*, *24*, 461–470.

Clark, D.M. (1996). Panic disorder: From theory to therapy. In P.M. Salkovskis (Ed.), *Frontiers of cognitive therapy*. New York: Guilford Press.

Ehlers, A., & Clark, D.M. (2000). A cognitive model of posttraumatic stress disorder. *Behaviour Research and Therapy*, *38*, 319–345.

Ehlers, A., Clark, D.M., Hackmann, A., McManus, F., & Fennell, M. (2005). Cognitive therapy for PTSD: Development and evaluation. *Behaviour Research and Therapy*, *43*, 413–431.

Falsetti, S.A., & Resnick, H.S. (1997). Frequency and severity of panic attack symptoms in a treatment seeking sample of trauma victims. *Journal of Traumatic Stress*, *10*, 683–689.

Falsetti, S.A., & Resnick, H.S. (2000). Cognitive behaviour treatment of PTSD with co-morbid panic attacks. *Journal of Contemporary Psychotherapy*, *30*, 163–179.

Falsetti, S.A., Resnick, H.S., & Davis, J.L. (2008). Multiple channel exposure therapy for women with PTSD and co-morbid panic attacks. *Cognitive Behaviour Therapy*, *37*, 117–130.

Hinton, D.E., Hoffmann, S.G., Pitman, R.K., Pollack, M.H., & Barlow, D.H. (2008). The panic attack-posttraumatic stress disorder model: Applicability to orthostatic panic attacks among Cambodian refugees. *Cognitive Behaviour Therapy*, *37*, 101–116.

Kessler, R.C., Sonnega, A., Bromet, E., Hughes, M., & Nelson, C.B. (1995). Posttraumatic stress disorder in the National Comorbidity Survey. *Archives of General Psychiatry*, *52*, 1048–1060.

Vujanovic, A.A., Zvolensky, M.J., & Bernstein, A. (2008). Incremental associations between facets of anxiety sensitivity and posttraumatic stress and panic symptoms among trauma-exposed adults. *Cognitive Behaviour Therapy*, *37*, 76–89.

Wald, J., & Taylor, S. (2008). Responses to interoceptive exposure in people with PTSD: A preliminary analysis of induced anxiety reactions and trauma memories and their relationship to anxiety sensitivity and PTSD symptom severity. *Cognitive Behaviour Therapy*, *37*, 90–100.

Cognitive therapy for post-traumatic stress disorder and obsessive-compulsive disorder

Blake Stobie

Many people will experience traumatic life events without developing post-traumatic stress disorder (PTSD), and the same is true for obsessive-compulsive disorder (OCD). However, clinicians and researchers have noted an association between trauma and the onset and maintenance of OCD. Trauma may contribute to the development of OCD, or comorbid OCD and PTSD (Gershuny et al., 2002), and the presence of traumatic life events is often associated with increased OCD symptom severity (Cromer, Schmidt, & Murphy, 2007). Stress can increase both the occurrence of triggering intrusive thoughts and relapse rates in OCD (de Silva & Marks, 1999), and whilst the content of obsessions and compulsions may be linked in an obvious way to the nature of the trauma (for example, people who check doors following an assault), this will not necessarily be the case. Similarly, the development of compulsions following a trauma can not necessarily be predicted by premorbid tendencies (de Silva & Marks, 1999).

The client in the case example that follows had mild premorbid tendencies towards perfectionism that had not interfered with her life. She developed PTSD after a trauma, followed by OCD. The case discussion focuses on techniques to highlight similarities in the treatment of both problems where they co-occur. The chapter concludes with a discussion of common traumas and their potential impact on the development and maintenance of obsessional problems.

CASE EXAMPLE

Claire is a woman in her 30s who worked as a carer for adults with learning disabilities. She was assaulted by a client in an unprovoked attack, in which she was knocked unconscious. Following her discharge from hospital for treatment of the injuries she sustained in the attack she was unable to return to work. She developed PTSD, and became progressively housebound. Claire was hypervigilant on leaving her home. She startled easily, and was not able to tolerate strangers walking behind her. Claire suffered from nightmares and flashbacks relating to the assault. Her sleep patterns became extremely disrupted, to the point that she would mostly be asleep during the day and awake at night.

Claire lives with her daughter Camilla, in her late teens, who is very supportive of her. Camilla stopped working in order to look after her mother. Nearly a year after the trauma she managed to persuade her mother to seek treatment. Fortunately the clinic was within walking distance of their home, and Camilla attended the first few sessions with her mother.

At assessment, Claire stated that she did not have any problems other than the PTSD, but Camilla added that following the trauma and the onset of the PTSD, her mother had developed a number of compulsions. These predominantly took the form of washing (particularly dishes etc. in the kitchen), spending an excessive amount of time hand washing and showering each day, and tidying items in the flat. Camilla stated that the compulsions took several hours per day, and were also contributing to her mother's disrupted sleep patterns, as she felt unable to go to sleep until the flat was in order. Claire met diagnostic criteria for PTSD and OCD. Prior to the trauma she had reportedly been somewhat perfectionistic. However, both Claire and Camilla reported that this had not interfered with her life prior to the trauma. At the start of the sessions she scored 36 on the PTSD Diagnostic Scale (PDS; 'severe'); 28 on the Beck Depression Inventory (BDI; 'moderate'); 30 on the Beck Anxiety Inventory (BAI; 'severe'); and a total of 99 on Distress ratings on the Obsessive Compulsive Inventory (OCI).

Claire also admitted that she had started to experience intrusive thoughts of harming others, for example of pushing strangers onto a train track, or stabbing her daughter with a knife. She was extremely distressed whenever she experienced these obsessional thoughts. She would try to suppress the thoughts from entering her mind, was avoiding holding sharp implements when near other people, and had stopped travelling on public transport other than buses. If the thoughts were particularly bad she would pray for strength, and would tense her body and try to 'take control' of her mind. At times when she wasn't experiencing the thoughts she would sometimes test herself, for example, by trying to remember events, or doing mental arithmetic, in an attempt to establish whether her mind was working properly. She sometimes sought reassurance from Camilla that she hadn't done anything wrong. She reported feeling constantly as if 'something about me isn't right', and she stated that she was constantly checking herself to determine whether this feeling of not being right had changed.

The OCD was formulated as a separate but related problem requiring treatment in its own right. The decision was made to treat the PTSD first, because the symptoms pre-dated the compulsive symptoms and Claire regarded them as more problematic than the compulsions. This suggested sequence of treatment was discussed and agreed with Claire.

Treatment for PTSD

There was an exclusive focus on PTSD for the first eight sessions. The cognitive therapy for PTSD included normalization, reliving, identifying and updating hotspots, and 'reclaiming one's life' (Ehlers & Clark, 2000; Ehlers et al., 2005). The main cognitive themes addressed were the fear of dying experienced during the assault and anger at the behaviour of her unsupportive employers. Claire's daughter Camilla was also present for three of these sessions, and was instrumental in implementing a programme to assist her mother in establishing some new routines, such as taking her out on social events and arranging to see friends and family again. By this point Claire was starting to become much more comfortable with going out; the frequency and distress of the flashbacks had diminished substantially. At session eight she scored 14 on the PDS (representing a shift from the 'severe' to the 'moderate range').

However, she was still spending several hours a day on compulsive rituals. She also felt unable to go to sleep until she had completed her compulsive cleaning of the kitchen. The intrusive thoughts of causing harm to others were also causing her significant distress, and these had increased as she spent more time with her daughter, who was the main focus of many of these concerns. Consequently, from this point, the OCD and remaining PTSD symptoms were addressed concurrently.

Treatment for OCD in the context of PTSD

Two formulations were completed based on the main obsessions of tidying and causing harm (Salkovskis, Forrester, Richards, & Morrison, 1998). The examples were discussed individually but are presented alongside each other here for comparison.

Claire described a recent instance in which she had been washing up in the kitchen. Camilla had come into the kitchen to urge her to finish. At this point Claire had experienced a sudden intrusive image of herself stabbing Camilla with one of the knives she was washing up. Intrusive images, urges, thoughts, or doubts such as these usually act as the trigger for obsessional episodes. Claire could not recall having experienced intrusions such as this in the past. The meaning (threat appraisal) which she attached to this thought at the time was 'the fact I've had this terrible image means I'm going crazy and could act on it and harm my daughter'. She believed this 40% at the time of the intrusion, and 10% when recounting the event.

Claire found it more difficult to recall a specific example of the tidying problem as this was occurring in a fairly uniform way on a daily basis, and hence the initial formulation was based on the previous night's cleaning and tidying of the kitchen, which had taken her several hours. Claire was unable to identify the intrusive thoughts that had preceded the compulsions. Instead she described the trigger as having felt 'out of control'. On some occasions this feeling was triggered by physical symptoms of anxiety, e.g., derealization and dizziness, and sometimes by depressive thoughts such as 'I'll never get over this'. The previous day Claire had not managed to go out all day and had been very anxious and upset. The meaning for Claire was, 'If I don't do something [i.e., washing] to regain control, I'll never get better [belief rating 70%] or go mad [belief rating 40%]'.

We discussed how both examples took place in the kitchen, and that the assault had also occurred in a kitchen. Although Claire had not previously made this connection, it seemed likely that stimuli in her kitchen were triggering reminders of the trauma, leading to an increased sense of threat. However, not all of Claire's obsessions and compulsions were occurring in the kitchen. The two different compulsions were being driven by similar threat appraisals: intrusive thoughts, 'feeling wrong', and PTSD symptoms and their consequences were causing Claire to believe that she was going crazy, and could cause harm unless she managed to increase her control of her mind and her environment. Linked to this were two key beliefs: (a) that the washing compulsions were making Claire feel more in control, and (b) that she would go mad if she didn't manage to reduce her anxiety and symptoms. The second belief had already been discussed earlier in the sessions during psychoeducation, normalizing symptomatology, and during the updating of the trauma narrative, but clearly further work was required with this belief given its central role in the maintenance of the compulsive symptomatology.

We drew out helpful and explicit parallels between the previously discussed maintenance factors for the PTSD and those maintaining her OCD (see Table 11.1).

Treatment approaches

Theory A/Theory B

This technique was used to present and contrast two opposing explanations of the OCD problem: first theory A, 'The problem is I'm going to lose control and I could harm somebody'; and then theory B, 'The problem is a worry problem. Although I may feel like I'm losing control sometimes, this is normal given what I've been through. I don't need to try to keep control as it's there even when it feels like it isn't'. We examined the evidence for each theory in turn subjecting it to rigid 'admissibility criteria' – would each piece of evidence stand up in a court of law? This led to some of the evidence supporting theory A being discounted, and some being tested further (see Table 11.2). The process highlighted important specific concerns. Claire admitted that she had sometimes fantasized about harming the man who had assaulted her. She was extremely ashamed of this, and she had taken this as evidence that she was capable of harming others.

After examining the evidence we considered what Claire would need to do

Table 11.1 Drawing links between PTSD and OCD responses

PTSD	OCD
Safety-seeking (trying to reduce threat): • walking close to walls • carrying keys in case of attack	Safety-seeking/neutralizing (trying to reduce threat): • tidying excessively • trying to control thoughts/my mind • testing myself • asking for reassurance • more generally, trying to get a sense of control or reduce feeling out of control
Avoidance: • of going out • lowers mood	Avoidance: • of untidy environments • sharp objects • public transport, especially train tracks where I could harm somebody • lowers mood
Rumination: • thinking about how I could have stopped the attack • thinking about how badly my employers treated me	Rumination: • worrying about the state of my home • worrying about my future and mental stability • worrying about harming others
These strategies are unhelpful because: • they make me unhappy • they make me believe I'm going to be attacked again • they stop me from living my life	These strategies are unhelpful because: • they make me doubt myself • they bring down my confidence • they make my fears seem more real/they stop me from finding out they're not true • they make me believe there's something wrong with me

if theory A were true, and what she would need to do if theory B were true. For Claire, as with many people with OCD, this presented an explanation for why the OCD persists. Responding to the obsessional problem using conflicting strategies, i.e., sometimes treating the problem as if theory A is true, and sometimes as if theory B is true, is sufficient to reduce confidence and maintain doubt, feeding the obsessional problem. Theory A/theory B also prefaced further goal-setting and behavioural experiments.

Further goal-setting

Claire was initially reluctant to acknowledge the extent of the OCD. Keeping a record of all of the rituals she was involved in carrying out, and discussing the issue openly with her daughter, was helpful in making her aware of how entrenched the problem had become. However, her expressed goals were

Table 11.2 Theory A/Theory B for Claire

Theory A: The problem is I'm going to lose control.	Theory B: The problem is a worry problem – although I may feel like I'm losing control sometimes, this is normal given what I've been through – the control is there even when it feels like it isn't.
Evidence supporting Theory A: • My heart races sometimes and I feel unreal and 'spacey' • I get really angry sometimes • I feel like I've 'lost it' since the attack	Evidence supporting Theory B: • BUT: this is normal when people feel anxious: I have felt like this before when I've been anxious before (e.g. on a roller coaster) and it didn't bother me then. • BUT: this is normal after what I've been through • BUT: again, people often feel like this after a trauma. A lot of this is because I'm worrying too much. These feelings are growing less all the time as my confidence increases. • I've never actually lost control (though this may be because I've managed to keep control) – behavioural experiment. • People don't lose control just in one room – the fact this feeling happens to me mainly in the kitchen (where I was attacked) suggests it is a worry problem (and so on).
What do I need to do if Theory A is true? • Try to regain control/make sure I don't lose control • Avoid going out	What do I need to do if Theory B is true? • Worry less • Go out more • Relax control etc.

initially focused on trying to do the same amount of cleaning (but in a shorter space of time), and trying to get rid of the distressing intrusions – i.e., she wanted to use the therapy sessions to become more efficient at doing her rituals! Following theory A/theory B, some time was spent with Claire agreeing a list of goals aimed at dropping her compulsions, safety-seeking behaviours and avoidances, and increasing her quality of life (i.e., acting as if theory B is true).

Stimulus discrimination

Claire's compulsions were sometimes triggered by intrusive thoughts and sometimes triggered by her interpretations of her emotional or physiological states. As much of the time spent on compulsions was being spent in the kitchen, and the assault had also taken place in a kitchen, stimulus discrimination was used to differentiate the two environments. The similarities and differences between the two kitchens were discussed extensively. This helped Claire to make sense of why she felt most at risk in her own kitchen. Then she deliberately triggered the memory of the assault whilst in her kitchen, focusing on what was different in the present (e.g., the kitchens are different in these ways . . .). Addressing the clearly overlapping PTSD and OCD symptomatology in this way reduced her sense of threat and hence the need for the compulsions. This also added further evidence for theory B: people don't lose control in specific rooms of the house, but it makes sense why you would worry more about losing control in a room that reminds you of a place where you felt you did not have much control.

Behavioural experiments

Claire acknowledged that the rituals may have been undermining her confidence in herself, decreasing her sense of control, and increasing her belief that she might be going crazy. However, this represented an intellectual knowledge rather than a firmly held conviction. Camilla was active in assisting her mother in setting up and executing some of the experiments aimed at testing out these ideas. Claire was encouraged to devise and carry out behavioural experiments, to test and gather evidence relating to theory A and B rather than to discover whether dropping the rituals would make her less anxious (in fact, several of the experiments predicted and required a heightening of anxiety).

Claire stated that the confidence to tolerate OCD-focused experiments came from the success of an earlier PTSD-focused experiment, in which she had allowed her nieces to hug her around the neck (this had been extremely difficult as she had been strangled during the assault). For example, she encouraged Camilla to have friends over for a meal and allowed her to wash up the following day. Previously she could not have left the washing up for more than five minutes, and would have had to do the washing up herself rather than allowing anyone else to do this. From this experiment she learned that, contrary to her predictions, her sense of control increased when she did not respond to the urge to wash up, and the number of intrusive thoughts, associated difficulty in concentrating, and sense of discomfort all increased initially but then rapidly dissipated. Claire also learnt that Camilla could be relied on to do tasks such as washing up, and this enabled her to relinquish responsibility for some of these tasks. Several of the experiments focused on testing the effects of deliberately inducing intrusive thoughts and then not responding to them, as opposed to attempting to suppress or otherwise respond to them.

One way of treating the cleaning compulsions would have been to use exposure with response prevention, and many of the homework tasks between sessions were focused on dropping compulsions such as cleaning, reassuring, praying, or ruminating. A strictly exposure with response prevention approach might have focused on the *effect on anxiety levels* of blocking rituals during exposure to feared stimuli. However, the focus of the sessions with Claire was on working cognitively with her fear of loss of control, which had been highlighted in her case formulation and theory A/theory B. Accordingly, what Claire discovered about rituals in her homework and behavioural experiments was always related back to their effects on her *sense of loss of control*, rather than to her *anxiety* levels. Dropping some rituals would make Claire more anxious (initially), whereas dropping others would make her less anxious. Irrespective of the changing anxiety levels, the therapy tasks were aimed at discovering the effects of safety-seeking behaviours on Claire's sense of control.

Acting 'anti-obsessionally'

A 'zero tolerance' policy towards compulsions is most likely to lead to stable improvements. If clients aim to reduce the time spent on their rituals rather than discontinuing them, the likelihood of relapse is far greater. As Claire gained increasing confidence through carrying out behavioural experiments and dropping rituals, she was encouraged to consider three different strategies dealing with each example of the obsessional problem that occurred: (a) the obsessional response – doing what the obsessional problem wanted her to do, i.e., doing all of the washing, cleaning, and checking rituals etc.; (b) the non-obsessional response, not doing the rituals and carrying on with whatever she was doing as she would have done prior to the onset of the problem; and (c) the anti-obsessional response, doing the opposite of the rituals, such as deliberately making a mess or not washing up all weekend, holding a sharp knife and deliberately thinking about stabbing Camilla with it. The behavioural experiments in which Claire acted in anti-obsessional manner were the most difficult but led to the greatest belief change and improvement.

Addressing worry and rumination

Worry and rumination were highlighted as common factors in Claire's PTSD, OCD, and depressive symptomatology. In addition to ruminating about the trauma and how she had been treated by her employers, Claire reported worrying compulsively about her mental health. She was also spending a significant amount of time each day planning the cleaning of her home in her head, and that these thoughts would sometimes occupy her mind even when she was out. Claire was encouraged to test out the effects of not engaging with the intrusive doubts or thoughts. Mental activity focused on past or future (hypothetical) events was likely to be unhelpful, and Claire was urged to try to live in the present and starve the unwanted thoughts of attention, without deliberately distracting herself, reassuring herself, or trying to suppress the thoughts. The analogy of a family member who arrives uninvited at a party was helpful. Claire was quick to point out that she would not try to turn the unwanted family member away (as this would cause too many problems), but would not spend the rest of the afternoon talking with them. She would leave them sitting in a chair until they got bored and left. Similarly, trying to stop the thoughts from entering her head would be an impossible task, but this didn't mean she had to engage with them.

Claire was guided to identify the beliefs 'I can't stop myself from worrying – it just happens', 'Worry is problem-solving', 'Worry shows that I care', and 'If I worry too much it will be bad for my mental health'. These conflicting beliefs were contrasted with each other. It was discussed that worry cannot be both automatic but also something that is done deliberately in an attempt to problem-solve. It was suggested to Claire that her beliefs about worry were causing her to try to improve her situation by thinking her way out of it. However, this was an impossible task, and was reinforcing her belief that she was in danger of losing control, was lowering her mood, and was making it difficult to concentrate.

Reassurance-seeking

Whereas PTSD treatment is often focused on helping clients to realize that they are not currently at risk, or that they are significantly overestimating their current risk in many instances, OCD treatment may emphasize this less, or not at all. Instead the objective of therapy is often to help clients to accept that things might go wrong, but this doesn't mean they now have a responsibility to act. Clients with OCD are often desperate to be reassured that they are not going to act on their intrusions, or that no harm is going to befall them or the people close to them. It is thus very easy for therapists to fall into the trap of repeatedly providing reassurance, which can then feed back into the client's threat appraisal and rumination. Obviously clients initially need to be provided with unambiguous, clear information (for example, that they are not going crazy). Once this has been thoroughly discussed, however, further discussion runs the risk of shifting from helpful assurance into unhelpful reassurance. We contracted that it was Claire's responsibility not to ask Camilla for reassurance in the first instance. However, if she did ask, Camilla was requested to not answer her.

Outcome

Claire received 16 weekly therapy sessions, plus three follow-up sessions at monthly intervals. Most of the work on the PTSD was done in the first eight sessions, with further 'reclaiming life' work and a site visit done in conjunction with the OCD treatment in sessions 9–16. By the end of the sessions she had stopped experiencing flashbacks and nightmares, she was no longer hypervigilant, she was socializing and going out much more, and her rumination about the attack had decreased substantially. At 3-month follow-up, the amount of time which she was spending on overt and covert compulsions was estimated at approximately 30 minutes each day, and was not interfering significantly with her life. Claire was able to let her daughter cook and wash up, and they had divided a roster for allocating chores, which previously she would not have trusted Camilla to do. She was experiencing significantly less intrusive thoughts of causing harm, but most importantly, was not responding to the thoughts or distressed by them when they did occur. She was able to use sharp implements, and travel on public transport. At the end of the sessions she scored 6 on the PDS ('mild'), 19 on the BDI ('mild'), 6 on the BAI ('minimal level of anxiety') and a total of 21 for the Distress ratings on the OCI.

SUMMARY OF POINTS ARISING FROM CASE EXAMPLE

Several points from Claire's case may be helpful to consider when treating comorbid PTSD and OCD:

- Claire sought help for PTSD, not OCD, and it was only because of feedback from her daughter and a detailed assessment that both problems were detected. It can be easy to neglect to assess for comorbidity when attempting to treat an obvious trauma. Asking clients at assessment about the amount of time they spent checking and washing things prior to the trauma, and whether this has increased, can be helpful. A more general question about whether they feel compelled to carry out any other physical or mental actions a set number of times can be useful for detecting other compulsions such as superstitious compulsions, hoarding, or praying. If uncertain, clinicians may wish to request their clients to complete an Obsessive Compulsive Inventory, which they can then use as the basis of further discussion.
- When clients with OCD and PTSD symptoms report 'unpleasant thoughts' or intrusions in assessment inventories, it is important to ascertain the content of these thoughts. It is common for the content of obsessional intrusions to be meaningfully linked to the precipitating trauma.
- Formulating how comorbid or interconnected problems overlap or contribute to each other should always be done from the outset, to determine the optimal point of initial intervention. Drawing comparisons between safety-seeking behaviours and other processes across disorders can be helpful in assisting clients to generalize findings from one problem to another.

- Contrasting the threat appraisal with a less threatening appraisal of the triggering intrusions using the theory A/theory B approach is a helpful way of contrasting strategies for dealing with obsessional problems. Approaches that encourage 'anti-' rather than 'non-' obsessional behaviour should always be encouraged. Theory A/theory B can also form the basis for behavioural experiments and reclaiming life work in PTSD. It enables clients with OCD and PTSD to recognize the similarities underpinning the work in identifying threat appraisals and testing out less-threatening alternative explanations.
- Worry and rumination are common to both OCD and PTSD, and can be treated using similar techniques.
- Emotional reasoning (e.g., 'I'm feeling anxious therefore there must be something to be anxious about') and needing to 'feel right' are common to both PTSD and OCD, and in these instances require psychoeducation, discussion, and testing with behavioural experiments when appropriate.
- Care should be taken by therapists to not become mired in reassurance-seeking and provision during the sessions.

DISCUSSION

The PTSD and OCD in the case example above followed an assault, and an association was forged between the type of trauma experienced and the obsessional worry, i.e., people sometimes attack other people without provocation, and if I get angry I could do that too. In some cases, the type of trauma that clients experience will have implications for the development and treatment of OCD. Examples of common traumas/traumatic life events that can trigger the onset or exacerbation of OCD are discussed below. Differences between OCD and PTSD responses to these trauma types are also considered.

Parenthood

OCD and PTSD are both common post-partum disorders. When post-partum PTSD occurs, the stressful experience is usually pain, but the focus may also be loss of control and fear of death, whereas in OCD the content of the concerns will often focus on fears of harming the vulnerable child (Brockington, 2004). When a parent is struggling with lack of sleep and a change in lifestyle, these intrusions may be interpreted by the parent as evidence that they wish to act on their thoughts or are capable of doing so.

Sexual abuse

Gordon (2002) notes that recurrent, intrusive, anxiety-provoking sexual ideation is common to OCD and PTSD. In both instances the intrusions can impair sexual performance, and lead to guilt and shame, particularly when the intrusions accompany or produce sexual arousal. Suppression and avoidance of triggering cues are common to both problems.

However, whereas PTSD represents the memory of a past event, obsessions in (non-comorbid) OCD may represent hypothetical events, for example in people without a history of sexual abuse who regard intrusive sexual thoughts as abhorrent. In these instances the graphic and detailed sexual imagery in PTSD is likely to contrast with vague imagery or ideation in OCD.

This guideline may not hold for people with OCD who have been abused. True imagery in OCD sometimes overlaps with flashbacks of previous traumatic events, or images of traumatic events that may have contributed to the problem (de Silva & Marks, 1999). Clients who have been abused may experience intrusive images or thoughts based on the abuse that they experienced. They are also at risk of interpreting these images as evidence that they wish to abuse children themselves, and their history of abuse may be interpreted by them as indicating that they are capable of doing this (based on the argument that many abusers have been abused themselves). In these instances it may be helpful to draw this evidence out and then critically challenge it using the 'theory A/theory B' technique described above. Discussing these issues in this way will not reinforce these ideas, but will critically address in them in a way that clients may be unable to do if avoiding them. Responsibility pie charts can be useful, in apportioning responsibility to events, e.g., if somebody who was abused believes that they were responsible for the abuse. For clients with OCD and PTSD, additional interventions such as imagery modification or restructuring may be helpful techniques for addressing the 'real' intrusive images that some authors have reported are common in OCD (Speckens, Hackmann, Ehlers, & Cuthbert, 2007). Rachman (2007) provides a clear overview of intrusive images in OCD.

A further possible consequence of sexual abuse as a trauma is a felt sense of having been contaminated, and in some cases these feelings of mental pollution may lead to the development of washing compulsions. Fairbrother and Rachman (2004) found that the majority of a sample of 50 female victims of sexual assault reported feelings of mental pollution. The mental pollution scores correlated significantly with PTSD symptom severity, and deliberate recall of the assault resulted in stronger reported feelings of 'dirtiness' and the urge to wash than deliberate attention to a pleasant memory. Feelings of mental pollution are not particularly accessible to exposure with response prevention, and the beliefs underlying these feelings may need to be targeted specifically within treatment (Fairbrother & Rachman, 2004). Feelings of mental pollution may also occur in cases of OCD that are unrelated to sexual assault (Fairbrother & Rachman, 2004). Claire's increase in her hand washing following a violent assault may be an example of this.

Accidents or injuries

The belief that our thoughts can cause or prevent harm from occurring is a risk factor for the onset of OCD following a trauma, but may also represent an attempt to regain control in response to feeling out of control, particularly when a person has been traumatized by an accident. Magical thinking or thought–action fusion can occur in both OCD and PTSD (Rassin, Diepstraten, Merckelbach, & Muris, 2001). For example, a man referred for treatment of PTSD had been repairing a car tyre on the motorway as part of his job. The man had been asked by the owner of the car whether he had ever had any accidents, to which he had replied 'No, never'. Immediately after saying this he was struck and injured by a tyre that had become detached from a passing truck. In addition to PTSD, the man developed a number of compulsive rituals based on magical thinking, such as refusing to answer particular questions in case he 'jinxed' himself. Treatment consisted of a discussion of the mechanism and how this might work (e.g., 'why does it only work for negative outcomes?', 'can you think of another explanation for what happened to you?'), followed by an invitation to test this out on the therapist, followed by behavioural experiments to test out whether thinking something really can make it happen.

CONCLUSION

The discussion above suggests that, in some instances, OCD and PTSD symptoms may superficially appear similar whilst differing significantly. For example, both may present with sexual imagery, which for an individual with PTSD may be vivid flashbacks of an actual event, and for a different individual with OCD may be vague imagery of a feared event. In other instances, PTSD and OCD may be maintained by similar processes, such as rumination, magical thinking, or mental pollution. These similarities and differences highlight the need for idiosyncratic formulations that adequately explain the presenting problems and how they relate to one another. De Silva and Marks (1999) argue that a dynamic connection exists between OCD and PTSD, such that treating one problem is likely to impact positively on the other. It is hoped that using some of the techniques outlined in the case example above may assist therapists in highlighting to their clients the maintenance factors and treatment strategies common to both of these problems.

REFERENCES

Brockington, I. (2004). Postpartum psychiatric disorders. *Lancet*, *363*(9405), 303–310.
Cromer, K.R., Schmidt, N.B., & Murphy, D.L. (2007). An investigation of traumatic

life events and obsessive-compulsive disorder. *Behaviour Research and Therapy*, *45*(7), 1683–1691.

De Silva, P., & Marks, M. (1999). The role of traumatic experiences in the genesis of obsessive-compulsive disorder. *Behaviour Research and Therapy*, *37*(10), 941–951.

Ehlers, A., & Clark, D.M. (2000). A cognitive model of posttraumatic stress disorder. *Behaviour Research and Therapy*, *38*(4), 319–345.

Ehlers, A., Clark, D.M., Hackmann, A., McManus, F., & Fennell, M. (2005). Cognitive therapy for post-traumatic stress disorder: Development and evaluation. *Behaviour Research and Therapy*, *43*(4), 413–431.

Fairbrother, N., & Rachman, S. (2004). Feelings of mental pollution subsequent to sexual assault. *Behaviour Research and Therapy*, *42*(2), 173–189.

Gershuny, B.S., Baer, L., Jenike, M.A., Minichiello, W.E., & Wilhelm, S. (2002). Comorbid posttraumatic stress disorder: Impact on treatment outcome for obsessive-compulsive disorder. *American Journal of Psychiatry*, *159*(5), 852–854.

Gordon, W.M. (2002). Sexual obsessions and OCD. *Sexual and Relationship Therapy*, *17*(4), 343–354.

Rachman, S. (2007). Unwanted intrusive images in obsessive compulsive disorders. *Journal of Behavior Therapy and Experimental Psychiatry*, *38*(4), 402–410.

Rassin, E., Diepstraten, P., Merckelbach, H., & Muris, P. (2001). Thought–action fusion and thought suppression in obsessive-compulsive disorder. *Behaviour Research and Therapy*, *39*(7), 757–764.

Salkovskis, P.M., Forrester, E., Richards, H.C., & Morrison, N. (1998). *The devil is in the detail: Conceptualising and treating obsessional problems*. N. Tarrier (Ed.) *Cognitive Behaviour Therapy for Complex Cases*. Chichester: Wiley.

Speckens, A.E.M., Hackmann, A., Ehlers, A., & Cuthbert, B. (2007). Intrusive images and memories of earlier adverse events in patients with obsessive compulsive disorder. *Journal of Behavior Therapy and Experimental Psychiatry*, *38*(4), 411–422.

Chapter 12

Cognitive therapy and suicidality in post-traumatic stress disorder

And recent thoughts on flashbacks to trauma versus 'flashforwards' to suicide

Emily A. Holmes and Gillian Butler

EXPLORING THE LINKS BETWEEN POST-TRAUMATIC STRESS DISORDER AND SUICIDALITY

When working with people suffering from post-traumatic stress disorder (PTSD) it is important to take into account the possibility that they may consider, plan, or attempt suicide, as there is an increased likelihood that they will do so compared with the general population. Tarrier and Gregg (2004) found a significantly higher incidence of suicidal ideation, plans, and attempts relative to the general population in 94 patients with chronic PTSD. Oguendo et al. (2005, 2003) report that patients with PTSD are 14.9 times more likely than those without PTSD to attempt suicide, and they also found that, in the context of major depressive disorder, those with a comorbid diagnosis of PTSD are the most likely to have attempted suicide. However, the precise nature of the links between the experience of trauma and subsequent suicidality has not been explored in great detail, with little clinical guidance as to how to reduce risk.

There are few empirically supported treatments for suicidality (for a meta-analysis see Hawton et al., 1998). To date, those few treatments demonstrated to be beneficial include a cognitive therapy intervention (Berk, Henriques, Warman, Brown, & Beck, 2004; Brown et al., 2005); dialectical behaviour therapy for people with borderline personality disorder (Linehan, Armstrong, Suarez, Allmari, & Heard, 1991); and sending routine postcards from a clinic to people who have attended hospital following a suicide attempt (Carter, Clover, Whyte, Dawson, & D'Este, 2007). There is currently a much-needed expansion of treatment developments for the prevention of recurrence of suicidal behaviour, such as mindfulness-based cognitive therapy (MBCT; Williams, Duggan, Crane, & Fennell, 2006) and acceptance and commitment therapy (ACT; Hayes, Strosahl, & Wilson, 2003). Further, treatment innovations for personality disorder more broadly include techniques that help to reduce suicidality, such as schema-focused cognitive therapy using imagery rescripting (Giesen-Bloo et al., 2006).

To our knowledge, there have been no treatment trials for suicidality in the context of PTSD. The studies mentioned above provide a spectrum of theoretically-driven techniques for working with suicidality generally, but none specifically addresses the links between suicidality and PTSD. Indeed, Tarrier, Taylor, and Gooding (2008) have argued that, across psychological disorders and all forms of cognitive behavioural therapy (CBT), there is a significant benefit of receiving CBT in reducing suicide. Our cognitive therapy techniques 'from basics to beyond' (J.S. Beck, 1995) may thus provide important and not-to-be-neglected tools for the assessment, management, and treatment of suicidality (see also useful assessment and treatment manuals for suicidality such as Chiles & Strosahl, 2005).

In this chapter we explore a new development in the use of mental imagery that could provide links between PTSD and suicidality. We present material from a case of Type 1 (single incident) trauma and describe recent research surrounding this new area. Then we provide a contrasting case, which enables us to consider the links between suicidality and Type 2 (multiple) trauma. Finally we end with a discussion of how to think creatively about improving the use and delivery of other available techniques. The main recurring theme is that the meaning of traumatic events, circumstances, or experiences can have a direct bearing on the decision to attempt suicide, but that these meanings are not always easy to discern.

CONSIDERING MENTAL IMAGERY: 'FLASHFORWARDS'

One current area we are interested in is to consider the mode of cognitive processing at times when people feel at their most despairing and suicidal thinking, particularly about mental imagery, which seems hitherto to have been neglected. This may be of particular interest to trauma clinicians given their familiarity with mental imagery, and their existing skills for working with it, for example in the form of flashbacks.

Why consider mental imagery in the context of trauma and suicidality? One answer to this question is that imagery-based processing can exacerbate extreme emotional states across psychological disorders. Our work is the first to determine experimentally that ideas in the form of mental images (usually visual, but including all sensory modalities) are more emotionally powerful than verbal cognitions about the same topic (Holmes & Mathews, 2005; Holmes, Mathews, Dalgleish, & Mackintosh, 2006; Holmes, Mathews, Mackintosh, & Dalgleish, 2008).

Imagery may have a special relationship with emotion for several reasons (Holmes & Mathews, 2005). First, brain systems for emotion evolved prior to language, and thus may encode information about threats in a perceptual or sensory form rather than as verbal representations (Öhman & Mineka, 2001). Second, mental imagery can be responded to as if it were actual perception (Kosslyn, Ganis, & Thompson, 2001). Third, autobiographical memory and action plans are imagery-based (sensory-perceptual episodic memories) reflecting one's self view (Conway, 2001; Conway, Meares, & Standart, 2004). Finally, we have argued that imagery may promote action – mental imagery can be causal in determining future behaviour, such as imagining voting and actually doing so (Libby, Shaeffer, Eibach, & Slemmer, 2007). Imagining an event has been shown to increase the likelihood of engaging in what is imagined for activities such as signing up for cable TV (Gregory, Cialdini & Carpenter, 1982) or doing exam revision (Pham & Taylor, 1999). Imagery can also make events such as winning an election or donating blood (Carroll, 1978) seem more probable. If, compared with verbal thoughts, affect-laden mental images have a more powerful impact on emotion and are more likely to promote action, then it seems important that we should investigate whether people report experiencing mental imagery when feeling suicidal.

To our knowledge, no previous literature had investigated whether patients with suicidal thoughts experience their suicidal ideation in the form of mental images as well as words (verbal thoughts). This is clearly different from just asking about suicidal 'plans' per se without distinguishing plans made in imagery form from those made in verbal form, and focusing on the content but not the form by which the information is being processed. Therefore, in a recent case series of patients with a chronic history of depression and suicidality (Holmes, Crane, Fennell, & Williams, 2007), patients were asked to describe what went through their mind at times when they were at their most despairing or suicidal, both for verbal thoughts and for mental images. That is, patients were asked about both the form and content of their suicidal thinking, using a structured clinical interview for imagery (cf. Day, Holmes, & Hackmann, 2004; Holmes, Grey, & Young, 2005). Strikingly, all of the 15 patients reported that they experienced intrusive, repetitive images related to suicide that came to their mind unbidden when feeling at their most depressed and despairing. For most patients these mental images involved acting out suicidal plans in the future, such as imagining hanging themselves, imagining taking an overdose of tablets, or imagining jumping off a cliff. Scores on a clinical measure of the severity of suicidal ideation (the Worst Ever Version of the Beck Suicidal Ideation Scale; Beck, Brown, Steer, Dahlsgaard, & Grisham, 1999; Beck & Steer, 1993; Williams, Barnhofer, Crane, & Beck, 2005) were associated both with preoccupation with their suicide-related imagery and with the perceived 'realness' of the imagery. These images appeared to pop to mind unbidden, with a high sense of 'nowness' – that is, clinically they appear to have features similar to the flashback images seen in PTSD. Such images describe mentally simulating a future suicidal (i.e. traumatic) behaviour. We have proposed in the context of suicidality that there may be a related phenomenon to flashbacks to past trauma seen in patients with PTSD: we have called these 'flashforwards' to suicide, referring to future-directed action images of suicide (Holmes, Crane, Fennell, & Williams, 2007).

A recent paper has reported a related observation in a study using an undergraduate student sample in which violent daydreaming about death in students was associated with high levels of depression (Selby, Anestis, & Joiner, 2007). Selby and colleagues argued that daydreams about suicidal plans, attempts, or about the way others will react to their death may increase people's positive affect in the short term, but may increase suicidal ideation and action in the longer term. Thus, violent daydreams about death may reflect a form of emotional dysregulation that contributes to suicidality. We suggest that it may also take the form of imagery-based mental simulations and thus link to the concept of flashforwards.

Intrusive imagery, such as that seen in flashbacks, is a hallmark feature of PTSD (Brewin & Holmes, 2003; Ehlers & Clark, 2000). Trauma-focused cognitive behaviour therapy targets this problematic imagery and is a recommended treatment for PTSD (National Collaborating Centre for Mental Health (NCCMH), 2005). It follows that we need to know more about the prevalence of imagery in suicidality, and also whether, as in the anxiety disorders, it may be amenable to cognitive therapy techniques such as imagery restructuring (Holmes, Arntz, & Smucker, 2007).

IMAGERY RESCRIPTING OF A FLASHFORWARD IN A CASE OF TYPE I TRAUMA

Jo was an asylum seeker who suffered a discrete traumatic event (a rape) and later attempted to kill herself using rat poison. Subsequent work with her revealed that the event had dramatically changed her self opinion. The theme emerging during therapy was encapsulated in her statement that she had been treated 'as a rat'. This made her feel as worthless as a rat, and subsequently she dealt to herself the treatment that she would have dealt out to a rat. This case illustrates well the importance of addressing the suicidality before treating the trauma.

The detailed assessment took more than one session, covering PTSD, depression, and suicidal issues. Jo expressed ongoing suicidal ideation and discussion of this topic was associated with high affect in the session. Following definitions of mental imagery and verbal thoughts, when asked to describe what was going through her mind at times she felt suicidal, Jo reported that as well as experiencing flashbacks to the rape, she experienced fleeting images in which she saw herself preparing and consuming poison again – i.e. 'flashforwards'.

Our understanding of the cognitive maintenance processes involved identifying and understanding the effects of both: (1) flashbacks to the rape and (2) flashforwards to preparing the act of self-poisoning (see also Holmes et al., 2007). The formulation was developed collaboratively with Jo, who described that her flashforwards kept the possibility of suicide 'close and real' in her mind, and thus potentially increased the likelihood of acting on the suicidal cognitions represented in her imagery.

Ways of keeping her safe included working on removing the means of suicide (throwing away the poison from her home), working on reasons for living and hopes for the future, and imagery rescripting for the flashforwards (see also Holmes et al., 2007). Later, imagery rescripting of the flashback imagery linked to the traumatic incident was also used.

Rescripting the flashforward

Jo deliberately brought the flashforward image to mind and it was explored in more detail for content and meaning. The flashforward in this case was an image like a short videoclip, in which she saw herself vividly preparing the act of self-poisoning and eating the poison, feeling worthless and humiliated, accompanied by the meaning that killing herself was the only way forward. The content, emotion, and meaning associated with the image were determined. These were explored further to develop her view of a viable alternative outcome to the suicidal situation depicted in the image ('what you would need to see/feel to not do this'). The alternatives included disposing of the poison and being able to focus on a positive alternative future to that represented in the suicidal imagery. In this case the alternative was a worthwhile future together with her young daughter.

The rescripting had two components. The first involved changing the ending of the existing image to imagery of an outcome in which she safely disposed of the poison (rather than harmed herself). The alternative outcome was decided by Jo and rehearsed verbally before using imaginal reliving. Imaginal reliving in this case started with describing the flashforward in detail, then in response to 'what can you do differently to keep yourself safe' recalling or 'inserting' vivid imagery of the constructed safe alternative, described in the first person present tense by the client ('describe what you can see right now. And what else/next? And what else do you need to happen to make sure you can see it's safe?') with high affect, with their eyes shut.

In the second component of the rescripting, the rescripted imaginal video clip was then 'run into' a new alternative image associated with opposite meaning. To do this, a new future-oriented image was constructed and elaborated. This involved vivid imagery of a positive, worthwhile future involving her young daughter growing up, including specific imagery of a hoped-for typical day with her daughter in a year's time. Thus effectively the rescripting involved changing the outcome of the toxic image so that it no longer resulted in suicide, and then 'glueing' this to a new positive, future-directed image.

This new imagery was rehearsed in therapy and as a homework assignment over approximately three sessions. In homework, Jo first listened to a tape of the therapy session using rescripting, and was asked to practise deliberately recalling the alternative imagery. She was also asked to keep a diary to monitor intrusive flashforwards (as well as flashbacks) in order to better understand trigger situations, as well as learn to notice and monitor intrusive cognitions. Jo was invited to practise the alternative, positive future-oriented imagery in response to her spontaneously experiencing flashforwards or other crisis situations. The aim was to make the alternative, rescripted imagery more accessible to memory in a range of situations outside the therapy session. The frequency of flashforwards dropped rapidly over the first two sessions targeting them, alongside an increased recognition that such suicidal thoughts 'were just mental events' and did not need to be acted on. Suicidal ideation was continually monitored for the remainder of therapy. The subsequent main focus of treatment was her PTSD symptoms using a standard trauma-focused cognitive therapy approach (NCCMH, 2005).

Discussion

A clinical concern in this case was that suicidality work was needed before the standard PTSD work, as imaginal reliving may have provoked even further distress that could have exacerbated the risk of suicide. According to the overall formulation, the PTSD flashbacks (to rape) and associated shame (feeling like 'a rat') were fuelling the suicidal flashforwards. In turn, the flashforwards (to self-poisoning) were increasing the risk of future suicidal action, and needed to be addressed in order to keep this patient safe (particularly since she had already attempted an overdose). Thus the imagery rescripting intervention was one technique used in breaking the cycle between flashforward and wanting to act accordingly. This flashforward imagery rescripting was helpful in reducing her preoccupation with harming herself as a response to her psychological pain. While only one component in the overall treatment, it allowed the therapist to move smoothly from first treating her suicidality, and then on to trauma-focused cognitive therapy involving imaginal reliving and imagery restructuring of her PTSD flashbacks. The overall formulation, including the 'microformulation' of how the flashforwards and flashbacks were linked, was crucial in deciding the sequence of treatment techniques, which will clearly vary from patient to patient. In this case, working in an imagery mode for the suicidal flashforward may have also had the benefit of helping the patient realize that her flashbacks were 'just images in the mind's eye' and thus would be equally amenable to treatment. Clearly, each case will vary and a detailed cognitive formulation will help guide the order of interventions as well as the choice of techniques.

LINKS BETWEEN PTSD AND SUICIDALITY IN
A CASE OF TYPE 2 TRAUMA

In this section we address suicidality in the context of long and enduring traumatic episodes, and consider the treatment options for clinicians working with people suffering from Type 2 trauma. A theme that consistently runs through these observations is that the meaning of traumatic events, circumstances, or experiences can have a direct bearing on the decision to attempt suicide, but that these meanings are not always easy to discern.

Anne, aged 35, had taken three overdoses in the year before she started treatment. She had initially refused offers of treatment, and her history and background only gradually became clear. Her father was an alcoholic who abused Anne's mother and older sister physically, and who abused Anne both physically and sexually. Her mother was neglectful and depressed. Anne dreamed of being rescued, but gave up hope after her bruising and absences were not noticed at school, and after the police, called to the house by neighbours, asked few questions and took no action. She concluded that she was not worth helping.

Anne left school at 16, and quickly married someone who was at first kind to her but who later became domineering and controlling, refusing to let her work or use the car and insisting that she account for every penny that she spent. He told her this was for her own good as she was incompetent and could not be trusted. She stayed with him for 12 years, becoming increasingly depressed. During the two years after leaving him she worked in a supermarket and met people with whom she wanted to make friends, joining a running club and a quilting group, and going to evening classes to catch up on missed schooling. At first she had been nervous, reserved but hopeful. Gradually her initial hopefulness dissipated. However, depression and intense anxiety increased, and she found herself unable to rest and was permanently exhausted. She said that thoughts of suicide were in her mind all the time. Overdoses had been triggered by difficulties in relationships with her new acquaintances. Later it was discovered that, in addition, she also used alcohol or exercise (running fast for long periods during the night), or depriving herself of food and warmth, to dull the pain on a regular basis (at least two or three times a week). Formally she did not meet criteria for PTSD.

Using CBT to reduce Anne's suicidality

Four aspects of this work will be distinguished here, and all of them were applied in the context of (relatively) standard methods for working with underlying schema and beliefs. Although these aspects of treatment can be distinguished, in practice they are more likely to be applied concurrently than consecutively.

Prioritising suicidality

Regular assessment of risk is clearly essential in such cases, and standard principles and techniques provide structured ways of doing this. Two particular difficulties arose in this case. The first was a product of Anne's reticence and reserve. She found it difficult to talk about herself, to think about her feelings, and to focus specifically on her attitude towards suicidality. The second difficulty was that, for Anne, it was commonplace to be living with suicidal thoughts and impulses. She was hardly ever free of such experiences, and the perceived difference between triggers for the overdoses that had brought her to the attention of others and triggers for other behaviours such as going for a run or missing meals, was barely noticeable.

The explicit nature of CBT is a valuable tool in these circumstances. Anne was later able to say that she found it helpful to hear the clear message that self-destructive behaviours are antithetical to the aims of treatment. The main task of the therapist is then to explain what treatment is, and what it will involve, and to adopt (and create) a sense of hopefulness. In these circumstances it may not be helpful to make a formal contract concerning suicidal actions, as impulsivity is hard to control and the self-harming behaviours, or emotionally numbing ones, carried out after the contract is in place may contribute to a sense of failure (or tempt patients to conceal them). It may be more helpful to attempt to make sense of thoughts, feelings, and behaviours of all kinds, and to start to consider other less dangerous or damaging options.

Making sense: Starting formulation work

The first purpose of this work when focusing on suicidality is to identify and to make sense of the links between traumatic events and experiences on the one hand, and self-damaging behaviours on the other. In cases such as that of Anne's it is almost impossible to do this without hearing her history. However for Anne, and for many like her, telling the story of the past tends to activate high levels of distress, and runs the risk of precipitating flashbacks, and further efforts to numb the pain. Anne was instead asked to start by exploring the thoughts, feelings, and behaviours surrounding the times when her suicidality was at its most extreme. Together Anne and her therapist then constructed a first hypothesis to make sense of what was happening when she acted so as to harm herself, focusing entirely on the present. Anne's first formulation focused on her belief that she was 'pernicious'. What she meant by this was that being around her was so unpleasant for others that they wanted to punish and hurt her. She saw herself as to blame when something went wrong within a relationship, even during relatively superficial interactions with others, and concluded that she deserved to be punished. Meting out the punishment to herself often made her feel that she had done the right thing. It also paved the way for her to interact with them in the future.

The next task is to find out what 'good reasons' Anne has to think of herself as pernicious. She was then asked to outline her story while her therapist focused on facts, and sometimes on their meaning, rather than on associated feelings. The reason for asking for an outline first, without knowing the details of her story at this stage, is to reduce the chance of activating intense distress, dissociation, or flashbacks – all of which could operate as precipitants for further suicidal behaviour. Adding this information into the formulation so far, again working together, suggested to Anne that she must be pernicious because of the ways in which she had been abused, neglected, ignored, and controlled by others. She also believed that if she punished herself it might prevent others punishing her. While accepting the internal logic of her argument the therapist offered an alternative view that (in brief) suggested that the 'badness' had been in the behaviour of those surrounding her rather than in Anne herself. Exploring the two ideas engaged Anne's interest, but she of course provided present-day evidence in support of her original view.

Identifying maintenance patterns in the present

The therapist specifically asked Anne for the details of the interactions with others that had precipitated her recent suicide attempts. She had borrowed a book from a member of the quilting group, forgotten to return it, and the person from whom she borrowed it had been publicly angry with her during a group meeting. Anne perceived the anger as an explosion of rage and a complete rejection. She felt ashamed and humiliated, and left the group early. At this point it is particularly helpful to identify assumptions. Those she had in mind at the time were: 'I should hide myself away', 'I should never ask anyone for anything', and 'I should annihilate myself'. Exploring where these assumptions came from, asking explicitly for links with her past, helped to reveal some significant maintenance patterns. Anne said that she had coped as a child by hiding, by never asking for anything or revealing anything about herself, and by remaining constantly on guard when with others. If she could keep others happy she was more likely to be safe. As might be expected her current patterns of interaction were similar. Predominantly she focused on trying to keep others happy, and she had revealed to nobody any of the details of her past life. She blamed herself, and made catastrophic predictions, if anything went wrong (however small). Anne made great efforts to make friends and to enter into different kinds of relationships with people, but with these assumptions intact her efforts failed, often leaving her feeling hopeless and suicidal.

As the collaborative formulation work proceeds the implications for treatment become clearer, and standard methods can be used to change old beliefs, to experiment with behaving in other ways than those dictated by the assumptions, and to build up stronger and more functional belief systems.

This work need no longer be focused on the suicidality, though it is important to remember that the normality of this way of thinking for people like Anne means that it quickly re-emerges at times of distress, and regular risk assessment is essential.

Showing you care and that you value the person you are working with

When people have experienced persistent traumatic abuse they tend to believe that others do not care about them, and that they have no value. They feel worthless, they have been treated as worthless, and so they know that this feeling of worthlessness is valid – and that they should punish themselves. Habitual suicidality, based in lifelong beliefs, is hard to shift. As therapists we need to show that we care, and that we value the person we are working with. Of course, we also need to be aware of appropriate boundaries, but this awareness should not prevent us showing that we care, and specifically focusing on those things that we consider valuable about the person we are working with. For Anne it was a revelation to discover that she and her therapist shared certain values (about not hurting others for instance, and about trying to help others in difficulty). This discovery helped her to feel, as well as to think, that she was not as pernicious as she had originally believed, and therefore did not need to annihilate herself, or to blot out her feelings when something went wrong.

Another of the elements of cognitive therapy that is helpful here is giving and receiving feedback. Used regularly, openly, and honestly, feedback enables both parties to learn from the interaction, and to become more flexible in the ways in which they relate to each other. With someone like Anne, who has a lifelong habit of hiding her thoughts and feelings from others but who still wishes to engage in a friendly way with them, practice with receiving as well as with giving feedback also helps to reduce the chance of taking potentially damaging action when feeling distressed by the behaviour of someone else.

It is of course likely that the links between past trauma and attempted suicide are complex and various, and there are also many more techniques available than those mentioned in the account of Anne's treatment. There are, in addition, a number of factors that can increase the risk of suicidality, many of which cannot be controlled or removed by a therapist. Formulation work can be used to make sense of them, and they can be explicitly discussed and appropriate preparations made. Among these factors are:

- Apparently trivial events can activate extreme levels of pain.
- Old schema can be re-activated even after 'successful' treatment.
- Adverse life circumstances (such as physical illness) can produce severe levels of hopelessness in people with histories of trauma.

- Strong feelings (good or bad) can increase risk in people who are unable to regulate affect.
- Habits (and skills) of dissociating or blotting out pain can be over-used, and misjudged.
- People who do not care whether they live or die tend to take big risks.
- Reliving can increase suicidality.
- Specific beliefs may increase the risk (believing that you don't deserve to live).

THINKING CREATIVELY ABOUT IMPROVING OUR TECHNIQUES

Working with people who have attempted suicide, or who might do so, is both difficult and worrying for therapists. Suffering from PTSD as well as feeling suicidal complicates the picture, and we are not yet able accurately to predict which of our patients are, or will become, most at risk. It is therefore imperative that we continue to research the links between trauma and suicidality, and to develop new techniques such as those using imagery. As described above, this may reveal specific, detailed images, or flashforwards that could indicate enhanced activation of beliefs associated with despair, and reduced ability to control associated impulses. There are also a number of other techniques that could be further developed, and their value estimated through detailed research, and some of these are described below.

First, clinical discussions suggest that many therapists switch quickly into using short-term strategies when they perceive their patients to be seriously at risk of making a suicide attempt. So, they may, for example, help the person to make links between therapy sessions, or 'create a bridge' between meetings, or develop a sense of continuity, or imagine how others might feel if they died. Or they might assess the current level of impulsivity and access to the means of killing oneself, and work to change these. The meanings taken from traumatic experiences, which include the impact, the implications, and the significance of these events (all aspects of meaning) are not addressed by these methods. Of course, safety must be the first consideration when people are at risk, but not at the expense of forgetting to focus on meanings. As illustrated in the examples provided above, the risk may be especially high when memories of the trauma are associated with a deep sense of shame (Lee, Chapter 15, this volume).

Second, a possible consequence of becoming active and taking a more controlling stance towards treatment when people are suicidal is that it switches attention away from the responsibility of the patient. In some circumstances this may echo the lack of control they had during traumatic experiences. In order to continue to behave in ways that are likely to be pleasurable, or to bring access to a sense of achievement, it can be important to continue to assume that the patient is capable of taking responsibility – for example, for initiating communication and contact with potential sources of help and support; for keeping themselves alive, as well as for responding catastrophically to the degree of pain that they experience.

A third point is closely linked to this one: curiosity about the future (any aspect of it) draws people into life again. Engaging a patient's curiosity about how this episode of despair could be brought to an end, or about the ideas the therapist and patient in collaboration might be able to come up with, encourages an external rather than an internal focus. It may be a source of new information, and bring relief from despairing rumination.

As cognitive therapists, we are interested in how people represent meanings to themselves, and have earlier in this paper described a new finding concerning imagery about the future (flashforwards). Meanings can be represented in words, in pictures, and in numerous other ways (reflected in all of the arts). A number of patients, when the therapist shows a serious interest in the way that they think and in the cognitive frameworks with which they approach the world, make creative and less inhibited attempts to express themselves. Some of them use drawings or pictures (see Butler & Holmes, 2009), and in a number of cases people struggling to deal with their suicidal impulses have used drawings to represent to themselves their feelings and the meaning to them of their current situation. In at least a few instances the patient has reported that creating the picture (often a violent and distressing object to look at) has enabled them to come through the suicidal crisis without taking more dangerous action. The action of creating an external representation of their pain appears to be capable, sometimes, of replacing, or bypassing, suicidal action. In a similar fashion drawings may be used as part of processing the traumatic memory in PTSD.

The far-reaching implications of early childhood trauma (abuse, violence, neglect etc.) often interfere with the development of a functional sense of self or identity. In extreme cases adults who have been extensively abused early in life may live predominantly in 'hypervigilant mode', on the lookout for danger from others while ignoring their own feelings and needs. These people may have little sense of their right to take action to reduce their pain; they may not even be aware of how to take such action. They may become at risk of suicide when unable to tolerate or deal functionally with times of intense distress, or with psychological pain. Then it is important to help them to recognize their needs, to feel that they have a right to act in their own best interest so as to meet their needs, and to care appropriately for themselves. It is also important to work on beliefs linked to the traumatic experience that might otherwise leave them exposed to future risk, such as beliefs about being bad, or evil, or responsible for the pain and trauma that surrounded them (and others). Building up functional belief systems is part of this work, and perhaps more ideas about how to do this could be sought from the recent research on positive psychology (e.g., see Seligman, 2006; Snyder and Lopez,

2005). Clearly it would seem insensitive to request that someone who is subject to strong suicidal impulses should think about their strengths and achievements, or focus on things that went well for them. But there may nevertheless be more ways than have yet been tried to help people find consolation in bad times and to create some foundations for a more enduring sense of hopefulness.

Working to build up functional beliefs, and to modify dysfunctional ones, can often be done at the same time as suicidal risk management. There is, however, (at least) one situation in which this work may temporarily increase the risk of suicide. This is when high anxiety comes to be associated with making functional changes (see also Fawcett, 2001). A patient described her more functional ways of living as coming to feel like 'not me' after a while. She then behaved in old familiar, self-punishing, and destructive ways, and found that these reduced her anxiety – an anxiety provoked by the novelty to her of behaving in more functional ways. In order to reduce the probability of such self-sabotage, therapists need carefully to time their interventions, explicitly to discuss the risk with each patient, and to guard against pushing for too fast a rate of change. Similarly, discussing the traumatic experiences themselves, whether in reliving or otherwise, leads to increases in anxiety, which if the client does not have some emotion regulation strategies can lead to an increased risk of suicide.

Of course these methods have yet to be evaluated, and clinical judgement is necessary in applying them. While we have highlighted the fact that cognitive therapists already have an extensive array of tools to use in this challenging area, it will be important to keep an eye on the exciting clinical research developments afoot in the literature. It would be a pity, however, if the fear of the issues around suicidality in a patient with whom one was working prevented therapists from sensitively using their creativity to best advantage.

ACKNOWLEDGEMENT

Emily A. Holmes is supported by a Royal Society Dorothy Hodgkin Fellowship.

REFERENCES

Beck, A.T., & Steer, R.A. (1993). *Manual for the Beck Scale of Suicide Ideation.* San Antonio: The Psychological Corporation.

Beck, A.T., Brown, G.K., Steer, R.A., Dahlsgaard, K.K., & Grisham, J.R. (1999). Suicide ideation at its worst point: A predictor of eventual suicide in psychiatric outpatients. *Suicide and Life-Threatening Behavior, 29*(1), 1–9.

Beck, J.S. (1995). *Cognitive therapy: Basics and beyond.* New York: Guilford Press.

Berk, M.S., Henriques, G.R., Warman, D.M., Brown, G.K., & Beck, A.T. (2004). A cognitive therapy intervention for suicide attempters: An overview of the treatment and case examples. *Cognitive and Behavioral Practice, 11*(3), 265–277.

Brewin, C.R., & Holmes, E.A. (2003). Psychological theories of posttraumatic stress disorder. *Clinical Psychology Review, 23*(3), 339–376.

Brown, G.K., Ten Have, T., Henriques, G.R., Xie, S.X., Hollander, J.E., & Beck, A.T. (2005). Cognitive therapy for the prevention of suicide attempts – A randomized controlled trial. *Journal of the American Medical Association, 294*(5), 563–570.

Butler, G., & Holmes, E.A. (2009). Imagery and the self following childhood trauma: Observations concerning the use of drawings and external images. In L. Stopa (Ed.), *Imagery and the damaged self: Perspective on imagery in cognitive therapy*. London: Routledge.

Carroll, J.S. (1978). The effect of imagining an event on expectations for the event: An interpretation in terms of the availability heuristic. *Journal of Experimental Social Psychology, 14*, 88–96.

Carter, G.L., Clover, K., Whyte, I.M., Dawson, A.H., & D'Este, C. (2007). Postcards from the Edge: 24 month outcomes of a randomised controlled trial of an intervention using postcards to reduce repetition of hospital treated self-poisoning. *British Journal of Psychiatry, 191*(6), 548–553.

Chiles, J.A., & Strosahl, K.D. (2005). *Clinical manual for assessment and treatment of suicidal patients*. Washington, DC: American Psychiatric Publishing.

Conway, M.A. (2001). Sensory-perceptual episodic memory and its context: Autobiographical memory. *Philosophical Transactions of the Royal Society of London Series B – Biological Sciences, 356*(3), 1375–1384.

Conway, M.A., Meares, K., & Standart, S. (2004). Images and goals. *Memory, 12*(4), 525–531.

Day, S.J., Holmes, E.A., & Hackmann, A. (2004). Occurrence of imagery and its link with early memories in agoraphobia. *Memory, 12*(4), 416–427.

Ehlers, A., & Clark, D.M. (2000). A cognitive model of posttraumatic stress disorder. *Behaviour Research and Therapy, 38*(4), 319–345.

Fawcett, J. (2001). Treating impulsivity and anxiety in the suicidal patient. *Annals of the New York Academy of Sciences, 932*(1), 94–105.

Giesen-Bloo, J., van Dyck, R., Spinhoven, P., van Tilburg, W., Dirksen, C., van Asselt, T., et al. (2006). Outpatient psychotherapy for borderline personality disorder: A randomized clinical trial of schema focused therapy versus transference focused psychotherapy. *Archives of General Psychiatry, 63*(6), 649–658.

Gregory, W.L., Cialdini, R.B., & Carpenter, K.M. (1982). Self-relevant scenarios as mediators of likelihood estimates and compliance – Does imagining make it so. *Journal of Personality and Social Psychology, 43*(1), 89–99.

Hawton, K., Arensman, E., Townsend, E., Bremner, S., Feldman, E., Goldney, R., et al. (1998). Deliberate self harm: Systematic review of efficacy of psychosocial and pharmacological treatments in preventing repetition. *British Medical Journal, 317*, 441–447.

Hayes, S.C., Strosahl, K.D., & Wilson, K.G. (2003). *Acceptance and commitment therapy: An experiential approach to behavior change*. New York: Guilford Press.

Holmes, E.A., & Mathews, A. (2005). Mental imagery and emotion: A special relationship? *Emotion, 5*(4), 489–497.

Holmes, E.A., Arntz, A., & Smucker, M.R. (2007). Imagery rescripting in cognitive behaviour therapy: Images, treatment techniques and outcomes. *Journal of Behavior Therapy and Experimental Psychiatry*, *38*(4), 297–305.

Holmes, E.A., Crane, C., Fennell, M.J.V., & Williams, J.M.G. (2007). Imagery about suicide in depression – 'Flash-forwards'? *Journal of Behavior Therapy and Experimental Psychiatry*, *38*(4), 423–434.

Holmes, E.A., Grey, N., & Young, K.A.D. (2005). Intrusive images and 'hotspots' of trauma memories in posttraumatic stress disorder: An exploratory investigation of emotions and cognitive themes. *Journal of Behavior Therapy and Experimental Psychiatry*, *36*(1), 3–17.

Holmes, E.A., Mathews, A., Dalgleish, T., & Mackintosh, B. (2006). Positive interpretation training: Effects of mental imagery versus verbal training on positive mood. *Behavior Therapy*, *37*(3), 237–247.

Holmes, E.A., Mathews, A., Mackintosh, B., & Dalgleish, T. (2008). The causal effect of mental imagery on emotion assessed using picture-word cues. *Emotion*, *8*, 395–409.

Kosslyn, S.M., Ganis, G., & Thompson, W.L. (2001). Neural foundations of imagery. *Nature Reviews: Neuroscience*, *2*(9), 635–642.

Libby, L.K., Shaeffer, E.M., Eibach, R.P., & Slemmer, J.A. (2007). Picture yourself at the polls – Visual perspective in mental imagery affects self-perception and behavior. *Psychological Science*, *18*(3), 199–203.

Linehan, M.M., Armstrong, H.E., Suarez, A., Allmari, D., & Heard, H.L. (1991). Cognitive behavioral treatment of chronically parasuicidal borderline patients. *Archives of General Psychiatry*, *48*, 1060–1064.

National Collaborating Centre for Mental Health. (2005). *Clinical guideline 26: Post-traumatic stress disorder (PTSD): The management of PTSD in adults and children in primary and secondary care*. London: National Institute for Clinical Excellence.

Oguendo, M.A., Brent, D.A., Birmaher, B., Greenhill, L., Kolko, D., Stanley, B., et al. (2005). Posttraumatic stress disorder comorbid with major depression: Factors mediating the association with suicidal behavior. *American Journal of Psychiatry*, *162*(3), 560–566.

Oguendo, M.A., Friend, J.M., Halberstam, B., Brodsky, B.S., Burke, A.K., Grunebaum, M.F., et al. (2003). Association of comorbid posttraumatic stress disorder and major depression with greater risk for suicidal behavior. *American Journal of Psychiatry*, *160*(3), 580–582.

Öhman, A., & Mineka, S. (2001). Fears, phobias, and preparedness: Toward an evolved module of fear and fear learning. *Psychological Review*, *108*(3), 483–522.

Pham, L.B., & Taylor, S.E. (1999). From thought to action: Effects of process- versus outcome-based mental simulations on performance. *Personality and Social Psychology Bulletin*, *25*(2), 250–260.

Selby, E.A., Anestis, M.D., & Joiner, T.E. (2007). Daydreaming about death: Violent daydreaming as a form of emotion dysregulation in suicidality. *Behavior Modification*, *31*(6), 867–879.

Seligman, M.E.P. (2006). *Learned optimism: How to change your mind and your life*. New York: Vintage Books.

Snyder, C., & Lopez, S. (Eds.) (2005). *Handbook of positive psychology*. New York: OUP.

Tarrier, N., & Gregg, L. (2004). Suicide risk in civilian PTSD patients: Predictors of suicidal ideation, planning and attempts. *Social Psychiatry and Psychiatric Epidemiology*, *39*(8), 655–661.

Tarrier, N., Taylor, K., & Gooding, P. (2008). Cognitive-behavioral interventions to reduce suicide behavior: A systematic review and meta-analysis. *Behavior Modification*, *32*(1), 77–108.

Williams, J.M.G., Barnhofer, T., Crane, C., & Beck, A.T. (2005). Problem solving deteriorates following mood challenge in formerly depressed patients with a history of suicidal ideation. *Journal of Abnormal Psychology*, *114*(3), 421–431.

Williams, J.M.G., Duggan, D.S., Crane, C., & Fennell, M.J.V. (2006). Mindfulness-based cognitive therapy for prevention of recurrence of suicidal behavior. *Journal of Clinical Psychology*, *62*(2), 201–210.

Chapter 13

Cognitive therapy for people with post-traumatic stress disorder to multiple events

Working out where to start

Pippa Stallworthy

INTRODUCTION

Many people presenting for help with post-traumatic stress disorder (PTSD) have re-experiencing symptoms relating to more than one traumatic event and this can be daunting to clinicians. Although there is now a substantial literature on working with single-incident PTSD, less is available to help clinicians working with those with PTSD to multiple events. The exception to this relatively neglected area is the literature addressing PTSD in survivors of childhood sexual abuse (Herman, 1992; Smucker, Dancu, Foa, & Niederee, 1995), personality disorders (Arntz & Weertman, 1999), veterans (Creamer & Forbes, 2004) and refugees (Schauer, Neuner, & Elbert, 2005). However, whilst these authors acknowledge that people may have PTSD to more than one event, and propose techniques to assist in their treatment, the developments that have improved outcomes for single-incident PTSD are only just beginning to be extended to the treatment of those with PTSD to multiple events (Lee, 2006; Duffy, Gillespie, & Clark, 2007).

Despite over 25 years of epidemiological research on the prevalence of traumatic events and PTSD, the proportion of this population with PTSD to more than one event remains unclear. Between 33 and 54% of the population have experienced at least two traumatic events (Resnick, Kilpatrick, Dansky, Saunders, & Best, 1993, cited in Carlson, 2001). Carlson also cites studies of psychiatric populations that found 67% of outpatients and 63% of inpatients report two or more traumatic events.

Many clinicians have argued that the psychological effects of isolated traumatic events and repeated trauma are different and require different treatment. Terr (1991) makes a distinction between single-event (type I) trauma and the experience of chronic trauma (type II). Herman (1992) proposed a phased model of treatment for people who have experienced multiple traumatic events. The first priority is ensuring safety. This includes reducing the risk of further trauma (e.g., organizing alternative accommodation for victims of domestic violence), reducing self-harm, improving affect-regulation, and controlling dissociation. The second phase, 'remembrance', involves providing a detailed account of the trauma so that it can be incorporated within an autobiographical narrative. In the third, 'reconnection' phase, a sense of self is (re-)established encompassing more than their identity as a trauma survivor.

Most guidance for clinicians working with people with PTSD to multiple events refers to themes likely to be important, such as trust and intimacy, or describes particular treatment approaches, such as testimony or narrative exposure therapy. Advice regarding the order in which to work on memories relates to constructing a hierarchy of trauma memories and collaborative decision-making with clients (Hembree, Rauch, & Foa, 2003). Control over treatment and sensitive pacing of the work are, clearly, essential for clients whose control was taken away during the trauma. However, greater attention to the cognitive factors within the formulation and the relationship between the traumatic events assists with this process. It can help identify which re-experiencing symptoms can be treated most quickly, giving the client an early experience of success, which can hearten them to tackle even more distressing memories.

People with PTSD to multiple traumatic events fall into different groups, which tend to have distinct presentations: (1) people with PTSD to multiple events in childhood, often physical or sexual abuse; (2) people with PTSD to multiple events in adulthood, including victims of domestic violence, people in high-risk occupational groups such as emergency personnel, and asylum-seekers and refugees; and (3) people with PTSD to traumatic events in both childhood and adulthood. The two cases presented in this chapter represent differing presentations of this third group. All aspects of treatment needed for PTSD to single events are also required for the treatment of PTSD to multiple events. The emphasis here is on additional elements useful with PTSD to multiple events. There are some issues particular to specific groups – those with histories of childhood abuse are likely to present with more dissociative symptoms, for example – but the same general principles apply across groups.

THEORY AND FORMULATION

Formulating the PTSD to each traumatic event (when possible) and the relationships between traumatic events and pre-existing negative beliefs enables clinicians to decide whether reliving will be effective without significant preliminary work. When entrenched negative beliefs were activated during the trauma, and continue to be strongly held, work to undermine these and develop an alternative, more helpful belief will be required so that the client is able to access an alternative understanding during reliving.

Recent developments in the understanding of PTSD have emphasized the importance of the thoughts and feelings people experience during the worst moments of the trauma (Ehlers & Clark, 2000). Assessment of these peri-traumatic 'hotspots' allows one to identify cognitions that are likely to interfere with successful 'reliving' of the traumatic event. Two types of peri-traumatic cognition can be problematic. First, thoughts (including images) associated with shame, guilt, or anger compromise the effectiveness of reliving (Jaycox & Foa, 1996). These cognitions are likely to need restructuring to reduce the intensity of these emotions and this new understanding will need to be incorporated into the trauma memory during reliving (Ehlers & Clark, 2000; Ehlers, Clark, Hackmann, McManus, & Fennell, 2005; Grey, Young, & Holmes, 2002).

When the number of traumas is so great as to render it impractical to assess the hotspots for each event separately, one can ask whether clients remember feeling guilt, shame, anger, or humiliation during the traumatic events. When people have experienced many traumas and have difficulty identifying their peri-traumatic emotions, identifying the emotions they experience during their intrusions is useful. Intrusions consistently accompanied by fear and humiliation suggest these emotions are likely to have been present peri-traumatically.

Second, if pre-existing negative beliefs about the self, world, or others were activated peri-traumatically, these cognitions are likely to be more difficult to re-structure. For example, if someone lost control of their bowels during an assault, and thought 'this means there's something wrong with me' but did not have significant pre-existing defectiveness beliefs, then they are likely to be able to consider information about common physiological reactions during trauma, and come to a different conclusion. Alternatively, if early experiences had left them with entrenched defectiveness beliefs, it is unlikely that challenging this thought would be effective, without an intervention targeted at undermining the underlying belief.

This means assessment of pre-existing beliefs and peri-traumatic cognitions (including whether these were activated during traumatic events) is essential in the formulation of PTSD. When people have PTSD to more than one event, one needs to understand the peri-traumatic cognitions involved in each trauma and the relationships between them.

If no negative core beliefs were activated peri-traumatically, one can take each trauma in turn, restructuring during reliving where necessary. When discussing with which event a client wishes to start, remember that an experience of successful reduction of PTSD symptoms serves to increase motivation for tackling more distressing events. Given the apprehension naturally felt about reliving, clients often decide to relive the least distressing event first. More rarely, people choose the maximum benefit in the reduction of their symptoms and wish to target the most distressing or most frequent re-experiencing symptoms first.

When people experience intrusions to more than one event, it is important to monitor the frequency of each intrusion separately. Subtle changes in the total frequency of intrusions are difficult for clients to detect and may pass unnoticed without monitoring. Sometimes, in the session after reliving a trauma, people describe their symptoms as 'the same as ever' because they still experience intrusions, even though their diaries show that they have not experienced any intrusions to the specific event relived in the previous session.

If well-developed negative beliefs were activated during all the traumatic events, and the client's conviction that these are true remains strong, then it may be necessary to employ techniques specifically designed to affect change at this level. These include schema-focused cognitive therapy (CT) prior to trauma-focused CT, imagery-rescripting techniques (Smucker et al., 1995; Arntz & Weertman, 1999), and compassionate imagery used within reliving (Lee, 2005).

First, one needs to establish the degree to which they hold a particular belief. Clearly, if someone believes 100% that they deserved the traumatic event(s), treatment is likely to take longer than if they believe it only 60%. In the latter case, one may be able to use techniques such as a responsibility pie chart to shift attributions of guilt. Sometimes even longstanding, strongly endorsed beliefs can shift relatively quickly. It is important to stress that the aim is to reduce the strength of the negative belief, and, ideally, to develop some conviction in a more helpful belief. It is not necessary to reduce the negative belief to zero to effectively 'relive' the trauma(s) in which the beliefs were activated.

If negative beliefs were activated during some traumatic events, but not all, it is easiest to start by reliving the event(s) in which the negative beliefs were not activated, which gives people a more rapid experience of successful reduction of PTSD symptoms.

CASE EXAMPLES

Jyoti: entrenched negative beliefs developed from childhood trauma but not activated during adult trauma

Presentation and history (two sessions)

Jyoti was referred for help with re-experiencing symptoms relating to a car accident en route to her father's funeral three months previously. Although she only wanted treatment in relation to the accident, she also described intrusive eidetic images and nightmares of physical abuse by her parents. Although there were times when she found herself ruminating about her childhood, the images and nightmares were clearly re-experiencing symptoms of PTSD. The younger of two children, she had been aware of her father's drinking and violence at home all her life. Her mother, Jyoti, and her aunts were all beaten. She was hospitalized during primary school, and was placed on the At Risk register. However, the violence continued. Jyoti was also repeatedly told that she was repulsive, worthless, and deserved to be mistreated. This was the more distressing since her brother was treated much better.

Jyoti also reported lifelong, frequent, out-of-body dissociative experiences, in which she saw things as if from the ceiling, for example in lectures. Despite many symptoms of depression, such as low mood, and feelings of failure and guilt, she was working full-time, studying for a degree, and teaching yoga. She scored 39 on the Beck Depression Inventory (BDI; severe range) and 99 on the Clinician Administered PTSD Scale (CAPS; extreme range. Blake et al., 1990).

One month before the assessment she had cut herself, and had done so frequently during adolescence, because 'physical pain makes it easier to deal with emotional pain'. She had since decided to stop self-harming and substituted intensive exercise at times when she felt the urge to cut.

Formulation (two sessions)

Her childhood experiences led Jyoti to believe that she was inadequate, repulsive, and the world would be better off without her. These beliefs were extremely painful and she developed a number of coping strategies, such as distracting herself by reading. As she got older, she would comfort eat, triggering feelings of guilt, sometimes resulting in her cutting herself or exercising for 2–3 hours a day. To compensate for her sense of inadequacy, she set herself extremely high standards. Her dependence on avoidant strategies also interfered with the processing of the memories of the car accident, thereby maintaining her PTSD to this event.

Recounting her traumatic history was, itself, distressing, so we discussed how to keep treatment tolerable. Amongst other ways of pacing the sessions, Jyoti decided to arrange appointments at three-weekly intervals.

Account of the accident (one session)

After the funeral, her brother drove to the crematorium at speed. She remembers him swearing, and watching, as from an observer perspective, a car hurtling towards them. She saw it approaching in slow motion and thought 'Oh God, they are never going to stop.' Next, she was aware of darkness, hearing a scream, and realizing it was hers. She watched what was happening both from an observer and her normal perspective. She fought to remain conscious as her vision began to turn blue. Finally, someone wrenched the door open, and pulled her out. Jyoti tried to call an ambulance and establish their location. She recalled feeling 'on automatic pilot', concerned to get everyone out. She heard ambulance sirens and someone saying 'I'm dying'. The paramedics praised the way she cared for the others, but she felt guilty for surviving. Jyoti and the others involved sustained minor injuries.

At assessment, Jyoti identified one hotspot: watching herself from an observer perspective, she thought 'I thought my life was supposed to flash in front of me.' Jyoti was clear that none of her longstanding negative beliefs had been triggered at this moment.

Intervention – PTSD to the car accident (six sessions)

Jyoti's intrusions were of the moment of impact, from her own and an observer perspective, and a moment of blackness, and panic. Having mapped out a formulation of the relationship between her experiences and her various

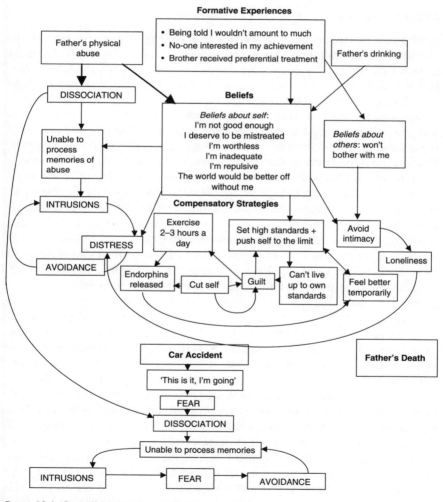

Figure 13.1 Overall formulation for Jyoti.

difficulties (see Figure 13.1), we agreed to try and relive the car accident without attempting to modify her longstanding negative beliefs first. Before this, we compiled a list of her intrusions to the accident, and she completed an intrusions diary, which established that she had 35 car accident intrusions per week. Given the risk of dissociation during reliving, we experimented with a range of grounding strategies, such as using essential oils (see Kennerley, Chapter 7, this volume). She learned to identify early signs of dissociation, and was often able to ground herself. We agreed she would use these strategies during reliving if necessary, and spent one session reliving the car accident. She did not dissociate, and these intrusions stopped.

PTSD to the childhood abuse (54 sessions)

Jyoti was still experiencing high levels of PTSD symptoms because of the intrusions of the childhood abuse, so decided to reduce these too. The next phase of treatment was much more difficult because of her entrenched negative beliefs (such as deserving maltreatment), which she was unwilling to consider might not be 100% true.

She was, however, prepared to experiment with compassionate imagery and generated an image fairly easily. She visualized a Buddha in a field with the sound of rushing water and birdsong, and felt calm and peaceful. Unfortunately, on opening her eyes, she dissociated. Initially, she had no idea what might have triggered this. In discussion, it emerged that after the abuse she would focus on an image of the Buddha and beg him to intervene, clarifying a link between the abuse, the image of the Buddha, and dissociation. We decided to postpone using compassionate imagery and began exploring how her beliefs about deserving abuse developed. Asked whether other family members were responsible for violence to them, Jyoti opted to finish the session, saying 'I don't like where this is going'. Before leaving, she explained she felt uncomfortable because she *was* responsible. However, a few weeks later, she was prepared to revisit the discussion and review the evidence. She considered her being a very active child who did not want to eat, evidence of responsibility for abuse. Evidence that she was not responsible included her father's violence to Jyoti's mother, grandmother, and aunts before she was born, and that 'it is wrong for parents to be violent to children'.

This led to a conversation about what more helpful belief she would wish to hold. When we next met, she was feeling 'on top of the world' (despite a BDI score of 32), saying 'I'm a good person who deserves happiness . . . if I'm feeling low and say it enough, it helps, even if I don't believe it fully'.

Unfortunately, a family argument before the next session triggered her negative beliefs again, and she found it hard to believe she could ever have said she deserved happiness. Fortunately, she had allowed me to tape the session (although she would not listen to the tapes herself). The tape and the notes of the last session helped remind her of the way she had been thinking and feeling. She described this as like having a positive and a negative magnet in her head, the latter being much stronger so that anything negative stuck, while the weakness of the other meant positive information had to be of a different order of magnitude and was easily lost. We discussed strategies for strengthening the 'positive magnet', such as a positive data log, but she baulked at this on the basis that believing you are good or worthwhile is 'arrogant'. We explored whether it was possible to hold such beliefs without arrogance, and also the criteria for being a worthwhile person. Drawing out a continuum for being a good person who deserves happiness, she placed people she knew along it. Discrepancies between her ratings and the way she thought people would rate themselves were examined. Then we began to think about what might account for a friend's lower estimation of himself and how it might affect his behaviour. She was reading Dave Pelzer's autobiography at the time and identified with one passage: 'I know deep inside that I do not now, nor will I ever deserve any love, attention, or even recognition as a human being' (Pelzer, 2000, 4–5). After consideration, she eventually disagreed with his estimation of himself and decided his belief was due to the way he was treated. This led to discussion of how his beliefs changed over time and what caused these changes. Jyoti found this distressing at times, but it also led her to re-evaluate her own entitlement to happiness. She visualized this as a protective bubble around her, but one easily punctured. As she disliked formal ratings and continua, she created her own scale of the 'strength of the bubble': gas, liquid, plastic, glass, metal, diamond.

Having agreed that a 'metal' bubble should be strong enough for us to work on the childhood memories, we concentrated on strengthening the bubble. Books about other people's experiences were particularly helpful. Reading Constance Briscoe's *Ugly*, Jyoti concluded that the way Constance was treated was totally unacceptable and undeserved (Briscoe, 2006). Reflecting on her own experience, she said, 'my parents had issues and took it out on me, and it was wrong, very wrong'. Considering the implications for the idea that she deserved it, she said that 'was the next station along', and that she 'wasn't there yet'. However, understanding the abuse as due to her parents' difficulties, made it easier 'like touching something very hot with oven gloves on'. By this stage, her 'bubble' was regularly 'metal', and we began planning work on the abuse memories. Nevertheless, when we tried to make an intrusions list, she became distressed and felt 'as though a shutter had come down' and could not remember any intrusions. Attempts to manipulate the shutter image were unsuccessful. We discussed 'testimony' (Cienfuegos & Monelli, 1983) and she started an account of her experiences. She noticed a change in her intrusions then, which became 'like having the TV on but with the mute button on'. At this point, she felt ready to relive one of the abuse memories.

Account of one childhood trauma

When she was ten, Jyoti was in a play and very anxious about her lines. Most of the performance went well and she could see her friends smiling in the audience. Her mother was also there, but impassive. Jyoti reversed the order of a line and saw her mother shaking her head. Jyoti felt ashamed and scared, knowing she would be beaten when she got home. On the journey back, her parents told her she was absolutely useless. Once home, she was hit by her mother, then her father.

She identified two hotspots. First, seeing her mother shaking her head and feeling shame, humiliation, and fear. Second, when her father reappeared, she thought the violence would escalate and was terrified. Given the shame and humiliation present, we discussed how she might 'update' the traumatic memory. She decided on the following: 'it's really good that I managed to carry it off in another language' and 'it's not my fault, I'm a good person who deserves happiness'. She inserted these updates at those moments during the reliving (Ehlers et al., 2005; Grey et al., 2002) and the intrusions to this event reduced and eventually ceased.

Outcome

We were not able to relive all the traumatic events before ending treatment, and her CAPS score remained high (68, severe range), but her intrusions were less frequent and less distressing and the nightmares reduced to once a fortnight. She described a marked improvement in her mood, 'I feel unstoppable now', and her BDI dropped to 15. She concluded 'my experiences have made me who I am, and who I am today is a strong and good person who deserves happiness'.

Jyoti's negative beliefs were very strong and slow to change. I suspect that the success with the PTSD to the car accident gave her the courage and confidence to persevere with treatment when the much more painful work began. The initial reduction of the PTSD to the accident was only possible because her negative beliefs had not been triggered peri-traumatically. Nonetheless, her treatment took 65 sessions over four years.

Rose: PTSD to traumatic events in both childhood and adulthood in which longstanding negative beliefs were activated during the adult trauma

Presentation and history

Rose, aged 37, presented for help following the premature birth of twins, who required resuscitation shortly after birth. At assessment it emerged that she did, indeed, have re-experiencing symptoms relating to the resuscitation, six months previously, but also to a rape by her uncle when she was six. Rose was particularly concerned about times when her head felt 'fuzzy', and her awareness of her surroundings reduced. On these occasions, she thought 'this isn't right' and worried that she was going mad. Her BDI score was 34 (severe) and her CAPS was 96 (severe).

The youngest of five children, she was treated as 'the black sheep' of the family, and always felt unloved and unwanted. Her parents drank heavily and left her alone for long periods from an early age. Even when present, her parents largely ignored her, and she was bullied by siblings and classmates. She believed it was her fault, and she deserved to be mistreated.

Rose explained that these experiences had left her with no self-respect and a great need to belong. This led to involvement with crime, drugs, and prostitution from the age of 12. At 13, she met a disc jockey with whom she had a sexual relationship. He kidnapped her for days at a time and mistreated her.

When she was nearly 16, she met Otis. He did not want her involved with drugs or crime, most of which she stopped. Three years later, she was convicted of an offence committed aged 16. She served six months in prison. This was the more difficult because being trapped triggered memories of the childhood rape. After her release, she learned that Otis had had an affair, which was devastating because he was the first person she had ever trusted. She coped with this by spending much of the next year taking drugs to numb her feelings.

Rose set up a business with a partner, which ran into financial difficulties, so she borrowed money from a 'friend'. A closure date for the business was agreed, and the 'friend' sent men round threatening violence and demanding the business' equipment as repayment. Rose was 7 months pregnant and feared for her life. She went into labour, was taken to hospital and given medication, but remained in considerable pain. After a sleepless night, her twins were delivered by caesarean section and taken to intensive care. A doctor explained that her babies were unable to breathe unassisted and needed ventilation. Rose believed they were going to die, that it was her fault, and had happened 'to teach her a lesson'. She was overwhelmed with fear, guilt, and grief. On a visit to the intensive care unit, she saw doctors huddled round resuscitating her baby. Fortunately, they were successful, although he remained in a critical condition for weeks.

She described one hotspot: seeing the doctors resuscitating her baby, and thinking 'he's going to die and it's my fault' and being overwhelmed by fear, guilt, and grief.

Formulation

Rose was adamant that she was 100% responsible for the twins' premature birth and the need for her son's resuscitation. It became clear that this emerged from lifelong beliefs that she was responsible for bad things happening to her and deserved to be mistreated. Mapping out a formulation it became apparent that we would need to address these beliefs before processing the memories of the resuscitation would be possible.

Intervention

Information about dissociation provided some reassurance about her fear that she was going mad, and gave her evidence with which to challenge those thoughts when they occurred.

We began by exploring how her belief that 'it's my fault' developed, and whether other children 'deserved' abuse. Reading about other people's experiences initiated a process of re-attributing responsibility for the abuse. Within a couple of sessions, she began to re-evaluate whether she 'deserved' other mistreatment. We then returned to discussion of the resuscitation. Rose identified four contributory factors: the person they borrowed money from; the men who tried to take the equipment; the business partner who left her in difficulties; and herself.

In the next session, we went through the list, working out what degree of responsibility they carried. Rose finally concluded 'it was partly my fault, but I made the best decision I could at the time'. When reliving the resuscitation and feeling intense guilt, she brought to mind the knowledge that she had done the best she could and a current image of her boys. At points, she needed some time to focus on these 'updates' before her distress reduced. Only one reliving session was required to get rid of the intrusions to the resuscitation.

We then focused on the intrusions to the rape. These memories were much more fragmented. She experienced intrusions of her uncle exposing himself and had no memory of what followed, although she always described it as rape. She identified one hotspot, when she thought 'no one would believe me' and felt confused, fearful, and 'totally alone'.

After discussing various ways to 'update' the memory, Rose decided to restructure it by bringing her adult self into the memory to incorporate her new understanding of what happened. We agreed her adult self would explain that it was not her fault (Arntz & Weertman, 1999). Reliving this, Rose became intensely distressed and needed to pause at frequent intervals to allow her adult self to provide comfort and reassurance. Bringing her adult self into the memory reduced her sense of isolation. She remembered her uncle cornering her in a garage and forcing her to touch him, but not what followed. After the reliving, she felt exhausted and tearful and the memories played on her mind for a few days. The frequency of her intrusions reduced.

During the second reliving, Rose became much more distressed and remembered the entire event in great detail, including aspects she had not remembered previously. This account was full of sensory detail, including a moment of extreme pain, when her head became very 'fuzzy'. After reliving, she was extremely disturbed by what she remembered, partly because she realized the rape must have been premeditated. After the first few days, her intrusions ceased, but coming to terms with the full implications of what happened and the impact on her life was very distressing. The 'fuzzy' dissociated sensation she experienced during the trauma helped account both for the dissociative symptoms she experienced as an adult, and why these were so distressing. After this reliving, the dissociative experiences gradually disappeared.

Outcome

After treatment (40 sessions) Rose no longer had any re-experiencing symptoms, but continued to have some low-level avoidance and hyperarousal symptoms. Her CAPS score was 18 (asymptomatic/few symptoms) and BDI score was 8 (minimal).

DISCUSSION

Progress was much slower with Jyoti and often felt as though we took two steps forward and one step back. Some techniques she did not wish to try, and others, such as using an image of the perfect nurturer (Lee, 2005), had unexpected pitfalls, triggering dissociation. This illustrates the need for creativity and flexibility with this type of work. Equally, there were a number of occasions when she became distressed and concluded the session early. Trying to pace the work to maximize progress while keeping her distress within manageable limits required constant attention.

In both cases, books significantly facilitated cognitive change. Self-help guides, autobiography, fiction, films, support groups and websites all provide access to other people's trauma experiences. Although some people do, initially, say that others also deserve abuse, this view usually changes fairly rapidly. Once they accept that someone else did not deserve abuse, it becomes hard to maintain the belief that they alone do.

Very occasionally, during one traumatic event, intrusions to earlier traumas are triggered. This is more likely when there are strong similarities between the events. This can mean that re-experiencing symptoms of one trauma includes intrusions to earlier events. Usually, it makes sense to relive the earlier trauma first, so that it becomes more manageable and less distressing before proceeding to other traumas.

Risk issues

Discussion of the traumatic event is distressing for most people and can lead to an increase in symptoms up to a few days afterwards. With people already at risk of self-harm, suicide, or harm to others, careful assessment of their ability to tolerate this is required and other interventions may be necessary before it is safe to proceed with trauma-focused work (see also Holmes & Butler, Chapter 12, this volume).

Affect-regulation difficulties

If people have PTSD to multiple events, their level of symptoms, including hyperarousal, is likely to be high. When this is present, it is important to check that they have the affect-regulation skills to tolerate the temporary increase in arousal associated with reliving. When these are insufficient, work on affect-regulation skills may need to precede trauma-focused work. Occasionally, people may be unable even to provide details of their trauma history, until after they have developed better strategies for managing distress.

Dissociation

Dissociation interferes with the processing of trauma memories, so grounding strategies may be necessary (see Kennerley, Chapter 7, this volume).

Trust and the therapeutic relationship

Repeated abuse experiences often lead to difficulties trusting others, therapists included. In these situations particular care needs to be devoted to the therapeutic relationship, and explicit validation of their difficulties and how to develop a trusting relationship can be helpful.

Alternative approaches

When there are re-experiencing symptoms of too many events to take separately, as is often the case for refugees, other approaches like testimony can be used. Once the total number of intrusions has reduced, reliving can be used with those that remain. Even those who have experienced years of abuse, however, may have re-experiencing symptoms to only two or three events.

Issues specific to particular groups

PTSD to multiple traumatic events in adulthood

The experience of persecution in adulthood is hugely different, depending on whether it is perpetrated by the state or a spouse. Refugees are less likely to feel that they have been singled out for abuse because of personal characteristics, although this may still occur. If, on the other hand, traumatic experiences occur in the course of employment, this is likely to be something that has been chosen, and training in dealing with dangerous situations may have been provided. Colleagues may have experienced similar events, although discussing them may not be easy. High-risk occupational groups, such as the armed forces, tend to have organizational cultures that expect staff to take traumatic events in their stride, minimize distress, and stigmatize mental health problems. Some also have a culture of heavy drinking.

Domestic violence

Rates of PTSD in this population are high, ranging from 33 to 84%. Between half and two thirds of female victims report histories of child sexual abuse, and those with childhood trauma histories are more likely to report feeling guilt and responsibility following experiences of domestic violence in adulthood (Follette, Polusny, Bechtle, & Naugle, 1996; Street, Gibson, & Holohan, 2005). Some level of safety is required (i.e., no longer at imminent risk from the perpetrator) before the processing of the trauma memories can take place.

High-risk occupational groups

Treating people currently employed in high-risk occupations, or planning to return to one, raises issues about the risk of exposure to further traumatic events, and the possibility of relapse or developing PTSD to another event. With those currently working, one may need to consider whether their symptoms could make them a risk to others. Carrying firearms may be undesirable for people who are irritable and/or hypervigilant.

Refugees and asylum-seekers

There are specific psychosocial and cultural issues relevant in this group (see d'Ardenne & Farmer, Chapter 18; Mueller, Chapter 17; and Young, Chapter 16, all this volume).

PTSD to events in childhood

Most commonly, people with PTSD to traumatic events in childhood have experienced physical or sexual abuse. Since the events occur when beliefs about the self, the world, and other people are still developing, childhood abuse is highly associated with shame and negative beliefs about the self and others. This may include a sense of responsibility for the abuse. Clinically, this is important because shame appears to be strongly related to treatment drop-out (McDonagh et al., 2005).

Childhood is when one learns how to cope with distress, so traumatic events may disrupt the development of constructive affect-regulation strategies. Those subjected to repeated abuse over which they are likely to have had little or no control may develop a more pervasive avoidant coping style.

Traumatic events in childhood, therefore, are a risk factor for borderline and other types of personality disorder, but it is important to be clear that many people have experienced physical and/or sexual abuse in childhood without developing personality disorders.

Nevertheless, abuse in childhood is associated with a wide range of psychological symptoms in adulthood and many authors suggest that it needs to be conceptualized in such a way as to capture the complexity of the comorbidity with more subtlety than the current ICD 10/DSM IV Axis I/Axis II distinctions allow (Briere & Spinazzola, 2005). Careful assessment is of paramount importance, focusing on the presenting phenomenology, rather than simply on diagnostic categories. Certainly, it should not be assumed that people who have experienced traumatic events in childhood will necessarily have PTSD.

When working with people with PTSD to childhood trauma it sometimes occurs that people, like Rose, remember other traumatic events, or parts of events, either during reliving or at other times. The recovered memories issue is contentious, but clinicians and researchers have a responsibility to investigate how to help clients distressed by 'new' memories. Although such memories can be distressing and disturbing to both client and clinician, it is important to remember that they respond to reliving in exactly the same way as other intrusions.

The memories of those exposed to childhood trauma, especially chronic trauma, are likely to be even more fragmented than those with PTSD to a single event in adulthood. Sometimes these are somatic or auditory intrusions (particularly if abuse occurred in darkness). The 'affect bridge' technique (Watkins, 1971) can help identify the source memory. For example, one client with PTSD to child sexual abuse always found herself becoming distressed and fearful when she caught a cold and felt mucus in her throat. Focusing on this sensation immediately triggered memories of being forced to perform oral sex. Reliving these memories reduced these reactions.

Whether or not people recall new information, once they start processing the trauma memories, there is often a period of distress as they come to terms with the implications of what happened. Even those who have always known about the extent of the abuse may have considered it impulsive. As their trauma memories become integrated in the wider autobiographical memory base, they may realize it must have been premeditated, causing distress. Alternatively, recognizing the myriad ways in which their lives have been affected may cause considerable grief.

PTSD to events in both child and adulthood

Women sexually abused as children are more likely to be assaulted as adults (reviewed in Follette et al., 1996). Compared with women sexually assaulted as adults, but without a history of child sexual abuse, re-traumatized women are more likely to report high levels of dissociative symptoms (Cloitre,

Scarvalone, & Difede, 1997). Forty-five per cent of women with histories of both child and adulthood abuse had attempted suicide, which underlines the need for careful risk assessment in this population.

Service-related issues

Even in the absence of complicating factors such as entrenched negative beliefs or difficulties establishing a trusting therapeutic relationship, the treatment of people with PTSD to multiple events will take longer than is needed for single-incident PTSD. When these complicating factors are present, treatment is likely to be significantly longer. Boos (2007) describes a phase-based treatment for multiply traumatized people with PTSD providing up to 60 sessions of treatment. Given the increasing pressures on psychological services in the UK, this is an issue for services, as well as individual clinicians. When services provide fixed limits on the total number of sessions clients can receive in one episode of care, some services offer clients that number of sessions per year, so that treatment is conducted in a series of episodes. However, that presupposes that it is possible to establish a sufficiently strong therapeutic relationship within that time-frame, and most clients and clinicians prefer to complete treatment within one episode of care. In the UK Health Service the National Institute of Health and Clinical Excellence (NICE) guidelines explicitly state that 'Healthcare professionals should consider extending the duration of treatment beyond 12 sessions if several problems need to be addressed in the treatment of PTSD sufferers, particularly after multiple traumatic events' (National Collaborating Centre for Mental Health, 2005, 129). To ensure that those with PTSD to multiple events receive the treatment they need, it may be helpful to provide more specific guidance about treatment length as more evidence about the treatment of people with PTSD to multiple events emerges.

There are many people like Jyoti and Rose with PTSD to multiple events, high levels of symptoms, and intense distress affecting all areas of their lives. Careful assessment of their hotspots, and whether or not cognitive restructuring is necessary before reliving, allows one to identify memories that may be treated relatively quickly. Accurate formulation of the relationship between beliefs and traumatic events facilitates efficient use of treatment, although this is still likely to require extending treatment considerably beyond the 12 sessions recommended in the NICE guidelines for PTSD.

Treating people with multiple-event PTSD requires creativity, flexibility, and regular, skilled, supervision. Cognitive techniques can change the beliefs of those convinced that they do not 'deserve love, attention, or even recognition as a human being' to the realization that they are good people who deserve happiness. This work can transform the lives of extremely distressed clients, and is highly rewarding for both clients and clinicians.

SUMMARY PATHWAY

1   Risk: Detailed discussion of traumatic events is distressing. Does the client have the distress-tolerance skills to do so safely? If not, work on reducing suicidality or developing better affect-regulation skills will be required.
2   Dissociation: If the client is having frequent derealization or depersonalization (out-of-body) experiences, preliminary work on grounding skills will be necessary.
3   Collect information regarding formative experiences and longstanding negative beliefs, including the current strength of the belief (out of 100).
4   If possible, given the number of traumatic events, collect information about peri-traumatic hotspots for each trauma, especially whether any longstanding negative beliefs were activated, and/or they experienced shame, guilt, anger, or humiliation.
5   Formulate how the various experiences, beliefs, and traumatic events relate to each other.
6   Provide the client with an explanation for their PTSD symptoms, and a rationale for treatment.
7   Discuss with the client which event to work on first. If they have re-experiencing symptoms to an event in which no longstanding negative beliefs were activated, and/or they did not experience shame, guilt, anger, or humiliation peri-traumatically, reliving is likely to be more effective.
8   If they have re-experiencing symptoms both to an event (or events) in which longstanding negative beliefs were activated and events in which this did not occur, it is usually best to reduce the PTSD to the latter before tackling those incorporating the activation of entrenched negative beliefs.

ACKNOWLEDGEMENTS

I would like to thank all the clients who have shared their experiences of trauma with me over the years, from whom I have learned so much. I am especially grateful to the clients who generously gave their permission for me to write accounts of their therapy.

REFERENCES

Arntz, A., & Weertman, A. (1999). Treatment of childhood memories: Theory and practice. *Behaviour Research and Therapy*, *37*, 715–740.
Blake, D., Weathers, F., Nagy, L., Kaloupek, D., Klauminzer, G., Charney, D., & Keane, T. (1990). A clinician rating scale for assessing current and lifetime PTSD: The CAPS-1. *Behaviour Therapy*, *13*, 187–188.
Boos, A. (2007). Characteristics of intrusive memories and non-memory intrusions

and their change in treatment in multiply traumatised patients with PTSD. V World Congress of Behavioural and Cognitive Therapies. Barcelona. 14 July.

Briere, J., & Spinazzola, J. (2005). Phenomenology and psychological assessment of complex posttraumatic states. *Journal of Traumatic Stress, 18*(5), 401–412.

Briscoe, C. (2006). *Ugly: the true story of a loveless childhood.* London: Hodder and Stoughton.

Carlson, E. (2001). Psychometric study of a brief screen for PTSD: Assessing the impact of multiple traumatic events. *Assessment, 8*(4), 431–441.

Cienfuegos, A., & Monelli, C. (1983). The testimony of political repression as a therapeutic instrument. *American Journal of Orthopsychiatry, 53*, 41–53.

Cloitre, M., Scarvalone, P., & Difede, J. (1997). Posttraumatic stress disorder, self- and interpersonal dysfunction among sexually retraumatised women. *Journal of Traumatic Stress, 10*(3), 437–452.

Creamer, M., & Forbes, D. (2004). Military populations. In S. Taylor (Ed.), *Advances in the treatment of posttraumatic stress disorder.* New York: Springer.

Duffy, M., Gillespie, K., & Clark, D.M. (2007). Posttraumatic stress disorder in the context of terrorism and other civil conflict in Northern Ireland: Randomized controlled trial. *British Medical Journal, 334*, 147–150.

Ehlers, A., & Clark, D. (2000). A cognitive model of posttraumatic stress disorder. *Behaviour Research and Therapy, 38*, 319–345.

Ehlers, A., Clark, D., Hackmann, A., McManus, F., & Fennell, M. (2005). Cognitive therapy for post-traumatic stress disorder: Development and evaluation. *Behaviour Research and Therapy, 43*, 413–431.

Follette, V., Polusny, M., Bechtle, A., & Naugle, A. (1996). Cumulative trauma: The impact of child sexual abuse, adult sexual assault and spouse abuse. *Journal of Traumatic Stress, 9*(1), 25–35.

Grey, N., Young, K., & Holmes, E. (2002). Cognitive restructuring within reliving: A treatment for peritraumatic emotional 'hotspots' in posttraumatic stress disorder. *Behavioural and Cognitive Psychotherapy, 30*, 37–56.

Hembree, E., Rauch, S., & Foa, E. (2003). Beyond the manual: The insider's guide to prolonged exposure therapy for PTSD. *Cognitive and Behavioural Practice, 10*, 22–30.

Herman, J. (1992). *Trauma and recovery: From domestic abuse to political terror.* London: HarperCollins.

Jaycox, L., & Foa, E. (1996). Obstacles in implementing exposure therapy for PTSD: Case discussions and practical solutions. *Clinical Psychology and Psychotherapy, 3*(3), 176–184.

Lee, D. (2005). The perfect nurturer: A model to develop a compassionate mind within the context of cognitive therapy. In P. Gilbert (Ed.), *Compassion: Conceptualisations, research and use in psychotherapy.* Hove: Routledge.

Lee, D. (2006). Case conceptualisation in complex PTSD: Integrating theory with practice. In N. Tarrier (Ed.), *Case formulation in cognitive behaviour therapy: The treatment of challenging and complex cases.* Hove: Routledge.

McDonagh, A., Friedman, M., McHugo, G., Ford, J., Sengupta, A., Mueser, K., Demment, C., Fournier, D., Schynurr, P., & Descamps, M. (2005). Randomised trial of cognitive behavioural therapy for chronic posttraumatic stress disorder in adult female survivors of childhood sexual abuse. *Journal of Consulting and Clinical Psychology, 73(3)*, 515–524.

National Collaborating Centre for Mental Health. (2005). *Clinical guideline 26. Post-traumatic stress disorder (PTSD): The management of PTSD in adults and children in primary and secondary care.* London: National Institute for Clinical Excellence.

Pelzer, D. (2000). *The lost boy.* London: Orion.

Schauer, M., Neuner, F., & Elbert, T. (2005). *Narrative exposure therapy: A short-term intervention for traumatic stress disorders after war, terror or torture.* Gottingen: Hogrefe.

Smucker, M., Dancu, C., Foa, E., & Niederee, J. (1995). Imagery rescripting: A new treatment for survivors of childhood sexual abuse suffering from posttraumatic stress. *Journal of Cognitive Psychotherapy: An International Quarterly, 9*(1), 3–17.

Street, A., Gibson, L., & Holohan, D. (2005). Impact of childhood traumatic events, trauma-related guilt, and avoidant coping strategies on PTSD symptoms in female survivors of domestic violence. *Journal of Traumatic Stress, 18*(3), 245–252.

Terr, L. (1991). Childhood traumas: An outline and overview. *American Journal of Psychiatry, 148*, 10–20.

Watkins, J. (1971). The affect bridge: A hypnoanalytic technique. *International Journal of Clinical and Experimental Hypnosis, 19*(1), 21–27.

Chapter 14

Trauma-focused cognitive therapy in the context of ongoing civil conflict and terrorist violence

Michael Duffy and Kate Gillespie

INTRODUCTION

Human conflict often involves groups that share the same territory and reside within the same region or state. In this chapter we consider how these inter-group processes have a bearing on the provision of a therapeutic response to people who, as a consequence of such conflicts, develop psychological problems, particularly post-traumatic stress disorder (PTSD). Such inter-group dynamics are not usually as relevant to the treatment of PTSD arising from traumas not related to civil conflict. As violence reduces, the improved context can assist the treatment of PTSD, for example, by facilitating the use of behaviour experiments. However, it is important to recognize that PTSD can also be effectively treated whilst conflict prevails. Indeed, as societies emerge from conflict, violence does not instantly end but remains in many forms for a considerable period of time.

The recent 30-year conflict in Northern Ireland has produced much suffering (McKitterick, Kelter, Feeney, & Thornton, 1999), significant numbers have experienced multiple traumas (Muldoon, Schmid, Downes, Kremer, & Trew, 2004), and have suffered from psychological problems including chronic PTSD for many years (Shevlin & McGuigan, 2003). One of the damaging effects of civil conflict is that communities are torn apart and inter-group attitudes become extremely polarized. In Northern Ireland today society is still divided along religio-political sectarian lines: more than 70% of public sector housing estates are comprised of more than 90% Catholic or 90% Protestant, and 95% of children attend exclusively Catholic or Protestant schools (Community Relations Unit, OFMDFM, 2003). At the height of the conflict, after a sectarian attack had been perpetrated against a member or members of one community, blame for the violation was often attributed by the victim's social group not only to the individual gunman or his paramilitary organization but to the entire ethno-religious group from which he emerged. These processes present a number of challenges for therapists. A society emerging from conflict contains a multitude of potential stimuli that can easily trigger the onset or relapse of PTSD symptoms. In Northern

Ireland, for example, the early release of hundreds of prisoners has been sanctioned as part of the current peace process. As a consequence, in small communities it is entirely possible for victims to meet a former perpetrator of violence walking the street, which can provide a cue for intrusive memories of past traumas.

Since 1998, the Omagh-based trauma team has been providing cognitive therapy (CT) for PTSD (Ehlers & Clark, 2000; Ehlers, Clark, Hackmann, McManus, & Fennell, 2005) to people affected by terrorism and other civil conflict. The team has published two studies of the effectiveness of CT for PTSD, first with victims of a single incident car bombing (Gillespie, Duffy, Hackmann, & Clark, 2002), and more recently with a chronic and comorbid population (Duffy, Gillespie, & Clark, 2007). This chapter addresses specific features of the application of the cognitive model in this context of ongoing civil conflict and terrorist violence.

The cases that follow demonstrate the importance of, and the idiosyncratic nature of, appraisals relating to a traumatic event. In the incident reported, several members of the same family were confronted by gunmen who left a hoax bomb at their family home. Until the police declared the device safe several hours later, the bomb was believed to be genuine! Three of the family members developed PTSD and were successfully treated individually by therapists using CT for PTSD at the Northern Ireland Trauma Centre in Omagh. An anonymized summary of therapy with father and daughter is reported below.

CASE OF JOHN – THE FATHER

Assessment

John is a middle-aged man who lives with his wife and two teenage children. On the day of the incident he was taking an afternoon nap because he had been up at 5 am that morning. At initial assessment 9 months after the incident, John described it as follows:

> I woke from a deep sleep and heard the children shouting – 'there's a gunman at the door'. Then I heard my wife's voice shouting, 'it's a bomb'. I totally panicked, I ran out of the bedroom, saw M. [wife] in the street, she told me she had moved the bomb to the other side of the street. I dialed 999; can't remember what I said. I went back into the house and went out into the back garden and jumped over the wall and into the street warning people about the bomb. Then I realized Jane was missing. I was calling for her then she suddenly appeared. I didn't know where she came from or who brought her back. Police arrived; stopped the traffic, told Mary 'you're lucky you got away with it this time'. A neighbour invited us into his home – he believed he was the intended target – the whole family were crying, asking 'What did we do to deserve

this?', then we were told there would be a controlled explosion, I worried about the damage to our home. Everyone was panic stricken – they were shouting, I felt so terrible.

Five weeks following the incident John's PTSD symptoms had escalated to a point where he felt exhausted and could no longer cope at work. His GP prescribed an antidepressant and recommended some time off work. Initially this helped a little, in that he could be 'more in control of the family', i.e., in closer contact with them during the day. However, he was spending more time ruminating 'why us?', and whether the family 'could ever get back to normal'.

He returned to work, partly to distract himself from his PTSD symptoms, but his intrusive thoughts and nightmares continued and he worried even more now about his family's safety as he worked longer hours in an attempt to improve the company's sales. He received a phone call from the police to say that the attack on his home had been a case of 'mistaken identity' and that the intended target had been a 'high-profile' figure who lived in the neighbourhood.

At assessment John met criteria for PTSD and Major Depressive Disorder. He scored 31 on the PDS (severe range) and 34 on the BDI (severe range). He was finding it increasingly difficult to go to work because of the fear that something might happen to his family. He suffered from insomnia and experienced nightmares in which he heard 'great commotion' and noise, ringing of the doorbell and the voices of his children calling for help. In all of these nightmares he felt 'paralysed' and helpless, unable to rescue his family. While at work, he worried constantly about the safety of his wife and family. He felt 'exhausted, distracted, and unmotivated'. He avoided the travel element of his work as much as possible and, as a result, failed to reach sales targets.

Course of treatment

Session one (PDS 28, BDI 28)

John reported that he had benefited greatly from reading an information booklet that he had been given at assessment and that he had shared some of this information with his wife and daughter.

John's key intrusions were: (a) nightmares of his wife surrounded by gunmen or confronting aggressors; (b) seeing her lifting a bomb and running with it; (c) hearing his children and wife shouting, 'gunmen, bomb'; (d) looking for but not being able to find Jane – 'they have done something to her'; (e) seeing the terror in the faces of his wife and children.

John's key appraisals were: 'my wife could have died'; 'they have done something to my daughter'; 'I'm responsible – I left them vulnerable'; 'I must protect my family at all times'; 'We will never get back to being a normal family again'.

John's key maintaining behaviours were: ruminating over different scenarios where his family could be at risk in the course of the day and checking on them regularly by phone; withdrawing socially (he even stopped visiting his parents for fear that they would see 'the state' he was in); avoiding going into the garden after dark; and trying to keep the family home together at night.

The formulation highlighted the need to reverse the maintaining strategies of avoidance and ruminating. He agreed to attempt to take up walking again with his wife and to visit his parents.

Session two: Imaginal reliving session (PDS 24, BDI 23)

Following a detailed 'reliving' account of his traumatic experiences, the key hotspots identified were: (a) hearing his daughter shouting 'There's a gunman at the door' and his wife calling out 'It's a bomb' and thinking they're in grave danger (fear 100%); (b) hearing the policeman say 'You got away with it this time' and thinking 'my wife could have died' (horror 100%); (c) realizing that his daughter Jane is missing and thinking 'they have done something to her' (fear 100%); (d) seeing the terror in the faces of his wife and daughter and thinking 'They should not have had to bear this'; 'They will never get over it' (sad 80%, anxious 80%); 'It's my fault – I did not protect my family' (guilt 80%). Hotspots (a), (c) and (d) all corresponded to intrusions or nightmares experienced.

The homework set was to continue to 'reclaim' his life by re-engaging with extended family and friends and to listen to the tape of the reliving and record any new information remembered.

Session three (PDS 29, BDI 28)

John had listened to the audiotape of the reliving session on two occasions and had remembered some additional detail from the incident. A young man, a neighbour whom he knew, had gone to lift the bomb after his wife had put it down. John pleaded with him not to touch it but the young man said 'I'm sure it's harmless, no one would want to harm you'.

This session focused on targeting a number of appraisals. The main appraisal was, 'It's my fault I did not protect them' (90%) with the associated emotion of guilt (80%). Initially the evidence for and against this was discussed (see Table 14.1).

A pie chart was then used to apportion responsibility for the family's traumatic experience. John realized that the perpetrators and the conflict situation were the main contributors. At the end of the session the belief that it was his fault dropped to 50% and he rated his guilt at 40%.

The second appraisal was 'Jane has followed them; they will do something to her'. Through Socratic dialogue, John was able to see her running from the

Table 14.1 Addressing John's self-blame: 'it's my fault. I did not protect them'

Evidence for	Evidence against
I was in bed asleep in the early evening.	In bed early because I had agreed to drive a relative to the airport, which meant getting up at 5.00 a.m.
I left them exposed and vulnerable.	I was at home with my family.
If I was visible they might have realized they were at the wrong house.	Even if I had not been in bed, I would not have been visible to the gunman, given the layout of the house.
I would have been in more control.	Being more in control could have delivered a worse outcome – for example, confronting the gunman.
Jane might not have seen them.	Jane was already in the street – even if I was not in bed asleep, I would not have stopped her going out. I could not have predicted what was going to happen that evening – this was only the second such incident in the neighbourhood in 19 years.

scene in the context of a 'fight or flight' reaction and in retrospect that it was better that she chose the latter rather than confronting the gunman. He was also now able to focus on the fact that she returned immediately unharmed.

The final appraisal was 'they will never get over this'. Through Socratic dialogue, John was able to draw on his newly acquired knowledge of trauma and how it affects individuals. He concluded that they may not have had the same reaction as he had, he had given them the literature to read, and he decided to talk directly to them. He was sure he could persuade them to access help in the same way that he had, if they required it.

John's homework was to reflect on the written reappraisals of the hotspots and to check out with his wife and daughter how they were feeling at this time in relation to the traumatic event.

Session four (PDS 4, BDI 5)

John had spoken to his wife and daughter and to his surprise they both disclosed that they were still 'deeply affected' by the event. He persuaded them to go to their GP. In this session the focus was on updating the trauma memory by using cognitive restructuring within reliving, i.e., inserting the reappraisals reached in the previous session immediately following the hotspots with 'I now know that . . .' (Ehlers & Clark, 2000; Ehlers et al., 2005).

Session five: Final session (PDS 2, BDI 2)

This session included a final reliving, which showed less emotional response than before, and also reinforced that appraisals were fully 'emotionally' believed. John asked an interesting question, 'I wonder if we are all thinking about it [the trauma] in the same way?'

One-year follow-up (PDS 2, BDI 0)

At follow-up, John presented with continued improvements in mental and physical health. He stated that 'I appreciate life more, am more sensitive to others' needs, and I am in a better place than before this happened'.

CASE OF JANE – THE DAUGHTER

Assessment

Jane is a young teenager and is achieving well at school. One afternoon she was standing outside her home when members of a paramilitary group left a parcel, which turned out to be a hoax bomb, on the windowsill of her family living room. At the time, her father was sleeping, but her mother observed the parcel being dropped off. When the men moved away her mother ran out, lifted the device and removed it to the end of the drive-way. The police used a controlled explosion to destroy the device some time later.

Six months after the incident, Jane developed PTSD and depression. Her referral for therapy was precipitated by an incident in which Jane was walking through town and she saw a group of youths burning a car. Jane became very anxious and had a panic attack.

At assessment Jane was hyper-aroused, easily startled, and physically appeared exhausted. She re-experienced the traumatic incident in the form of nightmares and flashbacks and her sleep was greatly disturbed. She scored 34 on the PDS (severe range) and 31 on the BDI (severe range).

At assessment Jane described the incident very briefly as follows:

> I saw the men walking up to our gate, a man stood outside with a gun and he pointed it at me. I first thought it was just a prank and then I realized it was not and ran to the house screaming, Mum shouts 'it's a bomb' and I panic I'm really afraid. . . . Mum goes out and lifts the bomb . . . I run down the road screaming.

Course of treatment

Session one (PDS 35, BDI 27)

The first session focused on a cognitive formulation of her problems. Jane's key intrusions were linked to three specific elements of the trauma: (a) the hoax bombers walking into her drive; (b) one of them pointing a gun at her; (c) her mother carrying the 'bomb' out and calling to her. She was confused about the sequence of events and her memory lacked detail particularly at the most distressing parts of the narrative, and she was unable to understand why some parts were so distressing.

Jane's main appraisals linked to the trauma were: 'I was stupid; I should have done something to stop the bombers' and 'I now have to be awake in case they [the hoax bombers] come to the house again at night time because I know they are going to attack our house again'. During the weeks after the trauma she ruminated about the incident with a theme of recrimination and self-blame: 'If I had not have just stood there watching them, they might have went away. I should have done something to make them go away. I should have warned my family.'

The intrusions and appraisals led to an increased sense of current threat (Ehlers & Clark, 2000). In order to cope with this she adopted a number of strategies, such as checking around the house every evening for similar devices, sleeping with the light on in her bedroom, leaving the television on in her room to distract her mind, looking over her shoulder as she walked through town to and from school, and not going out socially. However, these strategies did not allow any further processing of the trauma memory, any re-appraisal of her concerns, nor allow her to re-establish her previous life-style. Hence her PTSD and low mood were maintained.

For homework she was given information about PTSD and cognitive therapy to read.

Session two: Imaginal reliving session (PDS 29, BDI 27)

During a 'reliving' of the event, Jane described a more detailed narrative and identified associated appraisals. The therapist noted Jane's emotional re-action to further enquire about important emotional and cognitive material.

> I am standing with my friends. One friend tells us that two men with balaclavas are coming up hill. I turn around and see two masked men walking up the drive of my house. I stand at the gate, I move toward the house, I stand looking at one of the men, he points the gun towards us, I start saying that is my house. My friend says it's 'J's friends playing a joke'. I want to believe her. We walk over to a neighbour's house. I'm running into the house now, I'm feeling so scared.

[Peritraumatic cognitions remembered at this point] Who are they? What do they want? Why are they at our house? What are they doing? Oh my God, they are gunmen! I should do something, but what should I do?

I see mother and I know father is sleeping in his bed. I'm screaming 'two men are at the house'. Pat arrives – a friend, and my brother arrives. Mother shouts 'it's a bomb' and I panic. I am really afraid. I run down the road, screaming and crying. I go down the hill – questioning and blaming myself saying I should have done something more useful like call my parents.

What did they want? Why did they leave a bomb at our house? They must have a reason. How could I have thought the guy [bomber] was J's friend, I was so stupid, I should have stopped them.

It takes 5–10 minutes between the masked men leaving our house and me telling my parents about the bomb. What if it had exploded because I was so slow to tell my parents? I saw myself standing saying stupidly to the bombers 'that's my house'.

My friends come down to comfort me. I push them away and run over the road and C calls over to me and I tell her to go away as well. I go hysterical and roar at everybody. I say I want to be on my own. I sit on the ground. I go up to M's house in shock, feel sick, I am all shaky. I hear mother had thrown it away.

If I'd done something, she would have not had to do this. I should have done something like rung the police, roared at them, tried to stop them.

Somebody phones the police – we all go to neighbours' houses and tell them to get out. Brother J's at girlfriend's house. I was worrying about him, asking 'where is he?' Police perform a controlled explosion at 3 am. Until then, I believed it was a real bomb. At 4 am, I went to doctors at health centre and was prescribed tablets. I went to aunty and uncle's house, I was too afraid to go home. I stayed awake with parents, aunties, uncles etc. They talked about the incident – I just sat and listened. 7 am we went home. Still 100% fear – terrified and exhausted. Uncle had to carry me into the house I stayed up all night – could not sleep. Days later we attended my great auntie's funeral. I thought 'She was a different religion from us, maybe that's why we were targeted'.

Jane's worst moments were: (a) I see guy coming into our house: I realize they are not J's friends – who are they? Why are they here? He points gun at me – I am going to be killed (80%); (b) I see the parcel on the windowsill, it's a bomb – the whole family are under attack (80%); (c) I hear Mum calling out 'it's a bomb' and I run out – we are all going to die (90%).

For homework Jane agreed to continue to reduce her checking, listen to the audiotape of the reliving session, and record any new information that came to mind from this.

Session three (PDS 20, BDI 22)

After listening to the audiotape of the reliving session Jane recorded the following additional details.

> We came out to the door, to our friend Pat so that he could tell my mum what had happened. My mum noticed something on the window. She walked up towards it and started roaring 'it's a bomb'. My brother J ran into the house to tell my dad and sister to get out, because there was a bomb. My mum leaned towards the 'bomb' again and Pat started roaring at her to stay back and then he tried to hold her back but my mum got to it and threw it away. Then I began to panic and ran screaming down the hill.

This was an invaluable piece of new information because in Jane's opinion the previous incomplete narrative did not adequately justify her perceived extreme reaction of running out screaming down the hill. Now we were able to update the incomplete and inaccurate memory 'I hear Mum calling out "it's a bomb" and I run out' with the accurate account, 'I see Mum picking up the bomb and I run out', which made more sense to Jane in terms of explaining her behaviour. The new piece of missing data, now remembered – 'Mum picks up the bomb *before* I run down the street, causing me to scream *at her because I realized how at risk she was*'. In the immediate aftermath, this hotspot was accentuated by rumination and retrospection, generating further distress when new appraisals were added, 'What if the bomb had exploded? Mum could have been killed'.

This important new information filled a gap in the sequence of events and helped Jane understand why this part of the narrative was so distressing; the slow build up before her mum lifted the bomb, the attempts to hold her mum back, all contributed to the level of peritraumatic distress that Jane had experienced. This detail was important in helping to challenge two other unhelpful appraisals. First, in relation to the belief 'I should have done something to stop her', Jane now realized that if someone stronger and older than her had tried unsuccessfully to stop her mother, what chance was she likely to have had? Second, in relation to Jane's belief that she had been slow in alerting her parents to the threat, she now remembered that James had already done so, therefore there was no need for her to raise the alarm. In addition, through discussion with friends as part of a homework assignment, Jane also discovered that the actual time between the men leaving and telling her parents was only 1–3 minutes rather than the 5–10 she had previously thought.

Session four (PDS 12, BDI 22)

One of Jane's main appraisals was 'our house was the intended target and therefore it can happen again'. Due to her distressed emotional state and avoidance, she had previously refused to engage in discussions about the event or likely reasons for her home being targeted. Shortly after the incident she heard a police officer say to her mother 'you were lucky this time'. She assumed his remarks meant that the bombers would return. However, we were able to clarify that the police officer was referring to her mother's brave but highly dangerous behaviour in lifting the (hoax) bomb and was not suggesting that the incident might be repeated. We then discussed the evidence for and against the belief that it would be likely to happen to her again. This included reference to recent media reports about a campaign by a paramilitary group against people associated with the new regional Government in Northern Ireland. Jane's neighbour was linked with the new administration, but she only learned this some time after the attack on her home, by which time her trauma beliefs had become so entrenched that the newly acquired information could not be assimilated. Only in the process of therapy did the new information acquire sufficient meaning to enable her to challenge the accuracy of her beliefs (see Table 14.2).

Jane was also continuing to reduce safety behaviours, such as checking the windowsill at night.

Table 14.2 Jane's conflicting beliefs – supporting and opposing evidence

Bomb intended for Mr G (neighbour)	Bomb intended for our house
Mr G is linked with the Government	Somebody was offended by our family
Certain paramilitaries are targeting these Government officials	Even if these groups are after Mr G, we are friends of Mr G, so we are targets anyway
Paramilitary groups have issued warnings in local press against Government officials	
Several other Government officials have been targeted	
Don't know of any friends of Government officials who have been targeted	
What would be the point of targeting their friends, and where would the list end if they did this?	
In session Jane reads reports from local newspapers of five other officials who have also been targeted.	

Session five (PDS 5, BDI 12)

The work in the previous session led to significant reduction in PTSD symptoms. Jane only experienced one nightmare during the previous week.

A list was drawn up to distinguish between what Jane believed to be true during the trauma and what she now knows to be true (see Table 14.3). These were used to 'update' the trauma memory by bringing them to mind during a further reliving.

The remaining distressing appraisal was related to guilt: 'If I'd done something during the trauma, this would not have happened'. The potential advantages and disadvantages of Jane's suggestions for alternative actions were considered.

1 'I could have said something about this being the wrong house'

The possible consequences now accepted by Jane in session were that 'the gunmen might have panicked if confronted or might have gone inside to check whose house it really was and her parents might have been attacked, instead the gunman remained calm and walked away slowly'.

Table 14.3 Jane: what I thought then versus what I know now

Then	Now
See the guy coming towards our house He points a gun at me Maybe they're J's friends Why are they there?	A paramilitary group. No harm comes to us We are all safe
They are not J's friends	They are a paramilitary group leaving a hoax bomb at our house but it's a mistake
Who are these guys? Why are they at our house? What did they do?	
I see a bomb on windowsill It is a bomb Why is it on our windowsill?	It's not a bomb It was left on our windowsill by mistake
Mum picks up device. It's a bomb We're going to die	It's not a bomb We're all safe
Post-trauma appraisal – I should have done something, instead of stupidly saying 'that's my house'. They would have gone away.	I feel stupid

2 'I could have screamed at them'

The likely consequences now agreed were that 'they might have shot me and Mum may have ran out. They may have shot Mum also and Dad would have went after them and been shot'.

Jane concluded that there was nothing else she could have done during the event to prevent it.

Final treatment session (PDS 0, BDI 11)

Jane's PTSD symptoms were in the sub-clinical range and she was no longer employing safety behaviours. Her mood, sleep pattern, and concentration had improved significantly. Her schoolwork had recovered and she had recommenced social engagements with her friends.

Three-month booster session (PDS 0, BDI 2)

Jane now had no anxiety symptoms, and her mood, concentration, and sleep had all improved. Jane reported confidence about forthcoming exams.

One-year and 2-year telephone follow-up sessions (PDS 0, BDI 0)

Jane was still symptom-free and now abroad studying at university.

DISCUSSION

The cases illustrate the importance of idiosyncratic appraisals in the maintenance of PTSD. Despite long periods of discussion about the incident in the immediate aftermath, each individual within the same family had formed quite distinct appraisals of the incident and the aftermath. All three were self-critical about their own behaviours, and privately held some critical appraisals about the actions of another family member. Some of these appraisals may have been difficult to discover in a family group session, as they were linked to strong feelings of anger or shame. The cases also demonstrate the importance of professionals understanding the importance of the 'subjective' factors (appraisal of the event) as well as the 'objective' factors (nature of the event) when diagnosing or commenting on the severity of PTSD.

Treatment in the context of civil conflict and terrorist violence

There are a number of other important factors that are pertinent to the treatment of PTSD in the context of civil conflict and terrorist violence. One is the chronic and complex nature of the disorder with which clients who are exposed to repeated traumas present. In Northern Ireland, many clients have been exposed to several violent incidents over a 30-year period and meet criteria for PTSD and a range of other disorders. For example, one client's colleagues had been killed in an explosion 30 years ago, his uncle was later killed in a car bomb explosion, and more recently his son had been badly injured in a stabbing attack by a gang from the other side of the community. Comorbid conditions such as complicated grief, panic disorder with agoraphobia, and major depressive disorder are common amongst this chronic PTSD population (see Duffy & Gillespie, in press).

Establishing trust

In conflict scenarios, the therapist frequently must take more time to establish and develop trust, particularly with groups such as security personnel (army, police) and former combatants, who are extra vigilant in relation to their own personal security during the conflict. Trust is particularly important when the client and therapist are perceived to be members of the opposing ethno/religious social groups. During early stages of therapy, these clients often test out the genuineness, sincerity, and impartiality of the therapist and place great importance on confidentiality, safety, and security factors. These factors must be explicitly addressed to enable therapy to commence, by using Socratic dialogue to probe for cognitive biases such as over-generalized beliefs or dichotomous thinking. The following dialogue is an example with a client who had suffered multiple traumas and had a high level of suspicion of all members of the opposing group, including the therapist.

CLIENT: You know it is not easy to talk about these things. I have had to be careful all my life about who I talk to. If my uncle had been more careful, he'd still be alive today. What guarantees have I that I can trust you?

THERAPIST: OK, let's check for information that might be of help to you in this respect. When you were attacked on the street, who treated your wounds?

CLIENT: The local hospital staff, they were alright.

THERAPIST: And more recently, when your son was attacked, who treated your son's wounds?

CLIENT: The Casualty unit and right enough they were brilliant, they probably saved his life.

THERAPIST: Did the staff in the Casualty unit ask what religion your son was before they treated him?

CLIENT: Not at all.

THERAPIST: And did you think it necessary to check the religious background of the staff in the Casualty unit at the time.

CLIENT: No, why should I, they were only trying to help him.

THERAPIST: Could it be possible that your therapist might also only be interested in trying to help you?

CLIENT: I suppose so. We'll give it a go and see.

In such circumstances, therapy can be set up as a behavioural experiment to test out the over-generalized beliefs about the level of threat from out-group members, and often by the end of therapy result in a reduction of negative stereotype assumptions.

Therapists have to be more sensitive to issues that would not normally be associated with mistrust or generate suspicion in non-conflict zones. For example, a routine suggestion by the therapist to organize an appointment for the same time on the same day at the same clinic each week was misconstrued by the patient as placing him under an unnecessary form of threat. During the intense period of the conflict he had developed 'appropriate' security behaviours, such as varying his times and routes of travel. However, due to his PTSD, this patient had not adjusted his threat appraisals to take into account the reduced level of violence. Thus the therapist's appointment plans were appraised by him as abandoning a strategy he had employed for years and were viewed with extreme suspicion.

He retained the safety behaviour of arriving early for his appointment, but this backfired because as he sat in the waiting room in a perceptually primed state, he misinterpreted several 'normal' centre activities as evidence of a plot against him. As he entered the centre he observed a therapist giving a lecture and drawing on the whiteboard, which he misconstrued as someone drawing his different routes to the centre. Second, he saw another patient, whom he perceived to be from 'the opposing side of the community', and became more agitated. He concluded that the clinic was part of a conspiracy to harm him and that the therapist too was part of the perceived plot. These appraisals and the negative effects of the safety behaviours had to be addressed immediately at the start of the session because of his highly aroused state. Such intense levels of fear and suspicion associated with severe PTSD can sometimes be mistaken as paranoid psychotic features.

Appraisals about ongoing threat/objective risk

A complication for the therapist working in a civil conflict scenario where the level of violence is fluctuating is facilitating the client in the discovery of the actual, as opposed to the exaggerated, level of threat. One client believed that 'danger is always around and I can only cope with it by staying indoors at home'. Another stated 'Even though the terrorist activity is reduced, the level of threat to me will always remain high'.

One common feature of PTSD arising from conflict is that exaggerated appraisals about the level of threat remain constant and rigid, even as the conflict subsides. As these appraisals relating to threat are so varied and idiosyncratic, they are usually most effectively challenged by behavioural experiments to test out the actual level of threat. This may involve site visits to locations populated by the opposite side of the community to which the client belongs.

In the months after the Omagh bombing, 60–70 hoax bomb warnings were received relating to the town centre, some of which occurred whilst clients and therapists were undertaking such behavioural experiments. Although distressing at the time for some clients, these events were skilfully employed by therapists to assist clients to reappraise the meaning of the events and arrive at more balanced appraisals about the actual levels of threat ('the town was evacuated and we survived', 'the warning was a hoax and not an actual bomb' etc.).

Appraisals about the 'other community'

Behavioural experiments can also be used to challenge over-generalized appraisals of levels of threat attributed to the entire out-group members, and such experiments can involve visits to locations that are frequented by members of the opposing group. When designing such behaviour experiments, a collaborative assessment of legitimate safety factors is required so that the experiment does not put the client or therapist at risk, but it is also important that the therapist does not collude with the client's exaggerated threat appraisals.

One client had avoided his town centre for 10 years following a serious sectarian attack. An experiment was designed for him to purchase an item in a shop that was frequented by members of both ethno/religious groups. In the shop were four women whom he recognized. Three of the women (all members of the opposite religious group) were pleasant to him, whilst one was 'stuck up and distant' and he recognized her as a member of his group of origin.

The cognitive model acknowledges the important role of the environment in shaping the beliefs and the cognitive organization, or schemas, of an individual. Schematic structures develop not in isolation from the world we live in but 'through the continuous interaction of the organism with the environment' (Clark, Beck, & Alford, 1999, 65). During inter-group conflict, 'group think' processes influence individual appraisals in relation to traumatic events and beliefs that are formed about the conflict in general. Therapy can be challenging in a post-conflict society that remains divided retaining inter-group divisions and suspicions about members of the 'other community'. For these experiments, it is essential that therapists are in tune with changes in the community context.

Appraisals relating to anger

Many victims of terrorist violence, such as those who are traumatically bereaved, experience intense and often prolonged periods of anger. A common feature of conflict resolution scenarios is that former perpetrators of violence are given early release from prison. Some of these ex-prisoners become members of new post-conflict political establishments and for some victims the sight of ex-prisoners walking the street or holding prominent positions in society generates intense anger. Examples are: 'What was it all for?', 'Did my colleagues die for this? This was all a waste of time', 'The world is unjust, he is getting on with his life now and my son is dead'.

Following clear expressions of empathy, typically the therapist explores with the client what it would mean to be less angry (e.g., he'll be forgotten, they'll have got away with it), and ultimately what would be gained and lost by holding onto the anger? It is useful to ask clients to review a society emerging from conflict from a future time perspective. One extremely angry client was asked to use imagery and look back at today's level of violence through the eyes of his grandchildren 10 years from now.

THERAPIST: How do you think they will judge today's level of violence?
CLIENT: They probably won't even talk about it.
THERAPIST: How do you think they will feel about the conflict? Would you like them to feel as you do today?
CLIENT: No bloody way. I want them to be happy.

This session helped distance himself from his own personalized anger to more objectively appraise the process of a reduction in level of threat and violence, and divert his cognitive and behavioural strategies toward the future instead of continuing to ruminate on past traumas.

Therapist factors and supervision

In general, the needs of therapists must be addressed whilst working with trauma. In inter-group conflict scenarios it is important for therapists to remain impartial and neutral when dealing with clients from various sections of the community. In addition, the reliving of many gruesome traumas can vicariously traumatize therapists if teams and workloads are not managed carefully. Supervision is essential, in terms of support and workload management, but also importantly in enabling therapists to maintain high standards of competency in treatment and fidelity to treatment protocols and models. This is not just an important factor relating to patient outcome, but also a protective factor in relation to the well-being of the therapist.

REFERENCES

Clark, D.A., Beck, A.T., & Alford, B.A. (1999). *Scientific foundations of cognitive theory and therapy for depression*. New York: Wiley.

Community Relations Unit OFMDFM. (2003). *A shared future: Response by the Community Relations Council*. Belfast: CRC.

Duffy, M., & Gillespie, K. (in press). Treating PTSD in the context of civil conflict, terrorist violence and on-going threat: Cognitive therapy experiences from Northern Ireland. In A. Ehlers, D.M. Clark, A. Hackmann, F. McManus, M. Fennell & N. Grey, *Cognitive therapy for posttraumatic stress disorder: A therapist's guide*. Oxford: Oxford University Press.

Duffy, M., Gillespie, K., & Clark, D.M. (2007). Posttraumatic stress disorder in the context of terrorism and other civil conflict in Northern Ireland: Randomized controlled trial. *British Medical Journal, 334,* 147–150.

Ehlers, A., & Clark, D.M. (2000). A cognitive model of posttraumatic stress disorder. *Behaviour Research and Therapy, 38,* 319–345.

Ehlers, A., Clark, D.M., Hackmann, A., McManus, F., & Fennell, M. (2005). Cognitive therapy for PTSD: Development and evaluation. *Behaviour Research and Therapy, 43,* 413–431.

Gillespie, K., Duffy, M., Hackmann, A., & Clark, D. (2002). Community based cognitive therapy in the treatment of post-traumatic stress disorder following the Omagh bomb. *Behaviour Research and Therapy, 40,* 345–357.

McKitterick, D., Kelter, S., Feeney, B., & Thornton, C. (1999). *Lost lives: The stories of the men, women and children who died as a result of the Northern Ireland troubles.* London: Mainstream.

Muldoon, O., Schmid, K., Downes, C., Kremer J., & Trew, K. (2005). *The legacy of the Troubles: Experiences of the Troubles. Mental health and social attitudes.* Belfast: OFMDFM Victims Unit & CRC.

Shevlin, M., & McGuigan, K. (2003). The long term psychological impact of Bloody Sunday on families of the victims as measured by The Revised Impact of Event scale. *British Journal of Clinical Psychology, 42,* 427–432.

Chapter 15

Compassion-focused cognitive therapy for shame-based trauma memories and flashbacks in post-traumatic stress disorder

Deborah A. Lee

INTRODUCTION

It is common for clinicians to encounter difficulties in the effectiveness of traditional cognitive therapy when working with clients who experience profound shame and shame flashbacks in the aftermath of trauma. Therapists report patients who struggle to access and believe a more balanced and helpful perspective on their traumatic experience in a way that is meaningful to them and thus helps them feel differently about the experience. For example, patients may report that they understand or can see that they are not to blame for their trauma. Yet they still feel to blame, in that they suffer from affect, such as shame, which is congruent with the cognitions of self-blame. Therapists often report that the use of the Socratic method and guided discovery to facilitate a shift in perspective on self-blame can lead to 'dead ends' as patients report such things as that they are bad because they were born that way or they have always felt that way, or that they are different from everyone else.

This chapter will address some of these difficulties as they present in therapy for post-traumatic stress disorder (PTSD) by first exploring some theoretical concepts and then introducing the key features of compassion-focused work, illustrated by clinical work with shame-based trauma memories. The clinical work described is embedded within the National Institute for Health and Clinical Excellence guidelines for the treatment of PTSD (National Collaborating Centre for Mental Health, 2005), and is combined with compassion-focused cognitive therapy (Gilbert & Irons, 2005) to enhance clinical practice with those who are overwhelmed with feelings of shame related to their trauma experiences.

THEORETICAL CONSIDERATIONS

Shame is a distressing fear that other people hold you negatively in their minds (Gilbert, 1998) and a belief that such negative evaluations are true (e.g., other people think I am disgusting because of what I did and I think I am disgusting too). Thus shame is the response to threat, with the focus of the threat being on people's evaluation of you (*external threat*) and your own self-evaluation (*internal threat*). There is the possible consequence of rejection, abandonment, and isolation, and thus the focus of shame is on *social threat*. The experience of shame is associated with strong primary emotional responses to threat, such as fear, sadness, disgust, and anger as well as characteristic critical self-evaluation (Gilbert, 2000). People describe a feeling of being exposed and believe they are lacking, wanting, inadequate compared to others or lower down on the 'social status ladder'. They believe that others look down on them and will reject them if they 'found out' what they are 'really like'. As a general premise when working with shame, clinicians are aiming to help the patients overcome the fear of negative evaluation of self and others by developing a supportive, compassionate way of being with the self. Supportive self-soothing is associated with the stimulation of positive affect (probably related to the release of opiates), which appears to have the impact of reciprocally inhibiting the threat arousal and thus reducing the fear associated with the social threat. This idea will be explored more later on in this chapter.

Common experiences of those who suffer from shame are shame flashbacks, which may or may not be linked to trauma experiences. These are associated with reliving of vivid, painful, and emotionally intense memories linked to experiences of themselves as exposed, degraded, and inadequate in the eyes and mind of others. These may link to self-defining or self-working memories (Conway & Pleydell-Pearce, 2000) and they appear readily triggered by internal and external sensory cues that match an aspect of the current experience and convey matched meaning.

Self-criticism as a maintenance cycle in shame-based flashbacks

The way humans process threat-related stimuli is highly relevant in understanding shame and self-attack (Gilbert & McGuire, 1998) in the context of trauma. A signal from an external threat (e.g., someone wielding a knife) will be registered by the brain's threat system, located in the limbic system. The thalamus registers the 'threat' and sends signals both to the amygdala (the quick processing route; LeDoux, 1998) to release stress hormones (such as cortisol and neurochemicals), and to the cerebral cortex (the slower processing route). The hippocampus has a major role in contextualizing the meaning of the information received from the cortex and the amygdala. Under normal circumstances the hippocampus inhibits the function of the amygdala, which is responsible for producing the primary emotions. However, under extreme stress cortisol is released, which has the effect of enhancing the function of the amygdala and inhibiting the function of the hippocampus (see Figure 15.1). This allows us to react rather than think about danger (LeDoux, 1998).

The mobilization of the threat response involves the release of stress hormones (such as cortisol or nor-adrenaline), threat-focused thinking (narrowing of attention, rapid thinking), and safety seeking behaviours (fight, flight, freeze response). However, a signal from an internal threat (*an image* of a man wielding a knife) will produce the same effect on the limbic system, i.e., the stimulation of the threat response, especially if the image is related to real life experience of threat. This, of course, has useful implications for the use of imagery in therapy, which will be discussed later.

Our brains have evolved to process threat stimuli either from internal or external sources, and the amygdala is highly sensitive to both the tone and the content of speech. Thus self-critical thoughts such as 'you are despicable and disgusting' (a threat to the psychological integrity of the self and threat to social status) will be registered by the brain as highly threatening and consequently produce a threat response. Thus our own evaluations produce similar effects as to external attacks from others because we are capable of internalizing attacks from others, such as critical and abusive parents (Gilbert, 1989).

However, the amygdala, given its role in detecting threat, will also register stimuli from internal/external sources that are safe, and positive affect (linked to the self-soothing system and safeness) will be stimulated (Gilbert, 2000).

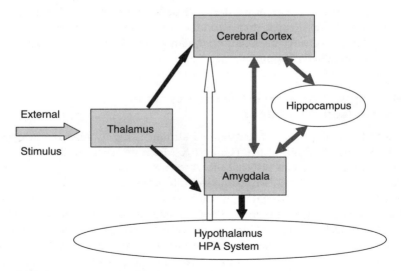

Figure 15.1 Brain areas involved in threat processing.

Gilbert's (1989) social mentality theory suggests that how we engage in social roles with our self and other people is shaped by experience and unless a child's processing systems for feeling warm and cared for are stimulated and elaborated through experiences, it is unlikely they will be available for use in 'self–self' relating (Gilbert & Irons, 2005). Hence the focus on the development of a compassionate relationship with the self is vital to providing people with the psychological resilience to deal with psychological threat-attacks on their self-integrity.

Trauma-related shame flashbacks are linked to experiences of psychological trauma in childhood and/or adulthood, which are represented in fragmented memory. Recent research suggests that most of the cognitive themes and associated emotions relating to threat in PTSD are in fact related to psychological threat to the self, such as 'I'm weak' (Holmes, Grey, & Young, 2005; Grey & Holmes, 2008), which may also be seen as a social threat from an evolutionary perspective. A significant number of people suffering from PTSD experience shame (Lee, Scragg, & Turner, 2001), are highly self-critical and lack the capacity to self-soothe (Harman, Lee, & Barker, 2008). For example, George, who was trapped in a car after a head-on collision, reported feeling ashamed and humiliated. His thoughts were related to feelings of being alone and frightened, whilst also thinking he was inadequate and foolish in his own mind and in the minds of others. The associated affect of shame also appears to be maintained by his self-criticism, and he feared that people would think badly of him and change their opinion of him if they knew about what had happened to him.

The ability to access feelings of safeness from psychological threat is key in the successful treatment of shame (Gilbert, 2000) and shame-based PTSD, as it ends the maintenance cycle of shame and self-attack (see Figure 15.2).

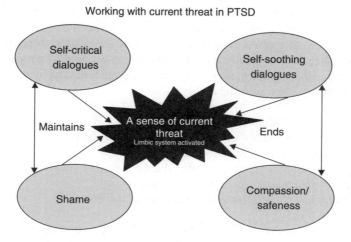

Working with current threat in PTSD

Figure 15.2 Self-dialogues and threat in PTSD.

Self-critical people often present with the heart/head lag in cognitive therapy, i.e., they understand that they are not bad, but they still feel they deserve to be punished. The development of a new belief, such as 'I am ok, I don't deserve this', does not trigger congruent emotional memories of the self as benign and deserving of care. This is probably because these key experiences are lacking from their childhood experiences and thus not stored on a bank of memories that relate to their sense of self. Consequently, this new perspective is effectively meaningless to them. Compassion-focused therapy offers ways to develop new emotional experiences and memories associated with positive affect in people who struggle to access such emotional memories.

COMPASSION-FOCUSED COGNITIVE THERAPY

Compassion-focused therapy was developed by Gilbert and his colleagues (Gilbert, 1989, 2000; Gilbert & Proctor, 2006; Gilbert, Lee, & Welford, 2006). The explicit goal is to develop, access, and stimulate positive affect associated with self-soothing in the mind and body of the patient in order to promote an inner sense of psychological safeness (Gilbert & Irons, 2005).

Gilbert (1989) suggests that the capacity to self-soothe and feel compassion for the self comes from the care-giving mentality and is learned in the context of the care-giving relationship. For example, the primary care giver offers validation, empathic understanding, care and soothing at times of distress, and this becomes an inner working model of self-soothing for the child. Consequently, how we self-soothe as adults will be directly influenced by our experiences of being cared for as a child (Bowlby, 1969). The ability to self-soothe as an adult is an essential skill needed to promote psychological wellbeing, as it allows us to deal with external threats from our social world (what other people think of us, how they treat us) and also internal threat (our own self-criticism). Being compassionate to the self is a state of mind, just as feeling threatened is a state of mind, and states of mind are related to physiological responses that govern behaviours, thought processes, and attention that are compatible with the needs and goals of the individual at that time.

Specific focus is given to the ability to:

1   tolerate and validate one's distress
2   be sensitive and know when one is upset and distressed
3   sympathize – to be moved by one's own distress
4   have warmth and genuine care for the wellbeing of yourself
5   be non-judgemental, as in non-condemning, and
6   be empathic – to understand the nature of the distress.

It is these qualities that, Gilbert suggests, create opportunities for growth and change in an individual through the development of a supporting, caring, kind, and warm relationship with the self, and that stimulates the affect system associated with self-soothing. The therapeutic relationship provides the foundation for this work and the compassionate focus mentality is demonstrated, modelled, encouraged, and reinforced by the therapist.

In those patients who struggle with profound feelings of shame, the ability to develop such qualities may take some considerable time. The most common stumbling block to the promotion of compassion is the patient's belief that they deserve to be punished because they are bad. Most people who struggle with profound feelings of shame and self-criticism believe that they do not deserve to treat themselves with genuine compassion, understanding, warmth, and care. Consequently they strongly believe, in spite of overwhelming evidence to the contrary, that they deserved/caused bad things to happen to them or were to blame for their trauma. The therapy focus is explicit in developing the insight that 'your struggles are not your fault', because traditional Socratic questioning is often limited in generating a more balanced and meaningful perspective on the issue of fault and blame in people who struggle to self-soothe. This is largely due to the lack of emotional experiences of themselves as feeling loved, soothed, supported, and validated, especially in childhood.

Thus one of the fundamental stages of the therapy is to develop the client's deep empathy for the non-intentionality of their difficulties and acts, and the understanding that their struggles, problems, and traumatic experiences are not their fault. Although this may seem obvious to some readers, most patients who experience profound levels of shame have spent their entire life blaming themselves for their perceived inadequacies, invalidating their own distress, and believing that there is something fundamentally wrong with them. The notion that their struggles are not their fault is often alien and frightening to them. Yet it is only when they are truly able to connect with the emotional understanding of the fact that their difficulties are not their fault that they can begin to offer themselves compassion, understanding, soothing, and in this context the development of kindness towards themselves for their suffering can activate profound grief for their loss. For the traumatized person who feels ashamed about their experiences, whether it be experiences of sexual abuse, adult rape, or torture, to understand that nothing about them made this thing happen to them is usually a turning point in therapy. Working from an emotional perspective in the first instance to help people develop positive affect, self-soothing capabilities, warmth, and kindness towards one's self, can have a profound impact on traditional trauma-focused cognitive behavioural therapy (CBT). The key phases of compassion-focused therapy are:

1   Explanation of the model
2   Shared formulation that 'it's not your fault'
3   Development of compassion for self
4   Compassionate focus on the self, goals, and future.

WORKING WITH SHAME-BASED FLASHBACKS AND TRAUMA MEMORIES

Exposure to the trauma memories, in one form or another, has been a predominant feature of cognitive behavioural treatment of PTSD for many years. Specifically, in trauma-focused CBT, trauma-related flashbacks are worked with by accessing the sensory-based memory using 'reliving' (Brewin, Dalgleish, & Joseph, 1996; Ehlers & Clark, 2000). Following Ehlers and Clark's (2000) model, the sense of current threat is reduced by bringing in new, updated information within reliving (Ehlers, Clark, Hackmann, McManus, & Fennell, 2005; Grey, Young, & Holmes, 2002).

For people who feel shameful and struggle to self-soothe, the successful updating of the meaning is achieved by accessing a more helpful and compassionate perspective to the traumatic experiences. In such cases the focus is the threat to the sense of self as viable, benign, and lovable. People often describe feeling ashamed, inadequate, and dirty as a consequence of their traumatic experiences. The sense of current threat is often maintained by self-critical dialogues, which activate the threat response. For example, the meaning conveyed in the flashback of a person who has been raped may not simply be 'I am being raped', but 'they must think I am dirty and disgusting and they must think I am worthless'. The task in therapy is to help the client to generate a new meaning that is connected to soothing emotional memories to help the person feel soothed and safe. For example, 'I am worthless' may be updated in a meaningful way, with the cognition, 'I am worthy', if this belief is associated with congruent emotional experiences, i.e., a sensory-based memory of the self as a worthy human being. In this way, one can update the meaning from psychological threat to psychological safeness and the experience of shame to one of self acceptance and soothing. Fundamental to the success of this intervention is the capacity of the individual to access emotional memories associated with self-soothing and self-acceptance.

Compassionate imagery, as well as being used to enhance the capacity of patients to access feelings of self-soothing as part of the therapeutic process (Gilbert, 2007; Lee, 2005), can also be used to work effectively with shame-based flashbacks – particularly as it uses imagery that symbolizes the emotional experience of safeness and self-soothing. It is quite usual to discover that patients struggle to develop self-soothing, and it is by no means an easy process in therapy. It can take a considerable length of time. This is particularly the case in traumatized people who have had experienced abuse in childhood. In some cases compassionate imagery, such as a 'perfect nurturer' (Lee, 2005) is used with the specific purpose and function of stimulating affect systems to create a sense of safeness in the mind of the person and thus reducing the threat response activation by reciprocal inhibition (akin to an on/off switch).

CASE EXAMPLES ILLUSTRATING THE INTEGRATION OF THEORY AND PRACTICE

Jo: Shame-based flashbacks relating to a single adult trauma

Jo, aged 28, came to therapy 4 years after she was raped in a horrific and brutal stranger attack. After this attack, Jo's world collapsed and she was no longer able to go to work or to go out with her friends. She felt depressed and very unsure of herself. She developed PTSD and she remained tormented by distressing memories and flashbacks to the attack. Her mind was plagued with thoughts of self-loathing and self-attack, and she experienced profound feelings of shame. She believed the attacker deliberately chose her because she was a horrible person and thus she thought the attack was her fault. A previous course of trauma-focused CBT had not significantly improved her symptoms.

Jo came from a loving family but she had been bullied at school, which mainly consisted of name calling, exclusion, and mocking from her peers. Consequently, Jo had suffered from poor self-esteem and a lack of confidence as an adult. However, she had made good friends as a young adult, had a full and varied social life, and was enjoying her work at a large department store prior to the attack.

Compassion-focused formulation

The focus of the shared formulation was to help Jo develop the insight that the rape was not her fault and that it was understandable that she blamed herself given her previous experiences in life such as bullying. We explored the notion that her self-attack could be seen as a safety behaviour in that if she blamed herself for her attack, perhaps that meant that there was something she could do to prevent such an attack happening again. We also hypothesized that the flashbacks to the rape were being maintained by thoughts of self-loathing and self-attack ('I am horrible, I am shameful, I am dirty'), which in turn were associated with overwhelming feelings of shame. Jo found this feeling so aversive that she engaged in attempts to avoid thinking and feelings related to the attack by cutting herself and misusing alcohol (see Figure 15.3).

Using an evolutionary-focused formulation (Gilbert & Irons, 2005), we discussed that as a result of Jo's early experiences of bullying it made sense that she had real fears about being hated and rejected by others and that she believed that she was a hateful person who deserved bad things to happen to her. We explored how, as a result of these experiences, her brain was highly threat-focused and that it responded to threat-related stimuli (such as fear of attack, other people's opinion of her, and her own thoughts about herself) by

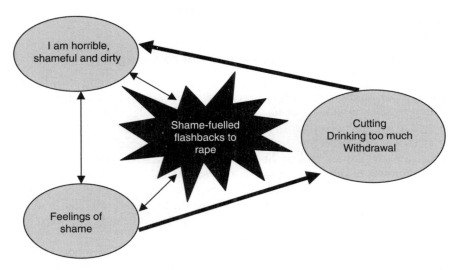

Figure 15.3 Jo's maintenance cycle.

releasing stress hormones and mobilizing the body's resources to manage the threat – such as withdrawal from other people and not wanting to go out, self-harm, and misuse of alcohol.

We developed a shared understanding that Jo's attempts to regulate the exposure to threat and experiences of shame by withdrawal and self-harm were not her fault, but that they had unintended consequences such as a sense of isolation. We hypothesized that Jo needed to develop other more helpful ways to manage perceived internal and external threat, namely by developing a compassionate and supportive self-dialogue to end the cycle of self-attack that was maintaining her flashbacks.

Compassionate reframe and updating the memory

Jo was very self-critical, struggling to 'believe' she was worthy and loveable. Although she understood objectively the stranger rape was not her fault, this did not change her emotional response to the attack. Jo struggled to self-soothe, had always feared that others did not like her because she was not good enough, and seemed perplexed by the notion that it was possible not to feel so fearful and scared of other people's opinion of you.

We embarked on a path of teaching Jo to self-soothe using the model of developing a compassionate mind. Jo was asked to consider the following questions in order to stimulate a care-focused mentality associated with self-soothing and warmth:

- What would compassionate 'attention' attend to or focus on?

- What would compassionate 'thinking' reflect?
- What would be a compassionate way to behave?
- How could you bring warmth, understanding, and acceptance into your experience?
- What would help you feel supported?
- What would you say/do to someone you care for?
- What would you like someone who cared for you to say/do?

In order to work effectively with Jo's shame-based flashbacks and to be able to 'update' them with a new emotional experience, two things needed to be present:

1 Jo's capacity to access a different meaning that not only has a cognitive component, but an emotionally congruent state and
2 Jo's ability to feel the new meaning of the event as a meaningful and helpful experience. For example, the statement 'I am worthy and loveable' would need to trigger emotional memories of her self as worthy and loveable in order for it to feel a meaningful and helpful statement.

It was essential to use examples, education, and demonstration to build insight into what would be a compassionate reframe of the meaning of events. The compassionate reframe is *not* about dismantling the evidence that supports the self-blame and building up a body of new evidence to support an alternative belief, rather it is about generating an alternative way of being with the self that is accepting, warm, caring, understanding, and supportive ('I understand why you want to blame yourself, it makes sense given what you have been through in the past and how hard you have found it to be kind to yourself. It's understandable that you are so sad and distressed but this is not your fault. Focus on the warmth, care, and kindness you have for yourself and how much you have suffered').

Once Jo was able to develop and use a self-soothing dialogue when she was self-critical, we were able to revisit the memories of the rape and specifically re-evaluate the meaning using Jo's compassionate part of her mind. Jo was able to update her thoughts of 'you are dirty and disgusting' with a compassionate reframe – 'this is so sad that you have suffered like this. You don't deserve this'. These new updates became meaningful to Jo because they triggered the congruent emotional response of soothing, compassion, and safeness. We then revisited the flashback by using the technique of reliving and updated the meaning by asking Jo 'what do you know now' while keeping the image in mind, to which Jo responded 'this is so sad that you have suffered like this. You don't deserve this'. Jo focused on the feelings of warmth, compassion, and safeness, whilst still reliving the flashback. Thus the memory of the rape became a sad memory as opposed to a shameful one.

Therapist comment

In total, Jo attended 20 sessions. The first 12 sessions focused on developing a compassionate mind. In some respects this work progressed relatively quickly as Jo had many experiences of being loved and valued by her parents as a child, but it was as if these emotional memories had been blocked by later experiences of bullying in her adolescence. Such work helped Jo resolve her feelings and re-evaluate the meaning of the attack. It also helped her work on her issues of low self-esteem by developing a relationship with herself that was helpful, supportive, and kind. The latter part of therapy focused on working directly with flashbacks by updating both the cognitive and emotional meaning, and helping Jo to re-engage with her pre-trauma life.

Gemma: Working with shame-based flashbacks to childhood sexual abuse

Gemma was a 34-year-old woman who had a history of childhood sexual abuse, anorexia, self-harm, and depression. Gemma's parents separated when she was 2 years old. Her mother went on to have other relationships, and Gemma was abused by her stepfather. Gemma recalled that she had always struggled to feel loved and wanted by her mother. As a child she felt desperate for attention from her mother and was often told by adults that she was attention-seeking and a 'drama queen'. At school, she was bullied and found it difficult to make meaningful friendships. She started to self-harm in her mid teens and at this time she began to restrict her intake of food. She first came to therapy 10 years previously, when she was suffering greatly and engaging in cutting and starvation as a way to regulate her overwhelming feelings of self-loathing and disgust, related to her experiences of childhood sexual abuse. At that time, Gemma received schema-focused therapy to help her develop new, more helpful beliefs about herself. She also worked on replacing self-harm with more helpful ways to manage emotional distress. She also revisited some of her painful memories of abuse, using her new beliefs to help her access the belief that the abuse was not her fault and that she did not deserve it. After 18 months of therapy, Gemma had made significant progress and was able to say, 'yes, I know I don't deserve the abuse', which she reported as reassuring and helpful to her. She said that she could forgive her stepfather for the abuse, as she could see that he had problems too.

Ten years later, Gemma re-engaged in therapy and had a further 12 sessions. Gemma had begun to experience difficulties again, which had been triggered by her involvement in an intimate relationship. She was struggling with overwhelming emotions and had strong desires to self-harm.

Compassion-focused formulation

It became apparent that Gemma had never really *believed* that the abuse was not her fault. Although she could say the words and objectively could understand that she was not to blame, this did not shift the feelings of shame and self-blame. At the end of her first course of therapy, she had been left with a profound inner sense of blame, which she knew she 'ought not to feel' but could not shift.

Gemma believed that she had caused her abuse and that is was her fault. She believed this because she relived a flashback in which she came downstairs one night, after being put to bed, because she was lonely and scared and wanted 'some attention'. She was pleased to be allowed to stay downstairs with her stepfather watching television. But as she sat on his knee he sexually abused her for the first time. This flashback conveyed the powerful meaning that the abuse was her fault and that she must be an awful person to have wanted attention so much that she would have allowed this to happen. Gemma was 4 years old when the abuse started.

Gemma's ability to forgive her stepfather was really a reflection on her own self-blame. How could she blame her stepfather when she *knew* on an emotional level that it was her fault?

Developing compassionate imagery

This time, therapy focused on developing Gemma's ability to self-soothe. We discussed that her brain was highly threat-focused and that her capacity to self-soothe was limited. I explained that her amygdala would respond to her own self-criticism by producing threat responses and that her self-critical dialogues maintained her shame. Through modelling and education in the therapeutic relationship, Gemma tried hard to develop her capacity to self-soothe. She developed a habit of 'talking to her amygdala' to try to soothe it when it became aroused. She loved the notion that her amygdala was trying to help keep her safe by responding to threats, but that it was overworking and over-sensitive. This was somewhat helpful in decentring from the intense emotions she felt in interpersonal situations. However, Gemma really struggled to self-soothe and one of the barriers to Gemma's ability to self-soothe was the profound belief she held: 'I don't deserve to be soothed as the abuse was my fault'. This belief was 'locked in' to the powerful emotional memory of the first time the abuse happened.

To explain the rationale for developing compassionate imagery, I asked Gemma to think about what happens in her body when she is hungry and sees a meal. She responded that her stomach starts to grumble and her mouth begins to water. I then asked her what happens when she is hungry and she merely *imagines* a meal. She responded that she still feels her stomach rumble and her mouth water. I then asked Gemma what happens in her body if someone shouts and criticizes her, and she responded that she feels anxious and afraid. I then asked what happened in her body if she *imagines* someone shouting and criticizing her, and she replied that she would still feel fearful and afraid. I then asked Gemma to comment on what she had learned from these questions, and she responded that her imagination makes her feel the same way as if the situation were actually happening. I then went on to ask what would happen in her body if she experienced a kind, empathic, and caring person helping her when she was distressed, and she responded that she would feel warm and cared for. I then introduced the notion that we can also imagine images of kind, caring, compassionate beings, or objects that have the capacity to stimulate the brain in the same way to produce the similar affect of feeling soothed and safe.

We developed an image of a 'perfect nurturer' to help Gemma access a more soothing and supportive feeling (Lee, 2005). Gemma considered the qualities and characteristics she would want in a fantastical image/inner helper that would always be able to nurture her and provide help/support when she needed it. Gemma wrote a list of attributes, such as unconditionally loving, strong, wise, accepting, and warm. I added to her list a sentient mind that can understand her struggles, genuine care for her wellbeing – and an image that has her mind in mind. We then used guided imagery to help Gemma create her perfect nurturer image using the following instructions:

- Sit comfortably and close your eyes.
- Focus on your breathing for a minute or so.
- Allow an image to come to mind that represent to you a 'perfect nurturer'. An image that would always have your best interests at heart and that would never let you down, an image that would support and comfort you when you are distressed, and offer you warmth and wisdom to deal with your struggles.
- Focus on the physical appearance of the image (size, colour), the texture of the image, and the smell (which I had previously discussed with Gemma to be one already associated with good feelings – such as an essential oil or perfume).
- Focus on the sound of the voice as it speaks to you and the relationship you would like to have with the perfect nurturer.
- Focus on the empathy and understanding your image has for you, focus on the feelings of warmth for you, focus on the fact that your image can tolerate your distress with you and that it is valid to feel this way.
- Focus on the feeling in your body generated by the image.

Gemma rehearsed and practised her imagery over several weeks and found it very helpful in 'calming her amygdala'. Once she was consistently able to use the imagery to access self-soothing affect, we began to work on the flashback that headlined the meaning 'the abuse was my fault'.

I discussed with Gemma what she would need in the flashback to help her feel safe and soothed; what would she like her perfect nurturer to say and/or do in the flashback; how would she like to feel in the memory. We also used a distinctive smell (lavender oil) conditioned to the image and affect to act as a trigger within the flashback. Gemma then described the key flashback in reliving while also bringing her perfect nurturer into the memory and triggering the associated affect by using her distinctive smell. Gemma had worked out how she wanted her perfect nurturer to support her and help her feel soothed and safe in the flashback.

At the end of the reliving, Gemma said: 'I need to report him to the police, as I think he still has contact with other children'. This was a profound moment in the therapy and Gemma went on to say that for the first time in her life she had now felt on an emotional level that the abuse was not her fault. Consequently, she was able to clearly say 'it's his fault and I need to act to protect others. I could not do that before as I believed that would not be fair as I had encouraged the abuse and that it had only happened to me'. This was a turning point for Gemma, as from then onwards this and other flashbacks ceased and she was able to accept that she did deserve self-soothing and compassion for her suffering.

To demonstrate the difference between compassion-focused and non-compassion-focused rescripting, two transcripts are provided. Gemma was working with another painful flashback to an incidence of sexual abuse. She felt overwhelmed with feelings of shame and dirtiness. A possible approach would be:

THERAPIST: How do you want to feel?
GEMMA: Powerful, disdainful, and in control.
THERAPIST: What needs to happen for you to feel like that?
GEMMA: I need to see him shrinking, being exterminated, looking very terrified and alone, begging – looking pathetic as I beat him.
THERAPIST: Can you hold that in your mind's eye?
GEMMA: Yes, he's gone – the pathetic, disgusting little man.
THERAPIST: And knowing that, how do you feel?
GEMMA: Good, I feel strong and powerful.

The potential problem with this rescripting is that it is highly likely to stimulate Gemma's threat arousal system because her response is coloured by anger. Whilst this may be useful in the interim, it would be important to encourage Gemma to access a more self-soothing re-enactment that 'turned off' the threat system, hence enhancing the likelihood of retrieval of a new emotional memory of self-soothing, rather than keeping Gemma locked in a cycle of shame–defensive anger.

The actual compassion-focused rescripting progressed as follows:

THERAPIST: How do you want to feel?
GEMMA: Safe, that it's not my fault, that I am not dirty.
THERAPIST: What needs to happen for you to feel like that?
GEMMA: I need to focus on the feelings of warmth, care, and kindness I have for myself, I need to focus on the sadness of this memory and to understand how hard this was for me to endure.
THERAPIST: Can you hold that feeling in your mind and body?
GEMMA: Yes, I am feeling stronger, he is going, and he can't harm me now.
THERAPIST: And knowing that, how do you feel?
GEMMA: Good, I feel strong and soothed.

Therapist comment

Gemma went from strength to strength in a fairly rapid time (12 sessions) and is still doing very well. Some patients who struggle to self-soothe and/or have little access to internalized images of loving others may find it useful to use compassionate imagery as a means to regulate internal responses to threat. Also given that flashbacks are a form of sensory-based memory, the use of other types of sensory-based memories (such as images of compassionate self-soothing others) can be helpful in updating the meaning of the flashback and thus the emotional experience associated with it.

The use of perfect nurturer and other types of compassionate imagery should occur in the context of a formulation that encompasses the reduced capacity to self-soothe and a heightened threat response. The imagery is not the intervention in itself, but it is a vehicle to enhance the arrival at the end point – the capacity to feel the affect of self-soothing.

DISCUSSION

This chapter has presented some theoretical considerations to help understand the role of shame and self-attack in shame-based trauma flashbacks. It has also presented two clinical examples that illustrate the clinical approach of compassion-focused cognitive therapy as a way of working with shame and self-attack in the context of trauma memories. In particular, the ability to self-soothe via self-dialogue and/or the use of compassionate imagery is highlighted as an important skill in working effectively with shame-based flashbacks and trauma memories. This is because those who struggle to self-soothe often struggle to feel the emotional valence of the new perspectives developed using more traditional cognitive therapy techniques. Traditional evidence-based practice, such as trauma-focused CBT for PTSD may be enhanced when working with shame if compassion-focused approaches are adopted. The use of compassionate imagery appears particularly effective when working with shame-based flashbacks, as it uses the same sensory modalities.

ACKNOWLEDGEMENTS

I would like to thank Gemma and Jo, who kindly gave me permission to write about their cases; Professor Paul Gilbert for his knowledge, support, and guidance in my development of this work with traumatized people; and Jenny Crofts for her administrative support.

REFERENCES

Bowlby, J. (1969). *Attachment and loss* (vol. 1). London: Hogarth Press.

Brewin, C.R., Dalgleish, T., & Joseph, S. (1996). A dual representation theory of posttraumatic stress disorder. *Psychological Review, 103*, 670–686.

Conway, M.A., & Pleydell-Pearce, C.W. (2000). The construction of autobiographical memories in the self-memory system. *Psychology Review, 107*, 261–288.

Ehlers, A., & Clark, D.M. (2000). A cognitive model of posttraumatic stress disorder. *Behaviour Research and Therapy, 38*, 319–345.

Ehlers, A., Clark, D.M., Hackmann, A., McManus, F., & Fennell, M. (2005). Cognitive therapy for PTSD: Development and evaluation. *Behaviour Research and Therapy, 43*, 413–431.

Gilbert, P. (1989). *Human nature and suffering*. Hove: Lawrence Erlbaum.

Gilbert, P. (1998). What is shame? Some core issues and controversies. In B. Andrews (Ed.), *Shame: Interpersonal behaviour, psychopathology and culture* (pp. 3–38). New York: Oxford University Press.

Gilbert, P. (2000). Social mentalities. Internal social conflicts and the role of inner warmth and compassion in therapy. In P. Gilbert, & K.G. Bailey (Eds.), *Genes on the couch: Explorations in evolutionary psychotherapy*. Hove: Psychology Press.

Gilbert, P. (2007). *Psychotherapy and counselling for depression*. London: Sage Publications.

Gilbert, P., & Irons, C. (2005). Focused therapies and compassionate mind training for shame and self attacking. In P. Gilbert (Ed.), *Compassion: Conceptualisations, research and use in psychotherapy*. London: Routledge.

Gilbert, P., & McGuire, M.T. (1998). Shame, social roles and status: The psychobiological continuum from monkey to human. In P. Gilbert, & B. Andrews (Eds.), *Shame: Interpersonal behaviour, psychopathology and culture* (pp. 3–38). New York: Oxford University Press.

Gilbert, P., & Proctor, S. (2006). Compassionate mind training for people with high shame and self criticism. Overview and pilot study of a group therapy approach. *Clinical Psychology and Psychotherapy, 13*, 353–379.

Gilbert, P., Lee, D.A., & Welford, M. (2006). *Overcoming shame and relentless self-attack*. A clinical aide download at www.compassioantemind.co.uk – available for free.

Grey, N., & Holmes, E.A. (2008). 'Hotspots' in trauma memories in the treatment of posttraumatic stress disorder: A replication. *Memory, 16*, 788–796.

Grey, N., Young, K., & Holmes, E. (2002). Cognitive restructuring within reliving: A treatment for peritraumatic emotional 'hotspots' in post-traumatic stress disorder. *Behavioural and Cognitive Psychotherapy, 30*, 37–56.

Harman, R., Lee, D.A., & Barker, C. (2008). The role of self-attack and self-soothing in the maintenance of shame-based PTSD. Manuscript submitted for publication.

Holmes, E., Grey, N., & Young, K.A.D. (2005). Intrusive images and 'hotspots' of trauma memories in posttraumatic stress disorder: An explanatory investigation of emotions and cognitive themes. *Journal of Behaviour Therapy and Experimental Psychiatry, 36*, 3–17.

LeDoux, J. (1998). *The emotional brain.* London: Weidenfeld and Nicolson.

Lee, D.A. (2005). The perfect nurturer: A model to develop a compassionate mind within the context of cognitive therapy. In P. Gilbert (Ed.), *Compassion: Conceptualisations, research and use in psychotherapy.* London: Routledge.

Lee, D.A., Scragg, P., & Turner, S.W. (2001). The role of shame and guilt in traumatic events: A clinical model of shame based and guilt-based PTSD. *British Journal of Medical Psychology, 74*, 451–466.

National Collaborating Centre for Mental Health. (2005). *Clinical guideline 26. Post-traumatic stress disorder (PTSD): The management of PTSD in adults and children in primary and secondary care.* London: National Institute for Clinical Excellence.

Chapter 16

Cognitive therapy for survivors of torture

Kerry Young

INTRODUCTION

Most people who receive treatment after surviving torture are refugees and asylum-seekers. This chapter focuses on their needs. However, much will also be applicable to other people who may have been tortured, such as following political imprisonments, and people working in the armed forces. Using a composite case example and referring to relevant literature, this chapter focuses on how you can work cognitively with the shame, alienation, and dehumanization that often follow torture. It also briefly addresses, first, whether you should focus on treating post-traumatic reactions while clients might also have a range of serious social, economic, legal, and/or physical difficulties, and second, how you can modify traditional reliving treatments for traumatic stress for clients with multiple traumas, often extending over months and years.

This chapter will not focus on the debate about using Western models of mental illness to understand the difficulties faced by traumatized refugees (e.g., Summerfield, 2001). Rather, it will take as its starting point the convincing body of research pointing to the effectiveness of cognitive behavioural therapy (CBT) for post-traumatic stress disorder (PTSD) in non-refugees (National Collaborating Centre for Mental Health (NCCMH), 2005), as well as the small but promising number of studies and articles suggesting that CBT can be used successfully to treat traumatized refugees and asylum-seekers (e.g., d'Ardenne, Ruaro, Cestari, Wakhoury, & Priebe, 2007; Grey & Young, 2008; Paunovic & Ost, 2001; Schulz, Resick, Huber, & Griffin, 2006). Issues concerning the delivery of CBT for PTSD through an interpreter are not examined in this chapter (see d'Ardenne and Farmer, Chapter 18, this volume).

CASE EXAMPLE

Assessment

Background information

Naseem is a 46-year-old refugee from Iran referred by his GP. At assessment, he presented as wary and distrustful. He asked for help with concentration, poor memory, low motivation, mistrust of others, and upsetting images of his torture experiences. He was seen for all sessions with a male, Farsi-speaking interpreter.

Naseem was born and brought up in Tehran, the youngest of nine children. His father worked as a doctor, his mother as a housewife. Both parents were liberal and open-minded, and encouraged their children to be the same. He briefly described a comfortable and happy childhood, and uneventful schooling. On leaving school, he went into business with one of his brothers.

In the build up to the Islamic Revolution in 1979, his whole family had been enthusiastic about deposing the Shah. However, over the next 10 years, Naseem became increasingly disillusioned by the new government and began to work illicitly for the opposition. In 1995, following a great deal of harassment, he was arrested and tortured for 13 months. On release, he went into hiding and fled to England.

Current circumstances

Naseem lives alone, in a one-bed flat on a large, inner-city estate. He has two enduring friendships, both with other refugees from Middle Eastern countries. However, he finds it hard to socialize and to make new friends. He becomes irritable if he thinks that others are letting him down. Naseem has regular telephone contact with his remaining family in Iran. He would like to be able to work, but doubted he would ever feel mentally alert or motivated enough to do so.

Naseem had Refugee Status and enough money to 'get by'. He was very unhappy with his accommodation, describing the estate as 'noisy, dangerous, and filthy'. He complained of some pain from torture injuries.

Current psychological difficulties

Naseem met criteria for PTSD and major depressive disorder (MDD). The PTSD symptoms had been present since his release from prison, but had reduced in frequency over time. The MDD symptoms had been present, at a stable level, for the last 3 or 4 years.

Naseem was most troubled by intrusive images of three mock executions that he had been subjected to and four or five 'particularly bad' beatings.

These images occurred several times each week. He also experienced night-mares of these experiences, at the same rate and reported distress, and physio-logical arousal at reminders (such as films about prison and news reports about the imprisonment of others).

He found it hard to concentrate for more than a few minutes at a time. His memory problems appeared to be exclusively for new information. He confirmed that he had not lost consciousness during any of his beatings nor suffered any after-effects (such as slurred speech, vomiting, and one-sided weakness) that might indicate neurological damage. He did, however, dissociate a few times during torture, for up to half an hour.

Naseem found it hard to picture himself being successful in the future (either occupationally or socially) due to poor concentration, sleep, and mistrust of others. Finally, he spoke about feeling permanently damaged by his experiences in prison: 'I am not a strong person any more, I am not fit to work like a man'.

Preliminary formulation

Growing up in a prosperous, liberal-minded, and well-functioning family, Naseem believed that others were essentially benevolent and that the world was largely predictable. He thought well of himself and, generally, expected others to share this view. After the Revolution, he was confused by the appar-ent misdeeds of the new regime. He thought that maybe he was mistaken when he heard about human rights abuses. Eventually, he began to view the members of the new regime as misguided and threw himself behind a move-ment to reinstate the old regime. Throughout this time, he did not change his optimistic view of himself or others; he merely ignored and/or made exceptions for bad behaviour.

Once he was imprisoned and tortured, the treatment that he received dra-matically contradicted his view of others as benevolent. Repeated experiences in which he was humiliated and terrorized by his torturers led him to abandon his belief in the goodness of others. Rather, he began to think that he could not trust anyone and that everyone was trying to do him harm. In addition, he began to believe that he was inadequate and weak because of his reactions to torture. The intense fear, anger, and shame that he felt during torture (together with periods of dissociation) made it hard for him to 'process' the memories of his imprisonment. Thus, on subsequent presentation of related material (e.g., emotional or environmental cues) the torture memories intruded. He found these terrifying and shaming, and so immediately pushed them out of his mind and/or avoided anything that might act as a trigger. Hence, his memory remained unprocessed.

Expecting others to harm him at all times, Naseem frequently checked others' behaviour for any sign of not treating him well (such as changing an appointment to meet or being late). He reacted aggressively to these signs and, as a result, he had few enduring relationships. Not only did this lead to an impoverished social life, but it also failed to challenge his unhelpful views about others and himself.

These problems had led to Naseem becoming increasingly isolated and having little meaningful activity. As his mood dropped, so too did his motivation and belief that he could improve his life. Thus, he was caught in a classic depressive vicious circle; memory, concentration, and sleep problems, leading to inactivity and hopelessness and *vice versa*.

Treatment plan

The treatment aimed to help Naseem with:

* Processing the memory of his time in prison.
* Challenging his unhelpful appraisals about himself (being permanently damaged) and others (that they cannot be trusted).
* Increasing his level of meaningful and pleasurable activity.

At the same time, several factors needed to be considered.

Should other concerns, such as pain from torture injuries or Naseem's housing, be worked on first?

Recent UK clinical guidelines recommend a phased approach to working with PTSD in refugees (NCCMH, 2005; see also Herman, 1992). In the first phase, the focus is on primary needs (such as housing, safety, and medical treatment). Only in the second phase would trauma-focused interventions be considered. While Naseem did report some difficulties with his primary needs, he was clear that he wanted to focus on working with his trauma-related psychological difficulties (Grey & Young, 2008).

Exposure-based therapies are highly effective for the treatment of PTSD (NCCMH, 2005). However, given the length of Naseem's imprisonment, to what should he be exposed?

One option would be to relive those moments of Naseem's torture experiences that intruded as images and nightmares. However, given the need to explain the shattering of his beliefs about himself and others, 'adapted testimony' was used to explore his entire imprisonment and earlier history (see Grey & Young, 2008). This is similar to Narrative Exposure Therapy (Schauer, Neuner, & Elbert, 2005; see also Mueller, Chapter 17, this volume) and to Testimony (Cienfuegos & Monelli, 1983). 'Adapted testimony' involves constructing a story of the person's traumatic experiences, over a number of sessions, focusing on exposing them to the memory of what happened while also attempting to examine unhelpful appraisals. Each session is taped and the client is asked to listen to *all* tapes between sessions.

How could Naseem's significant trust difficulties usefully be addressed within the therapeutic relationship?

Having discussed this issue with Naseem, it was agreed that he would complete a visual-analogue scale pertaining to his trust in the therapist at the end of each session. Any changes in the rating (for better or worse) would be discussed. In addition, we agreed that he should have the same interpreter through the treatment, and that he would also rate his trust in him every session. At the start of treatment, overall trust in the therapist and interpreter were both 20%.

The treatment plan for sessions with Naseem was:

- Adapted testimony, starting in his childhood and continuing until he had arrived in the UK.
- During the testimony, detailed exploration of the circumstances that had led to his unhelpful appraisals about himself and others.
- Once the testimony was completed, ways of increasing meaningful and pleasurable activity would be explored.

Due to difficulty getting appropriately translated and standardized self-report measures, Naseem monitored change over treatment with visual-analogue scales each session for concentration (initially 20%), motivation (20%), mistrust of others (90%), and upset caused by intrusive images (100%).

Clearly, full details of the content of Naseem's testimony cannot be given here. The focus here will be the cognitive restructuring aspect within the adapted testimony sessions. The two key meanings were, first, that others would try to harm him and could not be trusted, and second that he was deficient for his responses during his torture and has been permanently changed by them.

Work on trusting others

To help Naseem examine his appraisals about trust, we explored the events that led to him forming the conclusion that others were not trustworthy.

NASEEM: I thought that I understood people; I thought that I was clever, but I was a fool to believe in them. I cannot think how I could have been so stupid.

THERAPIST: How do you feel when you think about that now?

NASEEM: Devastated that I could have been so stupid ... ashamed of myself ... and scared.
THERAPIST: Scared?
NASEEM: Scared that no one can be trusted, that is frightening.
THERAPIST: Yes, it is a frightening thought ... you said that you felt ashamed of yourself ... how do you think you should have acted differently?
NASEEM: I should have seen what they were doing, how they were manipulating us all, may be then I could have tried to stop it earlier.
THERAPIST: What do you think you should have noticed that you didn't?
NASEEM: I'm not sure really, all of it, I don't know. There was no one thing.
THERAPIST: It seems quite important that we identify what it was that you missed, so that you would recognize it if it happened again.
NASEEM: Yes, that's the point, at the moment I can't trust my judgement, so I can't trust anyone ... or maybe everyone is bad ... but I know that's not right either.
THERAPIST: So, let me see if I understand you. If we could identify the point at which there is a warning signal that people may do harm to others, then, if you knew what that was, you would feel better able to trust others now?
NASEEM: Yes ... can we really do that ... how?
THERAPIST: Well, it's a big question; there probably isn't an easy answer. However, what others in your situation have found helpful is starting with their own explanation and then looking at some academic explanations, written by researchers who have studied these kinds of things.

It was clear that Naseem also felt ashamed of himself for trusting others when he thought that he should not have done so. However, the issue of trust was focused on first, to see if that discussion had any impact on his feelings of shame.

As we discussed the initial stages of the Islamic Revolution, Naseem surprised himself with how much he could, in hindsight, analyse the propaganda that had operated at the time. Our discussions focused on the incremental nature of the propaganda and it became clear that there was no one incident that he should have noticed that signalled danger.

THERAPIST: So you have identified a number of things that they did to create a thirst for revolution ... can we write them down on this sheet of paper, in order?
NASEEM: Yes (writes down list of five behaviours in Farsi, interpreter provides English version underneath).
THERAPIST: So, when they did this first one, how did you feel about it?

NASEEM: I didn't really notice it; just saw it as a fact.

THERAPIST: So did you think at the time that this would lead to them harming thousands of people in a year's time?

NASEEM: Not at all . . . it was nothing.

THERAPIST: What warnings were there of the harm to come at this time?

NASEEM: None . . . there weren't any.

THERAPIST: So was it reasonable of you not to be alarmed at that time?

NASEEM: Yes.

THERAPIST: So what about when they did this (points to third behaviour)? Cast your mind back, at that time, what warnings were there of the harm to come?

NASEEM: None . . . we believed they were just telling us the facts about the Shah, because what he was doing was wrong.

THERAPIST: So was it reasonable of you not to be alarmed?

NASEEM: Yes.

THERAPIST: So at what point did you sense danger?

NASEEM: Just there (points to last behaviour) . . . I could see that a lust for blood was forming.

THERAPIST: What did you do?

NASEEM: I started talking to the opposition group . . . to try to stop them.

THERAPIST: So you took action at the precise time that first you smelled danger . . . when you saw the warning signal?

NASEEM: Yes.

THERAPIST: On looking back over that time then, what else do you think that you could have seen sooner?

NASEEM: I can't think of anything . . . there was nothing, was there?

THERAPIST: Doesn't sound like it, no.

These discussions and the sessions so far had led to an increase in Naseem's trust in the therapist and interpreter (now 50%). He accounted for this increase by judging the actual behaviour he had received and observed in sessions. He was encouraged to equally judge others outside the session on their actual behaviour rather than simply assuming his immediate mistrust was correct.

Understanding tyranny

We then spent two sessions discussing research that tried to explain how such events take place; how ordinary people end up doing harm to each other. This was also recorded on tape for Naseem. The explanation is based on two main texts, Beck (1999) and Zimbardo (2007). It is presented according to the structure of a helpful television documentary, '5 Steps to Tyranny' (Sheena McDonald, 2000). Naseem also viewed this afterwards with the interpreter and therapist present.

Tyrannical behaviour is incremental. There is generally a very slow, subtle, step-by-step movement towards people harming others. In addition, there is little evidence of the existence of 'evil' people. Rather there is a mixture of dispositional and situational factors that explain why someone does harm. In the documentary, Sheena McDonald presents five steps that can lead to tyranny. They are:

- Separating people into in- and out-groups ('Us and them').
- People's natural tendency to obey authority ('Obey orders').
- People being instructed by leaders to harm the out-group ('Do them harm').
- The suppression of dissent ('Stand up or stand by').
- People being instructed to destroy/kill others in the out-group ('Exterminate').

Us and them

Humans have an age-old belief system that separates others into in- and out-groups. Presumably, there is an evolutionary advantage to the system. Tajfel (1981) randomly assigned a group of strangers to one of two groups. The groups had no meaning; they were simply two different groups of strangers. Immediately, he found that members rated their own group more highly than the other one. Moreover, on being given a group task to undertake, members reported increases in self-esteem following group success and increases in prejudice towards the group that failed.

An exercise with some similarities was carried out in 1968, on the day after Martin Luther King was assassinated. Jane Elliott, a primary school teacher in Iowa, USA, wanted to teach her class of all-white pupils about how it might feel to be judged negatively for the colour of their skin. She decreed that, just for one day as an experiment, the children with blue eyes were 'superior' to those with brown eyes. The brown-eyed children were not allowed to mix with the blue-eyed children and were denied various privileges. By the end of the day, the brown-eyed children were underperforming and were using negative adjectives to describe themselves. The blue-eyed children were arrogant and had begun to victimize the brown-eyed children. This exercise has been widely used in diversity training packages (see www.janeelliott.com).

Thus it seems that separating people into in- and out-groups can have a very powerful psychological impact. However, on the whole, researchers think that out-group prejudice is a largely unconscious process and needs to be activated by a stressor to have maximum impact. Stressors such as economic hardship, limited resources, or land disputes are thought to have been the setting conditions for most twentieth-century genocides. At times of stress, people may engage in 'primal thinking' (all-or-nothing thinking, personalization, magnification; Beck, 1999), which will increase prejudice. In-group leaders can then use propaganda to further reinforce the prejudice and to begin to de-humanize the out-group.

In summary then, the first step involves making conscious the largely unconscious tendency of humans to separate the world into in- and out-groups. Primal thinking will then begin to operate, reinforcing negative stereotypes of the out-group.

Obey orders

From a young age, children are socialized by their parents to obey them, in order to keep them safe from harm. Thus, as adults, most people have a natural tendency to obey authority. In 1963, Stanley Milgram carried out an experiment that demonstrated how strong the urge to obey orders was. He advertised for volunteers to take part in an experiment about learning. The volunteers were instructed to be 'teachers' and to give the 'learners' word pairs to memorize. The 'learners' were, unknown to the volunteers, stooges. The teachers were instructed to present the learners with a prime from the word pairs and told to say 'good' if the learners provided the correct answer. However, if they did not, the teacher was asked to deliver an electric shock to the learner. There were 30 switches for delivering the shocks, each one 15V higher than the next, up to 450V (Milgram, 1963).

Milgram asked 40 psychiatrists to predict how many volunteers would deliver the maximum shock. They predicted only 1% would do so. In fact, they found that 65% of subjects delivered the maximum 450V shock when instructed to do so, despite being able to hear the screams and entreaties of the 'learners' (stooges). The experiment has been replicated in nine different countries, with a mean rate of delivering maximum shock of 66% (for a review, see Blass, 2000). Variables that increase the rate of obedience are: the more authoritarian the person conducting the experiment appears to be (e.g., white coat, suit); the more 'prestigious' the study centre; the amount of physical distance between teacher and 'learner' (e.g., if 'learner' is in another building) and the teacher 'overhearing' experimenters discussing the 'learners' in animalistic terms.

In summary, the second step involves harnessing people's natural tendency to be obedient to authority.

Do them harm

Bandura (1986) argues that, in order to harm others in the out-group, individuals' natural moral deterrent against violence needs to be suspended, a process he refers to as 'moral disengagement'. Moral disengagement involves activating one or more of the following four cognitive mechanisms. First, redefining immoral behaviour as honourable (e.g., 'if we do not harm them, they will kill us'). Second, diffusing responsibility so that harmful outcomes are not seen as directly linked to individuals' actions. Third, minimizing or ignoring actual harmful consequences. Finally, dehumanizing or blaming the victims, thus making them not 'worthy' of normal human consideration.

Bandura, Underwood, and Fromson (1975) recruited 72 volunteers to make up three-person 'supervisory teams' tasked with evaluating the decisions of the 'team in the other room' (who did not really exist, but whose reasoning they were able to hear). They were instructed to give electric shocks to the decision-making team for poor decisions. The shocks varied in intensity from mild level of 1 to a maximum level of 10. The researchers varied the degree of personal responsibility the volunteers had for the shock level administered for poor decisions. They found that higher levels of shock were administered when volunteers thought that an average level would be computed from that assigned by each member of the supervisory team. Researchers also varied the language they used to describe members of the team in the other room. If they were described as animalistic, the shock levels increased.

In summary, the third step involves leaders helping individuals to suspend the moral rules that normally prohibit violence.

Stand up or stand by

Research reviewed so far has demonstrated that the majority of people, in the right circumstances, can be primed to do harm. But even stunning experiments such as Milgram's do not manage to yield 100% obedience. Social psychologists have conducted countless studies examining the factors that might determine who does and does not harm others. A recent meta-analysis of 1,500 studies pointed to the consistent and reliable impact of situational and not dispositional factors in this determination (Fiske, Harris, & Cuddy, 2004). For example, Darley and Batson (1973) took a group of students studying at Princeton's seminary. They were asked to deliver a speech on the Good Samaritan but, on their way to do so, had to walk past a stranger on the street 'in dire distress' (who was, of course, a stooge). Some of the students had been told that they were late for the speech, some had not. The researchers found that what determined whether or not the students did in fact behave as good Samaritans was their perceived time pressure. Ninety per cent of those who thought that they were late did not stop. Indeed, the situational variable of time pressure accounted for the majority of the variance in helping behaviour.

Thus those instructing others to cause harm must create robust situational factors to suppress dissent. Violent and swift responses to disobedience will deter many and widespread use of torture can create mistrust in an opposition group ('who betrayed whom under pressure?').

In summary, the fourth step involves creating situations that discourage dissent.

Exterminate

Once the other four steps are in place, many people will start to harm others. Zimbardo's iconic Stanford prison experiment demonstrates how quickly this can be achieved (see Zimbardo, 2007). He set up a mock prison in the psychology department at Stanford, wanting to study the social influences on behaviour in such a situation. He took a group of 24 volunteers and randomly assigned them either to being guards or prisoners. Prisoners were given uniforms and numbers. They were subjected to strict rules about when they could eat, sleep, smoke, and use the toilet. The guards were instructed only to keep order. Within minutes of the start of the experiment, the guards were psychologically bullying the inmates. By day 2, they were being physically violent. By day 4, Zimbardo had had to release half of the prisoners as they were suffering from stress. Zimbardo ended the experiment on day 5 when his girlfriend expressed disgust at the level of abuse of prisoners.

In summary, the fifth step involves leaders instructing members of the in-group to harm the out-group.

As we talked through each of these five steps, Naseem was encouraged to provide examples from the Revolution in Iran, which may correspond to the effects produced in such studies.

THERAPIST: So we started this conversation a few sessions ago. You were saying that you wanted to be able to identify the point at which there was a warning signal that others were about to do harm, so that you could identify it now and know who not to trust. What have we discovered about this warning signal from our discussions?

NASEEM: There isn't a single one . . . it's a series of slow steps that people go through over many years.

THERAPIST: Can you summarize those steps for me now? How does person X end up harming person Y?

NASEEM: There would have to be some separation of groups, which the leaders of the country would reinforce. They would have to say bad things about the other groups, but in a slow way, nothing too outrageous at any one time. Then the leaders would have to instruct person X to harm person Y. Person X would have to feel that, morally, that was reasonable and then they would have to be a bit afraid of what would happen if they did not do as instructed.

THERAPIST: So there are a series of situations that have to occur for person X to end up harming person Y?

NASEEM:	Yes.
THERAPIST:	Do you think that any of those situations exist in England now?
NASEEM:	Not in any major way. There is a bit of 'them and us' about refugees, but only in some bits of the press. It could never happen in England, there are no obvious in- and out-groups . . . it's too diverse.
THERAPIST:	So, the only situations that lead people to harm do not exist in England. How does that help you with trusting people now?
NASEEM:	Well maybe I can trust, can't I?
THERAPIST:	When should you be concerned about trusting people more generally?
NASEEM:	Only when all of those steps have been gone through.
THERAPIST:	How does that make you feel?
NASEEM:	Relieved, better . . . it makes more sense now.
THERAPIST:	Before you said that you felt stupid for not spotting the warning signal that this was happening in Iran. How do you feel about that now?
NASEEM:	How could I spot it – those 40 psychiatrists didn't think that people would give the electric shocks, how should I know?
THERAPIST:	So how do you feel?
NASEEM:	Not stupid . . . which is a great relief.

The ratings of trust in therapist and interpreter were now at 70%.

Work on mental defeat and perceived permanent change

Ehlers, Maercker, and Boos (2000) identified three appraisals that predicted PTSD symptom severity post-torture in former East German political prisoners: mental defeat, alienation, and permanent change. Mental defeat is defined as the perceived loss of all autonomy (e.g., 'they have destroyed me', 'I was an object'). Alienation refers to a perceived or actual inability to relate to others after trauma. Finally, perceived permanent change occurs when a person thinks that there has been a permanent change for the worse in their personality or that their former life has been completely destroyed (e.g., 'I am no longer the person I was'). People who experience mental defeat are more likely to interpret trauma as revealing something deficient about themselves, e.g., that they are weak. Thus they may see the event as signalling future global implications for themselves. They may avoid thinking and talking about the event, thus prolonging their PTSD and preventing any examination of the appraisals. Similarly, people who consider themselves to be permanently changed by trauma are unlikely to make efforts to 'reclaim' their former lives and personalities.

Naseem's comments about himself suggest elements both of mental defeat and of perceived permanent change. Discussion of this occurred in the section of testimony in which we discussed his torture experiences in detail.

THERAPIST: When they did that to you in prison, how did it make you feel about yourself?

NASEEM: There was the pain, but mainly I felt ashamed of myself for crying and begging them to stop. I even started to try to please them to make it stop.

THERAPIST: You felt ashamed of yourself – how would you liked to have behaved?

NASEEM: To not ever show them that they were getting to me, to never cry, to never scream out for them to stop, to be completely indifferent to them.

THERAPIST: Do you think that you should have behaved like that?

NASEEM: Yes I do.

THERAPIST: So given that you did cry out and so forth, you felt ashamed of yourself, which makes sense. Has it had any impact on how you feel about yourself more generally, not just how you felt about yourself in prison?

NASEEM: Because I fell apart like that, I now know that I am not a strong man . . . and I never will be again.

THERAPIST: Is that different from how you felt about yourself before you were imprisoned?

NASEEM: Yes, I used to think that I was a very strong character.

THERAPIST: So that's very serious then, isn't it? Because of how you behaved during that torture, you have changed your view of yourself. Because you 'fell apart', you no longer feel strong. So would you say that anyone who behaved like you did was not a strong man?

NASEEM: Yes.

THERAPIST: Have you talked to others about their time in prison?

NASEEM: No, not in detail, no one wants to remember.

THERAPIST: So you wouldn't know how common or otherwise your reaction was?

NASEEM: No, but I doubt it is common.

THERAPIST: If you had to guess, what percentage of Iranian prisoners on being tortured would behave like you did?

NASEEM: 10–20%.

THERAPIST: So most would behave in a stronger way . . . how do you think they would do that?

NASEEM: They wouldn't let it get to them, they would resist?

THERAPIST: How would they be able to do that?

NASEEM: I'm not sure.

THERAPIST: What if it weren't possible? What if most people reacted the way you did, would you feel less weak?

NASEEM: Yes, definitely.

THERAPIST: Perhaps we could discuss what we know about torture, what it is trying to do, and how it affects others?

NASEEM: I would like that.

Aims and process of torture

The overall structure of the explanation is adapted from Basoglu (1992). Despite the fact that torture is perpetrated in different places by different people, accounts of torture experiences bear remarkable similarity to one another. In most cases, the torture seems to have the following aims:

- Destroy the victim's sense of themself in relation to others.
- Foster a pathological attachment between the victim and the torturer.
- Affect a large population by the treatment of a few.

In essence, the torturer is attempting to break down the victim's defences, to make them feel weak and useless, before releasing them back to the population at large to tell others about their experiences (which will serve as a warning) and no longer be an effective dissident (because of the trauma they have suffered). The process by which this is achieved is as follows:

Induce terror

Torturers use a variety of techniques to maximize the terror they instil in their victims. In many cases there are parallels to the animal learning literature, which points quite clearly to the conclusion that the effect of trauma on animals is magnified if it is unpredictable (Basoglu & Mineka, 1992). If given a choice, animals show a clear preference for signalled versus unsignalled aversive events. Having a signal for when an aversive event will occur means that the animal can relax when that signal is not present. If the trauma is never signalled, then the animal will remain in a chronic state of fear.

Thus to maximize fear torturers deliver their torture in an unpredictable way. For instance, a person's actual time of arrest is unpredictable, as will be the time and duration of their torture sessions. Methods of torture might also be unpredictable, to avoid habituation to any one method. Blindfolding during torture also increases unpredictability. Very commonly, sham executions are used. The victim will be told that they are to be executed the following day, and then they will be taken from their cell, blindfolded, and a gun held to their head. The same procedure may be repeated for days or even weeks, leaving the victim in a chronic state of terror. Finally, rules may be enforced in an inconsistent way by the prison guards.

Limit autonomy and decrease initiative

Animals exposed to a long series of inescapable electric shocks behave differently from those exposed to the same amount of escapable shocks, and later these animals failed to learn how to escape shocks that were controllable in a different situation ('Learned Helplessness'; see Abramson, Seligman, & Teasdale, 1978).

Thus, to minimize resistance in prison and once released, torturers will attempt to take away as much control as possible from people. Clearly, the fact that the victim cannot escape from prison is a major loss of control. Torturers will often reinforce this by saying that the victim will be tortured until they die, that all of their comrades have been captured too, and so there is no hope that they will try to get them released. Holding prisoners in isolation will also break contacts with the outside world and with other prisoners. If others do not know that you are in prison, they cannot attempt to get you out of prison. Torturers will also attempt to control the victim's body and bodily functions, by stripping them naked, sexually torturing them, and limiting access to the toilet, to food and to sleep. By severely limiting food in particular, the torturer will make the victim's main aim to be survival. This may mean that they are much less likely to plot ways of resisting or escaping. Nevertheless, any signs of initiative will be harshly and publicly punished, to discourage others.

Ensure wide knowledge of torture and foster distrust in population

Some question why tyrannical regimes do not simply kill their opposition. Releasing a large number of traumatized torture victims may be a better deterrent than killing people (who may then come to be seen as martyrs). Survivors will tell their horrific stories and will often be visibly physically and psychologically damaged. Moreover, members of the population will not know what the victim did to secure their release – did they betray others or are they now an informant? This will foster effective distrust in the population, undermining the cohesion of the opposition.

As we talked through the aims and process of torture, Naseem was encouraged to provide examples from his own imprisonment and torture. He was genuinely surprised at how well his experiences matched the generic explanation.

THERAPIST: So when we started this conversation last session, you said that you felt ashamed of how you reacted to your torture. You thought that most others wouldn't react in the same way and, because you had, you were not and would never again be a strong man. What have you discovered from our discussion about the aims and process of torture?

NASEEM: It's amazing, these guys really know what they are doing. They design their torture to make everyone feel weak and broken.

THERAPIST: So what does it mean about you and your personality that the torture made you feel weak?

NASEEM: I felt weak and broken because I went through the torture, not because I am globally weak.

THERAPIST: What does that mean for your future? Can you see yourself as strong again?

NASEEM: I think that I might be able to.

THERAPIST: How does that make you feel?

NASEEM: Better, more hopeful.

Treatment outcome

Naseem was seen for a total of 18 sessions. A full verbal account of his traumatic experiences was completed. In addition, Naseem was encouraged to increase his level of activity as his trust in people slowly returned. At the end of treatment, Naseem no longer met diagnostic criteria for MDD or PTSD. He still had occasional nightmares about his time in prison and became distressed by news reports about the torture of others. He had just started working voluntarily for a friend's business, which was going well. His trust in others was greatly improved and he had not fallen out with anyone for the last 4 months. Finally, Naseem said that he was hopeful about the future: 'I feel much more my old self. I am a good, strong person, and I deserve to have a nice life here in England'. Ratings of his problems were now concentration (60%), motivation (80%), mistrust of others (30%), and upset caused by intrusive images (30%).

CONCLUSION

This chapter provides an account of work with a client who had been tortured and met criteria for PTSD and MDD. Within the work to treat his PTSD, particular attention was paid to addressing the themes of trust, shame, and alienation from his former self. While different clients present with their own idiosyncratic appraisals about their torture, clinical experience and research findings suggest that these issues are common in torture survivors with PTSD. Cognitive restructuring around these can then allow a fuller processing of the traumatic memories. Such restructuring often needs to include broader discussions of psychosocial understanding of people's actions than when treating other clients. Clients may have their own explanations for this, based on their own cultural understanding of such concepts as free will and 'good' and 'evil'. For some clients watching '5 Steps to Tyranny' may lead to a discussion of how they may be able to prevent such steps both in their country of refuge and homeland. This may lead to involvement in political activity, which for some may in fact be a return to such activity and as such helps them in the process of 'reclaiming' their life (Ehlers & Clark, 2000). While the focus in this chapter was on specific cognitive aspects of treatment, this is provided within a broader testimony/narrative of the traumatic experiences, and using other cognitive behavioural interventions as necessary. In addition, such trauma-focused treatment can only proceed when this is the main problem facing the person, rather than a preoccupation with primary needs such as housing or family reunion, or needing to establish safety in some other way.

REFERENCES

Abramson, L.Y., Seligman, M.E., & Teasdale, J.D. (1978). Learned helplessness in humans: critique and reformulation. *Journal of Abnormal Psychology, 87*, 49–74.

Bandura, A. (1986). *Social foundations of thought and action: A social cognitive theory.* Englewood Cliffs, NJ: Prentice-Hall.

Bandura, A., Underwood, B., & Fromson, M.E. (1975). Disinhibition of aggression through diffusion of responsibility and dehumanization of victims. *Journal of Research in Personality, 9*, 253–269.

Basoglu, M. (1992). Behavioural and cognitive approaches in the treatment of torture-related psychological problems. In M. Basoglu (Ed.), *Torture and its consequences: Current treatment approaches.* Cambridge: Cambridge University Press.

Basoglu, M., & Mineka, S. (1992). The role of uncontrollable and unpredictable stress in post-traumatic stress responses in torture survivors. In M. Basoglu (Ed.), *Torture and its consequences: Current treatment approaches.* Cambridge: Cambridge University Press.

Beck, A.T. (1999). *Prisoners of hate: The cognitive basis of anger, hostility and violence.* New York: Perennial.

Blass, T. (Ed.) (2000). *Obedience to authority: Current perspectives on the Milgram paradigm.* Mahwah, NJ: Lawrence Erlbaum Associates.

Cienfuegos, A.J., & Monelli, C. (1983). The testimony of political repression as a therapeutic instrument. *American Journal of Orthopsychiatry, 53*, 41–53.

d'Ardenne, P., Ruaro, L., Cestari, L., Wakhoury, W., & Priebe, S. (2007). Does interpreter-mediated CBT with traumatized refugee people work? A comparison of patient outcomes in East London. *Behavioural and Cognitive Psychotherapy, 35*, 293–301.

Darley, J.M., & Batson, C.D. (1973). 'From Jerusalem to Jericho': A study of situational and dispositional variables in helping behaviour. *Journal of Personality and Social Psychology, 73*, 100–108.

Ehlers, A., & Clark, D.M. (2000). A cognitive model of posttraumatic stress disorder. *Behaviour Research and Therapy, 38*, 319–345.

Ehlers, A., Maercker, A., & Boos, A. (2000). PTSD following political imprisonment: The role of mental defeat, alienation, and perceived permanent change. *Journal of Abnormal Psychology, 109*, 45–55.

Fiske, S.T., Harris, L.T., & Cuddy, A.J.C. (2004). Why ordinary people torture enemy prisoners. *Science, 306*, 1482–1483.

Grey, N., & Young, K. (2008). Cognitive behaviour therapy with refugees and asylum seekers experiencing traumatic stress symptoms. *Behavioural and Cognitive Psychotherapy, 36*, 3–19.

Herman, J.L. (1992). *Trauma and recovery*. London: Pandora Books.

McDonald, S. (2000). 5 Steps to tyranny. Available for free viewing at http://www.brightcove.tv/title.jsp?title=958764725 (July 2008).

Milgram, S. (1963). Behavioral study of obedience. *Journal of Abnormal and Social Psychology, 67*, 371–378.

National Collaborating Centre for Mental Health. (2005). *Clinical guideline 26. Post-traumatic stress disorder (PTSD): The management of PTSD in adults and children in primary and secondary care*. London: National Institute for Clinical Excellence.

Paunovic, N., & Ost, L.-G. (2001). Cognitive-behaviour therapy vs. exposure therapy in the treatment of PTSD in refugees. *Behaviour Research and Therapy, 39*, 1183–1197.

Schauer, M., Neuner, F., & Elbert, T. (2005). *Narrative exposure therapy: A short-term intervention for traumatic stress disorders after war, terror, or torture*. Göttingen: Hogrefe.

Schulz, P.M., Resick, P.A., Huber, L.C., & Griffin, M.G. (2006). The effectiveness of cognitive processing therapy for PTSD with refugees in a community setting. *Cognitive and Behavioral Practice, 13*, 322–331.

Summerfield, D. (2001). Asylum seekers, refugees and mental health services in the UK. *Psychiatric Bulletin, 25*, 161–163.

Tajfel, H. (1981). *Human groups and social categories: Studies in social psychology*. Cambridge: Cambridge University Press.

Zimbardo, P.G. (2007). *The Lucifer effect: Understanding how good people turn evil*. New York: Random House.

Chapter 17

The role of narrative exposure therapy in cognitive therapy for traumatized refugees and asylum-seekers

Martina Mueller

INTRODUCTION

Narrative exposure therapy (NET) is a short-term treatment for traumatic stress disorders following war, civil conflict, and political violence, including torture. NET has been developed by a team of researchers and clinicians at the University of Konstanz, in collaboration with the Vivo Foundation, an alliance of professionals specializing in the fields of trauma, humanitarian aid, and field research. NET is designed for traumatized adults, but there is also a child-friendly version in the form of KIDNET. NET is culturally sensitive because it builds on the universal tradition of storytelling. NET is manualized (see Schauer, Neuner, & Elbert, 2005) and was designed to be easily implemented, so as to make effective, trauma-focused intervention more easily available in refugee camps and settlements. It aims to address socio-political aspects of healing, and it fits well with working through interpreters, because it does not rely on finely tuned appraisals and meanings that may get lost in translation. It has a clear conceptual basis and a strong human rights focus and is designed to be delivered in a wide range of circumstances and situations, in the field as well as in more traditional therapeutic settings.

NET has a developing evidence base. Neuner, Schauer, Klaschik, Karunakara, & Elbert (2004), in a randomized study of a group of Sudanese refugees living in a Ugandan refugee camp, compared four sessions of NET (n = 17), four sessions of supportive counselling (n = 14), and four sessions of psycho-education alone (n = 12). NET was found to be more effective at the end of treatment, and furthermore this effect appeared to be sustained at 1-year follow-up, when only 29% of the NET group met criteria for post-traumatic stress disorder (PTSD) in contrast to 79% of the supportive counselling group and 80% of the psycho-education group. In a randomized controlled trial with elderly survivors of political violence in Romania, NET was found to be superior to psycho-education (Bichescu, Neuner, Schauer, & Elbert, 2007). Nunner et al. (2009) found that NET led to a significant reduction in PTSD in asylum-seekers six months post-treatment, whereas treatment as usual (psychotropic medication and supportive interventions) did not. In a controlled trial comparing NET with Interpersonal Psychotherapy, Schaal et al. (2009) found that NET was more effective in reducing symptoms of PTSD and depression on follow-up in a group of young adult orphans of the Rwandan genocide. In a randomized trial, Neuner et al. (2008) found NET to be an effective treatment of war-related PTSD when carried out in a refugee settlement by lay counsellors with limited training. KIDNET has also been found to be effective in a pilot study of six Somali refugees between 12 and 17 years old (Onyut et al., 2005).

NET is based on principles of habituation of the fear network by exposure to the trauma memories, in combination with the principles of testimony therapy to meet the needs of traumatized survivors of war, civil conflict, and political persecution (Cienfuegos & Monelli, 1983). Traditionally, prolonged exposure therapy has targeted a single traumatic event that the patient tries to remember in vivid detail on several occasions. Although more recently this approach has also been used with survivors of multiple traumas such as rape in the context of childhood sexual abuse, only one event (usually the worst event) is recollected in vivid detail on repeated occasions (Resick, Nishith, & Griffin, 2003; McDonagh et al., 2005). This focus may be less useful for asylum-seekers and refugees, as they tend to report multiple traumatic event types as well as events and often have great difficulty in identifying a single worst event (Neuner et al., 2004b). In NET, the patient constructs a *complete* narrative about his or her life from birth up to the present, with a particular focus on a very detailed account of all traumatic experiences. The entire narrative is documented by the therapist in writing and signed at the end of treatment by both patient and therapist. The narrative is usually written in English, and can be translated into the patient's first language if resources allow. Exclusion criteria are generally limited to active psychosis, current substance abuse, and learning disability. Patients presenting with suicidal ideation consequent to depression are not excluded.

NET has two key elements:

1   To facilitate habituation to the trauma memories by prolonged exposure to traumatic hotspots and, in line with Ehlers and Clark's (2000) model, to promote the elaboration and contextualization of the trauma memory by developing a chronological, coherent, and complete account of the person's experiences.
2   To help the refugee or asylum-seeker regain dignity by using narratives for prosecution of human rights violations by international criminal tribunals and awareness-raising purposes.

Ultimately, NET aims to promote a degree of recovery from PTSD and to lessen distress rather than a complete cure of multiple psychological and social problems.

CASE EXAMPLE

Introduction

Zevin is a Kurdish refugee who fled northern Iraq at age 27. He presented with a complex range of interacting difficulties including PTSD, comorbid depression, complicated grief, social isolation, and significant residual health problems following a gunshot wound and malnourishment. In the 2 years prior to starting treatment, Zevin had made two suicide attempts, the second leading to a brief compulsory admission under the Mental Health Act. After an earlier assessment for cognitive behavioural therapy (CBT), Zevin had been thought unsuitable for trauma-focused intervention because of the severity of his depression and the associated risk to himself, as well as his social isolation and associated lack of social support. At that stage he had been referred to the local Community Mental Health Team (CMHT) with the recommendation that he be re-referred for trauma-focused CBT when he was more stable.

A year later, Zevin was re-referred by his psychiatrist, who noted that whilst there had been an improvement in his housing and physical health, his mood had not lifted significantly despite help from an occupational therapist, several changes in medication, and ongoing support from CMHT staff, 'probably because of the severity of his PTSD, which appears to be maintaining the depressive symptoms'. Following further assessment, he was offered NET to see if this approach might aid his recovery. The decision to proceed with NET was made collaboratively with Zevin, who had expressed a desire to talk about his experience and had convincingly argued that he would be able to keep himself safe during the process with the ongoing support of CMHT staff. Importantly, Zevin also had resources that treatment might build on. He had leave to remain in the UK, his English was quite good, he seemed to have a sound understanding of the therapeutic process, and he was motivated and able to attend appointments regularly. The human rights orientation of NET also fitted well with Zevin's history of political activism and later also helped him overcome feelings of guilt and self blame.

Zevin came from a family with a strong tradition of political activism and his father had been killed in a Kurdish uprising against Saddam Hussein's regime when Zevin was a teenager. His father's death led to profound changes in Zevin's life as he had to leave school to support his mother and younger siblings, which meant that he had to give up his dream of studying medicine. He and his best friend were shot during a random attack whilst walking home. Zevin's leg was badly injured and his best friend died as a result of his injuries. Following medical complications that threatened the loss of his leg, Zevin agreed to a transfer to an Iraqi military hospital where staff had greater expertise in treating complicated gunshot wounds. Zevin endured several operations all performed without any anaesthetic, which Zevin believes to have been a deliberate act of maltreatment because of his ethnic origin and political affiliation. His wound eventually improved but did not recover fully, causing ongoing pain, and making it necessary for him to wear a calliper.

Zevin left Iraq when it became clear that he faced imminent imprisonment and probable execution. His younger brother, still a child at the time, was arrested after Zevin went into hiding, probably to persuade Zevin to give himself up to the authorities. Zevin and his family agreed that he would leave the country as his brother, being a child, was thought to be safe from execution. However, his brother was executed in prison, leaving Zevin with a profound sense of guilt and responsibility. His mother died of a heart attack shortly afterwards, of what Zevin believes to be a broken heart. This further fuelled his grief and feelings of guilt and self-blame. Zevin described eight traumatic events in total, some of which were predominantly fear-based (such as the shooting), whilst others led to grief and guilt.

Formulation

Zevin's formulation needed to take account of several interacting processes that acted to maintain his difficulties. The models of chronic PTSD (Ehlers & Clark, 2000), complicated grief (Boelen, van den Hout, & van den Bout, 2006), and depression (Beck, Rush, Shaw, & Emery, 1979) are all relevant in making sense of Zevin's presentation, and in considering options for treatment. The therapist needs to carefully consider which aspects of any model are most important and how they interact with each other, or when it would more useful to start from basic principles. Zevin's pictorial formulation attempts to describe key maintaining factors and their interrelationship relatively parsimoniously (see Figure 17.1).

Treatment plan

Zevin's key goals for therapy were:

- To be able to remember the traumatic events without reliving them in flashbacks or nightmares.
- To preserve his feelings of connection to his brother and mother without feeling overwhelmed by grief.
- To be able to lead a more normal life, including being able to watch media coverage of events in Iraq, meet up with other Kurdish refugees, and concentrate sufficiently to resume his English lessons (and perhaps one day return to full-time study).

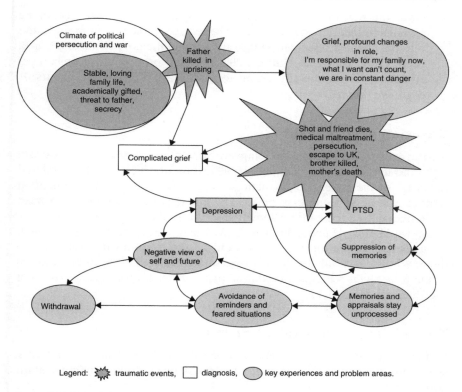

Legend: 🟊 traumatic events, ▢ diagnosis, ⬭ key experiences and problem areas.

Figure 17.1 Zevin's formulation.

In addition, therapy needed to provide Zevin with an opportunity to reflect on his feelings of self-blame and guilt. This was, however, not a goal identified by Zevin himself, because he firmly believed that his feeling of guilt and responsibility were a rightful punishment for failing to return to Iraq, and were therefore reasonable and justified. To help achieve these goals three main treatment strategies were used.

1   Construct a complete narrative of Zevin's life, to elaborate and contextualize his traumatic memories, and habituate to the fear elements within the trauma memory.
2   Address his grief and feelings of guilt and self-blame. The construction of a narrative offers an opportunity to carefully reconsider key decision points in his life, particularly the process of deciding not to return to Iraq. This helps to address hindsight bias and foster reflection on the reasons behind his decision. Further, the narrative permitted us to work directly on complicated grief by allowing Zevin to talk in detail about his relationships and key memories of his family (Boelen et al., 2006).

3   Once the narrative was completed we planned to use our remaining sessions to identify and work with the residual unhelpful appraisals and reinsert updated information into the trauma memory (Ehlers & Clark, 2000; Grey, Young, & Holmes, 2002) to help process his feelings more completely. Thus therapy aimed to interweave NET with elements of cognitive therapy.

Duration of treatment

Narrative exposure therapy is a relatively brief intervention, varying between eight and ten sessions, depending on the setting in which it is delivered and the needs of the patient. Outpatient settings usually permit more time than refugee camps. Sessions may be weekly, but it is not uncommon to meet more frequently for two (and sometimes more) sessions per week (see also, Grey, McManus, Hackmann, Clark, & Ehlers, Chapter 8, this volume). Each session lasts between 90 minutes and 2 hours, resulting in about 12 to 15 therapy hours in total. In Zevin's case we agreed that after 10 sessions we would reassess his remaining needs and plan further appropriate intervention together with his CMHT.

The role of psycho-education in NET

Following assessment the patient is given detailed information on PTSD symptoms, the nature and meaning of intrusive recollections, and an explanation of NET.

> I know that you have tried hard ever since {the traumatic events} to erase these feelings. They have been terrorizing you and leading a life of their own within you. However, we do not want them to do this to you any more . . . we are going to face them together. Up until now, it may have felt as though you have been held captive by them. This is often exactly what the perpetrators wanted. They want that you will remain a prisoner of these horrible events forever. But we are not going to let this go on. We are going to do something about it. If you can manage to vividly remember those memories, feelings and sensations you have had during the event long enough, those terrible emotions will eventually subside. They will lose their grip . . . They will fade away . . . I know this is hard to imagine, but I will help you and this can come true for you as it has done for many others.
> (Schauer et al., 2005, 30)

Patients are given an opportunity to ask questions, to discuss the structure of treatment, and to identify and deal with concerns about constructing a narrative. This is also a good time to clarify ground rules for interpreters (see also d'Ardenne & Farmer, Chapter 18, this volume).

Zevin's lifeline

Our intervention began in session two with a detailed discussion about the role of memory in the onset and maintenance of PTSD, perceptual biases in depression, and the process of NET, before going on to constructing Zevin's lifeline.

Constructing a lifeline

Before the narrative begins, a lifeline is constructed to act as a road map of key positive and traumatic events in chronological order. The lifeline is made from string or wool. Flowers or petals are placed on the lifeline to symbolize positive events, and stones are placed to symbolize traumatic events. The string represents the patient's life to date and is always coiled at the end to show there is a future. The patient lays out the rope in a shape which, in their view, best depicts their life so far, usually on the floor because a table is not large enough. The patient then puts down stones selected for size, shape, or colour to represent each traumatic event. The stones are spaced in chronological order on the lifeline, so as to roughly depict the age at which a particular traumatic event occurred. The same procedure is repeated with petals or flowers for positive events, and again different sizes and colours are provided to enable patients to represent the importance or meaning of an event.

The therapist observes the construction of the lifeline, usually without comment. How a patient constructs a lifeline can give useful clues about their approach to their traumatic memories. Some rush through the process, whilst others are slow to lay down some stones; others struggle to access any memories that might merit a petal or flower. The construction of a lifeline is a physical process that requires patients to take a step back from their experiences, rather than get lost in the detail of any one event. Patients report that this makes it easier to stay in the here and now, rather than getting stuck in hotspots, or overwhelmed by intrusive recollections. If a patient does 'get stuck', gently prompt them to move forward to the next experience. 'Where should the next stone go?', or 'Let's take a break from the stones and think about where some of the petals might go'.

When the lifeline is completed, the patient is asked to summarize, briefly, what event each stone or petal represents and at roughly what age the event occurred. The therapist documents the summary of the lifeline and this forms the beginning of the narrative. The patient can also make a simple drawing of the lifeline.

Zevin's lifeline

Stone 1 – age 8   A commando officer hit me when Iraqi soldiers came to my house looking for my dad.

Stone 2 – age 9	Bombs fell on our next-door neighbour's house. I was sleeping at the time but awoke to screaming in the street. The neighbours were taken to hospital and some survived.
Petal 1 – age 12	I received a very good report from my school. I was the best pupil in my school and had received 95% marks in all my lessons. My parents bought me a pen and new clothes as a treat. The pen had a train inside, which moved when the pen was tilted.
Stone 3 – age 13	My father was killed during the uprising against Saddam Hussein.
Stone 4 – age 14	I had to leave school to look after my family. The embargo had made it very expensive to buy things in the shops. I did not want to leave, but I was thinking about my family. Their lives were more important than school or my future.
Stone 5 – age 17	I was shot in the leg and then had many operations, some of these were very painful, because I wasn't given anaesthetic.
Stone 6 – age 23	Special Forces were looking for me. They couldn't catch me, but they did catch my younger brother.
Petal 2 – age 23	I managed to escape to a safe place.
Stone 7 – age 23	My brother was imprisoned and killed by Special Forces. He was only 14 years old.
Stone 8 – age 23	My mother died of a heart attack. I think it was too much sadness that killed her.
Petal 3 – age 27	Some people are helping me now that I'm here, the doctors and my friends.

Zevin's approach to the lifeline was methodical and carefully considered. He was slow to put down stones to represent the shooting and became visibly distressed when placing his biggest stones (stones 7 and 8) to symbolize the execution of his brother and subsequent death of his mother. The placing of the stones and his subsequent description of what they represented strongly indicated that he saw the two deaths as almost one event.

Constructing the narrative

The narrative was constructed over five sessions in the space of one month, each session lasting for around 2 hours. The imperative to complete the narration before moving onto anything else was useful in maintaining the momentum and focus of the intervention, although on one occasion it was tempting to do otherwise. Zevin had arrived feeling particularly upset and angry because several youths had been verbally abusive and thrown things at him on the way to the session. It would have felt more comfortable to talk in more detail about his feelings and reflect on options to help him deal with such events in the future; however, we refocused our attention on the narrative after a few minutes, with the explicit agreement that we would put 'coping with bullying' on our agenda for a session after we had completed the narrative. Fortuitously, the parallels between the narrative and that day's experience of bullying became very apparent during the session, which helped Zevin reflect on the impact it had had on him without requiring additional intervention later.

At the beginning of the narrative, Zevin tended to speak in a halting, almost inaudible manner. As the account progressed, however, the narrative would loosen, his voice became stronger, and his feelings would shine through more clearly.

Overview

The lifeline provides an outline of the number, nature, and severity of the traumatic events in the life of the patient. The time between events (positive or negative) is talked about at a fairly brisk pace. Events symbolized by flowers are described in greater detail, and hotspots are discussed in very fine detail with very careful attention to sensory memories, feelings, and detailed descriptions of who did what when. Questions about the meaning of an event are much less common than they would be in a reliving paradigm.

Each session finishes on a positive or at least calm point, rather than in the middle of a prolonged traumatic event or series of events. Thus it is important to talk about a particular traumatic event in its entirety in one session, regardless of how long that might take.

When describing traumatic hot spots, the therapist helps emotional processing by paying close attention to the patient's responses at all levels (sensory, emotional, cognitive, and behavioural) and by careful questioning to draw out and describe all aspects of the event. Careful observation of the patient's behaviour in session will provide useful clues about sensory experiences. For example: 'I can see that you are curling up in your chair as we are talking about this, is this something you did at the time?'

Usually the therapist takes notes in the session that are later used to type a fuller account of the narrative, although during hotspots note-taking may be inappropriate. The subsequent session begins with reading the documented narrative from the session before, to correct errors and integrate additional information, and to provide a further opportunity for emotional processing by further exposure to the traumatic memory. The patient reads the narrative aloud if he or she can read English, to reduce the likelihood of tuning out from any distress associated. Alternatively, the therapist slowly reads out the narrative, halting frequently to allow the patient to add to or correct the narrative and to allow time for translation by the interpreter. The final narrative is written in the past tense.

Beginning the narrative

The narrative begins at birth and includes family and cultural background details, to set the context of the person's life prior to the traumatic events. This provides a gentle introduction to the process of interweaving emotions, feelings, behaviours, and thoughts from the past with those in the present, and helps the patient become more familiar with the chronological structure of the narrative.

Detailed questions about the person's early life can be helpful. Sometimes early memories can be hard to access because they are overshadowed by later traumatic events. Cultural differences may make it difficult to understand an aspect of the person's life. Such occasions present a good opportunity to develop the therapeutic relationship, by demonstrating a genuine desire to understand.

Narrating a traumatic event

The lifeline guides the structure and pace of the narrative. 'I think we are coming up to the first traumatic event soon, is that right? Let's go really slowly now because I know this was a really frightening experience, which you relive every day. Tell me about the night before it happened . . .'.

The patient is encouraged to describe the traumatic event in sufficient detail to activate all its aspects and, by creating a complete narrative, to lead to habituation and to help the memory become more fully integrated into autobiographical memory. The therapist facilitates this process by:

- Asking questions to address all elements of the memory.
- Making observations about the patient's behaviour in the session.

Table 17.1 provides examples of useful questions.

Zevin's narration of a fear-based hotspot

During the narration of the shooting, Zevin experienced many sensory memories, including physical pain. He began prodding and poking the scars on his leg without initial awareness within the session that he was doing so. He was clearly feeling a great deal of fear but found it hard to show this openly in the session. Asking questions like 'How did you feel when you heard the first gunshot?' and 'Are you feeling like that right now?' helped a little, but reflecting on the interpersonal process was perhaps just as important in allowing him to recall his experience fully: 'I wonder if it is hard for you to show how vulnerable and afraid you are feeling right now? Is there any way I can help you feel safe in sharing your feelings with me?' This was particularly important because Zevin's trust in others had been comprehensively shattered by his

Table 17.1 Useful questions to help integrate and elaborate trauma memories

Type of memory	Elaborating details about the past	Contextualizing experiences in the present
Cognitive	'What did you think when you realized he was dead?'	'What is going through your mind as you remember the day your friend was shot?'
Sensory/ physiological	'What did you see when you looked at his body on the ground?'	'I notice you are holding your leg, are you feeling the pain of the wound you had then?'
	'What did you smell?'	'Can you smell the gunpowder right now?'
	'What did you hear?'	'Do you hear anything as we talk about what happened then?'
Behavioural	'What did you try to do?'	'Would you like to hide right now in the way you did then?'
	'What did you want to do?'	You seem quite cut off from your feelings right now, is that something that happened then as well?'
	'How did they react to that?'	
Emotional	'How did you feel?'	'What are you feeling as you are talking about this?'
	'Did you feel anything else?'	

Adapted from Schauer et al. (2005).

experiences, which made it essential to pay close attention to building and maintaining trust at every level of our work together. Below is an excerpt from Zevin's narrative of the shooting:

He is a dark, tall, big built man and has a moustache and a horrible face. He looked like a criminal person, like the Mafia. He holds a machine gun. I think he might be drunk, so I tell my friend to be careful. He is swearing saying 'All Kurdish people are bastards, we have to kill all of them . . . God damn Kurds, the dogs, I am going to kill them.' He opens fire and shoots my friend in the chest with many bullets. My friend falls over screaming. I try to catch him but can't. He is too far away and I'm so scared. People are screaming, running away. I hear my friend calling 'Zevin'. His face is contorted, looking at me. I feel an uncomfortable flick in the bottom of my leg; it was so powerful that I fell to the ground. I know that I've been shot, and I'm very scared. My friend tries to get up and is still shouting 'Zevin'. I think I'm going to die, this is my final day. I sense the direction of the shooting is changing and I cover my head with my hands and curl up. I can't see anything. Eventually the sound stops and I hear the screeching of tyres. I try to stand up. My leg twisted and I looked down and saw that my trousers were ripped. I lifted them up and saw a big wound because the bullet had exploded inside my leg (I did not know that at the time, but the doctors told me later). I touch my leg and my hand comes away with part of my bone which I throw away. I feel numb at the time and I'm not in pain.

Finding a safe end point for this traumatic event was difficult because the shooting was followed by nearly a year of very painful surgery, as well as Zevin's concern for the welfare of his family. In awareness of this we had scheduled a particularly long session so that we could finish the narrative at the point when he was discharged from hospital and able to support his family once again.

Narrating – loss and grief

Initially, Zevin found it hard to talk about the circumstances and implications of the losses, preferring to avoid details and thus keep a distance from his overwhelming feelings of grief. It was difficult to persist with questions when Zevin became tearful and said that he really couldn't face thinking about his dad or his brother. Pausing to reflect on why it might be important to acknowledge what has been lost encouraged both Zevin and the therapist to carry on.

My father was very kind and friendly with everyone. He was helpful to relatives and friends and he always advised me to do the right thing, to be respectful to people older than me. He helped me in my school work and was very proud of my reports from school. He was a tall man, of medium build. My nose looks like his, although because I fell over playing with my friend and broke my nose his nose was straighter than mine. Sometimes I heard my father swear and become very angry with Saddam Hussein. I miss his comforting presence; he made me feel protected from all the bad things around.

My father put us to bed earlier than usual because there was no electricity in the house as an American aircraft had destroyed the electricity supply. I couldn't sleep despite trying hard, but my sister and brother were asleep. My father had been more restless than usual. I felt nervous, maybe something was about to happen. My father came to our room, I opened my eyes 'You're still not asleep?' he said 'Yes' I replied, 'I can't sleep'. He kissed my brother and sister, and then he kissed me and cuddled me very hard. His face was different; he wasn't smiling or laughing but full of anger, very emotional. I asked him 'Daddy, are you ok?' He said 'Yes', put me back to bed and kissed my forehead and said 'Good-night', then he walked out of the room and shut the door. When I woke the next day he wasn't there . . .

At the end of this session we talked in some detail about the need for social support, and called one of Zevin's trusted friends to arrange a visit that evening. A follow-up call the day after the narrative provided much needed reassurance for everyone.

Troubleshooting

As with other forms of reliving or exposure, obstacles can arise whilst narrat-ing traumatic hotspots. Sometimes a patient may find it hard to put their experiences into words, either because the trauma memories are very poorly represented in a verbally accessible form, or because words (in whatever lan-guage) seem, quite simply, inadequate. The questions outlined in Table 17.1 can begin to help with this. The patient can also be asked to describe the experience in another form, e.g., 'It felt like a vice gripping my heart whilst I turned into stone'. The main aim is to find words that might *begin* to represent the traumatic event.

Several things can be helpful in holding particularly high levels of distress, and not avoiding the most traumatic material, including strong sensory memories of pain. First, therapists must feel that they are doing the right, helpful thing, which is greatly aided by supervision and a well thought-out case formulation. Second, the therapeutic relationship must be strong, so that therapists can feel confident in their ability to align themselves with the patient in support of recovery. It is important to feel comfortable with expressing distress when listening to very distressing material. To quote Frank Neuner (personal communication) 'It is OK [for the therapist] to cry. Just *start* crying after the patient does and make sure you *stop* before they do'.

Another difficulty encountered during the process of reliving or narrating a traumatic event is involuntary detachment from the trauma memories. The patient 'tuning out' from the traumatic event may be replicating a process that occurred at the time and is best treated as any other sensory memory. Sometimes, however, patients tune out because they feel overwhelmed. An early warning sign of this is often a growing emotional detachment from the narrative. The therapist needs to remain vigilant to this throughout the narra-tive and help reconnect the patient to the safety of here and now (see Schauer et al., 2005, 48).

If patients are experiencing flashbacks to the traumatic events during the narration, the therapist should reassure the patient that the event is over and provide sensory anchors to the present, by refocusing the patient's attention to sensations in the here and now (e.g., 'Can you hear the traffic noise outside?') and by providing discriminatory smells, sound, and touch sensations.

Cognitive components of Zevin's treatment

During the construction of the narrative, several important changes occurred. Zevin's voice and demeanour became stronger, he seemed to become more trusting of the safety of the therapeutic relationship, and he began to talk about feelings of anger, when earlier he had been entirely focused on guilt and self-blame.

Several, mostly fear-based, appraisals seemed to change as the narrative progressed, and Zevin began to talk about the role of Saddam Hussein's regime in causing so much harm to his family and the Kurdish people. Zevin found the idea of testing negative appraisals about his brother's death easy to understand and was able to participate actively in this process. This led to palpable changes in his degree of guilt, although for reasons which were not clear he refused to give belief ratings – however, a degree of rebellion on this (however small) was a pleasure to see as evidence of a reawakening spirit!

Finally, this new information (see Table 17.2) was used to 'update' his trauma memories within reliving (Ehlers & Clark, 2000; Grey et al., 2002).

Response to treatment

Zevin's progress in treatment was heartening. Although he still met diagnostic criteria for PTSD at 3-month follow-up, his scores on the Clinician Administered PTSD Scale reduced from 39 at assessment to 21 (frequency) and 37 to 19 (intensity), indicating a significant clinical improvement, and his score on the Beck Depression Inventory reduced from 43 at assessment to 31. Trial data suggest that further recovery might be expected between 3 and 12 months after treatment (Neuner et al., 2004a, 2009).

Zevin reported a reduction in the frequency and vividness of his flashbacks and nightmares. His feelings of grief appeared to have 'unfrozen' a little. There were also other unanticipated changes. He talked about feeling heard and understood, which by his report made it a little easier to reconsider some of his unhelpful appraisals. He became more trusting, not only in the therapeutic relationship, but also in his interaction with others, particularly other Kurdish refugees.

Zevin's progress appears to have been sustained. A recent report from his CMHT, written a year following discharge from psychological intervention, indicates that he has remained improved, his mood is stable, and he is physically much better. Zevin has now been discharged from care of the mental health services.

Table 17.2 Examples of Zevin's hotspots and updated meaning

Traumatic event	Hotspot	Emotion	Meaning	Updated meaning
Shooting	Being in the square	Guilt	'It was my fault that we were in the square'	'I could not have known what was going to happen' 'The regime and perpetrator are to blame'
	Man fires	Fear	'He might really hurt us'	'I survived and am safe now'
	Friend is hurt	Terror, helpless, guilt	'I can't help him' 'He is dying'	'No one could have helped him, his injuries were very bad'
	Shot in leg	Numb	'I don't understand this, but I know it's bad'	'I will keep my leg' 'More surgery will help heal it more'
Brother's execution	Decision not to return to Iraq	Guilt	'I should have known'	'I could not have known'
			'I am a coward for wanting to survive'	'It is ok to want to survive'
	Told that my brother has been killed	Disbelief, horror, guilt, despair	'I killed my brother'	'The regime killed my brother, and I must not let it off the hook'
			'I do not deserve a future'	'I need to live to show that Kurdish people will not be crushed'

DISCUSSION

The available evidence base to date suggests that NET is effective in its own right as a brief intervention for the treatment of PTSD in traumatized asylum-seekers and refugees. However, NET can also be used as one component within a broader cognitive-behavioural intervention.

The complex problems presented by traumatized refugees and asylum-seekers often lead therapists to move between talking about the trauma and working on stabilizing mood, or helping a patient solve a particular problem that has arisen. Although potentially helpful, these changes of focus can also make the therapy feel disjointed, and traumatic memories may remain unaddressed. Of crucial importance in incorporating NET within a wider CBT-based approach is that *once the narrative has begun it should be completed before moving on to anything else.* This guideline has two other advantages:

1   It allows both patient and therapist to keep the end of this process firmly in sight: 'This is difficult, but it will be over in two weeks'. Knowing that the narrative has a clear endpoint is important in enabling patients to persist with it.
2   It counteracts avoidance. Everyone who is faced with talking about or listening to detailed accounts of traumatic experiences would rather be doing something less distressing, demanding, and exhausting. This means that on many occasions therapist and patient alike will find themselves re-prioritizing issues, talking about interesting irrelevancies, or falling prey to other distractions. The simple rule of 'Finish once you've started' helps counteract this very understandable temptation.

However, there are occasional situations when one might reasonably consider diverting from this protocol. This is most likely when there is a real risk of harm to self or others that is *not* due to being stuck in a difficult and distressing part of the narrative. For example, an asylum-seeker who becomes actively suicidal whilst working on her narrative because she has just learned that her bother has been killed may need to discontinue the narrative for a time to help her cope in her present crisis. Another asylum-seeker who has been giving a detailed account of detention and multiple rape may be better served by helping her continue to process these memories more fully, thereby putting them more firmly in the past. Detailed knowledge of patients and their circumstances, and a sound therapeutic alliance, are crucial to helping therapist and patient make these difficult decisions collaboratively.

NET can also be a useful part of treatment for other traumatized populations, especially for patients who experience multiple traumas, domestic violence, or repeated occupational trauma, for example, over the course of their adult lives. The construction of a narrative helps to embed traumatic events in the broader experiences and context of a patient's life. It is also useful in identifying themes in meaning and their development, which informs cognitive components of treatment. However, as there is no documented evidence base as yet for the use of NET in this context, it is important to monitor and evaluate response.

ACKNOWLEDGEMENTS

I am grateful to the European Refugee Fund for their support of some of the work presented here, and to Frank Neuner and Elisabeth Schauer for their helpful comments on an earlier draft.

REFERENCES

Beck, A.T., Rush, A.J., Shaw, B.F., & Emery, G. (1979). *Cognitive therapy of depression.* New York: Guildford.

Bichescu, D., Neuner, F., Schauer, M., & Elbert, T. (2007). Narrative exposure therapy of political imprisonment-related chronic trauma spectrum disorders: A randomized controlled trial. *Behaviour Research and Therapy, 45,* 2212–2220.

Boelen, P., van den Hout, M., & van den Bout, J. (2006). A cognitive–behavioural conceptualization of complicated grief. *Clinical Psychology: Science and Practice, 13,* 109–128.

Cienfuegos, J., & Monelli, C. (1983). The testimony of political repression as a therapeutic instrument. *American Journal of Orthopsychiatry, 53,* 43–51.

Ehlers, A., & Clark, D.M. (2000). A cognitive model of PTSD. *Behaviour Research and Therapy, 38,* 1–27.

Grey, N., Young, K., & Holmes, E. (2002). Cognitive restructuring within reliving: A treatment for peritraumatic emotional hotspots in PTSD. *Behavioural and Cognitive Psychotherapy, 30,* 63–82.

McDonagh, A., Friedman, M., McHugo, G., Ford, J., Sengupta, A., Mueser, K., Denment, C.C., Founier, D., Schnurr, P.P., & Descamps, M. (2005). Randomized trial of cognitive-behaviour therapy for chronic posttraumatic stress disorder in adult female survivors of childhood sexual abuse. *Journal of Counselling and Clinical Psychology, 73,* 515–524.

Neuner, F., Onyut, P., Ertl, V., Schauer, E., Odenwald, M., & Elbert, T. (2008). Treatment of posttraumatic stress disorder by trained lay counsellors in an African refugee settlement – A randomized controlled trial. *Journal of Consulting and Clinical Psychology 76,* 686–694.

Neuner, F., Schauer, M., Klaschik, C., Karunakara, U., & Elbert, T. (2004a). A comparison of narrative exposure treatment, supportive counselling, and psycho-education for treating posttraumatic stress disorder in an African refugee settlement. *Journal of Consulting and Clinical Psychology, 72,* 579–587.

Neuner, F., Schauer, M., Karunakara, U., Klaschik, C., Robert, C., & Elbert, T. (2004b). Psychological trauma and evidence for enhanced vulnerability for post-traumatic stress disorder through previous trauma among West Nile refugees. *BMC Psychiatry, 4,* 34.

Neuner, F., Kurreck, S., Ruf, M., Odenwald, M., Elbert, T., & Schauer, M. (2009). Can asylum seekers with posttraumatic stress disorder be successfully treated? A randomized controlled pilot study. *Cognitive Behaviour Therapy* (in press).

Onyut, L.P., Neuner, F., Schauer, E., Ertl, V., Odenwald, M., Schauer, M., & Elbert, T. (2005). Narrative exposure therapy as treatment for war survivors with posttraumatic stress disorder: Two case reports and a pilot study in an African refugee settlement. *BMC Psychiatry*, 5, 7.

Resick, P.A., Nishith, P., & Griffin, M.G. (2003). How well does cognitive-behaviour therapy treat symptoms of complex PTSD? An examination of childhood sexual abuse survivors within a clinical trial. *CNS Spectrums*, 8(340–342), 351–355.

Schaal, S., Elbert, T., & Neuner, F. (2009). Narrative Exposure Therapy versus Interpersonal Psychotherapy – a treatment study with Rwandan genocide orphans. *Psychotherapy and Psychometrics* (in press).

Schauer, M., Neuner, F., & Elbert, T. (2005). *Narrative exposure therapy: A short-term intervention for traumatic stress disorders after war, terror, or torture*. Göttingen: Hogrefe & Huber.

Chapter 18

Using interpreters in trauma therapy

Patricia d'Ardenne and Elly Farmer

INTRODUCTION

This chapter is aimed at therapists working with traumatized clients in need of language support, and will show how to use interpreters to maximize therapeutic effect. We will inevitably refer to the issues of working with refugee experience and torture, since they interact with the interpreting process. We regard effective work with interpreters as a necessary but not sufficient skill for psychological therapists. Good interpreting can only take place within overall transcultural sensitivity (d'Ardenne, Capuzzo, Ruaro, & Priebe, 2005), which recognizes difference in perception, priority, and the meaning of emotion.

Recent post-traumatic stress disorder (PTSD) treatment guidelines recommend the use of interpreters and states that 'language . . . should not be an obstacle to the provision of effective trauma-focused psychological interventions' (National Collaborating Centre for Mental Health (NCCMH), 2005, para. 2.3.7.3.4), but has not detailed how this should be done. The clinical cases here will be based on our own protocols for interpreting (d'Ardenne, Farmer, Ruaro, & Priebe, 2007), which were designed to address this gap, and which can be applied to cognitive behaviour therapy (CBT) work based on the Ehlers and Clark (2000) model of PTSD. We have some evidence that interpreter-mediated CBT is effective and therefore hope readers will gain confidence in this practice, and ensure that language is not a barrier to effective trauma-focused work (d'Ardenne, Ruaro, Cestari, Wakhoury, & Priebe, 2007).

We will illustrate the application of these protocols for interpreting with fictitious cases based on authentic elements of our caseloads. The two cases outline many complex aspects of interpreting CBT, for example building rapport, reliving, and working with alternative realities. We demonstrate common difficulties with interpreting and how they can be prevented or resolved. It is not our intention to describe the entire therapeutic process, rather to describe these cases at points where interpreting issues are salient. We introduce dialogue, and when it is directly between the therapist and client, the reader can assume that interpretation has been literal and accurate. By contrast, we show three-way dialogues in which misunderstandings in language are arising. Throughout we share practice points, informed in part from our clinical mistakes and learning.

We use trained interpreters from a Local Authority, since psychotherapy demands a high level of fluency and accuracy for sequential interpreting. Well-intentioned but untrained people, including advocates and relatives, tend to summarize what they hear, to respond on behalf of the patient, and to gloss over nuances in language. Responsibility for well-interpreted psychotherapy lies primarily with the clinician, who has to ensure the linguistic competence of a neutral interpreter (Mailloux, 2004; Shackman, 1984). We therefore prefer professional interpreters, even though many have little mental health experience and no CBT training, and it is these on which we base our cases.

CASES

Background to referrals

Ahmed

Ahmed is a 27-year-old Kurdish man who lived in Turkey up until his recent flight to the UK, where he, his wife, and their 2-year-old son pleaded asylum and were granted refugee status. In Turkey he was a member of the PKK – a political organization fighting for the human rights of the Kurdish people. He was arrested and tortured by the Turkish militia and now suffers nightmares, flashbacks, and anger and anxiety attacks. He is scared to leave the house and trusts few beyond his immediate family. His symptoms are adding to both his and his family's depression and sense of hopelessness.

Ahmed is sent an opt-in letter in Kurdish, which summarizes assessment and trauma-focused therapy at the clinic. He sends back the accompanying slip indicating that he would like to attend and have a Turkish-speaking interpreter.

Asmara

Asmara is a 45-year-old Eritrean woman who fled her country because she was a Jehovah's Witness, and had been persecuted, arrested, and raped due to her religious beliefs. Her older son was shot in front of her following a struggle with Government-sponsored militia, and her husband and three other younger children were dragged away and placed under arrest. Asmara escaped and now lives alone in a hostel, and is working illegally as a cleaner. She is supported by her Church here and is seeking asylum. She is university educated, and speaks a little English. She was referred to the local Community

Mental Health Team by her GP, after she complained of hearing the voices of her attackers, continuing to humiliate her. The referral letter also describes traumatic grief, depression, and extreme shame about the rape. The letter says that Asmara can speak a little English, but a friend interprets for her. She is sent an 'opt in' letter, however, and when asked about her language needs, she requests a Tigrinya interpreter, and says that she would prefer a woman.

Practice points

- Ahmed was not explicitly asked in the opt-in letter whether he was willing to work with a Turkish-speaking national. Although we cannot offer unlimited choice, sensitivity to ethnic division can avoid tensions during interpreted psychotherapy.
- In Asmara's case, it is better to ask the client's needs directly (Patel, 2003), rather than rely on the referrer's evaluation. Sometimes clients request a spouse or sibling to interpret. This practice is unethical and inappropriate, as boundaries are broken regarding patient confidentiality, and because during trauma-focused CBT, interpreting a traumatic history places a considerable emotional and linguistic burden on a relative, for whom the therapist cannot be held responsible (Drennan & Swartz, 1999; Holder, 2002; Mahtani, 2003; Raval, 1996). Advocates, friends and next of kin may be very supportive and escort patients to the clinic, but cannot expect to be detached in assessment or treatment with CBT.

Preparation time with interpreters

Ahmed

Rema, the clinician, books a male Turkish interpreter, Farouk. She sends him some information on the service, traumatic reactions, and a list of key unusual English words that are likely to be used. They arrange to meet half an hour before the assessment, when she briefs him on Ahmed's background, current situation, and presenting difficulties. Farouk appears flustered, stating that he wholeheartedly condemns the way in which the Turkish militia have treated Kurdish people. Rema informally assesses Farouk's English to be of a high standard.

Asmara

Emma, the clinician, is informed by the interpreting service that there is a shortage of Tigrinya speakers; worse, very few are women, and of these, only one with mental health experience (Leila). Emma enquires about Leila's background and is told she is a Muslim and has interpreted for many clients from Eritrea and Ethiopia. Emma books Leila, despite concerns she has about religious differences between interpreter and client. Emma meets Leila before the assessment; she is a young black woman in Western dress and hijab. Emma asks her if she has experienced violence herself and Leila discloses that although she is from Ethiopia, she has not experienced violence personally. Emma checks her availability for assessment and intervention sessions over the following 3 months.

Transcript I

EMMA: In therapy we shall be re-visiting the worst parts of Asmara's experience many times. I need to know that you can interpret calmly and objectively.

LEILA: I have heard many terrible stories . . . killings and rape, and I know I must not interrupt or express any opinions about what has happened.

EMMA: Yes, good. Do you think Asmara might worry about you not being Christian?

LEILA: Yes, it has sometimes happened before, and I do understand why. I cannot change who I am. But I do not argue because I know people feel very strongly about these things . . .

Practice points

• Interpreters often come from the same wars as their clients. If Leila had disclosed personal victimization, Emma would have sought another interpreter to protect Leila's wellbeing. Emma would act before seeing Asmara, and explain that the interpreter was unavailable. Exposing traumatized interpreters to clients' torture compromises treatment and is unethical for all parties. Allocate enough briefing time with the interpreter and be ready to cancel the session if necessary.

• Both clinicians allowed adequate time for briefing and preparation for the type of work they will be engaged in. At a practical level, booking in 10–30 minutes with an interpreter beforehand saves time and avoids miscommunication and distress in session.

Engagement and assessment

Ahmed

Ahmed arrives early and sits opposite Farouk in the waiting room. Farouk initiates a conversation, eager to disclose his political position, believing that this will increase Ahmed's trust. Rema arrives and finds the two in animated discussion. Farouk turns and says in English 'we are all on his side'. Rema has set up the positions of the chairs in the consultation room so that Farouk is sitting slightly behind Ahmed, speaking into his ear whilst maintaining eye contact with her. Ahmed sits directly facing Rema at all times. She begins by outlining how sessions will operate, including confidentiality, length, and content. Early on, Rema observes that Ahmed makes little eye contact with herself, instead looking down and at times casting suspicious looks behind him at Farouk.

Transcript 2

REMA [English]: Ahmed, thank you for coming back to talk despite this being difficult. I was wondering whether you might be finding it hard speaking to both myself and Farouk at the same time . . .

FAROUK [Turkish]: Rema's wondering whether it might be difficult speaking to both me and her at the same time, and she says thank you for coming back.

AHMED [Tur] [eyes cast down]: hmm . . .

REMA [Eng]: I realize it's a difficult process and you may be wondering whether you can trust both of us with your experiences and feelings . . .

FAROUK [Tur]: She's wondering whether you can trust us with your experiences and feelings?

AHMED [Tur]: hmm [pause] . . . yes, I don't know who I can trust. There are many Turkish people in London and they have power, they are a cruel people. I don't even know about anybody else . . .

FAROUK [Eng] [shifting uncomfortably]: He doesn't know who he can trust as there are many Turkish people in London and he thinks we're cruel and powerful. He's also not sure about other nationalities. The thing is Rema is that – well you know – we're not all the same – I feel like him about the way the Turkish army's treating the Kurdish – it's not fair to lump us all together!

[Ahmed appears to be looking slightly scared of Farouk]

REMA [Eng]: Ahmed I need to speak directly with Farouk as I don't understand everything you've just said.

FAROUK [Tur]: She wants to speak to me on my own.

REMA [Eng]: Farouk, please remember to speak in the first person, saying exactly what the client and I have said. Thank you for helping here. Ahmed, given how people have treated you, I can see how it's extremely difficult to know whom you can trust. [pauses for Farouk to translate]

FAROUK [Tur]: [interprets to Ahmed word for word]

REMA [Eng]: Trust is a slow process and I can ask you to trust us as we show you our trustworthiness over time.

During this initial session, Rema checks whether the self-report questionnaires that were posted at the time of opting in have been completed. Ahmed shows her the blank forms and they agree that he will complete them at the end of the session with assistance from Farouk. At the end of the session, they are left for a further 40 minutes to complete these and return them to Rema.

Asmara: Transcript 3

EMMA: Asmara please sit opposite me and let Leila sit behind you.
ASMARA: I am not happy with this. Please change. I was blindfolded when being questioned in prison and I want to see everyone in the room . . . please!
EMMA: Of course! Where would you like Leila to sit?
ASMARA: Here, beside me, yes, that is good!

Asmara stands up and waits for Leila to move her chair and sit beside her, three-ways, round the table. Both women smile and look at Emma, who asks them both to move together a little and to continue looking at her even when Emma is speaking to and looking at Asmara.

During the assessment, Leila begins to shake her head and click her tongue as Asmara describes her emotional 'hotspots' during an attack. She rests her hand on Asmara's as a sign of solidarity. Then, the story is paused as Asmara begins to weep, and Leila also appears tearful. Emma tries to make eye contact with Leila, to no avail, and decides to wait until the end of the session, after Asmara has left the room.

Transcript 4

EMMA: How do you feel it went today?
LEILA: I felt so sorry for her . . . I just wanted to put my arms around her and share her grief.
EMMA: I guess it's very hard not to take a position about what she has suffered – but that is what I am asking you to do when you interpret for us.
LEILA: But we couldn't go on! She was becoming too upset to talk about what happened. She just wants to forget!
EMMA: I think *you* were more upset and once you expressed your feelings, it was impossible for me to explore her trauma any further today. Please remember that she cannot forget. We are doing trauma-focused work here. I realize this is difficult, but it is very important that you do not add your feelings when the patient is here, although I am always happy to talk about how you feel once she has left the room.
LEILA: I will try – but it is very hard – especially when I am right beside her. Today – I felt ashamed at what the government has done to her.
EMMA: Please try and look at me as much as possible during the session – and we can talk later – ok?
LEILA: Yes, yes, I will try.

Practice points

- Rema's difficulties during CBT could have been prevented by a full briefing with Farouk on the extent of confidentiality and self-disclosure. This should include what takes place in the consulting room, the waiting room, the journey home, and home and family and colleagues. Disclosure of any personal or political opinions can serve to weaken the effectiveness of the client-focused, Socratic techniques inherent within CBT. Although it can be tempting to disclose personal opinion in an area of work where injustices are rife, the premise of CBT is that clients are facilitated to explore and re-evaluate their own beliefs.
- Good therapy occurs when client and therapist feel communication has been direct, through the medium of unobtrusive interpreting. Part of this is the use of the first person; yet interpreters like Farouk may commonly slip into the third person, which can confuse the conversation (Bot, 2005; Bot & Wadensjo, 2004) and undermine the therapeutic alliance. Rema addresses both difficulties by halting the interpreting process to guide Farouk briefly. Therapists may need to keep prompting interpreters in this matter.
- At the start of assessment it is good practice to ensure that the interpreter is available to provide additional assistance with self-report questionnaires. Whilst it is recognized that interpretation does not entirely mean self-report, it is at least better practice for the clinician to be absent and to allow the interpreter to translate freely. In our experience interpreters provide more objective assistance than family or friends. In some parts of the world or some settings it may not be possible to access professional interpreters, and pragmatically family members may have to be used. However, this should be avoided if possible.
- Emma enables Asmara to control her immediate psychological space, and puts her at her ease – more important principles than conventional seating protocols. She quickly responds to Asmara's distress by inviting Leila to move forwards.
- Emma can quickly evaluate communication in this unusual session and also obtain feedback from Asmara when she escorts her from the consulting room.
- Emma uses debriefing not to directly challenge Leila; rather, she acknowledges that it is painful, and ascertains that talking does not mean re-traumatizing. Emma also uses debriefing time to focus on Leila's understanding about detachment. Professional interpreters add nothing, change nothing, and omit nothing. She repeats the invitation to use debriefing for her concerns and will continue this process throughout treatment.

Cognitive interventions

We have selected *reliving* (Ehlers & Clark, 2000) and *compassionate mind training* (Gilbert & Irons, 2005) as being two of the more challenging interventions for an interpreter. We explore how far we can use CBT without interpretation becoming a barrier to effective outcome.

Ahmed

In the assessment sessions and ongoing therapy, it has emerged that Ahmed's PTSD symptoms particularly focus around a mock execution he was subjected to. Rema has devoted therapeutic space to discussing the rationale for Ahmed re-experiencing this traumatic event (Harvey, Bryant, & Tarrier, 2003), and he has now chosen to take this step.

In order to prepare for the process of reliving with an interpreter, Rema, Farouk, and Ahmed practise reliving a neutral scene of Ahmed's choice: a walk he recently went on with his wife. Rema emphasizes to Farouk again the importance of interpreting as exactly as possible, including copying her use of the present tense. She also explains and models how reliving involves interpreting only one or two sentences at a time. Lastly, she speaks in a softer tone, and directs Farouk to do the same. After spending a session on this practice, the triad move to relive the execution.

Transcript 5

AHMED [Tur] [eyes glazed]: They were blindfolding me . . .

FAROUK [Eng] [quietly]: They were blindfolding me . . .

REMA [Eng] [quietly]: Remember to speak as if it is happening now. What do their hands feel like?

FAROUK [Tur]: [interprets word for word]

AHMED [Tur]: rough, cold. I can feel them pulling it so tight that my head hurts . . . And then, now they are taunting me, teasing me, telling me I'm going to die now, and that I deserve it and I am stupid for ever trying to challenge them. One of them has a really loud, particularly sneering voice. I feel so angry with them. How dare they? They are not men, they're like animals . . .

[Rema looks to Farouk, catching his eye and nodding for him to gently interrupt Ahmed by interpreting Ahmed's words back to Rema].

FAROUK [Eng] [quietly]: [interprets word for word]

REMA [Eng] [quietly]: Where can you feel your anger towards them?

FAROUK [Tur]: Can you feel the anger in your body? Where?

AHMED [Tur]: My stomach feels like it's in a tight knot, I feel like I'm going to faint . . .

FAROUK [Tur]: [picking up on Ahmed's words quickly, interprets word for word]

REMA [Eng]: Where in your body do you feel faint?

Although frequently in trauma-focused CBT reliving sessions are recorded for the client to listen to in-between sessions (to facilitate reprocessing), Ahmed decides against this as his interrogations were tape-recorded, and so therapy would feel like the same. Instead Rema adapts approaches from Narrative Exposure Therapy (Schauer, Elbert, & Neuner, 2004) to use with CBT and with an interpreter. Specifically, she writes down what Ahmed says during the reliving session, writing it up more fully afterwards whilst retaining the present tense and all details. In the subsequent session she gives Ahmed's account to Farouk to translate, and this version is given to Ahmed the session after, for him to read every day that week. During this process it transpires that Farouk's written Turkish is not completely fluent, impacting upon how vivid the account feels to Ahmed.

Asmara

Asmara has now been fully assessed by Emma with the help of Leila – and found to be presenting with significant depression and shame about her rape. Her thoughts about her history are particularly self-attacking. Leila's increasing adaptability to trauma-focused work allows Asmara to disclose these feelings more openly. Asmara, however, cannot describe fully the actual event, and her thoughts and feelings about this. During the fourth session, Emma asks Asmara for a detailed reliving of her rape. The rape represents for her the worst outcome of the war, as she believes it leaves her a defective and damaged individual. The memory therefore triggers extreme shame. Her avoidance of this emotion occurs when she begins to dissociate, as shown by her closing her eyes and falling forwards in a trance-like state, with her arms clinging to the table. Emma understands that she has not fainted, but Leila appears very frightened and immediately requests that the session be stopped and medical help sought. Emma as clinician takes control of the situation by firstly turning to Leila and reassuring her that Asmara has not fainted and that the session must continue and that she will be debriefed. Emma asks Asmara to locate herself in the here-and-now, by asking her whom she can hear in the room, what she can feel, what the temperature of the room is and makes reference to previous grounding exercises where she has felt safe. Emma continues to reassure her by providing an update on where she is, and the reliving is terminated. Gradually Asmara returns to the present time and leaves her fugue and a decision is made not to return to trauma-focused work for that session. After Asmara has left, Emma provides Leila with enough time to discuss the full meaning of what has happened.

In later sessions, Emma decides that compassionate mind training (Gilbert & Irons, 2005) using a *perfect nurturer* (Lee, 2005) would be an approach that might help Asmara with her extreme shame. Her shame is maintaining the intrusive symptoms by causing her to avoid processing her memories of being raped (Lee, Scragg, & Turner, 2001). There will inevitably be complexity in constructing an imaginal person to help Asmara reframe her critical thoughts with more compassion. Neither Asmara nor Leila has had experience of creating imagined people and states. Emma explains the rationale of the nurturer to Asmara and Leila several times during the initial session that this approach is discussed.

At the next briefing, Leila explains to Emma that Tigrinya has some grammatical irregularities. For example, in the second person pronouns, there is a separate vocative form that can be used to summon another person, and in particular to hold the attention of the person (or imagined person) being addressed. Emma decides to use this to good effect.

Transcript 6

EMMA [Eng]: Imagine your perfect nurturer, and when you feel comforted, ask her to change 'I got what I deserved' and 'I will never be good enough for my husband again'.

LEILA [Tig]: [interprets exactly and instructs Asmara to use the specific vocative form]

ASMARA [Tig]: You! (feminine) Please strengthen me and help me see how special I am. I know you love me. Stay here with me, and accept that I couldn't have known what would happen to the family.

However, not all of Emma's approaches work as well. In a later session, she re-evaluates Asmara's intrusive symptoms with the following question:

Transcript 7

EMMA [Eng]: What specific memories still haunt you from the arrest?

LEILA [Tig]: What ghosts visit you from the arrest?

ASMARA [Tig]: I see no ghosts! – why do you think I'm mad?

Practice points

- Rema's practising of a neutral scene before reliving Ahmed's trauma helps to reveal, and therefore resolve, any misunderstandings about the reliving process, thereby ensuring that the reprocessing of emotional material is not then subsequently hindered.
- This moves the attention away from any distracting discourse during the reliving for Ahmed.

- The frequency with which speech is interpreted needs to increase during reliving, to maintain *temporal proximity* between client and therapist. At one point, Rema is concerned that this proximity is decreasing as Ahmed goes deeper into reliving the past moment. There is a fine balance here between allowing this reprocessing, whilst at the same time needing to gently interrupt for interpretation so that the therapist can connect and so facilitate the client's experience.

- Interpreting during reliving demands discernment from the interpreter and therapist in knowing when to speak. Rema indicates the need for shorter interpreted 'chunks'. Farouk, like most interpreters in this situation, gets into the habit of picking up Ahmed's words quickly after small sections so that long, non-interpreted narratives do not occur.

- By its very nature, interpreted compared to non-interpreted reliving involves much more discourse, including that which the client cannot understand. This may increase the difficulty for clients to imagine being in a different time. Subtle differences, like speaking quickly and quietly, can help in working against this.

- Both reliving and compassionate mind training require clients and interpreters to work in an alternative reality (counterfactual thinking). Yet it is harder in some languages to speak of the world as how it might or could be. Emma uses the interpreter as a *linguistic consultant*, checking what is possible in the client's language. If this is done before the session, she can think creatively about what can be done given the language resources available.

- For Ahmed, therapy involves both written and oral forms of communication. It is therefore essential to clarify at the start that the interpreter is fluent in both language forms. It is not infrequent that a discrepancy occurs between a client and an interpreter's written competencies, which should be addressed to enable practising and reliving. Although not appropriate in Ahmed's case, audio-recordings can be made, enabling the client to write his story out at home.

- Emma should have prepared her interpreter for the risk of a dissociative episode (flashbacks or fugues), and the need to return to a safe place and offer reassurance. Any manifestation of fear is only likely to aggravate the client's belief that she is in an unsafe place.

- Emma shares with Leila the frequent use of metaphor in CBT. She also uses the interpreter as a *cultural consultant*, asking about metaphors and conditional tenses (Miller, Martell, Pazdirek, Caruth, & Lopez, 2005; Bjorn, 2005; Fox, 2001). Emma can then select an appropriate metaphor, one that is not too likely to lead to misunderstanding of a related meaning – e.g. psychosis. If in doubt, Emma can use the metaphor and then offer an expansion/explanation.

- The compassionate mind training requires much planning and practice for clients in interpreted CBT. We think it is wise to book in additional briefing and sessional time (perhaps twice as much time), which helps both client and interpreter understand the process of identifying the self-attacking thoughts, imagining the image of a compassionate re-frame, and the degree to which the client can agree with the re-frame.

• Emma watches Leila carefully to ensure that she does not 'rescue' Asmara before Asmara can rescue herself by her own efforts. She stops interpreting immediately if this process starts.

Endings, debriefing, and reflection

Ahmed

After walking Ahmed out of a reliving session, Rema returns to find Farouk looking absent. Farouk explains that he feels upset by what he has heard and does not know if he can carry on with the work. He has been feeling more distressed as the weeks have gone on, and he thinks that this is because he is powerless to improve the situation for the Kurdish in Turkey. However, he does think that it might help if he could use some of Ahmed's story as a testimony to the ongoing injustices. Farouk is talking very fast and looking visibly upset.

Rema firstly empathasizes with how Farouk has found the session, revealing her understanding of his feelings. She enquires further into the different emotions he has had at different points; these include anger, frustration, and hopelessness, and at times Farouk has found it difficult not to cry. As well as empathizing and normalizing, Rema is clear about the need to draw a boundary between Farouk's feelings and Ahmed's therapy. They explore options of increasing his power in challenging the human rights situation. Rema lastly affirms that he has a choice about interpreting; by this stage Farouk feels calmer and says he wants to continue until the end of therapy.

Asmara

At the start of the 15th session, Emma receives an answerphone message (in English) from Asmara to say that she has been resettled 20 miles away and that she cannot continue therapy. Emma decides to contact Asmara by telephone. She arranges a three-way conversation with two telephones and a double jack and asks Leila to call Asmara and to obtain more information. She does this so that she can hear Asmara speak, get some feeling for her mood, and continue to hold responsibility for the interpreting process (Bot & Wadensjo, 2004). It becomes clear that this therapy ending is unscheduled. Asmara and Leila become tearful again, and start to say goodbye directly to each other on the phone before Emma has had a chance to speak. Emma allows this conversation to take place, and then interjects with a request for factual information to enable Asmara to get healthcare in her new address. Leila is able to regain her composure, communicate with Asmara, as well as persuade her to return to the clinic for follow up once she has got settled and got her affairs in order. Emma makes sure that Leila and Asmara are available for follow-up in three months, to ensure some kind of closure to the case.

Practice points

- The issues arising for Farouk highlight the need for clinicians to have regular time alone with the interpreter after the session for debriefing. This time can also reveal any issues that the therapist should be particularly aware of; for example, the interpreter may have a child the same age as the client's who was killed.
- It may have been useful for Farouk to talk with other interpreters working in this area about his experience of interpreting, for example through a peer supervision group (Tribe, 1997). If possible, these should be initiated and facilitated by the service.
- In emotive areas, such as the use of testimony against further human rights abuse (Cienfuegos & Monelli, 1983), it might be tempting for therapist or interpreter to lose sight of confidentiality, as well as the centrality of client choice. Focusing on the Socratic techniques within CBT can be useful in ensuring that client choice and confidentiality remain central.
- Clinicians need to check throughout treatment the interpreter's commitment and fidelity to the CBT model. This is important when there may be reluctance or even resistance by the interpreter to trauma-focused CBT.
- Use interpreters to make telephone contact if there are unscheduled breaks in treatment, or crises, and remain engaged if possible, through the use of a second telephone and double jack.
- Always try to retain continuity with the interpreter and check availability to continue this type of work.
- Offer debriefing after the patient has been discharged.
- Consider organizing an interpreters' group to raise general as well as specific issues to do with the service.
- Above all, listen to everything interpreters have to say about their experiences and their needs. They remain an invaluable asset in the inclusion of all traumatized patients requiring CBT, and their work is difficult, delicate, and frequently undervalued.

Audit and supervision of interpreted CBT

Much of what has been described takes place at an individual level, but it would be impossible to provide effective interpreted CBT without consideration of the service and systemic issues within any clinical service, the wider healthcare organization, and the community. At the very least, clinicians should be able to provide interpreters with feedback about their performance after each session, as well as to the interpreting service, using feedback forms for each job. These can be sent back to the interpreters after each booking, but should also be kept by the service to monitor quality. Interpreting that is well below standard must be reported immediately by the service to the interpreting service, and followed up to clarify what has happened to an individual interpreter.

Many clinical services provide training, supervision, and support for their interpreters. Others argue that this is not always practical or affordable when these staff are employed elsewhere. Other models include quality circles (held less often but regularly), where interpreters are able to voice their anxieties with staff and generate some solutions for themselves, e.g., waiting room etiquette and privacy. Services can also fund and support the training of clinicians in the use of interpreting in CBT as part of their professional development.

Services should keep exact records of who is used and which languages are used most often, and to what effect. Case notes should record the fact that any sessions are interpreted, and with the name of the interpreter and the language used. Such monitoring ensures that more is known about how services are responding to need, and can be compared with other clinical services within the same geographic region.

Services need to establish boundaries around privacy, confidentiality, and the ever present requests to use relatives and friends as interpreters, and relieve the individual clinician of refusing requests from clients to avoid the use of a professional interpreter.

Services can send interpreters booklets about CBT and trauma, especially as so much of the work is counterintuitive, e.g., re-visiting the memories you most wish to forget. We have recommended Claudia Herbert's book *Understanding Your Reactions to Trauma*, because (1) it is written well in very clear English; (2) it is the same text we use for our clients, and ensures that clients and interpreters are sharing the same ideas (Herbert, 2002).

In addition to this, services should send protocols for working with CBT to the interpreting service for all staff to read, and these are provided more fully elsewhere (d'Ardenne et al., 2007). Lastly services are able to create an ethos that interpreted CBT is an important constituent of its provision, and enable referrers and service users alike to become aware of access to this important and effective treatment for PTSD. Services can become a stakeholder in treatment guidelines (e.g., National Institute for Health and Clinical Excellence), and provide a useful update to organizations about good clinical practice based on outcome research.

DISCUSSION

In this chapter we have aimed to go beyond what NCCMH (2005) recommends for the treatment of trauma-related difficulties. We hope we have shown that language does not have to be a barrier to CBT work. To overcome the barriers, we have shown that clinicians need a sound knowledge of interpreting practice coupled with clinical skill in applying it flexibly to suit individual need. There will no doubt be many clinical examples of when rules may need to be broken, but this can only be achieved if clinicians understand first principles. Specific adaptations of interpreting to CBT include:

- Temporal proximity within triadic communication
- Reliving past trauma through the first person in the present tense
- Interpreting the counterfactuals in trauma-focused CBT
- Communication of suitable metaphor in the creation of alternative perspectives
- Interpretation of clients' written materials, e.g., nightmare and mood diaries
- Interpretation of other materials, e.g., drawings, music, artefacts linked to traumatic memory
- Updating interpreted narratives as meanings change.

There is no reason to doubt that interpreting can be used and modified to other therapeutic approaches in trauma. Eye movement desensitization and reprocessing, systemic work, and group approaches, including creative art therapies, may also benefit from interpreting protocols designed for the particular approach. Inevitably, PTSD work will involve applying some of our common interpreting principles:

- Clinicians hold ultimate responsibility for the quality of the interpreting and any risks involved.
- Clinicians also have responsibility for interpreters' wellbeing through debriefing and feedback.
- Individual briefing of interpreters is required to establish language skill and emotional resilience, particularly in the context of interpreters with a refugee background.
- Education of interpreters about the model for trauma and its theoretical underpinnings, especially considering the counterintuitive nature of the work.
- Allocation of additional time as a resource.

Despite the additional cost, time, complexity, and skills required, interpreted psychotherapy allows non-English-speaking patients access to effective talking therapies and the benefits that these hold. We have some evidence to show that patients who need interpreting but who do not make full use of this service are actually more disadvantaged than those who accept it (d'Ardenne et al., 2007). CBT demands a high level of competence in a shared language; language barriers undermine temporal proximity and therapeutic rapport. Clinicians need to inform their clients of the benefits of interpreted therapy to make the best choice. Unfortunately we do not have such benefits for clients whose English is non-standard, when an advocate may be more appropriate. The benefits of interpreting for the clinicians and the service should also not be ignored (Miller et al., 2005). Clinicians have access to cultural experts in the room, who can provide invaluable background information about clients and their situation. Some have described the utility of a third party bearing witness to the patient's trauma (Miller et al., 2005). Pauses in verbal communication (due to interpreting) allow for attention to nonverbal signs, time for reflection, and written recording. Although therapy can seem slow, there are no empty moments in interpreted CBT. Nothing will work well without good briefing and debriefing, which must be structured and costed to existing services to ensure good quality interpreting.

We have aimed to cover some of the common difficulties using an interpreter raises, but clearly could not cover all issues and would recommend readers to further guidance (e.g., d'Ardenne et al., 2007; Tribe & Morrissey, 2004; Raval, 1996). There is a wider literature of cross-cultural papers defining good practice and ethical imperatives, not necessarily supported by any evidence about whether it is effective. As scientist-practitioners we need to be ever sceptical until we find a practice that is ethical, effective, and replicable. We hope that this chapter represents a first step in achieving these aims for interpreted trauma work, but recognize that good practice will invariably develop as more clinicians undertake interpreted therapy and test the contents and limits of current guidance.

Perhaps the best interpreter of our work is the poet Maya Angelou:

> The past, despite its wrenching pain, cannot be unlived, but if faced with courage, need not be lived again.
>
> (Angelou, 2006)

REFERENCES

Angelou, M. (2006). On the pulse of morning. In M. Angelou, *Celebrations: Rituals of peace and prayer*. London: Virago.

Bjorn, G.J. (2005). Ethics and interpreting in psychotherapy with refugee children and families. *Nordic Journal of Psychiatry*, *59*, 516–521.

Bot, H. (2005). Dialogue interpreting as a specific case of reported speech. *Interpreting*, *7*, 237–261.

Bot, H., & Wadensjo, C. (2004). The presence of a third party: A dialogical view on interpreter-assisted treatment. In J.P. Wilson, & B. Drozdec (Eds.), *Broken spirits: The treatment of traumatised asylum seekers, refugees, war and torture victims.* London: Brunner-Routledge.

Cienfuegos, A.J., & Monelli, Cristina (1983). The testimony of political repression as a therapeutic instrument. *American Journal of Orthopsychiatry, 53*, 43–51.

d'Ardenne, P., Capuzzo, N., Ruaro, L., & Priebe, S. (2005). One size fits all? Cultural sensitivity in a psychological service for traumatised refugees. *Diversity in Health and Social Care, 2*, 29–36.

d'Ardenne, P., Farmer, E., Ruaro, L., & Priebe, S. (2007). Not lost in translation: Protocols for interpreting trauma-focused CBT. *Behavioural and Cognitive Psychotherapy, 35*, 303–316.

d'Ardenne, P., Ruaro, L., Cestari, L., Wakhoury, W., & Priebe, S. (2007). Does interpreter-mediated CBT with traumatized refugee people work? A comparison of patient outcomes in East London. *Behavioural and Cognitive Psychotherapy, 35*, 293–301.

Drennan, G., & Swartz, L. (1999). A concept overburdened: Institutional roles for psychiatric interpreters in post-apartheid South Africa. *Interpreting, 4*, 169–198.

Ehlers, A., & Clark, D.M. (2000). A cognitive model of posttraumatic stress disorder. *Behaviour Research and Therapy, 38*, 319–345.

Fox, A. (2001). An interpreter's perspective. *Medical Foundation Series.* www.torturecare.org.uk, downloaded April 2006. Article first appeared in *Context, 54*, 19–20.

Gilbert, P., & Irons, C. (2005). Focused therapies and compassionate mind training for shame and self-attacking. In P. Gilbert (Ed.), *Compassion: Conceptualisations, research and use in psychotherapy.* London: Routledge.

Harvey, A.G., Bryant, R.A., & Tarrier, N. (2003). Cognitive behaviour therapy for posttraumatic stress disorder. *Clinical Psychology Review, 23*, 501–522.

Herbert, C. (2002). *Understanding your reactions to trauma: A guide for survivors of trauma and their families.* Oxford: Blue Stallion Publications.

Holder, R. (2002). The impact of mediated communication on psychological therapy with refugees and asylum seekers: Practitioners' experiences. MSc Dissertation, City University, London.

Lee, D.A. (2005). The perfect nurturer: A model to develop a compassionate mind within the context of cognitive therapy. In P. Gilbert (Ed.), *Compassion: Conceptualisations, research and use in psychotherapy* (pp. 326–351). New York: Routledge.

Lee, D.A., Scragg, P., & Turner, S. (2001). The role of shame and guilt in traumatic events: A clinical model of shame-based and guilt-based PTSD. *British Journal of Medical Psychology, 74*, 451–466.

Mahtani, A. (2003). The right of refugee clients to an appropriate and ethical psychological service. *International Journal of Human Rights, 7*, 40–57.

Mailloux, S. (2004). Ethics and interpreters: Are you practising ethically? *Journal of Psychological Practice, 10*, 37–44.

Miller, K.E., Martell, Z.L., Pazdirek, L., Caruth, M., & Lopez, D. (2005). The role of interpreters in psychotherapy with refugees: An exploratory study. *American Journal of Orthopsychiatry, 75*, 27–39.

National Collaborating Centre for Mental Health. (2005). *Clinical guideline 26: Posttraumatic stress disorder (PTSD): The management of PTSD in adults and children in primary and secondary care.* London: National Institute of Clinical Excellence.

Patel, N. (2003). Speaking with the silent: Addressing issues of disempowerment when working with refugee people. In R. Tribe and H. Raval (Eds.), *Working with interpreters in mental health*. London: Brunner-Routledge.

Raval, H. (1996). A systemic perspective on working with interpreters. *Clinical Child Psychology and Psychiatry, 1*, 29–43.

Schauer, M., Elbert, T., & Neuner, F. (2004). *Narrative exposure therapy: A short-term intervention for traumatic stress disorders after war, terror or torture*. Toronto: Hogrefe & Huber.

Shackman, J. (1984). *The right to be understood: A handbook on working with, employing and training community interpreters*. Cambridge: National Extension College.

Tribe, R. (1997). A critical analysis of a support and clinical supervision group for interpreters working with refugees located in Britain. *Groupwork, 10*, 196–214.

Tribe, R., & Morrissey, J. (2004). Good practice issues in working with interpreters in mental health. *Intervention, 2*, 129–142.

Index

absorption 97, 98
abuse: depression 78; dissociation 100–1, 102; imagery rescripting 89; intensive cognitive therapy 118, 120, 121; multiple trauma 194, 195, 197–202, 205, 206, 207–9; obsessive-compulsive disorder 174–5; psychosis 62; shame-based flashbacks 240–4; suicidality 184–8; *see also* trauma
acceptance and commitment therapy (ACT) 178
accidents 176; *see also* motor vehicle accidents
ACT *see* acceptance and commitment therapy
acute stress disorder (ASD) 3, 14–30; cognitive monitoring 18–20, 22; common trauma-related cognitions 21–6; diagnosis 14–15; dissociation 94, 95; normalization of symptoms 16–18; rationale for cognitive restructuring 18–20; treatment outcome 26
'adapted testimony' 250–1
adjustment disorder 4
affect: intensity of 33; positive 81, 231, 232, 234, 235; regulation 194, 206; *see also* emotions
'affect bridge' technique 208
affective disorders 4
agoraphobia: civil conflict situations 225; intensive cognitive therapy 112, 118, 125; panic attacks 148, 149, 161; permanent physical injury following trauma 132, 133; weekly treatment 128
alcohol use 6, 237, 238
amnesia, dissociative 14, 94, 97
amygdala 101, 231–2, 241
anger: civil conflict situations 224, 228;

motorcycle accident victim 116; multiple trauma 210; narrative exposure therapy 278; permanent physical injury following trauma 144; reliving 196; threat arousal system 243; torture survivors 284
anorexia nervosa 97
anxiety: acute stress disorder 16, 17, 21, 26; cognitive restructuring 19, 22; disorders 4; dissociation 106–7, 108; drug flashbacks 50, 51, 53; obsessive-compulsive disorder 167, 170, 171; suicide risk 190; torture survivors 284; transport-related trauma 42–3, 45, 46; travel phobia 31, 32, 33, 35, 37–8
anxiety sensitivity (AS) 147
appraisals: civil conflict situations 216, 219, 221–2, 223, 224, 226–8; depression 79; intensive cognitive therapy 112, 113, 115; massacre witness 151; obsessive-compulsive disorder 174; permanent physical injury following trauma 134, 136–8, 141, 142–3, 144; psychosis 56, 62, 67; transport-related trauma 42; treatment goals 131–2
arousal: acute stress disorder 14, 17–18; dissociation 98; threat perception 6; travel phobia 34–5; *see also* hyperarousal
AS *see* anxiety sensitivity
ASD *see* acute stress disorder
assessment 5–6; acute stress disorder 26–7; childhood trauma 208; civil conflict situations 214–15, 218; interpreters 286–9; multiple trauma 209; obsessive-compulsive disorder 173; panic disorder 148–9; permanent

'reconnection' 195
re-experiencing: acute stress disorder 14,
17; childhood abuse 197; civil conflict
situations 218; drug flashbacks 49, 50,
57; imagery rescripting 80; multiple
trauma 202–3, 205, 206, 210; panic
attacks 149–50; transport-related
trauma 33, 46; treatment goals 131; *see
also* reliving
refugees: interpreters 283–300; multiple
trauma 194, 195, 206, 207; narrative
exposure therapy 265–82; prevalence
of PTSD 2–3; risk of PTSD 74; torture
survivors 247, 248–53, 257–62
relapse prevention 78, 90
reliving 7, 8, 166, 236; acute stress
disorder 27–8; civil conflict situations
216, 217–18, 219–20; dissociation
104–5, 108; drug flashbacks 57;
hotspots 196; imagery rescripting
79–80, 89–90, 182; intensive cognitive
therapy 112, 114, 117, 119, 121;
interpreters 290–1, 292–3, 297;
multiple trauma 196–7, 200, 201–2,
204–5, 208; permanent physical injury
following trauma 140–1; shame 231,
239, 243; suicidality 182, 183, 188;
trauma-psychosis 75; travel phobia 37,
46, 47; war experiences 155; *see also* re-
experiencing
'remembrance' 195
Revised Impact of Events Scale (IES-R)
5
risk assessment: multiple trauma 205–6,
210; suicidal patients 185, 190
rumination 2, 6; civil conflict situations
216; cognitive restructuring 23–6;
depression 85; drug flashbacks 52, 55;
intensive cognitive therapy 113;
obsessive-compulsive disorder 168,
171–2, 173, 174; permanent physical
injury following trauma 137–9;
psychosis 66; transport-related trauma
41, 42, 43, 44

safeness 232, 233
safety behaviours: acute stress disorder
21; brain's response to threat 232; civil
conflict situations 222, 226; intensive
cognitive therapy 119, 122, 125;
obsessive-compulsive disorder 168,
169; panic attacks 158; transport-

related trauma 35–6, 38, 42, 43,
44–6
Scale for the Assessment of Positive
Symptoms (SAPS) 64, 65, 73
schema-focused cognitive therapy 197,
240
schemas 227
schizophrenia 61, 64, 75, 94
self-blame 5, 230; civil conflict situations
216–17, 219; intensive cognitive
therapy 119–20, 122–3; narrative
exposure therapy 267, 268, 269; sexual
abuse 241
self-criticism 231–4, 235, 236, 239
self-disclosure 289
self-esteem 74, 237, 240
self-evaluation 231
self-harm: dissociation 102, 103, 104,
105; multiple trauma 194, 198; shame
237, 238, 240
self-soothing 231, 232–3, 234–5, 236,
238–9, 241, 242–4
self-starvation 102, 103, 105
'semi-intensive' treatment 128
sexual abuse: depression 78; dissociation
100, 102; intensive cognitive therapy
118, 120, 121; multiple trauma 194,
195, 207, 208–9; obsessive-compulsive
disorder 174–5; psychosis 62; shame-
based flashbacks 240–4; suicidality
184–8; *see also* abuse
shame 230–46; acute stress disorder 16,
26, 27; civil conflict situations 224;
compassion-focused cognitive therapy
234–6, 237–44; drug flashbacks 53;
intensive cognitive therapy 119–20,
121, 122, 123; multiple trauma 210;
rape victims 291–2; reliving 196; self-
criticism as a maintenance cycle 231–4;
sexual abuse 119–20, 121, 175, 240–4;
suicidality 188; theoretical
considerations 231
site of trauma, revisiting 8; drug
flashbacks 50; intensive cognitive
therapy 116, 125; obsessive-
compulsive disorder 172; transport-
related trauma 33, 37
social anxiety 54, 133, 139–40, 143
social interactions 54, 55, 56
social isolation 62, 68, 75, 250, 267
social mentality theory 233
social phobia 31, 59, 132, 143